™

References for the Rest of Us

COMPUTER BOOK SERIES FROM IDG

Are you intimidated and confused by computers? Do you find that traditional manuals are overloaded with technical details you'll never use? Do your friends and family always call you to fix simple problems on their PCs? Then the ... *For Dummies*™ computer book series from IDG is for you.

... *For Dummies* books are written for those frustrated computer users who know they aren't really dumb but find that PC hardware, software, and indeed the unique vocabulary of computing make them feel helpless. ... *For Dummies* books use a lighthearted approach, a down-to-earth style, and even cartoons and humorous icons to diffuse computer novices' fears and build their confidence. Lighthearted but not lightweight, these books are a perfect survival guide to anyone forced to use a computer.

> *"I like my copy so much I told friends; now they bought copies."*
>
> **Irene C., Orwell, Ohio**

> *"Quick, concise, nontechnical, and humorous."*
>
> **Jay A., Elburn, IL**

> *"Thanks, I needed this book. Now I can sleep at night."*
>
> **Robin F., British Columbia, Canada**

Already, hundreds of thousands of satisfied readers agree. They have made ... *For Dummies* books the #1 introductory level computer book series and have written asking for more. So if you're looking for the most fun and easy way to learn about computers, look to ... *For Dummies* books to give you a helping hand.

IDG BOOKS ®

BORLAND C++
FOR
DUMMIES™

Paradx 5/27/95

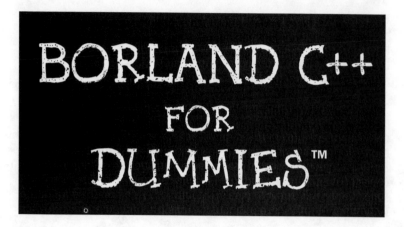

BORLAND C++ FOR DUMMIES™

Michael I. Hyman

IDG BOOKS

IDG Books Worldwide, Inc.
An International Data Group Company

San Mateo, California ♦ Indianapolis, Indiana ♦ Boston, Massachusetts

Borland C++ For Dummies

Published by
IDG Books Worldwide, Inc.
An International Data Group Company
155 Bovet Road, Suite 310
San Mateo, CA 94402

Library of Congress Catalog Card No.: 94-76646

ISBN: 1-56884-162-0

Printed in the United States of America

10 9 8 7 6 5 4 3 2 1

1B/QY/QV/ZU

First Printing, July, 1994

Distributed in the United States by IDG Books Worldwide, Inc.

is a registered trademark of IDG Books Worldwide, Inc.

About IDG Books Worldwide

Welcome to the world of IDG Books Worldwide.

IDG Books Worldwide, Inc. is a subsidiary of International Data Group, the world's largest publisher of business- and computer-related information and the leading global provider of information services on information technology. IDG was founded more than 25 years ago and now employs more than 5700 people worldwide. IDG publishes more than 200 computer publications in 63 countries. Forty million people read one or more IDG publications each month.

Launched in 1990, IDG Books is today the fastest-growing publisher of computer and business books in the United States. We are proud to have received three awards from the Computer Press Association in recognition of editorial excellence, and our best-selling ...For Dummies series has more than 7 million copies in print with translations in more than 20 languages. IDG Books, through a recent joint venture with IDG's Hi-Tech Beijing, became the first U.S. publisher to publish a computer book in the People's Republic of China. In record time, IDG Books has become the first choice for millions of readers around the world who want to learn how to better manage their businesses.

Our mission is simple: Every IDG book is designed to bring extra value and skill-building instructions to the reader. Our books are written by experts who understand and care about our readers. The knowledge base of our editorial staff comes from years of experience in publishing, education, and journalism — experience which we use to produce books for the 90s. In short, we care about books, so we attract the best people. We devote special attention to details such as audience, interior design, use of icons, and illustrations. And because we use an efficient process of authoring, editing, and desktop publishing our books electronically, we can spend more time ensuring superior content and spend less time on the technicalities of making books.

You can count on our commitment to deliver high-quality books at competitive prices on topics customers want to read about. At IDG, we value quality, and we have been delivering quality for more than 25 years. You'll find no better book on a subject than an IDG book.

John Kilcullen
President and CEO
IDG Books Worldwide, Inc.

For More Information

For general information on IDG Books in the U.S., including information on discounts and premiums, contact IDG Books at 800-434-3422 or 415-312-0650.

For information on where to purchase IDG Books outside the U.S., contact Christina Turner at 415-312-0633.

For information on translations, contact Marc Jeffrey Mikulich, Foreign Rights Manager, at IDG Books Worldwide; fax number 415-358-1260.

For sales inquiries and special prices for bulk quantities, contact Tony Real at 415-312-0644 or 800-434-3422.

For using IDG Books in the classroom, or for ordering examination copies, contact Jim Kelly at 800-434-2086.

The ...*For Dummies* book series is distributed in the United States by IDG Books Worldwide, Inc. It is distributed in Canada by Macmillan of Canada, a Division of Canada Publishing Corporation; by Computer and Technical Books in Miami, Florida, for South America and the Caribbean; by Longman Singapore in Singapore, Malaysia, Thailand, and Korea; by Toppan Co. Ltd. in Japan; by Asia Computerworld in Hong Kong; by Woodslane Pty. Ltd. in Australia and New Zealand; and by Transword Publishers Ltd. in the U.K. and Europe.

IDG Books Worldwide, Inc. is a subsidiary of International Data Group. The officers are Patrick J. McGovern, Founder and Board Chairman; Walter Boyd, President. International Data Group's publications include: **ARGENTINA'S** Computerworld Argentina, Infoworld Argentina; **AUSTRALIA'S** Computerworld Australia, Australian PC World, Australian Macworld, Network World, Mobile Business Australia, Reseller, IDG Sources; **AUSTRIA'S** Computerwelt Oesterreich, PC Test; **BRAZIL'S** Computerworld, Gamepro, Game Power, Mundo IBM, Mundo Unix, PC World, Super Game; **BELGIUM'S** Data News (CW); **BULGARIA'S** Computerworld Bulgaria, Ediworld, PC & Mac World Bulgaria, Network World Bulgaria; **CANADA'S** CIO Canada, Computerworld Canada, Graduate Computerworld, InfoCanada, Network World Canada; **CHILE'S** Computerworld Chile, Informatica; **COLOMBIA'S** Computerworld Colombia, PC World; **CZECH REPUBLIC'S** Computerworld, Elektronika, PC World; **DENMARK'S** Communications World, Computerworld Danmark, Macintosh Produktkatalog, Macworld Danmark, PC World Danmark, PC World Produktguide, Tech World, Windows World; **ECUADOR'S** PC World Ecuador; **EGYPT'S** Computerworld (CW) Middle East, PC World Middle East; **FINLAND'S** MikroPC, Tietoviikko, Tietoverkko; **FRANCE'S** Distributique, GOLDEN MAC, InfoPC, Languages & Systems, Le Guide du Monde Informatique, Le Monde Informatique, Telecoms & Reseaux; **GERMANY'S** Computerwoche, Computerwoche Focus, Computerwoche Extra, Computerwoche Karriere, Information Management, Macwelt, Netzwelt, PC Welt, PC Woche, Publish, Unit; **GREECE'S** Infoworld, PC Games; **HUNGARY'S** Computerworld SZT, PC World; **HONG KONG'S** Computerworld Hong Kong, PC World Hong Kong; **INDIA'S** Computers & Communications; **IRELAND'S** ComputerScope; **ISRAEL'S** Computerworld Israel, PC World Israel; **ITALY'S** Computerworld Italia, Lotus Magazine, Macworld Italia, Networking Italia, PC Shopping, PC World Italia; **JAPAN'S** Computerworld Today, Information Systems World, Macworld Japan, Nikkei Personal Computing, SunWorld Japan, Windows World; **KENYA'S** East African Computer News; **KOREA'S** Computerworld Korea, Macworld Korea, PC World Korea; **MEXICO'S** Compu Edicion, Compu Manufactura, Computacion/Punto de Venta, Computerworld Mexico, MacWorld, Mundo Unix, PC World, Windows; **THE NETHERLANDS'** Computer! Totaal, Computable (CW), LAN Magazine, MacWorld, Totaal "Windows"; **NEW ZEALAND'S** Computer Listings, Computerworld New Zealand, New Zealand PC World, Network World; **NIGERIA'S** PC World Africa; **NORWAY'S** Computerworld Norge, C/World, Lotusworld Norge, Macworld Norge, Networld, PC World Ekspress, PC World Norge, PC World's Produktguide, Publish& Multimedia World, Student Data, Unix World, Windowsworld; IDG Direct Response; **PAKISTAN'S** PC World Pakistan; **PANAMA'S** PC World Panama; **PERU'S** Computerworld Peru, PC World; **PEOPLE'S REPUBLIC OF CHINA'S** China Computerworld, China Infoworld, Electronics Today/Multimedia World, Electronics International, Electronic Product World, China Network World, PC and Communications Magazine, PC World China, Software World Magazine, Telecom Product World; IDG HIGH TECH BEIJING'S New Product World; IDG SHENZHEN'S Computer News Digest; **PHILIPPINES'** Computerworld Philippines, PC Digest (PCW); **POLAND'S** Computerworld Poland, PC World/Komputer; **PORTUGAL'S** Cerebro/PC World, Correio Informatico/Computerworld, Informatica & Comunicacoes Catalogo, MacIn, Nacional de Produtos; **ROMANIA'S** Computerworld, PC World; **RUSSIA'S** Computerworld-Moscow, Mir-PC, Sety; **SINGAPORE'S** Computerworld Southeast Asia, PC World Singapore; **SLOVENIA'S** Monitor Magazine; **SOUTH AFRICA'S** Computer Mail (CIO),Computing S.A.,Network World S.A., Software World; **SPAIN'S** Advanced Systems, Amiga World, Computerworld Espana, Communicaciones World, Macworld Espana, NeXTWORLD, Super Juegos Magazine (GamePro), PC World Espana, Publish; **SWEDEN'S** Attack, ComputerSweden, Corporate Computing, Natverk & Kommunikation, Macworld, Mikrodatorn, PC World, Publishing & Design (CAP), DataIngenjoren, Maxi Data,Windows World; **SWITZERLAND'S** Computerworld Schweiz, Macworld Schweiz, PC Tip; **TAIWAN'S** Computerworld Taiwan, PC World Taiwan; **THAILAND'S** Thai Computerworld; **TURKEY'S** Computerworld Monitor, Macworld Turkiye, PC World Turkiye; **UKRAINE'S** Computerworld; **UNITED KINGDOM'S** Computing /Computerworld, Connexion/Network World, Lotus Magazine, Macworld, Open Computing/Sunworld; **UNITED STATES'** Advanced Systems, AmigaWorld, Cable in the Classroom, CD Review, CIO, Computerworld, Digital Video, DOS Resource Guide, Electronic Entertainment Magazine, Federal Computer Week, Federal Integrator, GamePro, IDG Books, Infoworld, Infoworld Direct, Laser Event, Macworld, Multimedia World, Network World, PC Letter, PC World, PlayRight, Power PC World, Publish, SWATPro, Video Event; **VENEZUELA'S** Computerworld Venezuela, PC World; **VIETNAM'S** PC World Vietnam.

About the Author

Michael I. Hyman is Business Unit Manager for the Languages group at Borland. Before that, he was cofounder of Within Technologies, makers of Realizer, and a Program Manager in the Systems Group at Microsoft. Michael has written five other computer books, covering graphics, DOS, Windows, and OS/2.

When not busy slaving away at his "real" job, you can find Michael munching on pizza while creating strange multimedia applications, scaring the neighbors by droning on his digeridoo, playing CDs at far too high volume, and every now and then enjoying the fresh air.

Michael has a degree in Electrical Engineering and Computer Science from Princeton University and an incurable addiction to chocolate-chip cookies.

Credits

Vice President and Publisher
Chris Williams

Editorial Director
Trudy Neuhaus

Brand Manager
Amorette Pedersen

Project Editor
Susan Pink

Manuscript Editor
Teresa Frazier

Technical Reviewer
Bruneau Babet

Production Director
Beth Jenkins

Assoc. Production Coordinator
Valery Bourke

Production Quality Control
Steve Peake

Production Staff
Linda M. Boyer
Mary Breidenbach
Angela F. Hunckler
Gina Scott

Proofreader
Nancy Kruse Hannigan

Indexer
Liz Cunningham

Book Design
University Graphics

Cover Design
Kavish + Kavish

Acknowledgments

Ongoing thanks to my loving wife Sarah, not only for being a great person, but for putting up with all my long nights geeking out, whether for work, this book, or something else. To my parents Richard and Roberta, who despite being artists somehow ended up with a nerd for a son, and to my sister Betsy, who still calls me every time her computer burps. Also thanks to Bryan Willman for the occasional refuge at The Asylum, with or without the giraffe.

Thanks to Karen Offerman, who provided the Iaccoca joke. A special thanks to anyone in the press who reviews this — please say nice things. This book wouldn't be possible without all the incredibly hard-working folks in the Borland Languages group who have spent the last several years working 200 hours a day making Borland C++.

And finally, a thanks to IDG Books and in particular to Chris Williams, who's been involved with every book I've written. To Trudy Neuhaus, who's had to put up with me on both sides of the fence, to Susan Pink, who's learned even more about nerd humor, and to Teresa Frazier, who's read this manuscript more times than should be legal. Thanks also to Bruneau Babet, who was kind enough to spend his (lack of) copious spare time doing a technical review of this book.

Contents at a Glance

Cartoons at a Glance

by Rich Tennant

page 1

page 465

page 307

page 5

page 403

page 324

page 195

page 59

page 263

page 125

Table of Contents

· ·

Introduction

· ·

C++. Even though its name sounds like a cryptic joke, this language is the current rage in the computer industry. C++ is the critical tool used by hundreds of thousands of programmers, whether they're developers creating high-end products such as dBASE for Windows, MIS departments creating mission-critical applications, or the next generation of hackers creating multi-media masterpieces.

The 5th Wave   By Rich Tennant

IF BOB DYLAN HAD PURSUED A CAREER IN COMPUTERS.

©RICHTENNANT

"PUT HIM IN FRONT OF A TERMINAL AND HE'S A GENIUS, BUT OTHER-WISE THE GUY IS SUCH A BROODING, GLOOMY GUS HE'LL NEVER BREAK INTO MANAGEMENT."

There are a variety of reasons to learn C++. Some people want to learn C++ so they can get a high-paying job (or so they can *keep* their current job, whatever the pay). Other people need to learn C++ because it's a requirement for passing a class they're taking. Still other people (perhaps those with a high nerd potential) want to learn C++ because they crave a new, fun way to create applications on the weekends.

But learning C++ can be a pain. It's a complex language with lots of quirks and rules and confusing terms such as *operator overloading* and *class templates*. And in addition to learning "regular" programming, C++ requires you to learn object-oriented programming techniques.

Furthermore, C++ development tools can seem intimidating at first. Borland C++ features over 100 megabytes of tools, editors, debuggers, compilers, command-line tools, libraries, help files, frameworks, and so on. Sometimes it's tough just knowing where to start.

That's where this book comes in: it gives you the big picture. (You can think of it as your Cliff++ Notes.) Lots of other beginning programming books make you learn tons and tons of details. When you finally finish reading them, you might or might not be able to create fancy programs.

This book is different. When you're finished reading it, you probably won't be able to go off and create the next dBASE for Windows. But you *will* be able to read and understand a C++ program and you *will* have a really good idea of what object-oriented technology is all about. And, with a little help from your friends, you'll even be able to create some C++ applications of your own.

Who This Book Is For

You don't need programming experience to profitably read and learn from this book. But if you've done some programming-ish tasks before, such as creating spreadsheet macros or database programs, you'll feel much more comfortable than if you've never dealt with the concept of a program before.

If you already know BASIC, COBOL, Pascal — or even better, C — then this book will have you writing C++ in no time. (If you already know C++, however, this book probably isn't the best book for you because it's intended for beginners.)

Regardless of your programming background, this book assumes that you know how to run Windows programs and have a basic understanding of what files and programs are.

How This Book Is Organized

This book has four parts. *Part I* provides a quick guide to Borland C++ 4.0. It helps you get up and running, and introduces the main features of Borland C++ 4.0. *Part II* is an overview of C++ programming fundamentals (note that many of the topics are also applicable to C). *Part III* introduces the world of object-oriented programming — you'll learn about classes, templates, and other C++ features. If you're a seasoned C programmer, you could skim Part II and then jump to this Part. And last but not least, there's *Part IV*, the Part of Tens, which offers tips and solutions for various problems commonly encountered by beginning C++ users. It also provides some cool "top ten" lists of handy information.

Icons Used in This Book

Icons are pictures designed to grab your attention. Here's what the icons used in this book mean:

Heads up! This is information you should try to remember. Sometimes that's just because it's a cool bit of info, but other times it's because you might be sorry if you don't remember. ▪

Alerts you to nerdy technical discussions you can skip if you want to. ▪

Shortcuts and insights that can save you time and trouble. ▪

By the way, the little gray box — ▪ — is used to indicate the end of the iconed text. (If an entire section is iconed, though, the little gray box isn't used.)

The Accompanying Disk

There are lots of sample programs in this book that illustrate important aspects of C++ programming. All the code is listed in this book, but if you don't want to type the programs in by hand you can order the accompanying program disk and copy the sample code to your computer. The disk is inexpensive, so if you want to save yourself some time, you should probably go ahead and buy the disk. (There's an order form for the disk at the back of the book.)

Why Is It Called C++?

Choose one:

a.   It was going to be called D or D--, but the marketing folks figured that wouldn't sell well.

b.   It's the punch line of the inventor's favorite joke.

c.   The post-increment operator in C is written ++, so it represents the next step beyond C, in computer speak. (C++, which was designed starting in 1980, is based on a language called C. Which was based on languages called BCPL and B. Which were based on A. Before that there was darkness.)

If you guessed *c*, you may begin reading the book.

Part I

Quick Guide to Borland C++ 4.0

"ALRIGHT, NOW WE NEED SOMEONE TO PLAY THE PART OF THE GEEK."

In This Part

Part I gives you a whirlwind tour of Borland C++. It begins with an overview of everything that comes with Borland C++. Then it describes the different installation options and provides step by step instructions for installing Borland C++ on your computer.

Once Borland C++ is up and running, you'll create a simple Windows program. As you follow the steps in each chapter, you'll be adding functionality (cool features) to your program. Along the way, you'll be learning about the major components of Borland C++, such as the IDE, the Experts, Resource Workshop, the Project Manager, the editor, the debugger, and the browser.

If you've already installed Borland C++, you're ahead of the game: you can skip ahead to Chapter 3.

Chapter 1

What's in the Borland C++ Package?

In This Chapter

▶ Examine what's in the Borland C++ package

▶ Learn about the various Borland C++ features

So, you've decided to become a C++ programmer. That's a great idea. You'll be able to beef up your resume, create some cool custom applications, and meet all types of fascinating people. And most importantly, you'll be able to say you've installed one of the largest products ever created.

Borland C++ 4.0 is a *big* product. In fact, before Borland C++ 3.0 came out, the manufacturing folks (the people who put the product boxes together) toured supermarket aisles looking at laundry detergent boxes to find examples of sturdy box handles. This is a true story. And during the development of Borland C++ 4.0, the same folks examined luggage carts and skateboards just in case the product box needed wheels. Fortunately it didn't. But the research might come in handy for Borland C++ 5.0.

You'll learn how to install Borland C++ 4.0 in Chapter 2. First, though, here's a quick overview of all the cool stuff you'll be installing.

The 50,000-Foot View of What's in the Box

When you open the Borland C++ box, you'll find a number of C++ goodies. In addition to the manuals, roadmap, quick reference card, and the advertisements, you'll also find a stack of floppy disks (or a CD) containing the Borland C++ software. These disks contain a variety of features that help you create C++ programs:

✔ Compilers

✔ Debuggers

  ✔ Resource editing tools

  ✔ Integrated Development Environment (IDE)

  ✔ Application frameworks

  ✔ Libraries

  ✔ Windows utilities

  ✔ General utilities

  ✔ On-line help and documentation files

  ✔ Sample programs

The following sections of this chapter describe each of these features in a little more detail. That way, you'll have a basic idea of what all this stuff does before you install it.

That Old Compiler Magic

Compilers translate code from a form that programmers can understand (*source code*) into a form that computers can understand and run (a program called an *executable*).

What's a command-line compiler?

A command-line compiler is a compiler that doesn't have a user interface. Command-line compilers are fast, but not very user friendly. You tell them what to do by giving them some rather complicated-looking instructions, as shown in this example:

```
bcc -02 -vi- foo.cpp
```

In the previous line, the first item is the name of the command-line compiler you want to use, the next two items are options that tell the compiler what to do, and the last item is the file you want to compile. (You can tell if someone uses the command-line compiler instead of the IDE if they know that "-02" means faster and "-vi-" means turn off intrinsics. Anyone else will think these terms are just a bunch of gibberish.)

In the good old days, command-line compilers were the only compilers that were available. People who started programming a long time ago often continue to use the command-line compilers because they've gotten used to them and because they've developed all sorts of nifty tools to use with them. Beginners usually prefer the IDE because it's much easier to use.

Borland C++ has three compilers:

- A command-line compiler for creating 16-bit programs
- A command-line compiler for creating 32-bit programs
- An everything-wrapped-up-into-one Integrated Development Environment (IDE) that can create both 16- and 32-bit programs.

As you work through the tasks and exercises in this book, you'll be using the IDE compiler because its user interface is easy to use.

Those Bug-Zapping Debuggers

If your program has more than a few lines in it, it's bound to have some problems when you first compile it. If it doesn't, you're either a real *code jockey* (a hotshot programmer) or you copied your program from a book.

There are two types of problems you'll undoubtedly run into: syntax errors and logic errors. *Syntax errors* occur when you type something incorrectly, forget to supply information that the compiler needs, or use a command incorrectly. The compiler finds syntax errors for you and tells you what line they're on. You need to correct all the syntax errors or the compiler won't be able to create an executable.

Logic errors occur when you don't design or implement your program properly. Perhaps you forgot to read in an important piece of information. Or maybe you printed out the wrong variable. With logic errors, the program compiles perfectly, but some part of it doesn't work correctly when it runs.

For example, suppose you write a program to manage your checking account. When you deposit money in your account, you remember to have the program add that number to your balance. But when you withdraw money, you forget to have the program subtract the money from your balance. (A sort of Freudian withdrawal slip.) This is a logic error. You forgot an important step, and as a result your program reports you have more money in your account than you actually do.

Logic errors can be hard to find. It's usually difficult to track them down by looking at the source code for a program. Instead, you track them down by using a tool called a *debugger*. The debugger lets you run a program line by line, so you can examine the values in the program and pinpoint the location and cause of the problem.

Borland C++ 4.0 comes with four debuggers:

- ✔ A stand-alone debugger for DOS programs
- ✔ A stand-alone debugger for 16-bit Windows programs
- ✔ A stand-alone debugger for 32-bit Windows programs
- ✔ A debugger for 16-bit Windows programs; this debugger is integrated in the IDE and is called the integrated debugger

The stand-alone debuggers have more features than the integrated debugger (such as disassembly views and dual-monitor support). But for most programming tasks (in this book and in the real world), the integrated debugger will give you all the power you need.

Dialogs and Menus and Bitmaps, Oh My!

Resources define a Windows program's user interface. They're what distinguish Windows programs from DOS programs. Windows programs have dialog boxes (sometimes just called dialogs), menus, bitmaps, and all types of other fancy things to make it easier to use programs. (Actually, to keep things honest, resources aren't unique to Windows. The Mac, UNIX, OS/2, and a lot of other operating systems also have resources.)

To create and edit these resources, you need a *resource editing tool*. Borland C++ 4.0's resource editing tool is the powerful Resource Workshop, which lets you create and edit dialog boxes, menus, bitmaps, and about anything else you need to create a Windows user interface.

It's as Simple as I-D-E

Borland C++ contains an Integrated Development Environment (the IDE, pronounced by saying each letter: I-D-E) that combines the various development tools into a single easy-to-use environment. If you use the IDE, you don't need to learn how to use the various stand-alone tools.

The IDE contains eight major components:

- ✔ An editor, which lets you write and modify your programs without leaving the environment
- ✔ A compiler, which lets you compile your program (or find syntax errors that prevent your program from compiling)

✔ An integrated debugger, which helps you find mistakes so you can fix them

✔ A project manager, which lets you easily build executables (and DLLs and LIBs)

✔ A browser, which helps you understand the relationships of the various objects in object-oriented programs

✔ Visual programming tools (Experts), which enable you to easily create Windows applications

✔ Options notebooks, which make it easy for you to control the behavior of the IDE

✔ An integrated help system, which provides you with quick information about using the IDE or creating C++ programs

You can use and control any of these components just by selecting menu items and clicking on choices in dialog boxes. This makes it very easy to perform complex tasks, because you don't need to learn (and remember) the rather arcane command-line options (called switches). You'll use the IDE as you complete the various programming exercises throughout this book.

There's Even an OWL in Here

Application frameworks make it easier to create GUI programs because they provide a set of C++ classes that model the way a GUI program works. (A GUI program, or graphical user interface program, uses menus and dialog boxes so the user can control the program by just pointing and clicking. Windows programs are examples of GUI programs.) The application framework included with Borland C++ 4.0 is ObjectWindows, version 2.0. (ObjectWindows is sometimes called OWL for short, pronounced just like the bird name.)

Without using an application framework, it can be a real chore to create attractive GUI programs. Although graphical interfaces make it easier for users to learn and use programs, they are difficult for programmers to create. For example, it can take 2000 to 4000 lines of code to write a simple Windows program that contains menus, prints "Hello World" on-screen, and is able to be printed. (Programmers affectionately call this type of program Hello World. A Hello World program is often used to illustrate how easy or difficult a particular programming system is.)

Part of the reason a simple program like Hello World is so difficult to write in Windows is that there about a thousand (okay, around 750) different programming commands you need to learn in order to manipulate Windows. That's a lot to cram in your head.

Most programs are much more complicated than Hello World, though, and you need to do a lot of programming tasks to get them to work. For instance, you need to define a routine that receives Windows messages. You need to determine if these messages were caused by accelerator keys. You need to determine which parts of your program should receive these messages. You need to find out if there's another instance of your program running. You need to register the names of portions of your program. And that's only to *start* a program, not even to display something on-screen!

Application frameworks handle these and similar types of tasks automatically. For example, when you create a program, you can use the ObjectWindows TApplication class, which handles all the code for starting a program. You can use the TWindow class to create a window, and the TDialog class to create a dialog box. All these classes handle the details of Windows programming for you automatically, so you can concentrate on the unique features of your program.

No Need to Be Quiet in These Libraries

Libraries are predefined sets of functions and classes that handle many common programming tasks. Borland C++ includes a number of libraries. Some provide mathematical functions, and others provide basic data structures (ways to organize information in a program) that you can use throughout your programs. Libraries make your life as a programmer easier, because you can use these preexisting items instead of having to create your own.

There are two major groups of libraries. The runtime libraries (abbreviated RTL) include the various helper functions such as math, disk, and string-manipulation commands. These libraries have names that all start with a *c*. For example, cc.lib, ch.lib, and crtldll.lib are all RTL libraries.

The libraries of pre-built data structures (sometimes called the *container classes*, and sometimes called the Borland International Data Structures, or *BIDS*) all have names that start with bids. For example, bidsc.lib, bidsdbc.lib, and bidsm.lib are all BIDS libraries.

For Pros Only: Windows Utilities

Borland C++ includes a number of utilities that help you figure out what Windows programs do. Usually only advanced programmers use these utilities, the most important of which are WinSight and WinSpector. WinSight displays Windows messages and classes that are being used by a running program and WinSpector helps track GP faults. (A GP fault is the name of a particularly nasty

What are all those different library versions?

Many times, you'll discover that there are several different versions of each library. Each version corresponds to a different *memory model* — or way of building the program — and is represented by a letter (or letters) placed after the library name and before the .LIB extension. The version letters and the memory models they represent are described here:

S	Small model	F	Flat (32-bit) model
C	Compact model	W	Windows version
M	Medium model	D	Diagnostic
L	Large model	I	Import library (for use with DLLs)
H	Huge model	MT	Multithread version (Windows NT only)

For example, mathl.lib means that this math library is the large-model version. And bidsdf.lib means that this BIDS library is the flat-model version that also includes diagnostics.

If you're building small sample programs you can use the small-model libraries. If you're building real-world programs, you'll usually use only the large-model libraries. If you're building 32-bit programs, you'll use the flat-model libraries.

type of crash under Windows. GP, which stands for general protection, relates to the way computer chips work.) Tracking GP faults is very useful when you're debugging a program, because if the program goes sky high, you can figure out where (and sometimes even why) it died.

More Stuff for Pros Only: General Utilities

There are a number of other utilities that make it easier to write programs. Most of these utilities are for advanced programmers and are designed to be used in conjunction with the command-line tools. Three of the most often-used utilities are MAKE, GREP, and TOUCH. The MAKE utility is used in conjunction with the command-line tools to build programs. The GREP utility is used to search for text across files. The TOUCH utility is used to change the date and time on a program so that the compiler is tricked into rebuilding a file.

Some trivia you can use to impress people

There are lots of puns surrounding the Windows utilities. For example, the name WinSpector is a double pun: you can in*spect* Windows programs, and WinSpector helps you sift through the ghosts ("specters") of programs that have died (that is, GP faulted).

Microsoft has a similar program called Dr. Watson. Before Borland shipped WinSpector, it was called Dr. Frank and had an icon that looked like Frankenstein. This was partly a joke about Dr. Watson and partly a joke about a guy named Frank Borland, who some people say Borland was named after.

You can still find remnants of the Dr. Frank joke. For example, there's a program that works along with WinSpector called DFA.EXE. This stands for Dr. Frank's Assistant.

The Tree-Free Way to Get Information

Borland C++ 4.0 comes with many files that provide on-line information. These files come in three flavors: help files, explanatory text files, and on-line versions of the hard-copy (printed) manuals.

The help files, which all have an HLP extension, provide on-line access to information about Borland C++. The help files are context-sensitive — that is, they're smart enough to know what you need help about. For example, if you access help from a dialog box in the IDE, you'll be presented with help about the dialog box. Likewise, if your cursor is on a library or Windows function in the editor when you access help, you'll get help about those subjects.

You can read the help files either directly from the IDE (by pressing the F1 key) or by double-clicking on the help-system icons to load the Windows help program. You can search for topics, look at an index, and click on certain words (they'll be underlined) to get additional information.

The on-line text files are located in the DOC directory. Most of these files discuss esoteric details about various aspects of the product, such as compatibility with older versions and how to use the Windows NT RPC (remote procedure call) mechanism. These files usually have a DOC or TXT extension.

Two other on-line text files, README.TXT and INSTALL.TXT, are located in the \BC4 directory. README.TXT contains tips, last-minute information, and corrections relating to Borland C++. It's a good idea to read this file. INSTALL.TXT provides tips on how to install Borland C++ and suggestions on what to do if you have installation problems.

The CD version of Borland C++ 4.0 has a directory called BOOKS that contains complete on-line versions of all the printed manuals. Using on-line books is a convenient way to look through the documentation while you're at the computer. If you have the CD version, be sure to take advantage of this helpful feature by installing the on-line documentation.

Sample Programs to Get You Started

Borland C++ includes numerous sample programs that make it easier for you to learn and write programs in C++. Some of the sample programs illustrate a particular technique; others provide full working programs such as a simple video game. A handy feature of the sample programs is that you can cut and paste code from them to use in your own programs. This can save you lots of time and effort, and lets you focus on the more specialized parts of your program.

Chapter 2
Installing Borland C++ 4.0

· ·

In This Chapter

▶ Learn about the various Borland C++ installation options
▶ Install Borland C++
▶ Modify the system files to use the Borland C++ CD-ROM

· ·

*O*kay. You still have time to turn back, put away that stack of disks, and return to the land of mere mortals. Nah...

Before you use Borland C++ 4.0, you (obviously) need to install it on your computer. This chapter will help you do just that.

Borland C++ 4.0 comes with its own GUI installation program. (GUI, pronounced *gooey*, stands for graphical user interface, and means that you can use menus, dialog boxes, and buttons to easily specify how a program should operate.) Because Borland C++ 4.0 has so many features, the GUI install program contains lots of installation options. You can do a full installation (installing the entire Borland C++ 4.0 package) or you can install only those components you need (which can save you a lot of disk space). If you have the CD-ROM version of Borland C++ 4.0, you can also do a "bare bones" install (so called because most files stay on your CD).

Before you install Borland C++ 4.0, it's a good idea to read over this entire chapter so that you understand the various options and can choose the installation approach that's best for you.

Do You Have Enough Free Space?

Borland C++ takes up a lot of hard disk space when you install it. In fact, a full installation takes about 75 megabytes (abbreviated 75M) of disk space. Fortunately, you probably don't need to do a full install and can therefore use less disk space.

This chapter describes a number of different installation scenarios:

- Full install
- "Bare bones" install (for CD-ROM version)
- Install Windows tools only
- Install Windows tools only, but keep most files on the CD-ROM (for CD-ROM version)
- Install Windows and Windows NT tools only
- Install DOS tools only

The first two scenarios are described in their own sections, and the last four scenarios are described in the "Four Other Installation Scenarios" section. Read over each section before you start installing Borland C++ so you can select the scenario that's best for you.

You can save lots of disk space by choosing the appropriate installation scenario. For example, if you never plan to do DOS development, you don't need to install the DOS compilers. If you were to do a full install in this case, the DOS compilers would just be taking up valuable hard disk space on your computer. You might as well save the disk space by not installing them. Likewise, if you never plan to do Windows development, you can save many megabytes of disk space if you don't install the Windows help files.

Make sure you have enough disk space for the scenario you want. (The space requirements for each scenario are discussed in the beginning of each section.) For example, suppose you decide to do the "I want Windows tools only" install. This requires around 50M of free space on your hard drive. (You'll also need some extra space for temporary files used during installation. And don't forget that, after installation, you'll need some space for saving the programs you create.) So the first thing you need to figure out is: do you have 55-60M of free space on your hard drive? If you don't, either:

- Choose an installation option that consumes less disk space.
- Buy a new hard drive.
- Delete some files that you no longer use. Do you still use that recipe file? How about those bitmaps of your cousin's dog? Get rid of them so you can install Borland C++.

Which Install Do I Have?

Borland C++ 4.0 first shipped in December 1993. An update, called the Borland C++ Service Update (or version 4.02), shipped in June 1994. The install program in the Service Update is different from the install program in the original shipment. See the Appendix to determine which install program you have. If you have the original install program, use the install instructions in this chapter. Install instructions for the Service Update are provided in the Appendix.

Starting Install

You need to start Windows before you run the Borland C++ 4.0 install program. To start Windows, type:

```
WIN
```

(By the way, if you ever get tired of seeing the Microsoft logo flash by when you start Windows, just type `WIN :` instead.)

To run the Borland C++ install program, follow these steps:

1. If you have the floppy-disk version of Borland C++, put the first floppy disk in your disk drive.

   If you have the CD-ROM version, put the CD in the CD drive.

2. Select File|Run from the Program Manager.

3. If you have the floppy version, type `A:INSTALL` and click the OK button. (If your floppy isn't in drive A, use your drive letter instead of A. For example, if your floppy is in drive B, type `B:INSTALL`).

   If you have the CD-ROM version, type `E:\INSTALL\INSTALL` and click the OK button. (If your CD drive isn't drive E, then type its drive letter instead of E.)

4. When you see the message suggesting you read INSTALL.TXT, click the OK button.

The disk will chug for a while and then the install program will appear.

Now — *before* you select any options — continue reading this chapter so you can understand the various types of installs that you can do.

The Full Install (Or How to Fill a Disk in No Time)

This approach installs all the Borland C++ tools and requires around 75M of free space on your hard disk. Before you do a full install, it's a good idea to determine if this is really the best approach for you. Do you plan to use all the Borland C++ tools and utilities? Can you spare this much hard disk space? Many programmers (and almost all beginners) find that other installation scenarios are better suited for their needs. Simple step-by-step directions for each installation scenario are given in the following sections.

If you've decided that the full install is best for you, then follow these steps. Remember, you'll need around 75M of free space before you begin.

If you're installing from floppies:

1. Click the Install button.

2. Grab a good novel and place the disks into the machine when prompted.

If you're installing from the CD:

1. Make sure the Install Only Config Files option isn't checked.

2. Click the Install button.

3. Go for a short walk or grab a donut.

The Bare-Bones Install (Requires CD-ROM)

With the CD-ROM version, you can keep almost everything on the CD-ROM drive. A small number of configuration files will be stored on your hard disk, but everything else will stay on the CD. Performance will be a bit slow because you'll run the compiler and load libraries from the CD, and CDs are slower than disk drives. On the other hand, you'll only need around 75K (that's K, not M) of disk space!

To do the bare-bones install:

1. Make sure the Install Only Config Files option is checked.

2. Make sure the Create Borland C++ Group option is checked.

3. Click the Install button.

If you do the bare-bones install, you'll need to make sure the Borland C++ CD-ROM is in your CD-ROM drive every time you start Windows. That's because Borland C++ needs certain device-driver files that help its command-line programs run under Windows. These files are stored on the hard drive during a full install, but kept on the CD-ROM during the minimal (bare bones) install. If you do the bare-bones install, Windows will look for these files on the CD-ROM drive when it starts.

If you don't have the Borland C++ CD in the drive when you start Windows, you'll get two error messages before the Windows screen appears. These messages indicate that Windows can't find WINDPMI.386 and TDDEBUG.386.

You don't need to panic; just follow these steps:

1. Press Enter when you see each of these messages. Windows will then start.

2. If you're not going to use Borland C++, just keep using Windows as usual and nothing bad will happen.

3. If you do plan to use Borland C++, exit Windows, put the Borland C++ CD in the CD-ROM drive, and start Windows again.

Or, follow the steps in the "Free, free, set your CD free" sidebar. ▧

Four Other Installation Scenarios

This section describes the installation procedures for the four other installation scenarios. Selecting one of these scenarios can help you keep disk consumption down without impacting performance. Instead of installing the full set of Borland C++ tools, these scenarios install only the tools you'll use on a regular basis. If you use these scenarios, you'll be able to perform all the tasks discussed in this book (and in fact almost all programming tasks), yet use far less disk space than the full install requires:

✔ **I want Windows tools only:** Installs a reasonable set of tools for creating Windows applications. Requires around 50M of disk space.

✔ **I want Windows tools only, but keep stuff on CD:** Installs a reasonable set of tools for creating Windows applications, but keeps some files, such as the help files, on the CD to reduce disk consumption. Requires around 26M of disk space.

✔ **I need Windows and NT tools only:** Installs a reasonable set of tools for creating Windows and 32-bit Windows applications. Requires around 59M of disk space.

✔ **I want DOS tools only:** Installs what you need to create DOS programs. Requires around 26M of disk space.

The following sections show how to install these various options.

By the way, don't let the number of steps in each section scare you off; the individual steps are simple and easy to follow. Just take them one at a time and you'll be fine.

Free, free, set your CD free

Having to put the Borland C++ CD-ROM in the CD drive every time you start Windows is a pain. If you forget to replace the Seventh Guest game CD or Grateful Dead album you had in the drive, you'll get the two nasty error messages that were described in the "Bare-Bones Install" section of this chapter.

Here's what you can do to get back your CD freedom. Note that you need to do this only for the bare-bones install.

First, copy the two files Windows looks for on the CD when it starts. That way, Windows won't need the CD to be in the drive in order to find the files. If the E drive is your CD drive, and the C drive is where you installed Borland C++, copy the files as shown here:

```
COPY E:\BC4\BIN\WINDPMI.386 C:\BC4\BIN
COPY E:\BC4\BIN\TDDEBUG.386 C:\BC4\BIN
```

Next, modify SYSTEM.INI. This is a file located in the WINDOWS directory that tells Windows where to find all types of device drivers, video drivers, and other goodies. SYSTEM.INI thinks that the two special files are located on the CD-ROM, so you need to tell it that you moved them.

To do this, load SYSTEM.INI in NOTEPAD. Look for the following lines. They'll be in an area in the INI file that starts with [386Enh]:

```
device=E:\BC4\BIN\WINDPMI.386
device=E:\BC4\BIN\TDDEBUG.386
```

Change these lines to:

```
device=C:\BC4\BIN\WINDPMI.386
device=C:\BC4\BIN\TDDEBUG.386
```

That's it. Now you'll no longer need to have the Borland C++ CD in the drive when you start Windows.

The "I want Windows tools only" install

The following steps install the tools you need to create 16-bit Windows applications.

1. The Destination Directory entry lets you control where Borland C++ will be installed. By default this will be C:\BC4. You only need to change this if you want to install Borland C++ to a different disk drive.

2. If you have several disk drives in addition to a CD-ROM drive, you might need to change the CD-ROM Drive entry so it has the drive letter for your CD drive.

3. If you have the CD version of Borland C++, click the Install Only Config Files option off.

4. Click the Install Win32s option off.

5. If you're running Windows from a local area network, check the LAN Windows Configuration option.

6. Click the Customize Hard Disk Installation button.

7. Click the Borland C++ Tools button.

8. Click the following options off: 32-bit Target Command Line Tools, 16-bit Target Command Line Tools, 32-bit Turbo Debugger for Windows, 16-bit Turbo Debugger for Windows, and 16-bit Turbo Debugger for DOS. Click OK.

9. Click the Borland C++ Libraries button.

10. Click the 32-bit Specific RTL Header Files option off. Click OK.

11. Click the ObjectWindows Library Options button.

12. Click the following options off: 32-bit ObjectWindows Library, ObjectWindows 1.0 Conversion Utility, ObjectWindows Source Code. Click OK.

13. Click the Windows RTL Options button.

14. Click the following options off: 32-bit Library, 32-bit DLLs, 16-bit Small Library, 16-bit Compact Library, 16-bit Medium Library. Click OK.

15. Click the Class Libraries Options button.

16. Click the following options off: 32-bit Class Library, 1.0 Class Library API, Class Library Source Code. Click OK.

17. Click the DOS RTL Options button.

18. Click all the options off. Click OK.

19. Click the OK button again. (This will take you back to the Borland C++ Installation Options dialog box.)

20. Click the Utilities and Documentation button.

21. Click the Windows 3.1 DLL and HLP Files option off. Note, however, that if you plan to ship programs to customers who use Windows 3.0 (instead of Windows 3.1 or later), you should leave this option set on. Click OK.

22. Click the Examples button.

23. Click the following options off: Class Library Examples, IDE Examples, DOS Example Files.

24. Click OK. Click OK again. (This will take you back to the main install dialog box.)

25. Click the Install button.

The "I want Windows tools only, but keep stuff on CD" install

The following steps are very similar to those for the "I want Windows tools only" install, except that help files and sample programs are kept on the CD-ROM drive to save hard disk space.

1. The Destination Directory entry lets you control where Borland C++ will be installed. By default this will be C:\BC4. You only need to change this if you want to install Borland C++ to a different disk drive.

2. If you have several disk drives in addition to a CD-ROM drive, you might need to change the CD-ROM Drive entry so it has the drive letter for your CD drive.

3. If you have the CD version of Borland C++, click the Install Only Config Files option off.

4. Click the Install Win32s option off.

5. If you're running Windows from a local area network, check the LAN Windows Configuration option.

6. Click the Customize Hard Disk Installation button.

7. Click the Borland C++ Tools button.

8. Click the following options off: 32-bit Target Command Line Tools, 16-bit Target Command Line Tools, 32-bit Turbo Debugger for Windows, 16-bit Turbo Debugger for Windows, and 16-bit Turbo Debugger for DOS. Click OK.

9. Click the Borland C++ Libraries button.

10. Click the 32-bit Specific RTL Header Files option off. Click OK.

11. Click the ObjectWindows Library Options button.

12. Click the following options off: 32-bit ObjectWindows Library, ObjectWindows 1.0 Conversion Utility, ObjectWindows Source Code. Click OK.

13. Click the Windows RTL Options button.

14. Click the following options off: 32-bit Library, 32-bit DLLs, 16-bit Small Library, 16-bit Compact Library, 16-bit Medium Library. Click OK.

15. Click the Class Libraries Options button.

16. Click the following options off: 32-bit Class Library, 1.0 Class Library API, Class Library Source Code. Click OK.

17. Click the DOS RTL Options button.

18. Click all the options off. Click OK.

19. Click the OK button again. (This will take you back to the Borland C++ Installation Options dialog box.)

20. Click the OnLine Help button.

21. Click all the options off. Click OK.

22. Click the Utilities and Documentation button.

23. Click the Windows 3.1 DLL and HLP Files option off. Note, however, that if you plan to ship programs to customers who use Windows 3.0 (instead of Windows 3.1 or later), you should leave this option set on.

24. Click the Borland C++ Documentation option off. Click OK.

25. Click the Examples button.

26. Click all the options off.

27. Click OK. Click OK again. (This will take you back to the main install dialog box.)

28. Click the Install button.

The "I want Windows and NT tools only" install

The following steps install the tools you need to create 16- and 32-bit Windows applications. This install is similar to the "I want Windows tools only" install, but adds the 32-bit tools and libraries.

1. The Destination Directory entry lets you control where Borland C++ will be installed. By default this will be C:\BC4. You only need to change this if you want to install Borland C++ to a different disk drive.

2. If you have several disk drives in addition to a CD-ROM drive, you might need to change the CD-ROM Drive entry so it has the drive letter for your CD drive.

3. If you have the CD version of Borland C++, click the Install Only Config Files option off.

4. If you're running Windows from a local area network, check the LAN Windows Configuration option.

5. Click the Customize Hard Disk Installation button.

6. Click the Borland C++ Tools button.

7. Click the following options off: 16-bit Target Command Line Tools, 16-bit Turbo Debugger for Windows, and 16-bit Turbo Debugger for DOS. Click OK.

8. Click the ObjectWindows Library Options button.

9. Click the following options off: ObjectWindows 1.0 Conversion Utility, ObjectWindows Source Code. Click OK.

10. Click the Windows RTL Options button.

11. Click the following options off: 16-bit Small Library, 16-bit Compact Library, 16-bit Medium Library. Click OK.

12. Click the Class Libraries Options button.

13. Click the following options off: 1.0 Class Library API, Class Library Source Code. Click OK.

14. Click the DOS RTL Options button.

15. Click all the options off. Click OK.

16. If you have the CD-ROM version of Borland C++ and want to save space by keeping your help files on CD, follow these steps:

    (a) Click the OnLine Help button.

    (b) Click all the options off.

    (c) Click the OK button.

17. Click the OK button again. (This will take you back to the Borland C++ Installation Options dialog box.)

18. Click the Utilities and Documentation button.

19. Click the Windows 3.1 DLL and HLP Files option off. Note, however, that if you plan to ship programs to customers who use Windows 3.0 (instead of Windows 3.1 or later), you should leave this option set on. Click OK.

20. Click the Examples button.

21. Click the following options off: Class Library Examples, IDE Examples, DOS Example Files. (If you have the CD-ROM version of Borland C++ and want to save hard disk space, you can click off all the options in this dialog box.)

22. Click OK. Click OK again. (This will take you back to the main install dialog box.)

23. Click the Install button.

The "I want DOS tools only" install

The following steps will install the tools you need to create 16-bit DOS applications.

1. The Destination Directory entry lets you control where Borland C++ will be installed. By default this will be C:\BC4. You only need to change this if you want to install Borland C++ to a different disk drive.

2. If you have several disk drives in addition to a CD-ROM drive, you might need to change the CD-ROM Drive entry so it has the drive letter for your CD drive.

3. If you have the CD version of Borland C++, click the Install Only Config Files option off.

4. Click the Install Win32s option off.

5. If you're running Windows from a local area network, check the LAN Windows Configuration option.

6. Click the Customize Hard Disk Installation button.

7. Click the Borland C++ Tools button.

8. If you want to run only the command-line tools, you can save 22M of disk space by clicking the IDE option off and clicking the 16-bit Target Command Line Tools option on instead. In this case, skip step 9. Note that in most cases, and in all the examples in this book, you'll want to install the IDE.

9. Click the following options off: 32-bit Target Command Line Tools, 16-bit Target Command Line Tools, Resource Workshop, 32-bit Turbo Debugger for Windows, 16-bit Turbo Debugger for Windows. Click OK.

10. Click the Borland C++ Libraries button.

11. Click the 32-bit Specific RTL Header Files option off. Click OK.

12. Click the ObjectWindows Library Options button.

13. Click all the options off. Click OK.

14. Click the Windows RTL Options button.

15. Click all the options off. Click OK.

16. Click the Class Libraries Options button.

17. Click the following options off: 32-bit Class Library, 1.0 Class Library API, Class Library Source Code. Click OK.

18. Click the DOS RTL Options button.

19. Click the following options off: DOS Medium RTL, DOS Compact RTL, DOS Huge RTL.

20. Click OK. Click OK again. (This will take you back to the Borland C++ Installation Options dialog box.)

21. Click the OnLine Help button.

22. Click the following options off: ObjectWindows Help, Win32 & Windows 3.1 Reference, Resource Workshop Help, GUI Utilities Help, Creating Windows Help. Click OK.

23. Click the Utilities and Documentation button.

24. Click the following options off: GUI Utilities, Windows 3.1 DLL and HLP Files, Microsoft CTL3D Files. Click OK.

25. Click the Examples button.

26. Click the following options off: OWL Examples, Class Library Examples, IDE Examples, Misc. Windows Examples.

27. Click OK. Click OK again. (This will take you back to the main install dialog box.)

28. Click the Install button.

CD-ROM Installation Specifics

If you're using the CD-ROM version, you can take advantage of several extra installation features. (These features apply to both the original release and the Service Update.) First, because it's easy to copy files from the CD, you can do a bare-bones install (described earlier) and then copy additional files as you need them. Second, you can install on-line documentation for easy reference. And third, if you don't mind a little futzing with your files, you can save space by keeping your help files on CD-ROM. (The steps required to do this aren't difficult; you just have to be willing to do a little simple editing in your files.)

Installing just a few things from the CD-ROM

If you have the CD-ROM version, you can always install a few files and then install more later. It's easy to do this with the CD-ROM version because CDs store lots of information and therefore don't have to keep all the files compressed. (Floppy disks don't store much information, so files on the floppy version of Borland C++ are compressed. If they weren't compressed, it would take close to 70 disks to store Borland C++. And because the files are compressed, it isn't easy to copy an individual file from the floppies to your hard disk.)

The CD-ROM has a directory (INSTALL) containing all the compressed files. These files are used by the install program to install Borland C++ on your hard drive.

The CD also contains a directory (BC4) containing uncompressed files. This directory contains all the files you'd get by doing a full install. For example, BC4\LIB contains all the library files and BC4\BIN contains all the binary executables.

If you do a partial install but later want to copy more files to your hard drive, you can easily copy the uncompressed files from the CD-ROM to your hard drive. For example, suppose you only installed the large model library files. You could copy all the library files by copying the entire BC4\LIB directory from the CD-ROM to the BC4\LIB directory on your hard drive.

Installing on-line documentation

Installing on-line documentation is useful because if your desk is as messy as mine you can just read the Borland C++ documentation off your computer instead of having to search through letters, bills, and old pizza boxes to find your manuals. On-line documentation also lets you do such things as search the documentation for various words, or cut and paste examples into your programs.

To install the on-line documentation, run the INSTALL.EXE in the BOOKS directory.

If you use the on-line documentation, you'll find that the page numbers are slightly different from those in the hard copy. That's because the pages in the CD's table of contents count as pages, whereas in the hard copy they don't. All the cross-references in the on-line documentation are consistent — so you don't need to worry about an index entry in the on-line documentation giving the wrong page number — but if you flip back and forth between the on-line documentation and the hard copy you'll find the page numbers don't match exactly. ■

Save space by keeping your help files on CD-ROM

You can save 10-30M of hard disk space if you keep the help files on CD. But to be able to search these files from the IDE automatically, you'll have to do a few tricks.

First, load the WINHELP.INI file from the WINDOWS directory. You can use your favorite text editor, such as Notepad. Now change the drive for the Borland C++ help files so the CD drive is searched by the Windows help program. For example, if your CD drive is drive E, you would change the WINHELP.INI file to read:

```
[files]
BCW.HLP=E:\BC4\BIN
OWL.HLP=E:\BC4\BIN
BWINAPI.HLP=E:\BC4\BIN
WORKHELP.HLP=E:\BC4\BIN
WINSIGHT.HLP=E:\BC4\BIN
WINSPCTR.HLP=E:\BC4\BIN
MINDEX.HLP=E:\BC4\BIN
```

Now make similar changes to the BORHELP.INI file so that Borland C++ looks to the CD for the help index files. (Again, you can load and modify this with Notepad or another favorite text editor.) Change any 0's that are listed to 1's. If your CD is drive E, you would end up with:

```
[files]
BCW.HLP=1
OWL.HLP=1
BWINAPI.HLP=1
WORKHELP.HLP=1
WINSIGHT.HLP=1
WINSPCTR.HLP=1
MINDEX.HLP=1

[index path]
BCW.HLP=E:\BC4\BIN
OWL.HLP=E:\BC4\BIN
BWINAPI.HLP=E:\BC4\BIN
WORKHELP.HLP=E:\BC4\BIN
WINSIGHT.HLP=E:\BC4\BIN
WINSPCTR.HLP=E:\BC4\BIN
MINDEX.HLP=E:\BC4\BIN
```

Finally, you need to delete the help files in your BC4\BIN directory. (If you didn't install the help files in the first place, you'll have some really small place-holder files here. If you did install the help files, you'll have a bunch of really big files.)

To delete the help files, do this:

```
DEL BCW.HLP
DEL OWL.HLP
DEL BWINAPI.HLP
DEL WORKHELP.HLP
DEL WINSIGHT.HLP
DEL WINSPCTR.HLP
DEL MINDEX.HLP
```

The IDE will now know to load help files from the CD-ROM.

What to Do If It Doesn't Install

If you can't get Borland C++ to install, check out Chapter 39, which offers a number of suggestions and tips that can help you get Borland C++ installed and ready for work.

Chapter 3
Instant Windows Program!

● ●

In This Chapter

▶ Create a real Windows program

▶ Get acquainted with the basic IDE features

▶ Learn what the AppExpert does

▶ Change a program's color and title

▶ Use the AppExpert to generate a program

▶ Compile and run a program

● ●

*Y*ou've just spent a good chunk of time installing Borland C++ 4.0, and — in between feeding disks to the computer — you've probably consumed vast quantities of caffeine or sugar. So you're probably sitting on the edge of your chair, just waiting to get started.

That's why we'll jump right in and create a full working Windows application (or *program* — these two terms are often used interchangeably).

Fortunately, the Borland C++ tools do most of the hard work for you, so creating this application will be easy. This process will give you a quick overview of what it's like to create applications with Borland C++.

It's Time to Power Up Borland C++

All the steps discussed in this and the remaining chapters assume you have Borland C++ 4.0 running. If you want to follow along or try any of these things, make sure you've started Borland C++ 4.0.

When you install Borland C++, a large group is created inside the Windows Program Manager. To start Borland C++, double-click on the Borland C++ icon:

Whoa, Where Am I?

You've just started the Borland C++ IDE. You'll be spending a lot of time in the IDE (think of it as a comfortable armchair for programming), so it's worth taking a quick moment to look around it.

The IDE is made up of these parts:

- ✔ An editor, so you can write and modify your programs without leaving the environment.

- ✔ A compiler, so you can compile your program (or find syntax errors that prevent your program from compiling).

- ✔ An integrated debugger, so you can find and fix mistakes.

- ✔ A project manager, so you can easily build executables (and DLLs and LIBs).

- ✔ A browser, so you can understand the relationships of the various objects in object-oriented programs.

- ✔ Visual programming tools (Experts), so you can easily create Windows applications.

- ✔ Options notebooks, so you can easily control the behavior of all aspects of the IDE.

- ✔ An integrated help system, so you can get more information about using the IDE or creating C++ programs without needing to open a manual.

You use the menus and the SpeedBar buttons to access these various features — causing various new windows to appear within the IDE. For example, when you use the editor, an edit window appears. And when you compile, a dialog box appears, showing the status of the compiler.

There are several IDE features that make it easy for you to figure out what's happening: help hints, the help system, the SpeedBar, and SpeedMenus.

Help hints appear on the status bar (the gray bar that stretches across the bottom of the IDE). They provide quick information about what you're doing. For example, if you move the mouse across menu commands, the hints explain what the menu items do. If you're in the middle of opening a project, the hints help you with the various steps.

If you need more information than the help hints provide, you can press the F1 key to bring up the Borland C++ help system. The help system provides more information on tasks, as well as on the C++ language, library functions, and Windows functions. You can also access the help system by clicking on the help menu.

The SpeedBar (the bar containing icons that appears immediately below the menu bar), provides icons that you can click to perform various actions. As you move your mouse across the buttons, a help hint will appear to tell you what each button does. The SpeedBar contains icons for the most popular actions. Depending on what window you have active in the IDE, the SpeedBar will contain different icons. For example, if you're working in an editor window, the SpeedBar contains icons for editor actions, and if you're working with a browser window, the SpeedBar contains icons for browser actions.

You can also right-click on a window to bring up a SpeedMenu. The SpeedMenu shows the most common actions you can perform on a particular window. For example, if you right-click on a Project Manager window, you're given a list of commands for operating on projects.

In this chapter, you'll use the visual programming tools (the Experts) and the compiler to create a Windows application. In the following chapters you'll explore the various other parts of the IDE.

A Sneak Preview

Creating Windows programs can sometimes be a real pain. There are tons and tons of things you need to do just to get a simple window to appear on the screen. Getting an application to print text or graphics is even worse. A lot of tasks that seem simple in COBOL on a mainframe, or in any programming language in DOS, can become traumatic experiences in Windows.

Borland C++ provides lots of features that help reduce the mayhem. EasyWin, which is used throughout Parts II and III of this book, lets you program as if you were still under DOS. ObjectWindows 2.0 (OWL) provides high-level objects to handle things such as window display and printing. And the Experts (AppExpert and ClassExpert) help you create and modify Windows applications without requiring you to read enormous amounts of documentation.

In this chapter, you'll use AppExpert to create a basic Windows application. You'll then compile the application and try it out. In the next chapter you'll customize its user interface using the ClassExpert and Resource Workshop.

Bringing in the Expert

Most Windows programs have many things in common. They usually have a menu, a tool bar, a status line, and a help system. Some have printing and print-preview support, drag-and-drop capabilities, and help hints. Just these features, which are included in most commercial Windows applications, often require 30,000-70,000 lines of code!

But why create 30,000-70,000 lines of code from scratch if you can just borrow them from somewhere? (I'm talking about legal borrowing, of course.)

That's what the AppExpert is for. You describe the basic features of the application you want to create, and AppExpert creates the foundation — a full working Windows application ready for customization.

Ready to begin? Start the AppExpert by selecting Project | AppExpert from the Borland C++ menu. You'll first be asked for the name of the project you're trying to create. Type the name of the application you want to build. For example, type nohands, as shown in Figure 3-1.

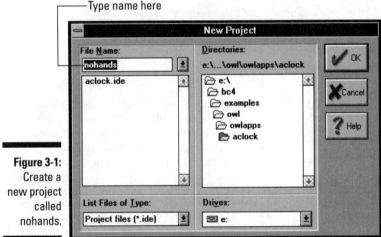

Figure 3-1:
Create a
new project
called
nohands.

In addition to typing a project name, you can also type the directory (including the entire directory path, if you choose) where you want the project to be stored. If that directory doesn't exist, Borland C++ will create it. ∎

Now Comes the Easy Stuff

Once you've typed in a name, the AppExpert appears, as shown in Figure 3-2. You just click the appropriate buttons to tell AppExpert what basic characteristics you want your application to have, and AppExpert creates it for you.

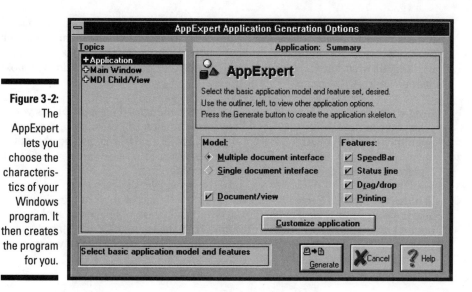

Figure 3-2:
The
AppExpert
lets you
choose the
characteris-
tics of your
Windows
program. It
then creates
the program
for you.

You can make a number of customization choices in AppExpert. The six main choices are listed here. Other choices (such as changing the background color, changing the title, and so on) are described in the following sections of the chapter.

As you read the descriptions of these six main options, don't change anything. Just keep the default settings for now.

Multiple document interface versus Single document interface: Multiple document interface (MDI) programs can have several windows open at once. Most word processors, spreadsheets, and even Borland C++ are MDI applications. Single document interface (SDI) programs have only one window in which things are displayed. In Windows, the calculator, Notepad, and Solitaire are examples of SDI applications.

Document/view: This is a fancy technique that lets you easily expand programs so that they can display different types of files (documents) in different ways (views). By default, the application will know how to view text files. You can add in viewers for databases, binary files, and all types of things. If you don't select this option, you'll still be able to view text files, but adding new viewers won't be as easy. (By the way, many people call this doc/view for short.)

SpeedBar: This is the gray bar that appears underneath the menus and contains icons you can click on. The SpeedBar icons provide a shortcut to common actions. For example, the default SpeedBar lets you click on a button to create a new file — rather than having to select File I New.

Status line: This gray bar at the bottom of the window displays helpful messages. For example, it might provide a help hint describing a particular menu choice or SpeedBar option. It might also indicate whether or not the Caps Lock key is pressed, or what line the cursor is on in an editor. You'll see status lines in most major Windows programs.

Drag/drop: Drag-and-drop support (usually pronounced *dragon drop*) lets you select files in the File Manager and then drop them on top of your application to open them. By default, the program that AppExpert creates knows how to open only text files. (That is, files with a TXT extension.) To make it understand other types of files, you need to do some programming.

Printing: When this choice is selected, your application can print files. It will also have a print-preview capability, so you can see what a page will look like before you actually print it. Printing support is one of the hardest things to program in Windows. Having AppExpert program it for you can really save a lot of time.

But I Want a Purple Background and a Fancy Title!

You can customize many aspects of the application that AppExpert will create. For example, if you click the Main Window item in the Topics list, you can change the background color and title of your application.

Although it's a matter of personal taste about whether you decide to change the default window background color (I'd suggest switching to a bright purple, personally), most people usually do change the default title.

The default title is the name that will appear in the title bar of your application. By default, the title is assigned the name of your project, with all lowercase letters. You might want to modify the title by adding words and spaces to make it more suited to your liking.

Follow these steps to customize the background color and title of your program:

1. Click Main Window in the Topics column.

2. Type `Look Ma, No Hands` for the Window title.

3. Click the Background color button.

4. From the Color dialog box, select bright purple and click OK.

Your screen should be similar to that shown in Figure 3-3. (The bright purple background doesn't show up in the figure, of course, but you get the idea.)

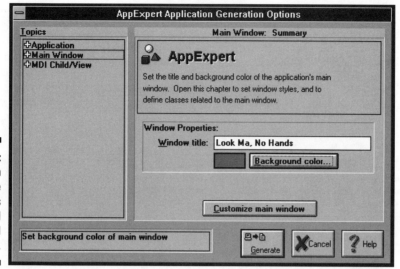

Figure 3-3:
You can change the application's background color and title.

Controlling the world

AppExpert offers a bazillion extra things that you can control. Most of these are advanced options that only hard-core propeller heads will want to touch. To look at the advanced options, click one of the pluses in the Topics list. This expands the topic to show additional items you might want to change.

For example, expanding the Application topic lets you control the author, copyright, and version information; whether or not a help file is created (this is an option you might want to use at some point); where and how the application is created; and what type of controls are used.

Expanding the Main Window topic lets you control whether the application is minimizable or maximizable, whether it has scroll bars, and all types of things about MDI and SDI class generation.

Expanding the MDI Child/View topic lets you control what types of classes are used when MDI child windows are created.

In most programs, you won't need to change these options. But you should definitely explore them if you're preparing for a nerd look-alike contest.

Let the Coding Begin

Now that you've described how you want AppExpert to create your program, it's time to let it begin the coding. Open a fresh Jolt cola, lean back, and click the Generate button:

As a safeguard, the dialog box shown in Figure 3-4 appears after you click the Generate button.

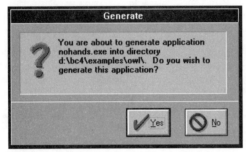

Figure 3-4: This dialog box gives you a chance to change options before the application is created.

Click the Yes button. (Most people end up talking to the computer at this point. Repeat after me — "Of *course* I want to generate it. If I didn't, why would I have clicked the Generate button?!") Actually, this *is* a useful dialog box. For example, you might find that you're about to create the application in the wrong directory, so this gives you a chance to go back and make AppExpert build the application in a different directory or on a different drive, or to correct some other mistakes you've made.

Now the AppExpert does its thing for a while. It builds a resource file, a bunch of C++ files, and related header files; it creates some bitmaps; and it does all types of other things. When it's finished, the Project Manager appears, showing you all the different files it created in order to make your application (see Figure 3-5). You're now ready to compile the application.

Project files (and the Project Manager) show you all the different files that make up a program you're creating. You'll learn more about project files in Chapter 5.

If you've been following the steps in this chapter, you've just generated your own C++ program called nohands. (When you clicked the Generate button, a

C++ program was automatically created for you. That AppExpert is pretty cool, huh?)

If you have the optional Borland C++ Programming for Dummies program disk, you could also look at a version of this program that's already been created; it's in the NOHANDS directory.

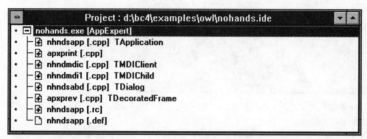

Figure 3-5: The Project Manager shows all the files the AppExpert just created. These are the files that make up your Windows application.

Run, Spot, Run

Now that you've created a program, it's time to compile and run it. To do this, click the lightning-bolt icon on the SpeedBar:

Clicking the lightning-bolt does two things:

✔ It compiles your program. In other words, it takes all the C++ source code that AppExpert created and turns it into an executable. (For background information on programming, you might want to refer to Chapters 12 and 13.)

✔ It runs the program.

While it's compiling, Borland C++ displays a dialog box that shows its progress, as illustrated in Figure 3-6.

The application you're creating has about 70,000 lines in it, so you'll need to wait until the number in the upper left part of the dialog box gets to around 70,000 before it's finished. ■

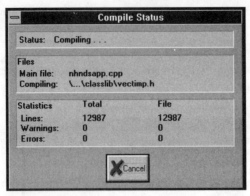

Figure 3-6: The Compile Status dialog box shows how many lines have been compiled, which helps you see how far along the compiler is.

So What's Going On and What's Taking So Long?

A number of things are happening while the numbers go whooshing by you on-screen. First, the C++ files are compiled. This creates a lot of things called object (or OBJ) files. Next, the OBJ files are linked together, along with some libraries. Then the resources are added in and the executable is created. If you stare at the Compile Status dialog box, you'll see messages related to these tasks flying by during these different stages.

Once Borland C++ has finished compiling the program, it runs the program.

After giving yourself a well-deserved pat on the back for creating yourself a nifty Windows program, you'll probably want to tinker a bit with your new creation. Here are two tasks you can perform with your new program:

1. Create a new text window by selecting File | New.

2. Open an existing file by clicking the open icon in the SpeedBar (it's the second icon). Open the APXPREV.CPP file; your screen should look like the one shown in Figure 3-7.

Experiment further, if you like. Look at the About box. Try printing and print preview (but before you do a print preview, read the following section).

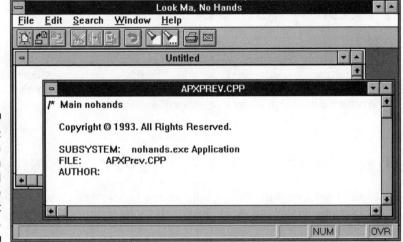

Figure 3-7:
The application you created can create or read text files.

Close That Print Preview Window Before You Leave, OK?

The Print Preview window shows you what a file will look like when it's printed, without your actually having to print the file. When you use the Print Preview window, you'll need to close it before you close or resize the program. To close the Print Preview window, double-click its system icon, as shown in Figure 3-8.

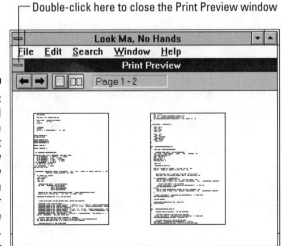

Figure 3-8:
You'll need to close the Print Preview window before you resize or close the application.

What to Do If You Get Errors

You shouldn't have received any error messages when you compiled this program. If you *did* receive error messages, however, the most likely reason is that the compiler can't find certain header files or libraries. You might need to use Options|Project to change the directories (see Chapter 11). You might also want to check out Chapter 41, which offers solutions for many common errors.

What to Do If It Takes Forever to Compile

Depending on your machine, compiling this program can take anywhere from one minute to one hour. If it's taking a very long time to compile, it's probably because you don't have much memory in your machine.

As a first step toward fixing this problem, make sure that Borland C++ is the only application you're running. As a second step, buy more memory. Realistically, you want 8M of memory to get good performance. If you have 16M, things should be really fast.

Table 3-1 provides some suggestions on hardware to use for compilation.

Table 3-1: Hardware to Speed Your Machine

Machine	*Suggestions*
386 with 4M	Get more memory. Ideally, you should get a 486, too. 386s are a little slow for development machines.
486/20 with less than 4M	Get more memory. Ideally 12-16M, though 8M will make a significant difference. Consider getting a faster machine, too.
486/66 with 16M	If this is slow, something else is going on. Maybe you are accidentally running from the CD-ROM drive?
Pentium with 32M	Send it to me.

Another alternative is to stick to the programs discussed in Parts II and III. They're much simpler and you won't spend very much time compiling them.

TECHNICAL STUFF

What *are* all those files that AppExpert generated?

AppExpert generates a number of different files for the different parts of the application. The last couple of letters in the file name tell you what the source code in the file does. Here's what all the files for the nohands program do. If you create other programs using AppExpert, you'll see that the same files are created, but with slightly different names:

nhndsapp.cpp: Contains code for where the program starts — this code is called *the main*. (Actually, for ObjectWindows programs, it's called the OwlMain.) Technically speaking, this is where things relating to the TApplication class are created.

apxprint.cpp: Contains code for printing.

nhndmdic.cpp: Contains code for the MDI client window.

nhndmdi1.cpp: Contains code for the MDI children (windows).

nhndsabd.cpp: Contains code for the About box.

apxprev.cpp: Contains code for print previewing.

nhndsapp.rc: Contains the Windows resources used by the program.

nhndsapp.def: The module-definition file for the program. You should never need to look inside this file.

This chapter has given you a quick overview of what it's like to program in Borland C++. In the next chapter, you'll continue working with your nohands program as you learn how to customize and enhance Borland C++ programs.

Chapter 4
Customizing Your Program

● ●

In This Chapter

▶ Customize a Windows program

▶ Learn how to use the ClassExpert

▶ Customize a dialog box with Resource Workshop

▶ Create a new dialog box with the DialogExpert

▶ Add a new menu to a program

▶ Add specialized functionality to a program

● ●

*I*f you followed the instructions in Chapter 3, you've just created a real nice Windows program. Unfortunately — and forgive me if this shocks you — you'll have a hard time selling this program to someone. It just doesn't have any custom features.

In this chapter you'll learn how to enhance the program's user interface. You'll change the About box and then add a new dialog box. You'll also see how you can add custom code to make your program stand out from the crowd.

Bringing Up Another Expert

The AppExpert makes programs. Its dashing twin ClassExpert customizes programs. So, since you now want to customize your program, you need to invoke the ClassExpert. One of the easiest ways to do this is to select View|ClassExpert. (A mouse shortcut is to double-click the EXE name in the project.)

The ClassExpert has three parts, or *panes*, as shown in Figure 4-1. The upper-left pane lists all the classes in the program. The pane at the bottom is a full working editor. You can use this editor to customize and debug your program. The upper-right pane lists events that happen. To customize your program, you can change what happens when these events occur.

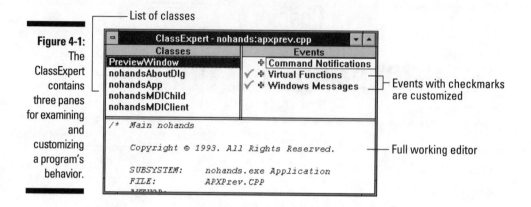

List of classes

Figure 4-1:
The
ClassExpert
contains
three panes
for examining
and
customizing
a program's
behavior.

Events with checkmarks
are customized

Full working editor

Instead of explaining these ClassExpert features in depth, this book uses a more hands-on approach: it has you use them. This will give you a good idea of what the various features are for and how to put them to work for you. Later, if you want more information, you can read the official Borland documentation.

What Are All Those Classes, Anyway?

Before you use the ClassExpert, glance again at the upper left pane in Figure 4-1. Five classes are listed there. These are the C++ classes that are used throughout the application.

Classes are one of the principal features of C++ programming — they let you model the way real-world objects behave. (Classes are described in more detail in Chapters 13 and 27.)

Each of the five classes has a specific purpose related to a critical part of the application, as shown in Table 4-1. All of these classes are ObjectWindows classes. (You'll be learning more about ObjectWindows in Part III.)

Table 4-1: The Classes Created by AppExpert

Class	Description
PreviewWindow	Controls the print-preview window.
nohandsAboutDlg	Controls the About dialog box that's displayed in the application.
nohandsApp	Controls the basic behavior of the application as a whole.
nohandsMDIChild	Controls how the MDI children (windows) behave.
nohandsMDIClient	Controls how all the MDI children relate to each other.

About boxes can hold secrets

Programmers often like to add special secrets to their About boxes. Usually, these are hidden screens that appear if you know the magic key combinations. For example, in Word for Windows, there's a screen where a whole bunch of Microsoft programmers jump up and down on a WordPerfect dragon. Borland C++ has a much less violent secret screen. If you bring up the About box and then press Alt+I, you'll get a list of the folks who helped create Borland C++.

Changing the About Dialog Box

One of the most important parts of an application is the About box. This is the box that appears when the user selects Help | About. It's where you can put a pretty picture of yourself and brag about how you wrote the application. So it's very important that you customize it.

To change the way your About box looks, just right-click the class that controls the About box (nohandsAboutDlg), and then select Edit dialog. This loads the About dialog box into Resource Workshop, which is a powerful tool for modifying resources.

Heeeeere's Resource Workshop

Resource Workshop lets you design the user interface for your application. You can add new controls, change the appearance of dialog boxes, draw bitmaps, and even edit menus. This book doesn't go into too much detail about the various Resource Workshop features, but you'll get a chance to try out a number of them.

Anyway, back to your application. After you select Edit dialog, Resource Workshop clanks and whirs for a while and then displays your About dialog box, as shown in Figure 4-2.

When Resource Workshop appears, you'll notice that it has a lot of windows. First, there's the dialog-box editing window. This is the big window that says DIALOG: IDD_ABOUT. There is also the dialog box itself — the window with the title that says About nohands. This is where you can directly manipulate the way your About box appears.

You'll also see a Tools palette. This contains a bunch of different controls that you can drop on the dialog box to give it extra capabilities. Finally, there's an Alignment palette to help you line things up inside your dialog box.

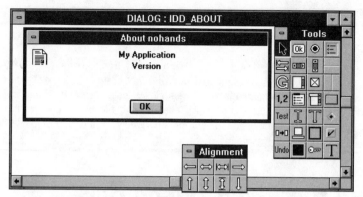

Figure 4-2: You can use the Resource Workshop tools to edit an application's user interface, such as by changing the appearance of a dialog box.

The Tools palette contains lots of different icons, with each icon representing a different tool. The icons in the left column control the process of creating and modifying the dialog box. The icons in the middle two columns let you add controls. The icons in the right column let you add special 3-D controls.

The Borland manuals contain a complete list of the tools. Table 4-2 shows the most important tools (the ones you're most likely to use).

Now that you've got a basic idea of what Resource Workshop can do, how about adding a new item to the dialog box:

1. Before you begin, select Options|Show properties. (If you just see Options|Hide properties, then you're okay — Options|Show properties has already been set.)

2. Click the static text tool icon (see Table 4-2 if you're not sure what it looks like). This indicates that you're about to add a new text field to your dialog box.

3. Now click the location on the dialog box where you want the next text field to appear. For example, click near the bottom right portion of the dialog box.

A new text field is then added.

If you placed the text field very close to the bottom or the right of the screen, portions of it might be overflowing the edge of the dialog box. To fix this, click the text item you just added and drag it back inside the screen. ■

Table 4-2: The Most Common Resource Workshop Tools

Tool	Description
	The selector tool lets you click on things to modify or move them.
	The button tool lets you add buttons to a dialog box. Buttons are used to invoke actions.
	The list box tool lets you add a list box to a dialog box. List boxes present users with a set of choices.
	The group box tool lets you put a clear box around a bunch of controls to indicate that they're part of a group.
	The edit control tool lets you add edit controls to a dialog box so users can enter text.
	The radio button tool lets you add radio buttons to a dialog box. Radio buttons let users choose whether an item is selected or not. Radio buttons are used for groups in which only one item in the group can be selected at a time.
	The check box tool lets you add check boxes to a dialog box. Check boxes let users choose whether an item is selected or not. Check boxes are used when several items in a group can be selected at a time.
	The combo box tool lets you add combo boxes to a dialog box. Combo boxes are a combination (hence their name) of edit controls and list boxes. You can type in values and also choose from a list. There are several variations of combo boxes.
	The static text tool lets you type text that appears on the dialog box. The user can't change this text. Static text is usually used for labels.
	The group shade tool lets you add a 3-D style group box to a dialog box. These are used to add an extra bit of snazz to an application.
	The Borland push button tool lets you add Borland-style buttons to a dialog box. These are the buttons with the checkmarks and big red Xs you see throughout Borland C++.
	The Borland radio button tool lets you add Borland-style radio buttons to a dialog box. These are radio buttons with a 3-D look.
	The Borland check box tool lets you add Borland-style check boxes to a dialog box. These are check boxes with a 3-D look.
	The Borland text static control tool lets you type some text for labels, with a 3-D look.

Now that the new text field is added, change what it says:

1. Click at the top of the Properties box (Figure 4-3).

2. Type in `My About`.

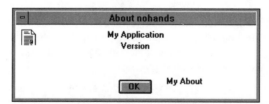

Properties	
My About	
Caption	My About
Height	18
Id Source	-1
Id Value	-1
Left	128
Style	
Tabstop	False

Figure 4-3: The Properties box, after you've typed in new text for the static text control.

You'll end up with an About box that looks like Figure 4-4. Ta da! That's all you need to do to customize your application's user interface.

About nohands

My Application
Version

OK   My About

Figure 4-4: Here's how your customized About box should appear.

Now switch back to the IDE:

1. Press Ctrl+Esc to get a list of programs that are running. (This list is called the Windows task list. The IDE will be listed as an item called Borland C++.)

2. Double-click the item that says Borland C++.

To prove that the changes you made actually worked, compile and run the program:

1. Click the lightning bolt in the Borland C++ SpeedBar.

2. When the program runs, select Help|About to look at the new About box.

3. Now close the program by selecting File|Exit.

Adding Some Panache with a New Dialog Box

Continuing along with our saga, we'll now add a completely new dialog box to your application. This task is going to require that you type a bit of code. If this seems a bit daunting at first, you might want to take a break, gulp down one or two caffeine-laden drinks to bolster your nerves, and then forge ahead. We'll take it step by step.

Ready to begin? Follow these steps to start creating a new dialog box:

1. Right-click on nohandsAboutDlg in the ClassExpert's list of classes.

2. Select Create new class.

This brings up the dialog box shown in Figure 4-5; this dialog box lets you add all types of new classes to your application. Follow these steps:

1. Don't change the Base class entry. (It should say TDialog.)

2. Type BlastIt for the Class name. The ClassExpert automatically fills in names for the source file and header file.

3. Type IDD_BLASTIT for the Dialog Id.

4. Click OK.

Figure 4-5:
The Add New Class dialog box lets you add new classes to your application. Here you'll add a new dialog-box class.

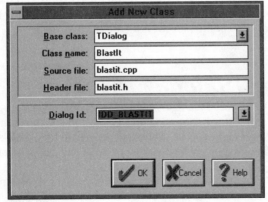

You've just told the ClassExpert that you want to create a new class that controls a dialog box. You therefore based the class on TDialog, the ObjectWindows class for dialog boxes. (At this point, those of you who've already read about object-oriented programming might want to know that you're creating a new class that's derived from TDialog. The rest of you might not want to know that yet.) You also associated a dialog ID with the class. The dialog ID tells what dialog box should be displayed when the class is used — that is, it associates a dialog resource with a dialog class. ■

Here are descriptions of each field in the Add New Class dialog box (Figure 4-5):

Base class: Lets you choose what type of item you want to add to your program. For example, you can add new dialog boxes, new editors, standard dialog boxes, VBX controls, and all types of other goodies by selecting classes from this drop-down list.

Class name: Lets you give a name to the new class. For example, in the previous steps you named your new class BlastIt. Don't use any spaces or funny characters in this field. (See the C++ naming rules in Chapter 16 if you have any questions about this.)

Source file: Unless you're a hard-core hacker, you never need to change this (hackers will intuitively know what this field does and why they might want to change it).

Header file: You never need to change this. (A *header file* is a special file that contains definitions that the program needs. You can find out more about header files in Part II.)

Dialog Id: Despite its name, this has nothing to do with the dialog box's subconscious personality or seat of psychic energy. The dialog ID is an identifying name for the dialog box. This name is used by the ClassExpert and by Resource Workshop. Most programmers use IDD_ to start the name of a dialog ID. (In case you're wondering, IDD stands for IDentification for a Dialog.)

And Up Pops the DialogExpert

When you type in a new dialog-box name, the DialogExpert appears, as shown in Figure 4-6. This is a special Expert that helps you create new dialog boxes quickly and easily. DialogExpert presents a list of different dialog-box styles.

DialogExpert lets you choose where to place buttons and what style of dialog box to create. The Borland-style dialog boxes all have a three-dimensional look to them.

1. Click on the option that says "Borland dialog. Buttons on bottom." This makes a 3-D dialog box with OK, Cancel, and Help buttons along the bottom.

2. Click OK.

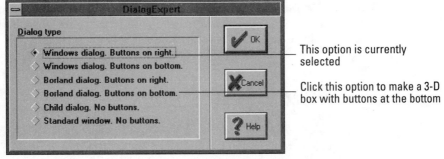

This option is currently
selected

Click this option to make a 3-D
box with buttons at the bottom

Borland C++ will now whiz and whirl as it creates a new C++ file and resource
file for the new dialog class. When it's finished, you'll be back in the ClassExpert.

Checking Out Your New Masterpiece

Let's take a look at this new dialog box.

1. Right-click on BlastIt in the ClassExpert.

2. Select Edit dialog.

Resource Workshop appears, showing your new dialog box (Figure 4-7).

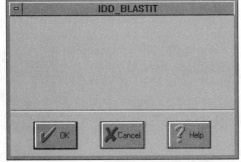

If you want, you can add some new controls to this dialog box. For example,
you might want to add some new text or some additional buttons.

Phew! Adding a new dialog box took a while to explain, but it really doesn't take
very long to do. Most applications have lots of dialog boxes in them, so it's a

good idea to practice this skill. You might want to experiment with creating different types of dialog boxes. After you've practiced a bit, you'll find that creating dialog boxes is really pretty easy.

Adding a New Menu Item

Now that you know how to add a dialog box to an application, you can add a new menu item to your application:

1. Switch back to the IDE: first press Ctrl+Esc to get a list of programs that are running, then double-click the item that says Borland C++.

2. From the ClassExpert, right-click on nohandsApp.

3. Select Edit menu.

In step 2, make sure you right-click on the App class. If you don't, your program won't work quite the way you expect it to.

After you complete all three steps, Resource Workshop and its menu editor appear, as shown in Figure 4-8. The menu editor shows what the menu bar looks like, and individually lists all the items that make a menu. Before you add the new menu items, there are two terms you need to learn: *popup* and *menu item.*

Popup menus are top-level menus that generally have other items (menu items) underneath them. Their text appears on the menu bar. For example, the File and Edit menus that appear in most Windows applications are popup menus.

Menu items are the individual items that are listed underneath the popup menus. Underneath the File popup menu, for instance, you'll see the Open menu item. Menu item text appears only when a menu is selected; for example, until you click on the File menu, you won't see the Open menu item. (Note that in Figure 4-8, and elsewhere in Borland C++, the term menu item is sometimes written as menuitem.)

Now let's add a new menu item:

1. Click on an existing menu item. For example, click on the Open menu item (this is a few items down in the File menu).

2. Press the Insert key on your keyboard. A new menu item is added after the one you selected. You can now change the new menu item's name, and even add a helpful message that will be displayed in the status line whenever you move the mouse over this menu.

3. Type Blast It as the Item text.

4. Type Display the Blast It dialog as the Item help, and press Enter.

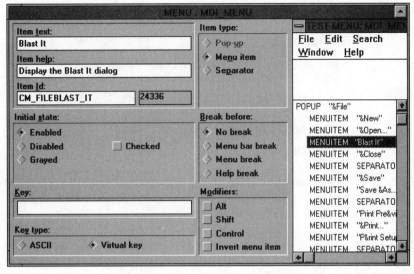

Figure 4-8:
Resource
Workshop
lets you
create and
modify menu
items.

You can set all types of parameters for menus. Most of the time, you can ignore all of them except for Item text and Item help.

Congratulations! If you were to recompile and run your program, you'd now have a new menu item and a new dialog box. (But don't do this yet.) Of course, all the menu item would do is sit there and look pretty, but that's a good start. And you'd have no way to prove that you created a new dialog box, because until you complete the next section, you won't have any way to display it.

Making Ends Meet: Hooking Up the New Dialog Box

Now it's time to make the new dialog box appear when the user selects the new menu item. It sounds like this should be pretty simple. Well, it is, as long as you don't mind typing a little code.

Here's what you do:

1. Right-click on the Blast It menu item, as shown in Figure 4-9.

2. Select ClassExpert. This pops you back into the ClassExpert, with a menu event highlighted.

3. Click on the little plus sign, and then click Command (Figure 4-10).

4. Right-click to bring up a SpeedMenu that shows actions for customizing events. In this case, you'll customize the event caused by the user clicking the Blast It menu item.

5. Select Add handler. The Add Handler dialog box (shown in Figure 4-11) lets you add a new function to perform some action when the menu is selected.

6. Select a name for this function, as shown in Figure 4-11.

   a. Type `ShowBlastIt`.

   b. Click OK.

This creates a new function that's called when the user selects the File | Blast It menu.

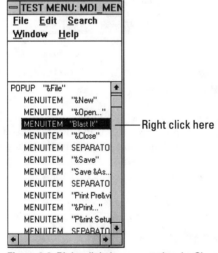

Figure 4-9: Right-click the menu to invoke ClassExpert.

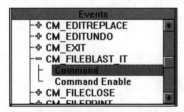

Figure 4-10: Click the Command item to modify what happens when the menu is selected.

Figure 4-11:
Type the
name of the
function to
handle the
menu event.

Next, you want this function to display the Blast It dialog box. To make this happen, you need to invoke some ObjectWindows magic:

1. Click in the ClassExpert editor, right below the line that says:

```
//INSERT>> Your code here.
```

2. Type:

```
BlastIt(MainWindow).Execute();
```

This tells the program to create and display the BlastIt class. (The BlastIt class is the class you created earlier; it displays the BlastIt dialog box.) In step 2 you passed in the name MainWindow and told the class to Execute. MainWindow is going to become the parent window for BlastIt. (Essentially, this just means that MainWindow is going to tell BlastIt where to appear on the screen.) Execute just runs some stuff inside of the BlastIt class that makes it display the dialog box. Did you write the Execute code? No — it was automatically inherited from TDialog. That's the magic of object-oriented programming at work.

After you've performed step 2, the ClassExpert editor window should look like the one shown in Figure 4-12.

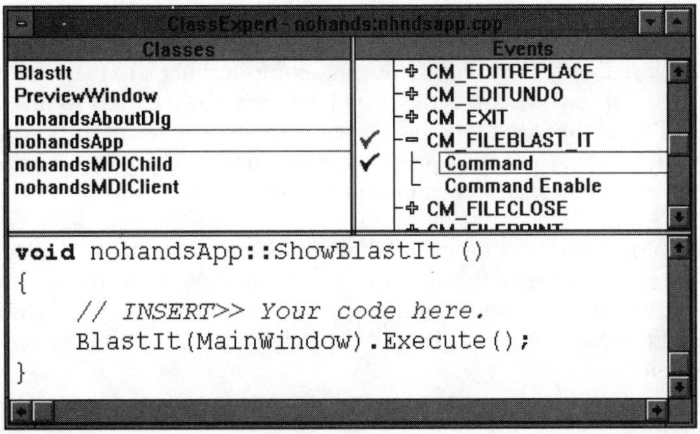

```
ClassExpert - nohands:nhndsapp.cpp

Classes                          Events
BlastIt                          ─⊹ CM_EDITREPLACE
PreviewWindow                    ─⊹ CM_EDITUNDO
nohandsAboutDlg                  ─⊹ CM_EXIT
nohandsApp                    ✓  ─═ CM_FILEBLAST_IT
nohandsMDIChild               ✓    ┌  Command
nohandsMDIClient                   └  Command Enable
                                 ─⊹ CM_FILECLOSE
                                 ─⊹ CM_FILEPRINT

void nohandsApp::ShowBlastIt ()
{
    // INSERT>> Your code here.
    BlastIt(MainWindow).Execute();
}
```

Figure 4-12:
Type the
special C++
code into
the editor
portion of
the
ClassExpert.

There's one more bookkeeping step you need to take care of. Because you're calling a new class, the application needs to know about the class. So you need to include the header file that defines the class. (As mentioned earlier, a *header file* is a special file that contains definitions that the program needs. You'll be learning about header files in Part II.)

The BlastIt class is defined in the blastit.h header file. Follow these steps to add it to your program:

1. Scroll to the top of the editor in ClassExpert, and then down a little until you see all the header file includes. (These all start with the word #include.)

2. Look for a line that says #include "nhndsabd.h". (If you think that looks confusing, just try to pronounce its full name: *no hands application about dialog header file*.)

3. Now click in the editor, right below the #include "nhndsabd.h" line, and type the following:

```
#include "blastit.h"
```

4. Because you've made a number of changes, save your program. Just select File|Save all.

(This complete program is in the BLASTIT directory on the separately available program disk.)

Running It Again

Now that you've customized the program, compile and run it once more. (To do this, just click on the lightning bolt.) Your program should now run. When you check out the program this time, note that there's a new menu item. Select File|Blast It, and your BlastIt dialog box should appear.

If for some reason your program doesn't compile, check to make sure you typed the source code correctly. (Compare your ClassExpert to that shown in Figure 4-12.) If you didn't type the code in correctly, click in the ClassExpert editor and correct the code. Then compile and run once more. If you still get compiler error messages, consult Chapter 42.

If your dialog box doesn't appear when the BlastIt menu item is selected, you probably skipped one of the steps in this chapter. Most likely, you forgot to click on the App class before creating the menu handler. Try the steps in the "Making Ends Meet: Hooking Up the New Dialog Box" section once more. Then compile and run.

If it still doesn't work, try going through all the steps in Chapters 3 and 4 again.

The 5th Wave   **By Rich Tennant**

PC DESCENDING
A STAIRCASE

"THE ARTIST WAS ALSO A PROGRAMMER AND EVIDENTLY PRODUCED SEVERAL VARIATIONS ON THIS THEME."

Summarizing What You Just Did

You just did a lot of stuff:

- Modified the About box.
- Created a new dialog box by creating a dialog class called BlastIt. This class inherited from TDialog, which is an ObjectWindows 2.0 class.
- Created a new menu item.
- Created a handler for the new menu item. In other words, you created a function that's called when the user selects the menu item.

    ✔ Created the BlastIt class, and made its dialog box display whenever the menu item is selected.

    ✔ Included the header file that defined the BlastIt class.

These are the basic steps for customizing your program:

1. You create new dialog boxes (or other types of classes).

2. You then cause these dialog boxes to appear, either after a button is clicked or when a menu is selected.

3. You can then add more and more specific functionality by adding more and more handlers for the various actions that can occur.

You've learned the basic framework for how to create a Windows program. Throughout this book, you'll learn additional skills for using the Borland C++ environment and you'll learn C++ programming. If you want to learn more about how to customize Windows applications, you might want to consult additional books or the Borland C++ manuals to understand the details of ObjectWindows classes and how Windows operates. The Borland C++ sample programs also illustrate many of the Windows programming techniques.

Chapter 5
Ready for a Brand New Project

● ●

In This Chapter

▶ Learn about projects and project files

▶ Create a new project

▶ Learn about the most common Project Manager tasks

▶ Examine a dependency list

▶ Learn some common file extensions

● ●

*B*y following the steps in Chapters 3 and 4 you created a Windows applica-tion. In the process, you used many different aspects of the Borland C++ development tools. Throughout the rest of Part I, you'll learn more about the various pieces that make up the Borland C++ environment. In this chapter, you'll focus specifically on project files.

Project files make it easier to organize programming projects. Large programs are often created by compiling several different source files. (Even the program you created in Chapters 3 and 4 was composed of several different source files.) Project files show the different source files that make up a program. They make it easy for you to add new source files to a program, and to change the various options that control how a file is compiled.

Who Needs Projects, Anyway?

Some programs consist of a single file. But most programs, such as the one you created in Chapters 3 and 4, are much larger. They involve many different source-code files and many different header files and libraries. To create the final executable, you need to compile each of these different source-code files and then link them.

There are two ways to do this. One is to use a command-line tool called MAKE and build something called a makefile. The other (kindler and gentler) way is to use project files.

A *makefile* contains a list of commands that are executed to create an application. For example, it might say compile *foo*, then compile *bar*, then link these together with library *muck*, and so forth.

Creating a makefile can be rather complicated. You need to know lots of details about how files are compiled and linked. You also need to learn a special makefile language! For example, here's an excerpt from a makefile for building the nohands program:

```
nhndsapp.obj : nhndsapp.cpp
    bcc -c $(CEAT_nohandsdexe) -o$@ nndsapp.cpp
```

Looks pretty intuitive, doesn't it? (I'm being sarcastic.)

The great thing about makefiles (and now I'm being serious) is that MAKE determines what files have been changed. So when you build your application, only the files that have changed are recompiled. This saves a lot of time.

Fortunately, project files provide this same capability, without requiring you to know all the nitty-gritty details about how the compiler goes about compiling and linking a program.

Making Your Life Easier with Project Files

Like makefiles, project files are used for organizing programming projects. But they're a *lot* simpler than makefiles. There are several reasons for this. For one thing, when you use project files, the compiler automatically looks through a source file and finds all the dependencies for you. For another thing, it's very easy to manipulate project files visually. Also, because Borland C++'s Project Manager automatically knows how to compile C++ files, how to link files, and so on, you don't have to tell it exactly how to do these things. In fact, all you have to do is simply add source files to a project file, and the Project Manager will handle the rest. Pretty cool.

Actually, you've already used a project file. When you created your program in Chapters 3 and 4, the AppExpert created a project file that listed every source file in your nohands program.

You can use the Project Manager to do all kinds of programming tasks. For example, you can look at or edit any of the source files listed in your project file. Or you can control details that determine how your application is built. Or you can compile or debug your application. See the "Common Things to Do from the Project Manager" section of this chapter for more information.

Creating a New Project

You need to create a project file whenever you build a program. The project file tells the compiler what source files to compile when building an application. It also tells the compiler what libraries to link in. When you use the AppExpert, the AppExpert creates a project file automatically. (If you're not using the AppExpert, you'll need to create a project file by hand. For example, you'll need to create project files for the various programs discussed in Parts II and III of this book.)

Creating a new project is easy. Just select Project|New project to bring up the New Project dialog box (Figure 5-1).

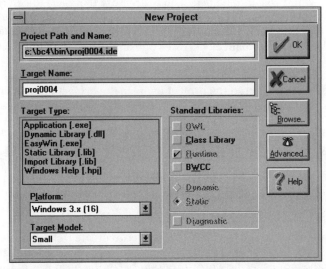

Figure 5-1: The New Project dialog box is where you specify details about the project you are about to create.

Specifying details about the new project

You specify details about a new project in the New Project dialog box. For simple projects, you need to provide a project path and name as well as a target name. You also need to indicate what type of project you're creating and the platform you want.

This section describes the New Project dialog box fields and list boxes where you enter this information.

Project Path and Name field: Use this field to indicate the location and name for the new project file. Before you enter anything into this field, you need to figure out where you want to keep all the source files associated with this project file. In general, it's a good idea to create a separate directory for each project. And you usually name the project the same name you've given the application you're building.

For example, suppose you want to create an application called PIZZA9, and you want to store it in the MYAPPS\PIZZA9 directory. Here's what you would type to do this:

```
MYAPPS\PIZZA9\PIZZA9.IDE
```

If you want your project to be placed in a directory that hasn't been created yet, that's okay. If you type in a directory that doesn't exist, Borland C++ creates a new directory for you. For example, if the MYAPPS\PIZZA9 directory doesn't exist, Borland C++ automatically creates one and places the project file in it. ■

Target Name field: This field contains the name of the application that's being created. When you entered the project name in the Project Path and Name field, Borland C++ automatically created the target name for the resulting executable.

If you want to change the name, you can type in whatever name you want. For example, you might type PIZZA, CHESS, or DBASE.

A *target* is a file that's created by the Project Manager when you compile a project file. Typically, a target is a program (an executable).

You might be wondering why a target isn't just called a program. Well, that's because you can also use the Project Manager to create DLLs, libraries, and help files. Since these aren't really programs, the generic word "target" is used instead of the more specific word "program." (For the purposes of this book, though, you can always think of target as meaning program.)

Target Type list box: This list box lets you specify whether you're creating an application, a DLL, a library, a help file, or an EasyWin program.

The two most common choices you'll make are Application and EasyWin. Application lets you make DOS and Windows programs, and EasyWin lets you write a DOS-style program that runs under Windows.

Chapter 6 provides a little more detail about the target type choices.

Platform list box: This list box is where you specify whether your application will run under DOS, Windows, or NT. For example, if you choose Application as your target type, you can then choose whether the application will be a Windows program, a DOS program, or an NT program.

(By the way, if you choose EasyWin as your target type, you don't need to look at the Platform list box — EasyWin programs are always Windows programs.)

Chapter 6 provides a little more detail about the platform choices.

Other parts of the New Project dialog box

For now, you won't need to fill in the target model type (in the Target Model list box). Just accept the default.

Likewise, for now you can just accept the default library information in the Standard Libraries group box. (When you indicate the type of application you want to create, Borland C++ automatically chooses the libraries that you need.)

Okaying the new project

Once you've supplied the necessary information, just click the OK button to create the new project.

What's All That Stuff That Just Happened?

The new project appears in a window called the Project Manager window, which is shown in Figure 5-2. Note that project files always have the letters IDE for their extension (for example, FOO.IDE and SL.IDE).

The Project Manager window contains a hierarchical diagram showing the name of the executable (at the top) and the names of the source files that are part of the project (below and connected to the executable).

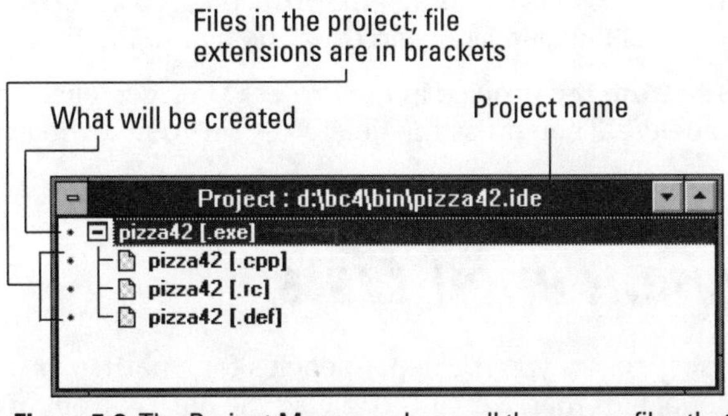

Figure 5-2: The Project Manager shows all the source files that are part of a project.

When you create a new project, some files are automatically placed in it, as outlined in Table 5-1. These are the basic files you need to create an application. For example, if you create a DOS program, a C++ source file is automatically listed in the project file. If you create a Windows program, a C++ source file, resource file, and module-definition file are automatically placed in the project file. Initially, these files are empty.

Table 5-1: Files Created When You Create a New Project

Target	Files created automatically
Application (Windows)	cpp, def, rc
Application (DOS)	cpp
EasyWin	c

Common Things to Do from the Project Manager

You can use the Project Manager to do a myriad of tasks. Here are some common tasks you'll probably do over and over again with project files:

✔ **Look at or edit one of the files in the project:** Double-click on a file name in the Project Manager to load the file into an editor. (Or, if the file is a resource file, Resource Workshop is loaded to edit it.)

✔ **Add a new file to the project:** Right-click on the target (the EXE, DLL, or wherever you want to add a new source file) in the Project Manager and select Add node. You can then choose a single file or a group of files to add.

✔ **Add a file to the project with drag and drop:** Select a group of files from the Windows File Manager. Drag and drop them onto the Project Manager.

✔ **Remove a file from the project:** In the Project Manager, click on the file you want to delete. Then press the delete key on your keyboard.

Looking at Dependency Lists

The Project Manager shows you the dependencies for a particular file. *Dependencies* are the set of files that, if changed, cause the file to be out of date. For example, if the file is a source file, the dependencies are usually all the header files that get included when the file is compiled.

To illustrate this, suppose that you change something in a header file that the source file includes. This will change the way the source file behaves, because something is now defined differently in the header file. (A header file contains a list of definitions used by a source file. The text in a header file is treated as if it were typed directly in the source file. Changing a header file that's included by a source file is essentially the same as changing the source file itself.) Thus, the source file is dependent on the header file, and the source file needs to be recompiled so the changed header file is accounted for.

If a file has dependencies, it has a + (plus) or a – (minus) inside its icon in the Project Manager. The + means that you can click on the icon to show its dependencies. The – means that the dependencies are currently shown; if you click on the icon when it has a – in it, the list collapses to hide the dependencies.

Before a program is compiled, none of the source files have a + in their icon. When the program is compiled, Borland C++ builds up a list of dependencies. You can then expand the source files to see their dependencies (the header files they include), as shown in Figure 5-3. Sometimes the number of header files that's included can be amazing!

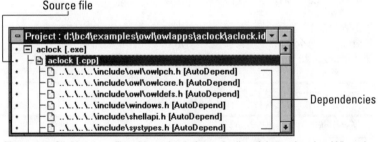

Figure 5-3: Clicking on a file with a + icon shows its list of dependencies. When the dependencies are showing, the + changes to a –.

Something You Don't Need to Worry About: Multitargeting

There are two types of files inside projects: targets and nodes. *Targets* are files that are created. For example, if you've written a bunch of files to create a program called ACLOCK.EXE, then ACLOCK.EXE is a target.

Targets are created by compiling nodes. *Nodes* is just a fancy word for source files. For example, ACLOCK.CPP is a node inside the ACLOCK.EXE target.

If your program is very complex, you might want to break it into a lot of different library files. In Windows, these are called DLLs. For example, Resource Workshop consists of an executable called WORKSHOP.EXE and a set of DLLs.

You can have several targets within a project file. This is useful when you have a large complex program and you therefore want to keep the EXE and the related DLLs within the project.

Multitargeting is also useful when you want to create both a 16-bit and a 32-bit version of a program at the same time.

But (now that you know all about it), multitargeting isn't something you really need to worry about. Not in this book, anyway.

A Quick Guide to File Extensions

File extensions are the three letters that appear at the end of a file name, after the period. They are often used to indicate what a file is. You'll see many different extensions when you use the Project Manager.

Table 5-2 shows the most common extensions that you'll see in the Project Manager, as well as a few others you might run across while you're poking around inside directories that contain project files.

Table 5-2: Common File Extensions

Extension	Description
BAK	A backup file. Backup files are usually copies of text files; they represent what was in the file before it got changed. You can use these files to get back an earlier version if you didn't really mean to save. Or you can delete them to save disk space.
BMP	A bitmap file. Bitmap files define bitmaps used by a Windows program.
C	A C source file.
CPP	A C++ source file.
CSM	Precompiled header file. Precompiled header files are used by the compiler to speed compilation.
DEF	A module-definition file. Module-definition files are used in Windows. They indicate whether a file is a DLL or an EXE, what routines in the file can be called by outside applications, and some other complex stuff.
DLG	A dialog file. Dialog files define dialog boxes used by a Windows program.

Extension	Description
DLL	A dynamic-link library. Dynamic-link libraries are sets of routines that can be linked into an application. Unlike a LIB, the routines aren't sucked into the EXE. As a result, the EXE isn't larger, but the DLL needs to be around in order for the application to work.
DOC	A documentation file. These files usually explain something about a program. Sometimes this extension means that the file was written with Microsoft Word for Windows, but not always.
DSW	A desktop file. Desktop files describe what files and options were set when Borland C++ was last used. This isn't something that you'll ever need to touch.
~ES	A temporary or backup file created by Resource Workshop.
EXE	An executable file (program).
H	A header file.
HLP	A help file.
IDE	A project file. Project files contain information about the files that comprise a project.
LIB	A library. Libraries are sets of routines that can be linked into an application. (Sometimes this extension is pronounced like the beginning of liberation, and sometimes like the beginning of library.)
MAK	A makefile. Makefiles are used in conjunction with the command- line MAKE tool.
OBJ	An object file. OBJ files are created by the compiler and are linked together to create EXEs. (In the UNIX world, these are called .O files.)
RC	A resource file. Resource files contain Windows resources (such as bitmaps, menus, and dialog boxes) that are used by the application.
RES	A compiled resource file. Before resources can be used by an application, they must be compiled into a RES file. The RES file is then linked into the executable.
RTF	A rich text file. Text to be converted into help files must appear in this format.
TMP	A temporary file. Here today, gone tomorrow. Usually, it's safe to delete temporary files, thus freeing up disk space. If you're in the middle of using an application (such as Borland C++), however, it's *not* a good idea to delete temporary files that application has created. The application might still need them. Wait until you shut down the application before you delete any temporary files associated with it.
TXT	A text file.
WRI	A documentation file written with Microsoft Write.

Chapter 6

Three Minutes with the TargetExpert

In This Chapter

▶ Learn about the TargetExpert

▶ Create a DOS project

▶ Create an EasyWin project

▶ Create a Windows project

*B*orland C++ 4.0 lets you create a variety of different types of programs, from DOS to Windows to Windows NT applications. Setting up the correct libraries and compiler options to create an application would be a real headache if it weren't for a special Borland C++ feature called the TargetExpert. When you create a new project, the TargetExpert asks you what type of application you want to create. It then does all the busy work for you.

What Type of Program Would You Like Today?

You can create many different types of applications with Borland C++, including:

- DOS programs
- EasyWin Windows programs — you use these for Windows programs that don't require menus and dialog boxes, such as for simple Windows utilities or to port DOS programs to Windows quickly
- Windows programs
- 32-bit Windows programs

The following sections describe how to create a simple DOS program, a simple Windows program, and a regular Windows program.

Creating a Simple DOS Program

Follow these steps to create a project for making a simple DOS program (one without overlays):

1. Select Project|New project. You'll see the dialog box shown in Figure 6-1.

2. Select Application [.exe] from the Target Type list.

3. Select DOS Standard from the Platform drop-down list.

4. Click the OK button.

Edit the CPP file that is created or add new CPP files.

Figure 6-1:
When you create a new project, the TargetExpert lets you select the type of program to create.

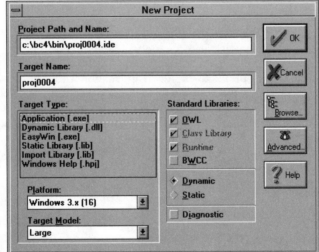

Using EasyWin to Start a Simple Windows Program

Follow these steps to create a project for making an EasyWin program:

1. Select Project|New project.

2. Select EasyWin [.exe] from the Target Type list.

3. Click the OK button.

Note that this creates a C file. You can edit the C file that's created or add new C files.

If you want to make a C++ EasyWin application, follow these steps:

1. Select Project|New project.

2. Select EasyWin [.exe] from the Target Type list.

3. Click the Advanced button.

4. Select .cpp Node and click OK.

5. Click the OK button.

Creating a Regular Windows Program

Follow these steps to create a project for making a regular Windows program:

1. Select Project|New project.

2. Select Application from the Target Type list.

3. Select Windows 3.x (16) from the Platform drop-down list.

4. Optionally, you can change the memory model by choosing an item from the Target Model drop-down list. Most often, you'll want to select Large.

5. Click the OK button.

Edit the CPP file that is created or add new CPP files.

Creating a Windows application can be a lot of work. Fortunately, Borland C++ includes visual programming tools that do most of the hard work for you. See Chapters 3 and 4 for more information on using the AppExpert and ClassExpert.

Chapter 7
Editing Files

• •

In This Chapter

▶ Learn what an editor does

▶ Load and save files with the editor

▶ Perform basic and programming-specific editing tasks

▶ Use color syntax highlighting to identify various program elements

▶ Get context-sensitive help

▶ Search for text

▶ Use macros to avoid having to repeat keystrokes

▶ Emulate other programmer's editors

• •

*W*hen you get right down to it, the process of writing programs consists largely of typing code into an editor. And, just as a good word processor makes it much easier to write a book, a good programmer's editor makes it much easier to write a program. A programmer's editor, as its name implies, is an editor that lets you do special programming-related tasks in addition to the usual editing tasks such as cutting, copying, and pasting text.

Borland C++ 4.0 contains a sophisticated, customizable programmer's editor that you can use to do programmer-type tasks (such as indenting groups of lines or quickly loading header files) in addition to the usual editing tasks. (For short, the Borland C++ programmer's editor is just called "the editor" in this book.) This chapter provides a quick guide to the most important features of the Borland C++ editor.

Powering-Up the Editor

You can edit as many files as you would like (well, not quite an infinite amount but an awful lot of them) with the Borland C++ IDE. If you edit several files at once, each will appear in an editor window within the IDE. An editor window is a plain-looking window into which you can type text. Figure 7-1 shows the editor window with some text in it.

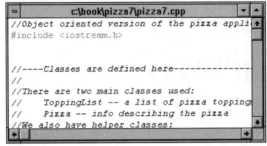

Figure 7-1:
Use the
editor to
display,
enter, or edit
text.

The three most common ways to bring up an editor window are:

- ✔ **Edit a file that's in a project**: Double-click on a file name in the Project Manager. This loads the file into an editor window.

- ✔ **Create a new file**: Select File|New. The file is given a default name. Be sure to give it a new name when you save the file.

- ✔ **Load an existing file**: Select File|Open. Select the name of the file you want to edit.

Once you've edited a file, you can easily save it. You can also save all the files you've edited in one fell swoop. Here are several ways you can save:

- ✔ **Save a file**: Select File|Save.

- ✔ **Save a file, giving it a new name**: Select File|Save as. Type in the new name you want to give the file, and click the OK button.

- ✔ **Save any files that have changed**: Select File|Save all. It's usually a good idea to do this before you run a program you've created, just in case the program crashes the system.

Become an Editing Taskmaster

As you program, you'll find yourself performing a number of editing tasks over and over (and over!) again. Some of these tasks are basic, such as cutting and copying text. Other tasks are very specific to programming, such as indenting a group of lines or opening a header file.

Table 7-1 lists and describes both basic and programming-specific editor tasks. The more basic tasks are described first.

Table 7-1: Editing Tasks for Nerds and Non-Nerds Alike

Editing task	*Description*
Select text.	Click where you want the selection to begin. Hold down the mouse button, move to the end of the selection, and lift up with the mouse.
	Or, click where you want the selection to begin, hold the shift key down, and click where you want the selection to end.
	Or, click (or arrow key) until you get to where you want the selection to begin. Hold the shift key, and arrow key until you get where you want to end.
Cut text.	Select text. Then select EditlCut or press Ctrl+Del. You can then paste the text somewhere else.
Copy text.	Select text. Then select EditlCopy or press Ctrl+Ins. You can then paste the text somewhere else.
Paste text.	Select Editl Paste or press Shift+Ins. This pastes text from the Clipboard into the editor.
Move to top of file.	Ctrl+Home
Move to end of file.	Ctrl+End
Move up a page.	PgUp
Move down a page.	PgDn
Move right one word.	Ctrl+$\rightarrow$
Move left one word.	Ctrl+$\leftarrow$
Find where text runs off right side of the page.	Look for the gray vertical bar in the window. By default, this shows the 80th column. You can change where the bar shows up. If your code is wider than 80 columns, the columns will often wrap when the code is printed (unless you use a really small font).

(continued)

Editing task	Description
	If you keep your code within the gray bar, you can usually be sure it will print out okay.
Look at top and bottom of the file at the same time. (Split the window horizontally.)	Click on the ▤ in the SpeedBar. This breaks the window into two panes. You can scroll each pane separately, and thus be able to look at the beginning and end of the file at one time.
Look at the left and right side of a file at the same time. (Split the window vertically.)	Click on the ▥ in the SpeedBar. This breaks the window into two panes. You can scroll each pane separately, and thus be able to look at the left and right of the file at one time.
Get rid of split windows.	Move the cursor over the bar that shows where the windows are split, until the cursor changes shape. Then click and drag to the bottom right side of the screen.
Indent a group of lines.	Select the group of lines and then press Ctrl+Shift+I. You might do this if you've just added an *if* statement and you need to indent a section of code so that it's easier to read.
Outdent a group of lines.	Select the group of lines and then press Ctrl+Shift+U. You might do this if you've copied a group of lines from one place to another, and now you don't need them indented so much.
Look for matching ( ) { } < > or [ ].	When the cursor is to the left of a ({ < or [, press Alt+] to find the matching) } > or]. When the cursor is to the left of a) } > or], press Alt+[to find the matching ({ < or [. You might do this if you have a lot of nested statements and you want to find where the block started. Or, you might want to make sure that you remembered to end a function call with).
Set a bookmark.	You can set up to ten bookmarks. Move the cursor to where you want to place the bookmark. Press Ctrl+Shift+0 to set bookmark 0. Press Ctrl+Shift+1 to set bookmark 1, and so on.

Editing task	Description
	This lets you mark a place in the code that you easily pop back to. For example, if you want to copy code from one part of a file into a routine, you might set a bookmark at the beginning of the routine, scroll to find the code, copy it, jump to the bookmark you set, and paste in the code.
Jump to a bookmark.	Press Ctrl+0 to go to bookmark 0. Press Ctrl+1 to go to bookmark 1, and so on.
Open a related header file.	Click in the header file name in the source file. For example, if you had the line #include "foo.h", click by the *f* or by one of the *o*'s. Then right-click and select Open source.
	When you write C++ programs, you often need to modify the header file as well as the C++ file. Or you might want to check a header file real quickly to see what has been defined.
Get help for a command.	Click somewhere inside the call you need help on. Press the F1 key.
	For example, you might want to know the syntax for a library call, a Windows API call, or a C++ command.

Colorful Language Allowed Here

The editor in Borland C++ uses something called color syntax highlighting to make it easier for you to read the programs you've written. *Color syntax highlighting* highlights the different program elements — such as comments, keywords, numbers, variables, and so on — so that you can easily identify them. Highlighting also helps you to quickly find common syntax mistakes.

For example, if your code always appears in black and your comments in blue, it's easy to see if you've forgotten to turn off a comment because you'll see a seemingly endless ocean of blue text before your eyes. Likewise, if you set up highlighting so your keywords are italic, you'll know that you've misspelled a keyword if it isn't italic. For instance, if you type clasp when you meant *class*, it won't show up italic. And if a variable shows up as italic, you'll know it's a bad variable name because variables can't have the same name as keywords. (Naming conventions for variables are discussed in Chapter 16.)

If you want to customize the syntax-highlighting colors, just select Options | Environment and move to the Syntax Highlighting page. (You'll learn more about how to do this in Chapter 11.)

Help Is Just a Click Away

If you're using either a C++, runtime library, Windows, or ObjectWindows command, but you can't remember how that command works, help is just a click away. For example, suppose you're trying to use the TWindow class from ObjectWindows, but for the life of you, you just can't remember how to use it. Let's suppose this is the line in question:

```
TWindow foo;
```

Just click somewhere on the word TWindow, then press F1, and on-line help appears.

As another example, suppose you had this line:

```
while (strlen(bar) > 10)
```

You could either click on *while* and press F1 to get help about the *while* command, or you could click on *strlen* and press F1 to get help about *strlen* library function.

Seek and Ye Shall Find

If you're like most programmers, you'll often find yourself in a situation where you need to locate a particular block of code in your file. Instead of scrolling through the file until you find it, you can have the editor search through the code for you.

Use Search | Find to find a particular piece of text. Use Search | Replace to find the text and replace it at the same time. For example, you could use Search | Replace to replace every variable named foo with one named goo.

The Find Text and Replace Text dialog boxes let you enter a number of options to control how the search is done. Figure 7-2 shows the Find Text dialog box; its options are described in the following list.

Case sensitive: C++ is a case-sensitive language. This means that, for example, C++ considers Boogs and boogs to be two different variables. If you set case

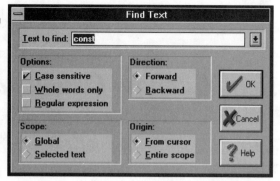

Figure 7-2:
The Find
Text dialog
box lets you
search
through an
edit window
for specific
text.

sensitivity on, the search (or the replace) finds words only where the capitaliza-
tion is exactly matched. Use this option if you know exactly what you're looking
for (that is, if you know the case). If you can't remember whether a name you're
searching for is capitalized or not, turn off case sensitivity.

Whole words only: If this option is on, the search matches the word only when
it's a separate word by itself (a word that's separated from other words by
either a space, a comma, or a bracket). When this option is off, the search finds
the text even if it's embedded inside another word. For example, if you're
searching for const when this option is off, the search finds const in the words
constant and deconstruct.

Regular expression: This is a fancy search feature that lets you look for
wildcards. *Wildcards* are special characters you use to represent other characters. For example, let's say you're looking for a particular variable that you
know starts with an *S* and ends with an *h*. But you're not sure what's in the
middle. You can use wildcards to find all the words that match this characteris-
tic. You've probably used wildcards to search for filenames before (for example, the asterisk in *.bat is a wildcard. When you do a DEL *.*, both asterisks
are wildcards). In the world of C++, wildcards are often called regular expression matching commands and are used to find text quickly. (Table 7-2 lists
some of the most useful expression-matching commands.)

Direction: This option lets you specify whether the editor should search
forward or backward through the file for the text you specified.

Scope: Usually, you search (or replace) through the whole file. Thus, the Global
option is on by default. If you instead set the Selected text option on, the editor
searches only through the text that's selected. (This is probably most useful
when you're replacing, because you can limit your changes to a particular part
of the file.) If you want to search through the whole file, make sure the Global
option is set on.

Origin: This option determines if the search begins where the cursor is or at the beginning of the file.

Regular Expression Matching Commands

Regular expression matching lets you look for wildcards inside text. To see the regular expressions you can use to control searching, turn on the Regular expression option in the Find Text dialog box. Table 7-2 lists the most common of these regular expressions.

The regular expressions in Table 7-2 are sometimes called *GREP-style regular expressions* because they're the same as the expressions used by the general text-searching program called GREP.

GREP is a tool that became popular on UNIX systems. Many UNIX tools have rather gutteral-sounding names, like MAWK, SED, DIFF, and GREP. When you're around computer people, feel free to use the word grep instead of search, as long as you're referring to searching text. You don't grep for signs of intelligent life in the universe, for example. Or anyway, most people don't.

You can also use *BRIEF-style regular expressions,* as shown in Table 7-3. Such expressions are the same as those used by BRIEF, a popular programmer's editor. (To do so, you need to turn on BRIEF-style regular expressions by using BRIEF emulation, or by clicking BRIEF Regular Expressions in the Options | Environment Editor Options dialog box. See Chapter 11 for more information on how to do this.)

Why do they use such fancy words?

Wildcards are sometimes called *regular expression matching commands*. This rather unwieldy term comes from the world of compilers.

When you build a compiler, you often need to build something called a *lexical analyzer,* which is a program that scans over the text in your source files and breaks it into pieces the compiler can understand. The lexical analyzer breaks the file into pieces by searching for patterns. These patterns are called (you guessed it) *regular expressions.*

Thus, regular expression matching just means looking for regular expressions, or patterns.

But you can just say wildcards.

Table 7-2: Regular Expression Matching Commands

Command	Example	Meaning
.	S.ip Matches Slip, Skip, Sbip, and so on.	Matches any single character.
*	Sl* Matches Sl, Slug, Slip, Sliding, and so on.	Matches any number of characters. It must be used at the end of a word; for example, you can't do Sl*g.
+	Sl+ Matches Slug, Slip, Sliding, and so on, but doesn't match Sl.	Matches any number of characters, but it must be followed by at least one more character. It must be used at the end of a word.
-[ ]	S[ml]ug Matches Smug and Slug.	Matches to one of the characters that appears inside the brackets.
[^]	S[^ml]ug Matches Saug, Sbug, and so on, but not Smug or Slug.	Matches to any character, except the character(s) inside the brackets.
[-]	S[c-l]ug Matches Scug, Sdug, Seug, ... Slug, but nothing else.	Matches any letter in the range of characters separated by the hyphen (including the specified letters themselves). So c-l means all the characters between c and l, inclusive.

Table 7-3: BRIEF-Style Regular Expression Matching Commands

Command	Example	Meaning
?	S?ip Matches Slip, Skip, Sbip, and so on.	Matches any single character.
*	Sl* Matches Sl, Slug, Slip, Sliding, and so on.	Matches any number of characters. You can use it to match characters in the middle of a word, such as sl*g to match slug or sloog.
+	Sl+ Matches Slug, Slip, Sliding, and so on, but doesn't match Sl.	Matches any number of characters, but it must be followed by at least one more character. It must be used at the end of a word.
|	Slug|cat Matches either Slug or cat.	Matches either the word on the left or the word on the right.
[ ]	S[ml]ug Matches Smug and Slug.	Matches to one of the characters that appear inside the brackets.
[^]	S[^ml]ug Matches Saug, Sbug, and so forth, but not Smug or Slug.	Matches to any character, except the character(s) inside the brackets.
[-]	S[c-l]ug Matches Scug, Sdug, Seug, … Slug, but nothing else.	Matches any letter in the range of characters separated by the hyphen (including the specified letters themselves). So c-l means all the characters between c and l, inclusive.

Repeating Keystrokes, Repeating Keystrokes

Sometimes you'll need to repeat the same set of keystrokes over and over again. For example, you might need to change the path for a long list of include files. Or you might want to delete the last parameter of a number of function calls.

When you're doing repetitive tasks like these, you can save yourself a lot of time by using macros. A *macro* is a set of keystrokes that you can record and play back. Macros can include letter and symbol keys, and even menu commands such as search.

Start the macro by pressing Ctrl+Shift+R. This records your keystrokes until you press Ctrl+Shift+R again. You can press Ctrl+Shift+P to play back what you just recorded.

Different Keystrokes for Different Folks

The Borland C++ editor is extremely flexible and can emulate several popular editors. For example, it can easily emulate BRIEF or Epsilon (EMACS).

If you don't like BRIEF or Epsilon emulation, you can design your own editor emulation. For example, you could make an EDLIN emulator. Creating your own editor emulation is pretty advanced, though, so it isn't discussed in this book.

To make the editor emulate the BRIEF or Epsilon editors, select Options | Environment and go to the Editor page. Click the appropriate button to choose the editor style you want (the buttons are shown in Figure 7-3).

Figure 7-3: Click these buttons to change the editor emulation.

For example, you could click BRIEF emulation to make the editor emulate BRIEF. To use the default editing keys, click Default keymapping.

Table 7-4 shows the commonly used editor keystrokes for the default, BRIEF, and Epsilon editor settings. (The default keystrokes were described earlier in Table 7-1, but they're repeated here so you can compare them with the other two editor settings.)

Table 7-4: Common Editing Keystrokes for the Default, BRIEF, and Epsilon Editor Styles

Action	Default Editor	BRIEF	Epsilon
Cut text.	Ctrl+Del	-	Ctrl+k (cuts whole line)
Copy text.	Ctrl+Ins	+	Alt+w
Paste text.	Shift+Ins	Ins	Ctrl+y
Move to top of file.	Ctrl+Home	Ctrl+PgUp	Ctrl+Home
Move to end of file.	Ctrl+End	Ctrl+PgDn	Ctrl+End
Move up a page.	PgUp	PgUp	PgUp Alt+v
Move down a page.	PgDn	PgDn	PgUp Ctrl+v
Move right one word.	Ctrl+→	Ctrl+→	Alt+f Ctrl+→
Move left one word.	Ctrl+←	Ctrl+←	Alt+b Ctrl+←
Indent a group of lines.	Ctrl+Shift+I	Tab	Ctrl+X+Ctrl+I Ctrl+X+Tab
Outdent a group of lines.	Ctrl+Shift+U	Shift+Tab	n/a
Undo.	Ctrl+Z	Gray *	Ctrl+x+u F9 Ctrl+F9

Action	Default Editor	BRIEF	Epsilon
Look for matching ({ < or [.	Alt+] Alt+[	Ctrl+Q+] Ctrl+Q+[	Ctrl+Alt+f Ctrl+Alt+b
Set a bookmark.	Ctrl+Shift+0 Ctrl+Shift+1 ⋮ Ctrl+Shift+9	Alt+0 Alt+1 ⋮ Alt+9	n/a
Jump to a bookmark.	Ctrl+0 Ctrl+1 ⋮ Ctrl+9	Alt+J+0 Alt+J+1 ⋮ Alt+J+9	n/a
Record a keyboard macro.	Ctrl+Shift+R	F7	n/a
Playback a keyboard macro.	Ctrl+Shift+P	F8	n/a

Chapter 8

Compiling the Night Away

. . . .

In This Chapter

▶ How to compile a program

▶ Syntax errors and warnings

▶ The difference between makes, builds, and compiles

. . . .

*W*riting programs can be wickedly good fun. You can include all types of zany formulas and approaches in your programs, and then type them up and share them with your friends at parties. And if you're a student, you can submit them to the creative-writing department as avant-garde poems. For example, if Shakespeare were a programmer, he might have written something like "if (_2B) { } else { };".

But if you want the programs you write to actually *do* something, you need to compile them. Compiling a program turns source code — which is code that humans can understand — into machine instructions that the computer can understand.

The process of turning source code into machine code is very complex. It involves figuring out how to turn a set of high-level instructions into very specific low-level machine instructions. When the process is complete, an executable is created. This is the program you can run.

Entire books are written on how to convert high-level programming languages into machine language. Fortunately for you, compiler vendors have read these books, so you don't have to understand how this process works. You just take the programs you've written and compile them with Borland C++.

Recycling, Composting, and Compiling

Well, okay. This chapter is actually just about compiling. Compiling a program with Borland C++ is easy. In fact, you've already done it: when you followed the steps in Chapters 3 and 4, you compiled several times.

To compile a program, first open the project file for that program. (See Chapter 5 for more information on Project files.) Then, select Project|Make all.

Borland C++ will go through all the source files in the project file and convert them into machine code. The end result will be an executable program. You won't see anything on-screen (except for a message telling you that the compilation was successful), but the program will now be on your hard disk. You can run the program, copy it to a disk and give it to a friend, or do whatever else you like doing with programs. (Nothing *too* wild, I hope.)

If you want to compile *and* run the program, click on the lightning bolt instead:

Durn! Syntax Errors

If you made a mistake while writing your program — for example, if you passed the wrong number of parameters to a function, or misspelled a command, or used the wrong name for a variable or a class — then the compiler won't be able to understand your program.

If this happens (or actually, I should say *when* this happens, because it's going to happen), the compiler displays a Message window showing you a list of syntax errors, as shown in Figure 8-1. *Syntax errors* are messages telling you that you've messed up somehow. You can click on a syntax error to go to the line containing that problem. You'll need to fix each syntax error before the program can compile correctly.

Sometimes it's pretty clear what's wrong. Other times, you might have a hard time figuring out how to fix syntax errors, especially when you're new at it. This

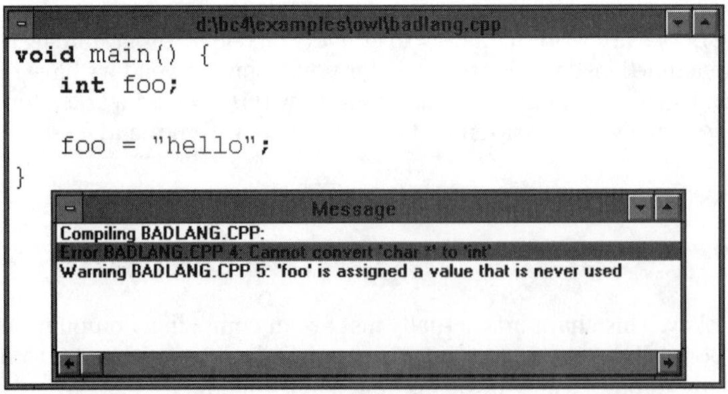

Figure 8-1:
If you have syntax errors, they'll be displayed in the Message window.

```
d:\bc4\examples\owl\badlang.cpp
void main() {
    int foo;

    foo = "hello";
}
```

```
Message
Compiling BADLANG.CPP:
Error BADLANG.CPP 4: Cannot convert 'char *' to 'int'
Warning BADLANG.CPP 5: 'foo' is assigned a value that is never used
```

is one of those things where, after you mess up enough times, you start to be able to see patterns and to better figure out how to fix the problems. The nice thing is that you can usually take your time, so — unless you have someone looking over your shoulder — you don't need to feel embarrassed about your mistakes.

Some simple rules:

- ✔ If the line you're on looks perfectly fine, sometimes it's the previous line that's messed up. Be sure to check it, too.

- ✔ Check for missing or extra ; and } characters.

- ✔ Messages that say "cannot convert ... to ..." usually mean you're trying to assign the wrong type to a variable. For example, you might have a variable that's an integer but you're trying to turn it into a string.

- ✔ Make sure you've typed things correctly. A common mistake is to name a variable one thing, but then spell it wrong or use some other name later on.

- ✔ Check out Chapter 41. It contains a list of many common errors you might encounter and offers solutions for how to fix them.

- ✔ Sometimes one simple problem can cause the compiler to find tons of errors. For example, putting in the wrong path for a header file can lead to 30 error messages. And just fixing that one line can make all those errors go away. So if you compile a program and see screen after screen of problems, there's no need to panic. Often a simple change will fix them all.

- ✔ If you can't figure out what's wrong, ask someone else for help. If you're embarrassed about this, just say something like "Geez, I've been up all night staring at this code and everything is just swimming. I sure could use help from a fresh pair of eyes." Fellow programmers will understand.

Warning, Will Robinson

Sometimes when you compile, you get warnings instead of (or in addition to) errors. *Warnings* occur when the compiler can understand what you're doing, but it thinks you might be making a mistake. For example, if you created a variable but never gave it a value, the compiler warns you to say "why did you do that?" Or perhaps you used a variable before you assigned it a value — if you did this, you'd get a message similar to the one in Figure 8-2.

It's usually a good idea to heed warnings. Sometimes warnings occur because the compiler is just being overprotective, but they usually occur because you've done something careless.

For example, if you accidentally forget to add a line to initialize a variable that you use, you'll get a warning. If you don't heed the warning, the variable will

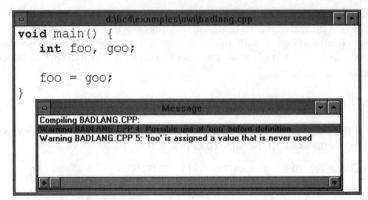

```
                d:\bc4\examples\owl\badlang.cpp
void main() {
    int foo, goo;

    foo = goo;
}
```

```
                         Message
Compiling BADLANG.CPP:
Warning BADLANG.CPP 4: Possible use of 'goo' before definition
Warning BADLANG.CPP 5: 'foo' is assigned a value that is never used
```

Figure 8-2: Borland C++ displays warnings in the Message window if the compiler finds code that it thinks might lead to problems.

have a meaningless value wherever it's used, which can lead to all sorts of troublesome complications.

A good rule of thumb is to fix things until you have no warnings and no errors.

If the Compiler Knows There's an Error, Why Doesn't It Just Fix It?

Even though the compiler knows where an error occurs and what type of error it is, the compiler doesn't know *why* the error occurred. For example, the compiler might detect that a semicolon is missing. Why doesn't it just add one? Well, the semicolon could be missing because you forgot to type one in. Or perhaps the entire line that's missing the semicolon wasn't meant to be there. Or maybe you forgot a few other things in addition to the semicolon. Rather than hazard a guess and get you into real trouble, the compiler just points out the problem and leaves it up to you to fix it.

Compiles, Builds, and Makes: What's the Diff?

You can compile files in three different ways: by compiling them, by building them, and by making them.

Compiling (Project | Compile) compiles a single file. It doesn't create a full program. You use this option when you want to check a particular file for syntax errors. If you successfully compile a file, the end result is an object file (OBJ).

Building (Project | Build all) compiles all files in a project and links them together to create an executable. The end result is either a bunch of syntax errors or a full working program. Even if you just built a program, if you build it again, then every single file is recompiled from scratch. (The result is a fresh OBJ for every single source file, plus an EXE formed by linking all the OBJs.) Building is usually done when you want to make sure that everything in your project has been completely rebuilt.

Making (Project | Make all) compiles any files that have changed, and then creates a new executable if any files changed. In other words, it creates fresh OBJs if any of the source files changed. And if there are fresh OBJs, the program is linked to create a new EXE. As with building, the end result is either a bunch of syntax errors or a full working program. When you're working on a project and changing first one piece and then another, you usually use Project | Make all. That's because making rebuilds only those things that have changed, so you don't have to waste lots of time watching the compiler do unnecessary work.

Most likely, you'll usually do a Project | Make all after you've changed source files and need a new executable. If you press the lightning bolt, it's the same as doing a Project | Make all followed by a Debug | Run.

Chapter 9
Getting the Bugs Out

• •

In This Chapter

▶ Learn about the basic features of the debugger

▶ Understand the overall debugging process

▶ Set a breakpoint

▶ Step through a program

▶ Inspect an object

▶ Create a watch

▶ Debug and fix an actual program

• •

*Y*ou're walking down a maze of twisty passages all alike. Your flashlight batteries are running low. And all you hear is "click, click, click." That's when you look down and see that you're knee deep in a nest of menacing giant cockroaches. Aggghhh!

That might sound like Kafka meets Zork or Stephen King does virtual reality, but when you've been up all night programming, it's amazing how quickly your code can become filled with nasty bugs. And then when you try out your program the next morning, blam! Nothing works.

At this point you have four choices:

✔ You can give up. (Wimp.)

✔ You can get a really slow computer in the hopes that you'll be able to see what's going wrong. (Bad idea.)

✔ You can fill your program with print statements, so that after every line executes, something will be printed and you can figure out what's going on. (Works, but is a real pain.)

✔ You can use a debugger. (Works, and isn't a pain.)

A *debugger* is a tool that lets you execute your program line by line. This makes it easier for you to look at the logic in a program and figure out how it operates, pinpoint what's going wrong, and then fix the mistakes.

What's the Difference between a Syntax Error and a Bug?

As described in Chapter 8, a syntax error occurs when you write something that the compiler doesn't understand. Usually you've just spelled something wrong, left out a portion of a command, or incorrectly used a variable or a class. You can't run a program when it has syntax errors because the program can't be compiled.

A *bug*, on the other hand, is an error in logic. The program is written in perfect C++, but what it's doing doesn't make sense. Or perhaps it just doesn't do what you wanted it to do.

Reporting bugs and flamotherapy

If you're using commercial software and run across a bug, it's a good idea to report the problem to the vendor. That way they can try to fix the problem in the next version of the software.

To report the bug, you can either call the vendor, send them a letter, or send electronic mail on a bulletin board. Most vendors maintain bulletin boards on services such as CompuServe, so you can send bug reports and — if you're lucky — get a work-around sent to you electronically.

Hidden behind the anonymity of an electronic account, bug reports occasionally become pretty nasty. Nasty electronic-mail pieces are known as *flames*. They're designed to get a lot of attention by resorting to hyperbole. For example, I've seen plenty of mail messages saying things such as "Whatever marketing weasel designed this utter piece of garbage deserves to be strung up by their toenails and shot." In real life, the person who wrote this message is probably a real nice person. It might even be the grandmother who lives next door. But behind the disguise of an e-mail account, the person becomes a *flamer*.

When a lot of flamers get together, and things get very toasty, it's called a *flame fest*. Some people practice flaming. These people become *flame meisters*. Watch out for them.

On the one hand, flames can reduce a programmer's stress. (This is called *flamotherapy*.) On the other hand, electronic bulletin boards are being used by more and more people, many of whom don't appreciate flaming.

What's more, it's not exactly a good idea (or very nice) to insult a person who's trying to help you. The people who staff technical-support lines often endure lots of flaming and rude calls, and can become pretty battle-hardened as a result. (They're said to have *asbestos underwear*.)

In general, when you post messages, avoid flames. Usually a polite request gets you as much attention as a big flame.

For example, consider the following instructions for baking a potato:

1. Take potato.
2. Wrap in aluminum foil.
3. Microwave for three hours.

This is a perfectly understandable set of instructions. There are no syntax errors. On the other hand, if you did what it said, you'd blow up your microwave (not to mention the potato). That wouldn't be the desired result.

To fix the problem, you need to analyze the various steps to see what doesn't make sense. That's what debugging is all about: looking at a problematic piece of code line by line until you see what isn't working right.

When programs get large, it's hard to remove all of their bugs. That's because some bugs occur only under strange circumstances. That's where users come in. If you have a lot of people using your program, they'll undoubtedly find bugs in it. And they'll undoubtedly let you know about them.

An Overview of the Debugging Process

The debugging process basically consists of figuring out where bugs occur. The goal is to isolate each problem to a particular area, and then to examine exactly how the program operates in that area. For example, if you know you have a bug in a particular routine, you could have the program stop whenever that routine starts. Then you could step through the routine one line at a time, so you could see exactly what's happening. You might find out that something you intended to happen just isn't happening correctly. You could then change the code, recompile, and try again.

There are a number of tools in the debugger that you can use during this process:

- *Breakpoints* tell the debugger to stop when a particular line is reached. You use them when you want to run a program uninterrupted, but still be able to stop whenever you reach a particular section you need to examine in detail.

- *Stepping* and *tracing* let you run a program one line at a time. You use these features to determine the results of every minute action that occurs, so that you can see exactly when something incorrect happens.

- *Inspectors* display the values of variables. While you're stopped at a breakpoint, or while you're stepping through a program, you can look at the values of any of the variables that are in use.

> ✔ *Watches* let you display the value of variables while the program is operating. You can use watches to get a live view of a variable as it changes. You can also watch expressions, so you can see how a particular expression changes when variables change.

What Does the Debugger Look Like?

Editor windows double as debugger windows. In other words, when you want to perform a debugging action such as setting a breakpoint or examining the value of a variable, you do so directly from an editor window.

The editor and debugger are tightly linked together. This makes great sense. After all, when you debug a program you need to examine the source code to see what's happening. Because Borland C++ combines the editor and debugger, you can use any of the editor features (such as scrolling, window splitting, and searching) to look through your program as you debug. Heck, you can even type in fixes directly when you find the mistakes in your code.

Of course, not all information will show up in the editor window itself. Many debugging activities will cause debugger-specific windows to appear. For example, if you set a watch, a watch window will appear.

Stop, in the Name of Bugs

Use breakpoints when you want to stop at a particular line. For example, let's say you have a routine that returns the factorial of a number. For some reason, though, it always returns 0. To figure out why this is happening, you could set a breakpoint at the beginning of the routine. Then, when you run the program, the program will stop when the factorial routine is called, and you'll be placed inside the debugger. You can then use the power of the debugger to figure out what's going wrong. Toward the end of this chapter, you'll actually use the debugger to solve a problem like this.

To set a breakpoint on a particular line:

1. Click the line where you want to set a breakpoint.
2. Right-click to bring up the SpeedMenu.
3. Select Toggle breakpoint.

The line is then highlighted in red.

To clear a breakpoint:

1. In the editor, click the line that contains the breakpoint.

2. Right-click to bring up the SpeedMenu.

3. Select Toggle breakpoint.

The line will no longer be highlighted in red.

Breakpoints are saved between development sessions. So if you set a breakpoint but don't clear it, and then load the project later, the breakpoint will still be set.

This is great, because if you're in the middle of debugging, you don't have to reestablish all of your breakpoints from scratch if you decide to take a break from programming and do something else — such as eat or sleep. On the other hand, if you forget that you have breakpoints in your code, you might get some surprises. (Your program will unexpectedly stop while you're running it.)

If you're not sure whether or not you've left some breakpoints in your program, use the View | Breakpoint option. This brings up a dialog box that shows any active breakpoints. ■

Stepping and Tracing (and Grooving to the Music)

Once you've reached a breakpoint, you might want to examine how each line of code operates. You can do this by running a program one line at a time. This is called *stepping* through an application. Stepping runs one line at a time. If there are any functions called by the line, the functions are executed, but you won't stop inside them.

Tracing is a variation of stepping. Tracing also runs the program one line at a time. But, with tracing, if functions are called, the debugger stops at the first line in the function.

Tracing is used when you know something's broken, but you aren't sure if that something is in the routine you're debugging or in one of the functions that's called by the function you're debugging. Stepping is used when you want to look at each line in a function as a single unit.

For example, suppose you have the program:

```
foo = MySquareRoot(x);
foo = foo + 1;
```

If you know that MySquareRoot is correct, and you just aren't sure whether the foo + 1 should be done, you should step. Execute the first line — including any lines that are part of MySquareRoot — and then stop before getting to the foo = foo + 1 line.

If you suspect that MySquareRoot could be the source of your problems, you should trace. That way, when you trace the first line, you would stop at the first line inside MySquareRoot. You can then see all the different things that MySquareRoot does, and if you're lucky you can find out what's going wrong.

When you step and trace through a program, the line that's about to run is highlighted in blue.

To step, press F8 or click the step icon pictured here:

To trace, press F7 or click the trace icon pictured here:

Note that you don't need to set breakpoints to step and trace. If you want, you can step or trace as the first action you make, instead of running a program. This will stop you on the very first line in the program.

Inspector Clue So...

Inspectors are a valuable debugging tool because they show you the value of variables and expressions. So if you're wondering if the result of a formula is correct, or what's stored in some variable, or what all the values in an array are, you can inspect the variable to see.

To inspect an object:

1. Click the name of the object in the editor. This puts the cursor somewhere in the object's name.
2. Right-click to bring up a SpeedMenu.
3. Select Inspect object.

The inspector appears, showing the value of the object. For example, if you had a program with a variable named foo, and you followed the steps just shown, you'd see something similar to the inspector shown in Figure 9-1. As the program runs, the inspector window is updated to show the current value of the item being inspected. This is a very powerful tool for examining how values change as the program runs.

You can inspect simple variables as well as very complex objects. If an object contains other objects, you can double-click to expand further and further. For example, suppose you have a class that contains a coordinate and an integer. You can look at the object, and then expand further to look at details of the coordinate, as is shown in Figure 9-2.

Figure 9-2: Double-clicking in the inspector lets you get more information about structures

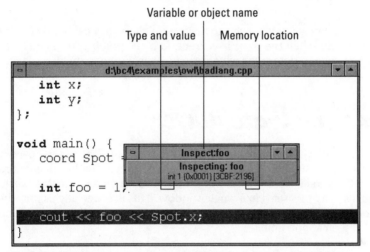

Figure 9-1: The inspector lets you examine values of classes and variables.

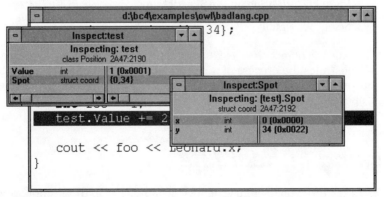

within structures.

Changing Your Values

If you want to, you can even change the value of a variable when you inspect it:

1. Right-click the name of the variable inside the inspector window.

2. Select Change value.

3. Type in a new value.

4. Click OK.

This is useful when you want to make a quick fix to see if the rest of the program works when the value is correct. At some point, you'll need to go back to the program to determine why the value was wrong in the first place.

All Along the Watchtower

Watches are very similar to inspectors. When you want to see how several items change as a program executes, you can set individual inspectors for each item. This will create several windows. If you set watches instead of inspectors, you'll see all the items in a single window. This is especially useful when you need to watch several values at once, because there will be fewer windows on the screen at one time.

To watch the value of an object:

1. In the editor, click the name of the object you want to watch.

2. Right-click to bring up the SpeedMenu.

3. Select Set watch.

Any time the object changes, the watch window is updated. For example, Figure 9-3 illustrates the process of watching an object named test that contains an integer and a pair of integers. Whenever the value of test changes, the watch is updated.

Debugging in Real Life

Let's see how you might use debugging in real life. In this section, you'll walk through the various techniques you can use to examine a program, determine where the bugs are, and then fix them.

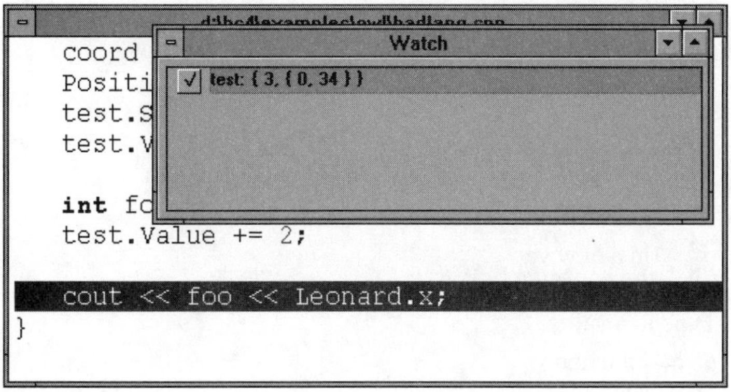

Figure 9-3:
Watches let
you see the
values of
variables as
a program
executes.

```
coord
Positi
test.S
test.V

int fo
test.Value += 2;

cout << foo << Leonard.x;
}
```

Watch

☑ test: { 3, { 0, 34 } }

Setting the scene

Begin by creating a new EasyWin project and typing in the following C++ code.
This is a program for displaying the factorial of a number:

```
#include <iostream.h>

//Returns the factorial of n.
int Factorial(int n) {
    //Loop variable.
    int i;
    int Result;

    //Initialize the result.

    Result = n;
    //Now multiply by 1 .. n.
    for (i = 0; i < n; i++)
        Result *= i;

    return Result;
}

void main() {
    int n;

    //Get a value.
    cout << "What value?";
    cin >> n;

    //Print the factorial.
    cout << Factorial(n);
}
```

(If you can't figure out what this program does, be sure to read through Part II,
which will help you understand C++ programs. If you need help creating an
EasyWin project, check out Chapter 6. And note that this program is located in

the BADFACT directory on the separately available disk. You can open it by
loading the BADFACT project.)

Finding your first bug (eek!)

Now run this program a few times:

1. Click the lightning bolt.

2. Type in a value.

3. Examine the result.

4. Close down the badfact program.

5. Click the lightning bolt again and repeat the process.

You'll find that no matter what value you type, the result is always 0. Hey, that
doesn't seem right!

Looking for clues

Let's figure out what's broken. Well, the input and output lines look pretty simple:

```
//Get a value.
cout << "What value?";
cin >> n;
```

You probably don't need to step through these. Instead, let's concentrate on
what happens in the Factorial routine. You can begin by setting a breakpoint at
the beginning of this routine:

1. Scroll in the editor until you get to the beginning of the Factorial routine
   (it's close to the top).

2. Click this line:

   ```
   int Factorial(int n) {
   ```

3. Right-click to bring up the SpeedMenu.

4. Select Toggle breakpoint.

You'll set a breakpoint on this line, as shown in Figure 9-4.

Now run the program:

1. Click the lightning bolt. The program then runs and asks you for a number.

2. Type in a number.

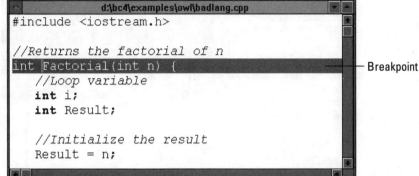

Figure 9-4:
Breakpoints
show up as
red lines in
the editor
window.

Breakpoint

```
#include <iostream.h>

//Returns the factorial of n
int Factorial(int n) {
    //Loop variable
    int i;
    int Result;

    //Initialize the result
    Result = n;
```

At this point, the program calls the Factorial routine. This causes your break-point to be reached, and the debugger to appear. The line that's about to run is highlighted in blue, as shown in Figure 9-5. (You'll undoubtedly notice that the "red" and "blue" lines in Figures 9-4 and 9-5 show up as gray in this book. You'll have to use your imagination to color them in.)

Figure 9-5:
When you
step through
a program,
the line that
is about to
execute is
highlighted
in blue.

This line is
about to
execute

```
#include <iostream.h>

//Returns the factorial of n
int Factorial(int n) {
    //Loop variable
    int i;
    int Result;

    //Initialize the result
    Result = n;
```

Now you can step through the Factorial routine one line at a time, so you can see what's going wrong. Since you know that the result returned by the routine is bad, and you know that the result is stored in the variable called Result, you need to set a watch on Result:

1. In the editor, click the name Result.
2. Right-click to bring up the SpeedMenu.
3. Select Set watch.

A watch window will appear. You should end up with a screen that looks similar to the one shown in Figure 9-6.

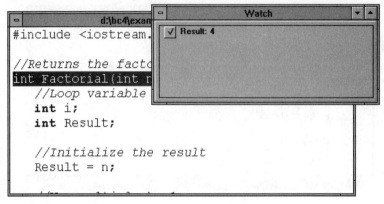

Figure 9-6:
As you
debug the
program, the
value of
Result is
displayed in
the watch
window.

Now step through the program one line at a time by clicking the step icon several times. As you do this, you'll see the screen of the running application, and then after a brief pause you're placed back into the debugger. The value of Result is displayed in the watch window and is updated anytime it changes.

You'll quickly see that after you run the following line, Result becomes 0, which is hardly what you expected:

```
Result *= i;
```

Worse, it never changes from 0. How do you know Result became 0? Simple — your watch window told you so. Your screen should look like the one shown in Figure 9-7.

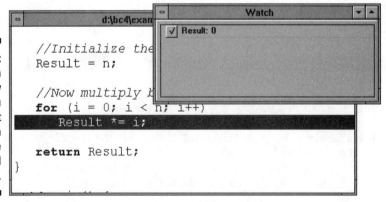

Figure 9-7:
The watch
window
shows you
that Result
is 0, which
isn't the
expected
value.

Because Result is being set to a bad value inside the *for* loop, you know that something is going wrong inside the loop. Since the first (and only) line in the loop is multiplying Result by *i*, maybe something is wrong with *i*. If you look at the beginning of the *for* loop, you can see that *i* starts at 0 and goes to *n*:

```
for (i = 0; i < n; i++)
```

This means that the first time through the loop, *i* is 0. So Result *= *i*; sets Result to 0. No wonder there are problems!

You're getting close...

By mistake, the program has a bad *for* loop. Instead of going from 0 to *n*, it should go from 1 to *n*. Now change the code directly in the editor:

1. Click the editor window to bring it up front.

2. Change this line:

```
for (i = 0; i < n; i++)
```

to this:

```
for (i = 1; i < n; i++)
```

Your screen should look similar to the one shown in Figure 9-8.

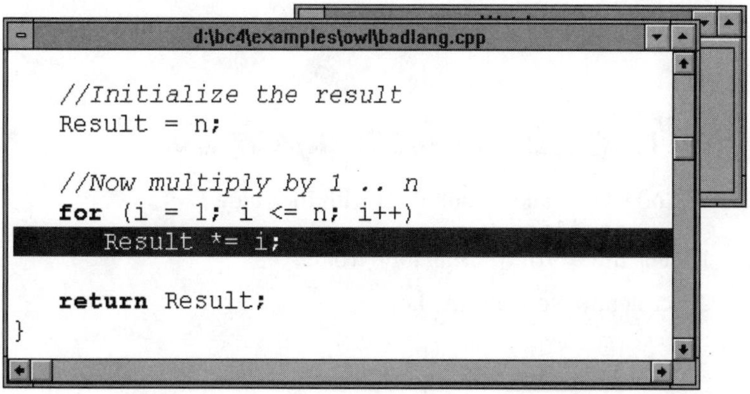

Figure 9-8:
You can fix the program by typing in the corrected line in the editor.

```
//Initialize the result
Result = n;

//Now multiply by 1 .. n
for (i = 1; i <= n; i++)
    Result *= i;

return Result;
}
```

d:\bc4\examples\owl\badlang.cpp

Now that you've fixed the line, you need to run the program again to make sure your change fixed the problem. End the program and then run it again:

1. Select Debug | Terminate program. This ends the program (it's still in the middle of working because you set a breakpoint).

2. Click the lighting bolt to compile and run again.

Note that instead of stopping the program as you did in step 1, you can also just click the step or run icon. The debugger knows that the program has changed, so it asks if you want to rebuild. Naturally, you *do* want to rebuild so your fix can take effect, so say Yes. The debugger then terminates the program, rebuilds, and starts the program running again.

Now that your program is running again, step through it several times to see if it's working correctly. Well, lo and behold, the value of Result is no longer 0 — so it *looks* like things are fixed.

Close but no cigar

But wait a minute. Something's still wrong, because the value is becoming enormous very quickly.

Once again, things go bad the first time you run the loop. Result starts at 5 and then becomes 10, 20, and so on. By looking at the value of Result in the watch window, you can clearly see that you again need to examine how it's being set and changed. Why does Result start with the value 5? To compute a factorial, you really want it to start with the value 1. As you look over the code, you'll see that Result is initially set to *n*:

```
//Initialize the result.
Result = n;
```

But you actually want Result to start with the value 1.

You're getting close, again...

Here's how you make Result start with the value 1:

1. Click the editor to bring it up front.
2. Scroll until you find the line:
   ```
   Result = n;
   ```
3. Change it to this instead:
   ```
   Result = 1;
   ```

By George, I think you've got it!

Now run the program once more, stepping several times when you hit the breakpoint. You'll see that your debugging session has been quite valuable because now the correct result is returned. For example, if you enter the number 4, the program runs correctly, as shown in Figure 9-9.

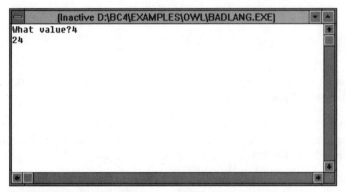

Figure 9-9: Once you've fixed the program, it runs correctly.

Taking care of business

Now you need to remove the breakpoint and the watch that you've set. First, select View I Breakpoint to see a list of the breakpoints you've set (Figure 9-10).

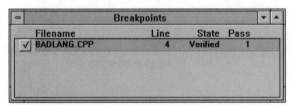

Figure 9-10: When you select View I Breakpoint, you can easily see all the breakpoints in your application.

Now remove the breakpoint:

1. In the Breakpoints window, right-click the breakpoint you want to clear. This brings up a SpeedMenu.

2. Select Delete all breakpoints.

Your breakpoint (and any others you had set) then goes away. (If you want to delete only this specific breakpoint, you can instead right-click on that particular breakpoint and select Delete breakpoint.)

Now get rid of the watch:

1. Click the watch window.

2. Right-click and select Delete all watches.

As with breakpoints, you can delete a specific watch by selecting Delete watch instead.

Now when you run the program, it runs to completion without stopping at any breakpoints. (If you don't believe me, try it.)

As you can see, debugging a program isn't hard. But it does take some practice and experience to see why a program isn't working correctly. The more you program, the easier this process will be.

Singing the Debugging Blues

At one time or another while you're debugging, you might run into one of several common debugging problems. This section describes these problems and tells you how to solve them.

Problem 1: You're trying to debug a program and you get an error message that says, "No debug info at program start. Run anyway?"

This message means that you don't have debug information in your program. To solve the problem, you'll need to turn on debug info, rebuild your application (in this case, you'll need to select Project|Build all), and then try debugging again. (For information about turning on debug information, see Chapter 11.)

Wondering why that error message occurred? Well, to debug a program, the debugger needs special debugging information to be placed inside the EXE. (By default, the compiler adds this information.) The debug information, however, makes the EXE much larger. So before a program is released to the public, most vendors turn off debugging information and rebuild the program. (Not only does this make the programs smaller, but it makes it a lot harder to reverse engineer a program.)

Problem 2: You're trying to inspect a variable and you get the error message "Cannot access an inactive scope."

This message means that you're trying to find the value of a variable the compiler doesn't know about. Typically, this means that you're trying to inspect a variable inside some function that isn't active. To solve this, you can usually just continue stepping along. When you get into the function, you'll be able to inspect the variable.

The technical reason this message occurs is because the object is out of scope. To find out more about what this means, check out Chapter 26.

Problem 3: You load a program, run it, and then all of a sudden you start hitting breakpoints that you never set.

Breakpoints and watches are saved when you shut down a project. Thus, they're active when you start working on the project again. To solve this problem, clear out any breakpoints that you no longer want set.

But Wait, There's More

You can do many, many more things with the debugger. For example, you can view the values of CPU registers and you can set conditional breakpoints. To learn more about the debugger, you might want to experiment with some of the features in the Debug and View menus, or read the debugging sections of the Borland C++ manuals.

In addition to the integrated debugger described in this chapter, Borland C++ includes stand-alone debuggers for DOS programs and for 16- and 32-bit Windows programs. You can use these to debug across a network, across a communications line, or with two monitors. You can also use them for fancy things such as hardware debugging and reverse execution. This stuff is mostly for the hardcore folks, but you might want to read up on it in the Borland manuals.

Chapter 10
Just Browsing, Thanks

● ●

● ●

C++ programs are composed of classes (objects). When a program is large and has many classes, it can sometimes be difficult to understand how one class relates to another. And, if you use application frameworks (such as ObjectWindows) or libraries that you didn't write yourself, you might discover that you need to rely on classes that you've never even heard of before.

Borland C++ includes a tool called the ObjectBrowser that displays the different classes in your application. You can use the ObjectBrowser (which is often just called "the browser") to figure out how different classes are related. For example, you can determine what class any given class is derived from. You can then use this information to figure out the various capabilities that a class has inherited. (For more information on base classes, derived classes, and inheritance, see Chapters 27 and 30.)

Displaying the ObjectBrowser

You display the ObjectBrowser by selecting View|Classes. Figure 10-1 shows the browser for a very simple application.

In the browser, each class is shown inside a box. Lines show what classes are derived from other classes. For example, you can see that ostream is derived from ios.

Naturally enough, programs that are more complex also have class hierarchies that are more complex — and thus more things inside the browser. For example,

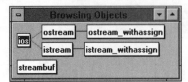

Figure 10-1: The ObjectBrowser shows the class relationships in an application, as in the simple program shown here.

if you were to browse an ObjectWindows application (such as a program created by AppExpert), you'd see something similar to the elaborate class relationships shown in Figure 10-2.

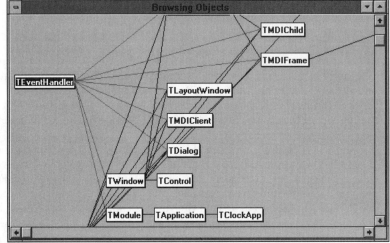

Figure 10-2:
Large applications often have complex class relationships.

Checking Out a Particular Class

You can follow these steps to browse a particular class or variable:

1. Click the class or variable name in the source file.

2. Right-click to bring up the SpeedMenu.

3. Select Browse symbol.

This brings up a browser for the class or variable you selected.

Get It in Writing

If you have lots of classes in your program, you might find it useful to print the overall hierarchy shown in the ObjectBrowser:

1. Right-click on the ObjectBrowser to bring up the SpeedMenu.

2. Select Print class hierarchy.

Pull Out the Magnifying Class

You can find out more information about a particular class by double-clicking on it in the ObjectBrowser. This brings up a list of all the member functions and data members, and indicates the parameters they require and what they return. This information is very valuable for figuring out what you can do with a particular class.

For example, Figure 10-3 shows what you would see if you double-clicked on TDialog.

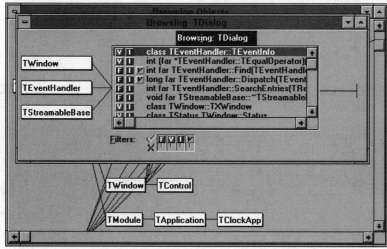

Figure 10-3:
Double-clicking on a class displays more information about that class.

As you can see in Figure 10-3, the ObjectBrowser also displays all types of letters in colored boxes next to the data members and member functions. The meaning of the various letters is explained in Table 10-1.

Table 10-1: The Meaning of the Colored Letters in the ObjectBrowser

Letter	Description
F	This item is a function.
T	This item is a type. (This shows up only when you browse globals.)
V	This item is a variable.
C	This item is an integral constant.
D	There is debug information available for this item.
I	This item is inherited from a different class.
v	This item is a virtual function. (This letter looks like a checkmark, but is actually an italicized v.)

These letters are repeated at the bottom of the browser window in an area called Filters. By turning a particular filter on or off, you can determine whether or not that type of item is shown. For example, if you click off the I filter button, then no inherited items are shown — you'll just see the data members and member functions unique to the class. If you click off the I filter for TDialog, you'll see only the data members and member functions that are unique to TDialog, as shown in Figure 10-4.

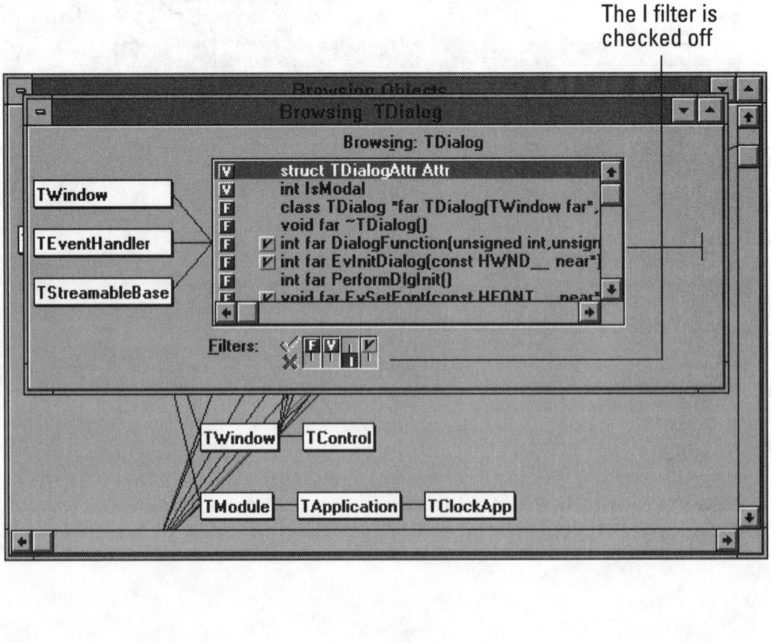

The I filter is checked off

Figure 10-4: Use filters to select the types of data members and member functions you want to see in the browser.

Some Common Things to Do with the Browser

Table 10-2 lists the three most common ObjectBrowser tasks, and describes how you can perform each of these actions.

Table 10-2: Common ObjectBrowser Tasks

Task	Action
Find out more information about a particular item.	Double-click the item.
Look at the source code where an item is defined.	Click the item. Then right-click and select Edit source.
Look at a list of all places in the code where a particular item is used.	Click the item. Then right-click and select Browse references.

Here's How To Get Yourself a Global Perspective

To browse all the global variables and types, select View|Globals. You'll then see all the different global variables, types, and classes in your program, as shown in Figure 10-5.

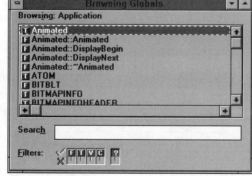

Figure 10-5:
You can examine all the globals in your application.

Sometimes Things Don't Work

You might occasionally run into problems when you're using the Object-Browser. This section describes several of the most common problems and tells you how to solve them.

Problem 1: You select View|Classes and get the message "No EXE found."

The browser can only browse a program if it was successfully compiled. If you get this message, you need to do a Project|Make all to build an executable from your source files. If you get syntax errors, you'll need to fix them so you can build an EXE.

Problem 2: You select View|Classes and get the message "The executable does not contain symbolic debug information."

To use the browser, your project must be built with debug information turned on. Therefore, you need to turn on debug information and do a Project|Build all.

Problem 3: You click a symbol in a file, right-click, select Browse symbol, and get the message "Don't know this symbol!" (Or, you double-click on an item in the ObjectBrowser and it tells you it doesn't have any browse information for that item.)

The particular file defining the symbol was built without debug information turned on. Turn on debug information and do a Project|Build all. If the item without browser information came from a library that you purchased, you might need to contact the vendor to get a version of the library that does have the vendor information included. Or, if the vendor supplied source code for the library, you could rebuild the library yourself with debug information turned on.

Chapter 11
Exploring Your Options

● ●

In This Chapter

▶ Examine the Project Options Settings Notebook

▶ Examine the Environment Options Settings Notebook

▶ How to change options for all files in a project file

▶ How to change options for a single file

▶ The most important project and environment options

● ●

Compilers are very complex beasts. When you compile a program, you can control numerous aspects of the compilation process. For example, should debug information be used? What type of error messages should be generated? Should code be optimized for the Pentium?

Accordingly, there are many different options you can set to control what happens when a file is compiled. This isn't as overwhelming as it sounds: of the hundreds of available options, there are only a few you'll end up using over and over again. And, if you want to change the options you're using, Borland C++ makes it easy to do so.

Options fall into two main groups: project options and environment options. *Project options* affect the way source files are built. These include options that control what directories are searched for header files, what types of optimizations are used, whether or not exception handling is turned on, and so on.

Environment options control the development environment. These include things such as whether the editor uses BRIEF-style keystrokes, what colors are used in syntax highlighting, and what icons show up on the SpeedBar.

How Do I See What the Options Are?

To look at project options, select Options | Project. You'll see the Project Options Settings Notebook, as shown in Figure 11-1.

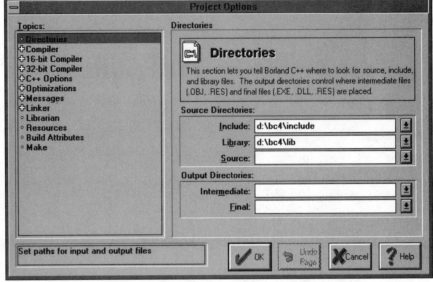

Figure 11-1:
The project options let you see all the settings related to how a particular project is compiled.

To look at the environment options, select Options|Environment. You'll see the Environment Options Settings Notebook, as shown in Figure 11-2.

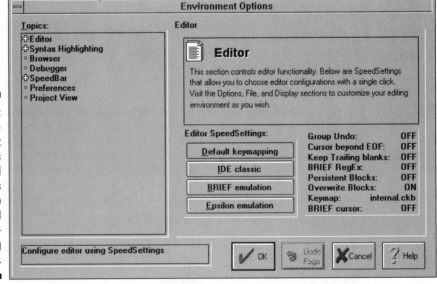

Figure 11-2:
The environment options show all settings relating to the Borland C++ programming environment.

You've already seen similar Settings Notebooks; they're used throughout Borland C++.

The left side of the Settings Notebook presents a list of topics. Some topics have additional items underneath them. If you click the plus sign, you can view these items. The right side lists things you can select and change.

If you change the value of one of the options, the change will take effect for all the files in the project file.

One of the nice things about the Settings Notebooks is that the top-level topics (the topics on the front page that you don't need to expand out to see) contain almost everything beginners might need. When you're setting or changing options, you can usually just scan down the list of these top-level topics to find what you need.

Beginners might also want to keep in mind a couple of tips about Settings Notebooks. First, if you don't understand a topic or its explanation, you don't need to change it. And second, if the option isn't listed on the top page (that is, if you have to expand out to see it), you're probably better off not experimenting with it. ■

Changing Options on a File-by-File Basis

When you select Options | Project from the menu and make changes to options settings, the changes affect all files in the project file. If you want, you can change project options for individual files instead. For example, you might want to turn on special optimizations for a particular file. Or you might want to have debug information available for one file, but not for others.

To change options for a particular file:

1. In the Project Manager, right-click on the file you want. This brings up the SpeedMenu.

2. Select Edit local options.

The Project Options Settings Notebook that appears shows the project options for the file you selected.

Note that when you change options for a single file, the upper-left corner of the Settings Notebook points out what file you clicked on. That way, it's pretty clear what file the changes will affect. For example, Figure 11-3 shows what appears if you change local options for a file named badlang.cpp.

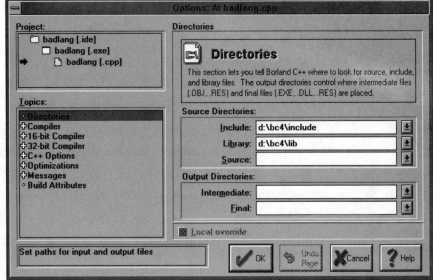

Figure 11-3:
You can
change
options for a
single file,
as shown
here.

What Are Some Good Options to Change?

You usually don't need to change the project options. From time to time, though, you might need to change one or two of them. This section describes the most common project options that you might need to change; of these, it's most likely that you'll change the Directories and Resources options.

Directories: This option is where you tell the compiler where to search for header files and libraries. Usually the defaults are fine, but you might want to set the include path to \bc4\include and the library path to \bc4\lib. If you have special areas for include and library files, type them in here. For example, you could have \bc4\include;\vfwdk\inc.

If, during compilation, you get error messages about header files not being found, you probably need to change or add something to the include path.

Resources: This option is where you indicate whether you want to create resources for Windows 3.1 or for Win32.

Compiler: (This is a subtopic under Debugging.) If you're finished with a program and now want to give it to other people, you should turn off debug information. This will save space and make it harder to reverse engineer your application. Turn off debug information by unchecking the Debug information in OBJs option. You should also uncheck the Browser reference information in OBJs option. Finally, go to the Linker topic, select the General subtopic, and uncheck Include debug information. Then rebuild your application using Project | Build all. One pleasant side-effect of doing this is that your executable will be much smaller.

On the other hand, if you get messages about not being able to debug a program because there isn't any debug information, or messages from the ObjectBrowser about not having browser information, you'll want to turn on these items and rebuild so that your application has debug information.

Compiler: (This is a subtopic under Precompiled headers.) Precompiled headers make it much faster to compile applications. When the compiler compiles header files, it sticks the result in a database. Then, if it runs into these same header files later on in a different file, it loads them from the database rather than recompiling them. This saves lots of time.

By default, precompiled headers are turned on. If you're running low on disk space, though, you might want to turn them off because the precompiled header file can get pretty large.

The Important Environment Options

This section describes the environment options that you're most likely to want to change. Unlike the project options, the environment options don't affect the way your application works — they just affect the way the Borland C++ environment looks.

Editor: This option lets you change the way the editor behaves. For example, you can have it emulate BRIEF or Epsilon. Just click the button for the particular editor you want.

Editor: (This is a subtopic under Display.) This is where you can change the font that's used in the editor. For example, if the font is too small, you can increase its point size. Use the Font and Size drop-down lists to choose what you want.

Syntax Highlighting: This page is fun to play with. It lets you choose the highlighting colors from a variety of different predefined sets. You can also turn highlighting off altogether.

Syntax Highlighting: (This is a subtopic under Customize.) This is where you can change everything relating to color syntax highlighting. If you don't like the predefined color sets, this subtopic gives you everything you need to create your own color sets.

A sample code fragment is provided; you click on an item in the code fragment and then click on a color to determine how that item is highlighted. (You can also select the type of item for which you want to set the color.) For example, if you click on Integer in the Element list and then click on red, all integers in your program will show up red.

Clicking a color with the left mouse button sets the foreground color. Clicking with the right mouse button sets the background color.

You can also set what program elements are bolded and italicized. For example, you can bold the reserved words and italicize the comments, if you like.

One fun trick is to set comments so that their foreground and background color is white. That makes all your comments disappear. That way you can feel like a real hacker.

You could also set the background color of the comments to yellow to make it look like you've highlighted them.

SpeedBar: (This is a subtopic under Customize.) This option lets you determine which icons appear on each SpeedBar. (As you've probably noticed, different Borland C++ windows have different SpeedBars associated with them. For example, when the editor window is the topmost window, the editor SpeedBar appears, and when the ObjectBrowser window is the topmost window, the browser SpeedBar appears.) Each SpeedBar has its own set of icons suited to its own particular purpose. You can select the SpeedBar that you want to customize from a drop-down list.

Since SpeedBars provide shortcuts, you might want to customize them so they include icons for the tasks you do most often. Scroll through the list of Available Buttons to see if it includes icons for these tasks. If so, just click the right-arrow button to add each icon to the SpeedBar.

Oops, I Didn't Mean to Change That

If you just clicked on an option but you didn't really want to change it (and now you've forgotten what you clicked), hit the Undo Page button to revert to what it used to be. Or, hit the Cancel button and start again.

Part II
Overview of C++ Fundamentals

REAL PROGRAMMERS

Real Programmers eat only junk food.

In This Part

*I*n Part II, you'll learn the basic fundamentals of C++ programming, starting with what programs are and leading through variables, statements, and pointers.

Lots of sample programs are provided in this Part. It's a good idea to try them out to make sure you understand what's being discussed in each chapter.

One of these sample programs, affectionately dubbed "the pizza program," appears throughout the chapters in this Part and in Part III. The pizza program begins life as a fairly basic program for ordering fairly basic pizzas. Then, as you learn about the various C++ language features, they're added to the program until voila! you've got a pretty cool program on your hands at the end of Part III. But more importantly, as you track the changes made to the pizza program, you'll get a great opportunity to see these language features in a real-life program.

And finally, if you've never programmed before, you'll get a glimpse into nerd humor. In fact, by the end of this Part, you'll be laughing uncontrollably at jokes like:

What would you get if Lee Iaccoca were bitten by a vampire?

a. Winged convertibles with an aversion to garlic

b. Cujo

c. AUTOEXEC.BAT

Chapter 12
What's a Program, Anyway?

In This Chapter

▶ Programming fundamentals

▶ Learn about statements, variables, comments, and libraries

▶ Read a program

*C*reating a program boils down to four basic steps: designing, writing, compiling, and debugging. You've already learned about these techniques in Part I, but let's review them quickly.

Designing a program (sometimes called *analyzing*) is when you figure out what a program is supposed to do. You examine the problem you're trying to solve and figure out a strategy for solving the problem.

Writing (often called *editing*) is when you sit down and write the program. Usually you do this by typing high-level instructions using a computer language. For example, you might tell the computer to print some text to the screen. Throughout this and the next section, you'll learn many C++ commands so you can tell the computer what to do.

Next, you *compile* the application. In this step, Borland C++ converts the high-level C++ program into a low-level program that the computer understands.

Programs are often broken into several files during the development process (because it's easier to manage them that way). During the compilation phase, these separate files are linked together into a single application. After a program has been compiled, the computer understands how to run it.

Now you run the program. If your program is more than a few lines long, it will probably have some errors in it. Because errors are par for the course, you'll need to test your program to make sure it behaves properly.

The process of finding and fixing mistakes is called *debugging*. You'll usually use the debugger to help you track down the cause of these problems. If you find problems, you go back to the editing stage to fix them.

For existing nerds only: the difference between high- and low-level languages

In case you'd like to see the difference between a high-level language and a low-level language, here's a simple C++ line (high level) followed by the equivalent in assembly language (low level).

C++ example:

```
a = 3*a - b*2 + 1;
```

Assembly language equivalent:

```
mov     ax,word ptr DGROUP:__a
imul    ax,3
mov     dx,word ptr DGROUP:__b
add     dx,dx
sub     ax,dx
inc     ax
mov     word ptr DGROUP:_a,ax
```

Actually, even the assembly language code is at a higher level than the computer can understand. The computer only understands machine language, which is the numeric equivalent of the assembly language instructions. Here's what machine language looks like:

```
A1 74 00
6B C0 03
8B 16 76 00
03 D2
2B C2
40
A3 74 00
```

Now how would you like to program like that?

Basic Structure of a Program

Computer programs are composed of commands telling the computer what to do and how to manipulate data. In fact, all that most programs do is acquire, process, and display (or store) data.

Even a video game does this. It acquires your keystrokes (commands), processes them to determine what to do, and then displays the resulting data (for example, a screen showing the next room in a maze).

The place where a computer program starts is called the *main*. When a program begins, the first *statement* (a statement is a line of code — it's essentially an instruction to the computer) in the main executes. Then, all the following statements are executed, one statement at a time.

Some statements tell the program to execute different sections only when certain conditions are true. (These type of statements are called *conditional statements*.)

For example, there could be a line that says the equivalent of "print out the document only when the user selects the Print Command."

Variables represent data in programs. For example, if you want to store the name of a user, you could create a variable called "name" to do so. Then, any time you needed to know the name of the user, you could examine the value of the variable called name. The value inside a variable can change as the program runs. So you could store "Betsy" in the name variable at one point, and "Sarah" in the same variable at another point. (The value in a variable doesn't change out of the blue without your knowing it, though. If you want to change the value in a variable, you have to write a statement in the program to specifically do so.)

Program *comments* explain what's happening in a program. You use comments to describe the purpose of a section of code, to discuss assumptions, or to point out particular tricks. When you comment code, it makes the code easier for other people to read. Comments also help when you're trying to fix something you wrote late at night — you might have written terrible code at that point, and the comment might be the only way you can tell what on earth you were trying to do. Comment lines are ignored by the compiler, which skips over them when it converts C++ to machine code.

Figure 12-1 shows a small program, with the main, statements, and variables pointed out.

```
#include <iostream.h>

int MyInt ──────────────────────── Variable

int main ( ) { ──────────────────── Main starts here
    //This is the first line in the program ── Comment line
    cin >> MyInt; ──────────────── Statement
    if (MyInt > 0) ──────────────── Conditional statement
        cout << MyInt
}
```

Figure 12-1:
The basic features of a program.

Look for It in the Library

Routines common to most programs are stored in files called *libraries*. For example, almost every program prints values to the screen. Printing to the screen can, believe it or not, involve a lot of steps for the computer. Instead of always reinventing these steps each time you write a program, you can just use the routine already provided in one of the Borland C++ libraries.

There are two types of libraries, *static* and *dynamic*. With static libraries, routines that are used by your program are copied into the program itself (thus increasing the program's size). With dynamic libraries (called DLLs), the routines aren't copied into your program, but are accessed when the program runs.

How Do I Figure Out What to Do in My Program?

When you begin the process of creating a program to solve a particular problem, you first need to break the problem down into logical pieces and then write routines to handle each piece. At first, you might find it difficult to chunk the program down into pieces. But the more you program, the more you'll develop your problem-solving skills. (And Computer Science courses teach all kinds of cool tricks and problem-solving strategies you can use.)

As a real quick example, here's how you might convert a real-world problem into a program.

Real-world problem: A plain pizza costs $10. Additional toppings cost $2 each. If I know the number of toppings, how much will a pizza cost?

The program that solves this problem needs to figure out the price for a pizza. Two components are needed to do this: the base price ($10) and the number of toppings. The cost of the pizza is $10 plus $2 times the number of toppings.

The logical steps you need to take to solve this problem are:

1. Find out the number of toppings.
2. Calculate the cost of the toppings by multiplying the number of toppings by $2.
3. Calculate the cost of the pizza by adding $10.
4. Display the cost, to make the result known to the user.

Now that you've broken the problem into logical steps, you need to convert it into a computer language. For example, in C++, this program would be:

```
//Compute the cost of a pizza
#include <iostream.h>
```

```
void main() {
    int NumberOfToppings;
    int CostForToppings;
    int Cost;

    //Find the number of toppings.
    cout << "How many toppings do you want?\n";
    cin >> NumberOfToppings;

    //Calculate the cost for the toppings.
    CostForToppings = NumberOfToppings * 2;

    //Calculate the total cost.
    Cost = 10 + CostForToppings;

    //Print the result.
    cout << "Your pizza costs $" << Cost << "\n";
}
```

(This program is in the PIZZA1 directory on the separately available program disk.)

You could then make the program more complex by letting the user choose a large, medium, or small pizza. Or, you could vary the prices for the toppings. That way, adding onions wouldn't cost as much as adding rare mushrooms from the Northwest.

How to Read That There Program

Just a moment ago you took a look at a real, live C++ program. If you've never read a program before, here's how you do it:

1. Start at the top.

2. Read the program one line at a time.

3. Try to figure out what each line does.

4. If you can't figure something out, move on to the next line.

This is just what the compiler does. Only the compiler usually doesn't do step 4.

The following scenario shows what might happen if you were to read the pizza program line-by-line. Here's the first line:

```
//Compute the cost of a pizza.
```

You might say: hmm, that looks pretty reasonable. This is a program that computes the cost of a pizza.

```
#include <iostream.h>
```

Beats me. This line looks pretty technical. I'll probably learn about it in a later chapter.

```
void main() {
```

That looks pretty strange too. I guess I'll skip it for now.

```
int NumberOfToppings;
int CostForToppings;
int Cost;
```

Not sure what these do, but they seem to represent something that's part of the problem I'm trying to solve.

```
//Find the number of toppings.
cout << "How many toppings do you want?\n";
cin >> NumberOfToppings;
```

This looks pretty bizarre, but I guess it's finding out the number of toppings.

```
//Calculate the cost for the toppings.
CostForToppings = NumberOfToppings * 2;
```

Ah hah, something I understand! This is a formula multiplying the number of toppings by $2 per topping.

And so forth.

In this chapter you've learned that programs are composed of statements. These statements manipulate data so you can solve real-world problems. You examined an actual C++ program to get a feel as to how these statements are combined in a program. In the next chapters, you'll learn more about the various types of statements you can employ to create sophisticated C++ programs.

Chapter 13

An Introduction to Object-Oriented Programming

· ·

In This Chapter

▶ The fundamentals of object-oriented programming

▶ Encapsulation, inheritance, and polymorphism

· ·

*M*ost people buy Borland C++ to take advantage of the object-oriented capabilities of C++. Why? There are lot of reasons — here are some of the main ones:

- ✔ With object-oriented programming, you'll be able to reuse code and thus save development time.

- ✔ Object-oriented programs are well structured, which makes it easy to figure out what a particular routine does.

- ✔ Object-oriented programs are easy to test. You can break an application into small components, and isolate testing to specific components.

- ✔ Object-oriented programs are easy to expand as your needs change.

How It All Works

The basic idea of object-oriented programming is simple. Data and the routines to process the data are combined into a single entity called a *class*. If you want to access the data in the class, you use the routines from the class.

With the older style *procedural programming*, on the other hand, the data and routines are separate and are thought of separately.

Take a quick look at Figure 13-1. The top portion of the figure shows what the pizza application from Chapter 12 looks like when procedural programming

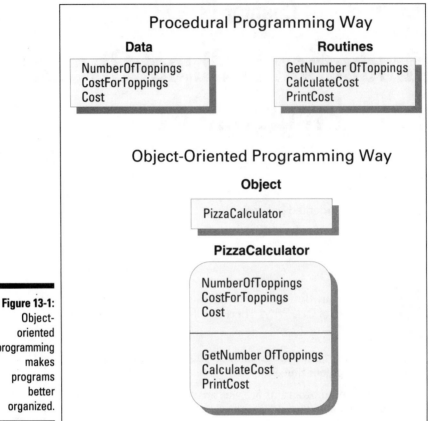

Figure 13-1:
Object-
oriented
programming
makes
programs
better
organized.

methods are used. The bottom portion of the figure shows the same application when OOP methods are used. (OOP, by the way, is the abbreviation for object-oriented programming.)

The two diagrams don't look too different. One nice thing about the OOP picture is that you can clearly see there's a single object in the program, and that the various data and routines are related. This isn't obvious in the procedural programming picture on the top.

For simple situations like the one depicted in Figure 13-1, the diagrams of the two approaches don't look too different. But Figure 13-2 shows what happens when things become a little more complex. With procedural programming, things start to get confusing as you add new variables and new routines. There are more data items, but to whom do they belong? What are the new routines for? And is it okay for the routine called GetCustomerName to change the CostForToppings value?

With object-oriented programming, you can quickly see that all that's happened is that the program has now added an object for taking orders. Also, it's pretty clear that the GetCustomerName routine isn't allowed to change the CostForToppings value.

As more and more capabilities get added to the application, the benefits of object-oriented programming increase.

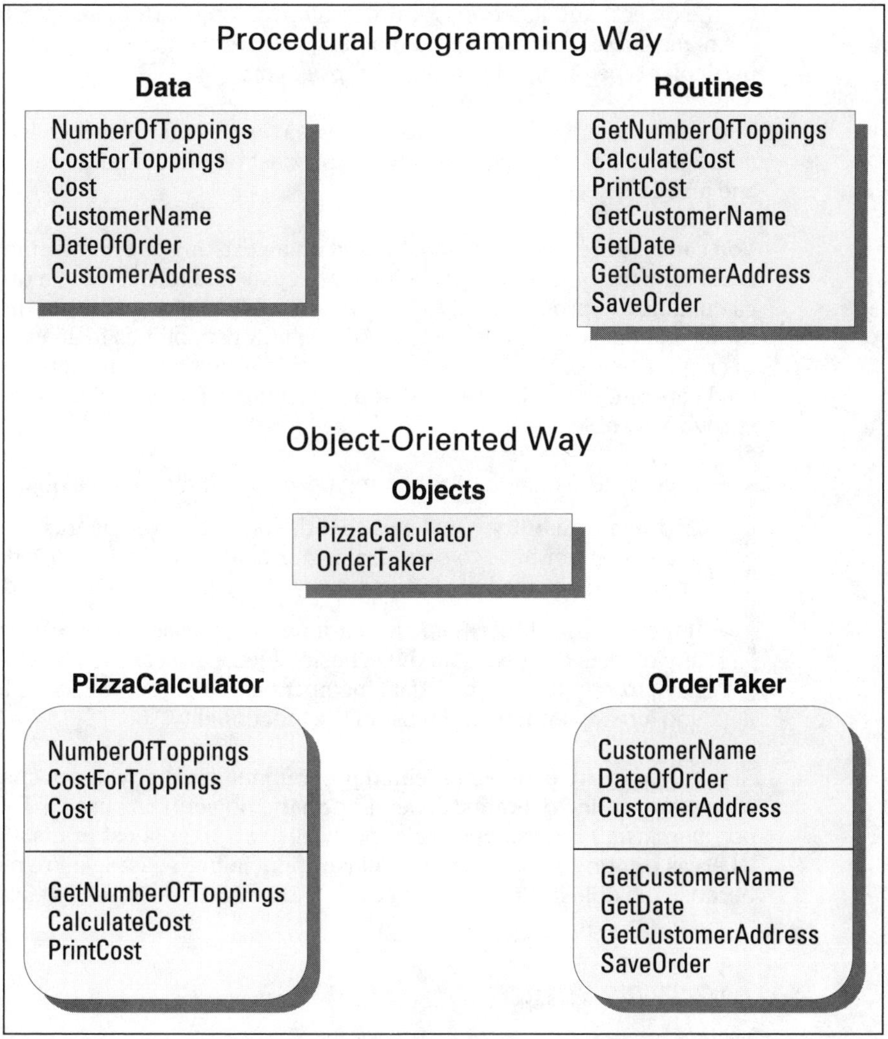

Figure 13-2:
As the program grows in complexity, the object-oriented program becomes far easier to understand.

Procedural Programming Way

Data

NumberOfToppings
CostForToppings
Cost
CustomerName
DateOfOrder
CustomerAddress

Routines

GetNumberOfToppings
CalculateCost
PrintCost
GetCustomerName
GetDate
GetCustomerAddress
SaveOrder

Object-Oriented Way

Objects

PizzaCalculator
OrderTaker

PizzaCalculator

NumberOfToppings
CostForToppings
Cost

GetNumberOfToppings
CalculateCost
PrintCost

OrderTaker

CustomerName
DateOfOrder
CustomerAddress

GetCustomerName
GetDate
GetCustomerAddress
SaveOrder

That's All?

That's the basic idea behind object-oriented programming: you break a problem into a group of objects. Objects contain data and the routines that process the data. So a pizza-ordering program, for example, could be composed of objects for getting and processing information describing pizzas. The program could have objects representing a pizza and pizza toppings. Each of these objects could have data further describing them (for example, indicating the price for the object) and functions for processing the object (for example, to print out the name and cost of an item). Combining data and functions for processing a particular type of object is called *encapsulation*.

You can combine several objects to create new objects. This is called *composition*. For example, you could create a Breakfast object containing a Pizza object and a Soda object.

You can also create a new object based on an existing one. For instance, you could take the object for calculating pizza costs and turn it into an object for calculating the profit of a pizza business by adding information on the manufacturing and delivery cost for pizzas. Adding new capabilities to an existing object to create a new object is called *inheritance*. Inheritance is one of the most powerful capabilities of object-oriented programming. By inheriting from an existing, working object, you:

- ✔ **Save code:** You don't have to retype what's in the original object.

- ✔ **Improve reliability:** You know that the original object works, so any bugs you encounter have to come from your new code. And if you find bugs in the original object, the fixes automatically affect any object inherited from it.

- ✔ **Improve readability:** You can learn how a basic set of objects work. Then, any objects derived from those basic objects are easy to learn — you only have to examine the new data members and member functions because you already understand most of the functionality.

Another property of object-oriented programming is that you can change how a particular routine operates, depending on the object being used. (This is called *polymorphism*.) For example, printing a cell in a spreadsheet prints a value, whereas printing a chart prints an illustration. In both cases you're printing, but because the objects are different (a cell and a chart), the results are also different.

More on encapsulation

Encapsulation refers to combining data and the functions that process the data into a single entity, called a *class*. The data are called *data members* of a class. The functions are called *member functions* of a class.

The challenge in designing an object-oriented program is to define classes so they accurately model the real-world problem you're trying to solve, and so they can be reused frequently. This might be a bit difficult at first, but after you've programmed for a while, it will become second nature.

More on inheritance

Inheritance is one of the coolest things about object-oriented programming. With inheritance, you create new objects by expanding existing ones. When you create a new class from an existing class, the new class is called a *derived* class. The previously existing class is called the *base* class. (Sometimes derived classes are called *children* and base classes are called *parents*. And sometimes the act of creating a derived class is called *subclassing*.)

In Figure 13-3 there are eight classes. The Food class is the most elemental. All it describes is the weight and number of calories for a particular food. Solid Food is based on Food, so it too has a weight and number of calories. But it also has some extra items describing the dimensions and color of the food. Pizza is a solid food. It contains all the items from Solid Food (which contains all the items from Food) in addition to other items. As you can see, you can use inheritance to build up complex things, such as a pizza, out of much more elemental items. (In fact, here I show the programmer's version of the five basic food groups.) At each step, the derived class inherits the features and capabilities of its base class.

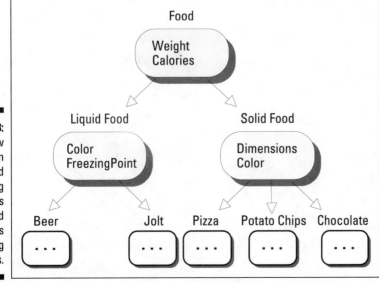

Figure 13-3:
New classes can be created by inheriting the features and capabilities of existing ones.

More on polymorphism

Not only can you build up classes through inheritance, but you can use polymorphism to specialize behavior for each class. For example, the Solid Food class might have a member function called GetMe. For the Pizza object, this function would dial the local pizza deliverer. For the Potato Chip object it might instruct you to drive to the nearest supermarket. (Or, if you live in California, to the nearest Fry's, where you can get soda, chips, and software all at once.)

The combination of inheritance and polymorphism lets you easily create a series of similar but unique objects. Because of inheritance, such objects share many similar characteristics. But because of polymorphism, each object can have unique behavior. So, if polymorphism is used, common functions, such as GetMe, behave one way for one object and another way for another.

If polymorphism isn't used for a particular function, the base class functionality is used. For example, if a particular object derived from Solid Food doesn't override GetMe, Solid Food's GetMe routine will be used for that object. Because of this, functionality in base classes tends to be generic so it can be used across derived classes. If it's not generic, the derived classes almost always use polymorphism to override the behavior of the base class.

The programmer who designs the Pizza or Potato Chip class determines what the GetMe call will do. The person who uses Pizza or Potato Chip doesn't need to understand all the details about what GetMe does, merely that it performs the correct function for finding food. This additional benefit of polymorphism — namely, that the user of a class doesn't have to understand its details — is sometimes called *information hiding*.

Chapter 14

The Parts of a Program

The two principal parts of C++ programs are source files and header files. The *source files* (sometimes called CPP files, for C Plus Plus files) contain the main parts of the program. They're where you type in routines, define data, and decide how the program flows (program flow refers to the order in which your routines should be called).

Sometimes source files use routines that are created in other source files or in libraries. When you use such routines, however, the compiler doesn't recognize that these routines exist. That's because the compiler only understands what's happening in the particular file it's compiling.

To remedy this situation, you include a *header file*. The header file tells the compiler the names and characteristics of routines you're using from other files or from libraries. For example, let's say you want to use a routine called foo, and that foo is in a library. To do this, you'd include a header file that tells the compiler that foo is a routine, and that describes what types of data you might pass to foo.

If you create routines in one file that you plan to use in another file, you need to create a header file describing these routines. By reading the header file in the other source files, you'll be able to access the routines you created.

The (not) missing linker

When you define an external function in the header file, you just give the function name and its parameters, not the name of the library or the source file containing the function. The compiler generates a list of all functions that it needs for a particular file, both external functions and those that are defined within that file.

After compilation, the linker is called. Among other things, the linker looks at all the functions that are needed and searches for a match across all files and libraries. If it finds a match, it uses that function automatically. If it doesn't find a match, it spits out an error message.

What Do I Put in a Source File?

Source files are composed of *statements*. Statements are program lines that tell the computer to do something.

For example, the following line is a statement that tells the computer to calculate the cost by adding 10 to the value of CostForToppings:

```
Cost = 10 + CostForToppings;
```

Each statement needs to end with a semicolon. The semicolon tells the computer where one statement ends and the next statement begins, just like a period does in a sentence.

You can group a set of statements together by surrounding them with { and } (a left curly brace and a right curly brace). For example, let's say you have a statement like "if the pizza is cold, reheat it;". (The *if* command, which is described in Chapter 19, lets you tell the computer to execute a particular statement if a particular condition holds true.) If you want to tell the computer to execute another statement at the same time, you could say something like: "if the pizza is cold {reheat it; take a 5-minute nap;}". The two statements are grouped together inside the { and }.

You also use { and } to define where functions begin and end. You'll learn more about this in Chapter 21.

When you pass parameters to a function, you surround the parameters with (and). For example, you could say "if the pizza is cold {reheat(5 minutes); take a nap(5 minutes);}". This tells the reheat routine how long you want to cook the pizza. You'll learn more about this in Chapter 21.

Here's a summary of the rules about statements:

✔ End lines with ;

✔ Group lines with { }

✔ Pass parameters with ( )

Where It All Begins

When you run a program, the computer needs to know where the first line of the program is. Instead of numbering the program lines (which is a real pain), you put the first line in a function called *main*. The first line in main is the first line that executes when you run the program. For example, here's a simple program that does nothing:

```
void main() {
    //This does absolutely nothing.
}
```

You can see this program has a routine called main. That's where the program starts. Because main can take parameters, you put ( ) after it. (You usually won't put anything inside the ( ) for main, however.) Next you see a {, which tells the

Hey, that's not legal!

The C++ standard (called the ANSI/ISO standard) requires main to return a value. In most cases, though, you really don't need to return a value, so Borland C++ lets you declare that main doesn't return a value, by declaring it a void. This book takes advantage of this by using void to make programs easier to read. But note that if you try out these programs with other compilers, you might get a message indicating that main needs to return a value. To make main return a value, you'd do something similar to this:

```
int main() {
    //Statements here
    return Value;
}
```

Actually, you can choose to not bother returning a value *and* to not declare main as void—this will let you have routines that are easier to read and that are ANSI/ISO compliant. But if you do this, you'll get a warning from the compiler telling you that you didn't return a value. (And, to make things even more explicit, if you don't list the int before main, the compiler will assume that main returns an int.) Although as a rule it's not a good practice to ignore warnings, you can ignore this particular warning in this particular case.

Also, any time that you *do* indicate that a routine returns a value, you should return a value.

computer that the lines that follow are part of main. The closing } tells the computer that this is the end of main.

You might be wondering what *void* means (it appears before the main in the program you just saw). It has to do with functions, which you'll learn more about in Chapter 21.

Functions are self-contained routines that perform some type of functionality, such as print, or process data, or ask for input. Functions can return values; for example, the *sin* function returns the sine of a number.

Anyway, void means that nothing is returned. Because the main function isn't returning a value, it's a void routine; you put void before the main to alert the compiler that main won't return a value.

Read on, and you'll see how to do something in main.

It's Alive! Sending Output to the Screen

If you want to display something for the user to read, you need to print it to the screen. Fortunately, this is real easy. A thing called *cout* (pronounced either see-out or to rhyme with gout) represents the screen. When you send a value to *cout*, *cout* happily prints it. You use the << command to send a value to *cout*.

To print text, enclose the text that you want to print within double quotes. (By the way, computer people frequently refer to text as *strings*, which is short for strings of characters.)

Let's look at some examples. Any time you see *cout* <<, the value that follows will be printed:

```
//print "Hello World"
cout << "Hello World";

//print "The meaning of life is:  42"
cout << "The meaning of life is: 42";
```

You can also print several values out at the same time. In the following two examples, two values are being passed. In the first of the two examples, "My name is" and "Michael" are two separate values. And, as the second example shows, the values can be either text ("The meaning of life is") or numbers (42).

```
//print "My name is Michael"
cout << "My name is " << "Michael";

//print "The meaning of life is:  42"
cout << "The meaning of life is: " << 42;
```

Well, aren't *these* characters special?

There are a number of special characters you can use while printing. Here are a few:

\n   Start a new line

\t   Tab

\b   Go back one space

\f   Start a new page

\\   Print the \ character

\'   Print the ' character

\"   Print the " character

For example, to print:

```
He said "Ahoy"
```

you would do this:

```
cout << "He said \"Ahoy\"\n";
```

As you can see, you can combine text and numbers very easily. Also note that every statement ends with a semicolon.

Ta da! That's all you need to do to start printing things with C++.

What's My New Line?

You can print a number of special characters. The most commonly used special character is "\n", which starts a new line. (As you might expect, this character is sometimes called the *newline character*.) For example, if you wanted the previous examples to print text on separate lines you would type this:

```
//print "My name is Michael"
cout << "My name is " << "Michael\n";

//print "The meaning of life is:  42"
cout << "The meaning of life is: " << 42 << "\n";
```

The "\n" is treated like normal characters are treated. In other words, you can use a \n by itself, as in the 42 << "\n", or you can put it in the middle (or end) of any text, as in the "Michael\n". (You could also do something such as "Mich\nael". This will print out Mich on one line, start a new line (when the \n is encountered), and then print ael.) Unlike normal characters, \n doesn't print anything to the screen — it just forces a new line to start.

At first, all of these << and "\n"s might look rather outlandish, but you'll get used to them pretty quickly.

Getting Input from the User

Reading characters from the keyboard is as easy as writing them to the screen. You use *cin* and >>. (This is pronounced *see-in* or *sin*. Your choice.) For example, to have the user type in the number of toppings, you could do this:

```
cin >> NumberOfToppings;
```

When you get input from the user, you typically save it into a variable. Variables are discussed in Chapter 16.

Adding Helpful Comments

You might know exactly how your program operates. But if someone else looks at it, or if you return to it in a few years, you might forget what a particular line or function does. That's why it's important to put comments in your programs. Comments explain in English (or in whatever language you speak) what you've written in Computerese.

You've already seen lots of comments in the sample programs so far. Comments are indicated by // (two slash marks); when you see this, you'll know that all the following text on that line is a comment. (See the "Sure, use the old-fashioned comments" sidebar for information about the older C-style comments.)

Sure, use the old-fashioned comments

C++ uses // to indicate comments. You can also write comments using the older C style, in which you enclose comments between a /* and a */. Here are several examples:

```
/* This is a C style comment */
a = 10;  /*Give the variable a the value 10*/
/*a is my variable*/ a = 10; /*give it the value 10*/
```

If you use the older C style comments, be sure that you end them! If you forget the */ at the end, the compiler ignores everything that you've typed after the first /*.

Note that, unlike /* and */, when you use // you don't need to end the line with a special character. // indicates that all the following text on that line is a comment. But, unlike using /* and */, you need to start each comment line with //.

Comments can be entered on their own separate lines, as in:

```
//This is a comment.
```

Comments can also occur at the end of a line, as in:

```
a = 10;   //Give the variable a the value 10.
```

Using Functions from a Library

At this point you're almost ready to write your first program. But the routines *cout* and *cin* are part of a library. As discussed earlier in this chapter, this means that, to use them in a program, you need to include the header file that defines them. You do so with the *#include* command. (This is pronounced *include* or *pound include*.)

Any command that starts with a # is called a *preprocessor directive*. This is a fancy term for a command that tells the compiler to do something. Preprocessor directives don't get turned into code: they just control how the compiler operates.

For example, the *#include* preprocessor directive tells the compiler to load an include file. The definitions for *cin* and *cout* are made in an include file called *iostream.h*. (The .h is the standard extension for a header file.) So to load these definitions, you'd add this line to the beginning of your program:

```
#include <iostream.h>
```

This loads the definitions for *cin*, *cout*, and many other routines that are part of the iostream library.

Future hackers read this: " " versus < >

The *#include* command is followed by the name of the header file to load. If the header file is one of the standard header files — that is, if it comes with the compiler — put the name inside < and > (a left and right angle bracket):

```
#include <iostream.h>
```

The compiler knows where to find its own header files and will search there. If you're loading a header file you created, put the name inside quotation marks. This tells the compiler to look in the current directory before searching the directory containing the standard header files:

```
#include "foo.h"
```

You can also give a full path name:

```
#include "\michael\pizza\foo.h"
```

Note that preprocessor directives aren't followed by a semicolon. Preprocessor directives can only be one line, so the compiler always knows that when the line ends, the preprocessor directive ends.

C++ is composed of a small number of commands and a lot of library functions. Many library functions are common across all C++ compilers — no matter what C++ you use, you'll always find these helper functions. Other library functions are extra. For example, you can buy a library that contains functions for doing statistics.

At Last: Hello World

It's time to create your first program. This program will print "Hello World" on the screen:

```
//My first program.
//Prints "Hello World" on the screen.

//Include definition for cout.
#include <iostream.h>

void main() {
    //Print "Hello World" to the screen.
    cout << "Hello World\n";
}
```

(You can type this program in, or load it from the HELLOW directory in the separately available program disk.)

Note (as discussed in the "Hey, that's not legal!" sidebar) that if you aren't compiling with Borland C++, you might need to remove the void that comes before the main. If you do this, you can ignore the warning message that will tell you that you need to return a value from main.

Do It to It with Borland C++

Here's how to create and run this program with Borland C++ 4.0. If you don't understand what these steps do, you might want to reread some of the chapters in Part I.

1. Start Borland C++.

2. Create a new project file by selecting Project | New project. The New Project dialog box appears.

3. In the Target Type list, select EasyWin. (This lets the *cin* and *cout* in the program work under Windows. You could also create a DOS program instead.) Your screen should look like Figure 14-1.

4. Now click the Advanced button. (Not bad — you're just getting started and you're already using advanced features!)

5. Click the .cpp Node button on, as shown in Figure 14-2.

6. Click OK to close the Advanced Options dialog box.

7. Click OK to create the new project.

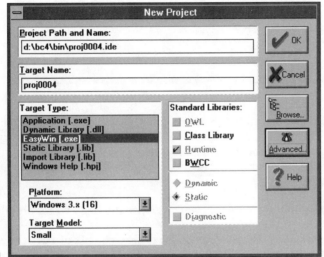

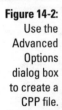
Figure 14-1:
Start the
Hello World
program by
creating a
new project.

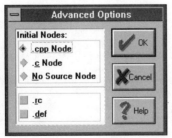
Figure 14-2:
Use the
Advanced
Options
dialog box
to create a
CPP file.

By default, the new project will have a single CPP file in it. Double-click on that file and an editor will appear. Type the Hello World program into the editor. You should end up with something like the program in Figure 14-3.

(If you're using the separately available disk, just select Project I Open and then load the HELLOW.IDE file from the HELLOW directory on the separate disk. This will load a project file containing the same program you get if you follow steps 1 through 7, above.)

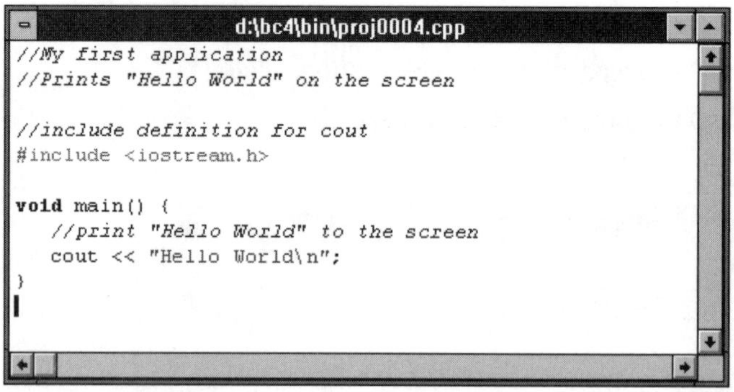

Figure 14-3:
Type the
Hello World
program into
the editor.

```
d:\bc4\bin\proj0004.cpp
//My first application
//Prints "Hello World" on the screen

//include definition for cout
#include <iostream.h>

void main() {
    //print "Hello World" to the screen
    cout << "Hello World\n";
}
```

Now you can compile and run your program. Just click on the lightning bolt. Unless you messed up, the program will run. (If you do run into errors, however, bring up the editor again and make sure you've typed the program in correctly. Also check out the "Those sooner-or-later-gotta-happen syntax errors" sidebar.)

After you've admired your work, you can close the Hello World program.

In this chapter, you've learned about the basic elements of a C++ program. In the next two chapters, you'll learn about adding variables to your program so you can store information.

Those sooner-or-later-gotta-happen syntax errors

If you type a program incorrectly or use C++ commands improperly, the compiler will tell you that you've got a *syntax error*. This just means that the compiler doesn't recognize the words you've used or that you've left something out of a command.

There are many different types of syntax errors that can occur. Chapter 41 discusses the most common syntax errors and describes how to fix them.

Chapter 15

Data Types

In This Chapter

▶ Learn about the different C++ data types

▶ Declare a variable's type

▶ Learn about type protection and typecasting

▶ Add variables and constants to a program

Computer programs process data — and there can be a lot of different types of data. For example, floating-point numbers in a spreadsheet program, order records in an order inventory system, and album titles in a music-search program are all of a different *data type*.

Strongly typed languages, such as C++, are computer languages that require the programmer to describe what a piece of data is before using it. For example, if you want to save a number, you first need to tell the computer to expect a number.

There are many advantages to using a strongly typed language. For example, if you make a mistake and treat an item that's a number as if it were an employee record, the compiler generates an error. That's good.

Here's an example that explains why it's good: suppose that an employee record uses eight bytes of memory, while a number uses only two bytes of memory. If you clear an employee record, you clear eight bytes of memory. So if you cleared a number as if it were an employee record, you'd end up clearing the number *plus* six additional bytes in memory. And the six extra bytes you cleared might very well have contained important information. Clearing them could lead to some unexpected and undesirable results.

Some other languages, such as BASIC, are *loosely typed*. In loosely typed languages, the computer figures out what an item is when you use it. For example, if you set a variable to contain the text "foo", the compiler makes the variable a string.

Loosely typed languages can be a little easier for new programmers. But they don't catch mistakes as well as strongly typed languages, so the resulting programs tend to be less robust.

Tell It What It Is: Declaring a Variable's Type

In C++, you must *declare* each variable's type before you can use it. To declare a variable's type, you simply indicate the type followed by the variable name; this is called a *variable declaration*. (You'll learn more about variables in Chapter 16 — in the meantime, just know that a variable is a thing you store information in. Think of a variable as a cell in a spreadsheet. Only with a name.)

Several examples of variable declarations are provided here. For example, this example shows a variable declaration for a variable foo that is of type integer:

```
int foo;
```

This variable declaration is for a variable bar that is of type character:

```
char bar;
```

And the following variable declaration is for a function, min, that takes two integers as parameters and returns an integer. (You'll learn more about what functions do and how to declare them in Chapter 21.)

```
int min(int first, int second);
```

If you plan to use variables (or routines, or classes) in more than one file, you'll probably want to make a header file containing the various definitions. You'll learn more about this in Part III. ■

The Basic Data Types

C++ provides a number of predefined data types that you can use. You can also create more complex data types by combining data types, as discussed in Chapter 17. Here are the three most commonly used data types:

char	A character. a, b, and * are all characters. (By the way, *char* can be pronounced either like the char in charcoal or like the care in caretaker.)
float	A floating-point number. These are the numbers with decimal points, such as 3.14, -1.78, and 25.0. Floating-point numbers are sometimes called real numbers.
int	An integer. Integers are whole numbers (they can be positive, negative, or 0). For example, the numbers 0, 1, 3, 39, and -42 are all integers, but 1.5 isn't an integer.

Getting back to our favorite subject, let's say that you want to have a variable that stores the number of toppings for a pizza (the number of toppings is an integer). Here's what you'd do:

```
int NumberOfToppings;
```

Then you could find out how many toppings there are, and store this information as an integer:

```
cin >> NumberOfToppings;
```

When you write your application, you need to figure out what data types you need for the various data you're going to be using.

For example, if you don't want customers to be able to order half a topping, use an integer for the NumberOfToppings. If you might charge a fractional amount for a pizza (such as $12.19), then use a float for the Cost. And if you need to store text, you'll need a character pointer. You'll learn more about character pointers in Chapter 22.

Data Types That Avoid the Limelight

There are a number of other data types you might want to know about, but which you won't use as often as those types you just learned.

double	An extra large float. (And no, that doesn't mean it comes with two scoops of ice cream.) Normally, floats represent numbers between +/–3.4×10^{-38} to +/–3.4×10^{38}. Doubles can represent numbers from +/– 1.7×10^{-308} to +/–1.7×10^{308}.
long	Can precede an int to tell it to use 32 bits to represent the number. (This lets you store much larger numbers — those ranging from -2,147,483,648 to 2,147,483,647, to be precise.)
long double	(This is sometimes called *double long*.) It makes a floating-point number use 80 bits. This extends the range to be from +/–3.4×10^{-4932} to +/–1.1×10^{4932}.
short	Can precede an int to tell it to use 16 bits to represent the number.
signed	Can precede an int to indicate that the number is either positive or negative.
unsigned	Can precede an int to indicate that the number is always positive. This lets one more bit be used to represent the size of the number.

void   No type. Used to indicate that a function doesn't return a
                value. (See Chapter 21 for more information on functions.)
                For example:

```
void main()
```

Type Protection and Other Strong-Arm Tactics

Machine language doesn't care about data types. To machine language, data is just locations in memory. That's why a machine language program will blithely write integers all over your employee records, or write characters all over your program, or whatever else a program might tell it to do. (Many computer viruses are designed to destroy data in just this way.)

But C++ *does* care about types. If you declare a variable as one type and then try to use it as another type, the compiler will generate an error. This is a very helpful feature of C++, because it means that the compiler finds some very common errors. (This is certainly better than having the compiler ignore the errors, only to have your program crash as a result of them.)

So, the following program works well:

```
//Use an integer for the number of toppings.
int NumberOfToppings;
//Make there be 7 toppings.
NumberOfToppings = 7;
```

But, if you tried the following, you'd get an error, because NumberOfToppings is an integer, so you can't set it to a string:

```
//Set number of toppings to "Hello World".
NumberOfToppings = "Hello World";
```

For some operations, the compiler automatically converts from one data type to another. For example, the compiler converts a floating-point number to an integer in the following situation:

```
int NumberOfToppings;
NumberOfToppings = 6.3;
```

After running this code, NumberOfToppings is set to 6. (The compiler automatically rounds down to the nearest integer.)

You can also explicitly tell the compiler to convert from one type to another.

This is called *typecasting*. To do this, you just put a type name in parentheses prior to the item to convert:

```
int NumberOfToppings;
float MyInput;
NumberOfToppings = (int) MyInput;
```

One of these types is not like the others

Borland C++ goes to great lengths to make sure there aren't type mismatches. As the compiler compiles a C++ source file, it creates something called a *symbol table*. The symbol table contains detailed information about all the variables and functions used in the source file. Whenever you use variables (or functions), the compiler finds their type from the symbol table and makes sure that the correct types are used. The compiler also contains very detailed rules on how to convert data from one type to another. For example, if you have a function that expects a float (see Chapter 21 for more information on passing parameters to functions), and you pass in an integer, the compiler knows how to convert an integer to a floating point value. If the compiler finds a type mismatch in a situation where it doesn't have a rule for converting the data, it reports an error.

When you compile a program that uses more than one source file, the situation is a bit more complex. One source file might use a function or variable that is declared in a different source file. The compiler needs to be able to match functions and variables across source files — and to make sure correct types are used. Technically speaking, this step is performed during the linking phase.

Type checking across files (called *external resolution*) is done with a technique called *name*

mangling. When you declare a variable, function, or other item, the compiler converts the name you've given the item to an internal name. The internal name includes information describing the type of the item. For example, suppose the compiler uses the character *i* to indicate an item is an integer and *cp* to indicate an item is a character pointer. Suppose you have this function in one source file:

```
int NumberOfToppings();
```

Also suppose that, in a different file, you have this code:

```
char *MyText;
MyText = NumberOfToppings();
```

The compiler would convert the name NumberOfToppings to iNumberOfToppings and the name MyText to cpMyText. You never see these internal names (unless you're looking at assembly language listings), but the linker does.

As a result, the linker sees this:

```
cpMyText = iNumberOfToppings();
```

By looking at the mangled name, the compiler sees that there is a type mismatch (since type integer doesn't match type character pointer), so it prints out an error.

Some Things Never Change: Constants

You'll find that you'll use certain numbers or words over and over again in an application. For example, if you're doing mathematics, you know that π is always 3.141592.... If you're writing a philosophy program, you know that the meaning of life, the universe, and everything is 42. And if you're writing a pizza program, you might know know that pizza toppings always cost $2 each. (Sure, in real life, some toppings cost more than others, and there is that funny thing called inflation. But we'll deal with the real-life cost of pizza toppings later.)

For cases like this, you can create a *constant*. A constant is just a name for an item that never changes. To make an item a constant, precede its declaration with *const*. For example, the following code makes the CostPerTopping a constant that always has the value 2:

```
//Pizza toppings are always $2.
const int CostPerTopping = 2;
```

Constants make your programs a lot easier to read, because you can provide a name for a particular value. Also, if you change the value of a constant, the change "ripples out" and affects the whole program. For example, if the cost of a pizza topping increased to $3 (horrors!), you'd only need to change the constant. All the related calculations would be updated automatically, saving you from having to read through your whole program to find each place where it calculates the cost of a pizza.

You can use a constant in a program anywhere you could use an item of the same data type as the constant. For example, if you have an integer constant, you could pass in that constant anywhere that you could use an integer in an equation. Thus, you could multiply the number of toppings on a pizza by the constant CostPerTopping to determine the cost for all the toppings.

Easier to Read Pizza

Let's revisit our pizza application, this time using constants. You can type and run this application just as you did with the program in Chapter 14:

```
//Compute the cost of a pizza.
#include <iostream.h>

void main() {
    //Toppings are always $2 each.
    const int PricePerTopping = 2;
    //A plain pizza costs $10.
    const int PlainPrice = 10;
```

```
        int NumberOfToppings;
        int CostForToppings;
        int Cost;

        //Find the number of toppings.
        cout << "How many toppings do you want?\n";
        cin >> NumberOfToppings;

        //Calculate the cost for the toppings.
        //use the constant so that it is easier to read
        CostForToppings = NumberOfToppings * PricePerTopping;

        //Calculate the total cost.
        //note that the constant makes it easier to read
        Cost = PlainPrice + CostForToppings;

        //Print the result.
        cout << "Your pizza costs $" << Cost << "\n";
    }
```

(This program is in the PIZZA2 directory on the separately available program disk.)

This program works just the same as the previous pizza program, but it's easier to understand because of the constants. Also, if you wanted to raise the price of the pizza, all you'd need to do is change the constant PlainPrice.

Another nice thing about constants is that if you inadvertently try to change them, the compiler complains. For example, let's suppose you accidentally include the following line in the middle of the program:

```
    PlainPrice = 65;
```

When it saw this line, the compiler would generate an error telling you that you're trying to change the value of a constant. This kind of early warning can prevent lots of hard-to-find bugs later on.

Chapter 16

Some Things Always Change: Variables

In This Chapter
▶ Learn what variables do
▶ Name variables
▶ Declare and initialize variables

*P*rograms read, write, and manipulate data. When you want to save a particular value, or save the results of a calculation, you do so by using a *variable*. A variable is a name used to represent a piece of information. There are all types of things you can store in variables, such as information about an employee, price for a plain pizza, number of bicycles ordered, and so on.

Variables often have descriptive names. For example, the name NumberOfToppings lets you quickly know that this variable represents the number of toppings a customer wants to place on a pizza. On the other hand, C3PO is not a great variable name. It could be a serial number, a license plate, a robot, or who knows what.

Whenever you want to access the information stored in a variable, you use the variable's name. Because C++ is strongly typed, you need to declare a variable's data type before using the variable.

The Programmer's Guide to Variable Names

You can name a variable pretty much anything that you want, with only a few (quite reasonable) limitations:

 ✔ Variable names can't start with numbers.

 ✔ Variable names can't have spaces in them.

✔ Variable names can't include special characters, such as . ; , " ' and +. In fact, it's easiest just to assume that _ (the underscore) is the only non-alphanumeric character you can use in a name.

✔ Variables can't be named the same name as words that are part of the C++ language.

✔ Variables shouldn't be given the name of C++ library functions either.

Table 16-1 shows the Borland C++ keywords. Keywords are the commands that are part of the C++ language. You'll learn what most of these keywords do by the time you finish this book! The keywords that start with one or two underscores (_ or __) are special Borland extensions that make personal-computer programming easier. Don't use these keywords for variable names.

Table 16-1: The C++ Keywords

__asm	__slowthis	_seg	far	short
__cdecl	__ss	_ss	float	signed
__cs	__stdcall	_stdcall	for	sizeof
__ds	__thread	asm	friend	static
__es	__try	auto	goto	struct
__except	_asm	break	huge	switch
__export	_cdecl	case	if	template
__far	_cs	catch	inline	this
__fastcall	_ds	cdecl	int	throw
__fastthis	_es	char	interrupt	try
__finally	_export	class	long	typedef
__huge	_far	const	near	union
__import	_fastcall	continue	new	unsigned
__interrupt	_huge	default	operator	virtual
__loadds	_import	delete	pascal	void
__near	_interrupt	do	private	volatile
__pascal	_loadds	double	protected	wchar_t
__rtti	_near	else	public	while
__saveregs	_pascal	enum	register	
__seg	_saveregs	extern	return	

Conventional wisdom on bestowing names

There are a number of conventions for how you name variables. Some people suggest that variables should all start with a lowercase letter, and functions with capitals. Other people suggest using a few characters at the beginning of a name to help clarify what it is. A particularly popular notation is the *Hungarian notation*. This is often used with Windows and OS/2 programming. With Hungarian notation, you precede pointers with a p, far pointers with an lp, functions with an fn, handles with an h, and so on. For example, you might have hInstance for an instance handle or lpRect for a far pointer to a rectangle.

Hungarian notation was developed by a Microsoft programmer named Charles Simonyi. In Microsoft's early days, Charles was famous for giving helicopter rides at company picnics.

Here are some examples of legal variable names:

way_cool

RightOn

Bits32

And here are some bad names:

case	This is a reserved word.
52PickUp	This starts with a number.
A Louse	This has a space in it.
+−v	This has illegal characters in it.

Variable names are case sensitive. So bart, Bart, bArt, and BART are all different variables.

Defining Variables

Before you use a variable you need to define it. To do so, just state the data type for the variable, followed by the variable's name; for example:

```
int    NumberOfToppings;
float  CostPerTopping;
long   Johns;
```

Initializing Variables

When you define a variable, you can also provide an *initial value*. This is the value the variable will have when it's first used. You provide an initial value by following the name with an = and a value; for example:

```
int    NumberOfToppings = 3;
float  CostPerTopping = 1.8;
long   Johns = 32700;
```

In this chapter you've learned how to define and initialize variables. In the next chapter you'll learn how to combine variables into structures and use them in a program.

Chapter 17

Structures
(Building Blocks for Variables)

● ●

In This Chapter

▶ Learn what structures are

▶ How to declare structures

▶ How to combine structures

▶ Add structures to an application

● ●

*S*o far you've learned about simple data types and seen that you can store information in a variable. But suppose you want to store something more complex than a simple data type — for example, a user's name, address, and phone number. You *could* do this by storing three separate variables: one for the name, one for the address, and one for the phone number.

This strategy is awkward, though, because in the real world it's natural to group things together. For example, let's say you want to read in or print an employee record. Although that record probably contains lots of parts (like name, address, phone number, salary, and so on), you probably think of it as a complete entity in and of itself. After all, it's a lot easier to say "print the employee record" than it is to say "print the employee name, address, phone number, salary ...".

The process of grouping a set of related variables into a single entity is called creating a *structure*. Structures are a very powerful feature of C++ that make it easy to organize and process information.

Declaring Structures

Declaring a structure is similar to declaring a simple data type (as discussed in Chapter 15). To declare a structure, you use the *class* keyword, followed by the name of the structure. Then, in curly brackets (some people also call these braces), you type *public:* followed by a list of the variables that make up the structure.

For example, you could have:

```
class Financials {
public:
    float       Bonds;
    float       Stocks;
    float       MoneyMarkets;
    BankList    Banks;
};
```

Note how the { } (the curly brackets) are used to contain all the statements that make up the class declaration.

Here's another example:

```
class Pizza {
public:
    int NumberOfToppings;
    int CostForToppings;
    int Cost;
};
```

To define a variable to be a structure, just follow the structure name by the variable name:

```
//Make a pizza variable.
Pizza       MyPizzaInfo;

//Make a financials variable.
Financials   MyFinancialInfo;
```

Wait, my instuctor is teaching me about struct!

In this book, you'll use the *class* keyword when you create structures. You'll also use the *class* keyword when you create classes. (See Chapter 27 for more information on classes.)

C++ actually has two different commands that you can use to declare structures (and classes): *class* and *struct*. *struct* is similar to *class*, except that you don't need to use *public:* before you list the items that make up a structure. Some people use *struct* any time they declare structures and *class* any time they declare classes (which are structures that also have functions within them). Note, though, that you can just as easily use *struct* to declare classes.

When you read about classes, you'll learn what the *public* keyword means. You'll also learn about *private* and *protected*, and use these keywords frequently. *struct* items are *public* by default, whereas *class* items are *private* by default. Rather than remember which is which, it's easier to just use *class* any time you declare a structure or a class.

Why are there two different keywords for doing almost the same thing? *struct* is a holdover from C. It's kept so you can compile C programs with a C++ compiler; it was given some new functionality that makes it similar to *class*. Since you're a C++ programmer, you might as well use *class*.

Defying clarification by defining declaration

In C++, declaration and definition are technical terms. They have slightly different meanings and are often used interchangeably (although doing so is incorrect).

Declaring a structure means telling the compiler what's in the structure, as in:

```
class Pizza {
public:
    int NumberOfToppings;
```

```
    int CostForToppings;
    int Cost;
};
```

No memory is set aside for the structure.

Defining a variable means telling the compiler to create a variable. This causes memory to be allocated for a variable:

```
Pizza           MyPizzaInfo;
```

Using Structures

Once you've created a structure you can access its *members* (the variables within it) by typing in the structure variable, followed by a . (that's a period), followed by the member name.

For example, to print the number of toppings, you could type in:

```
//Define a Pizza variable.
Pizza MyPizzaInfo;

//Now print out the value of the data member called
//NumberOfToppings.
cout << MyPizzaInfo.NumberOfToppings << "\n";
```

Likewise, to print the cost for the toppings, you could do this:

```
cout << MyPizzaInfo.CostForToppings << "\n";
```

Combining Structures to Make Bigger Structures

You can combine structures to create more complex structures. Sometimes this is called *nesting* structures.

For example, let's say you create a structure like the one in Figure 17-1. This structure, called Financials, tracks personal finances and contains variables about stocks, bonds, money market accounts, and bank accounts. As you can see (in the figure), the bank accounts variable (called Banks) is itself a structure that lists entries for each bank account.

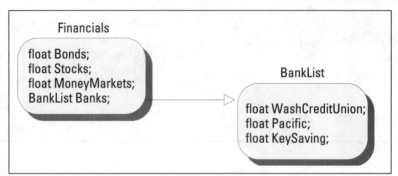

Figure 17-1:
Structures
can contain
other
structures.

You can include any structure within another structure, as long as it has already been declared. For example, in the Financials structure in Figure 17-1, the BankList structure needs to be declared:

```
class BankList {
public:
    float       WashCreditUnion;
    float       Pacific;
    float       KeySaving;
};

class Financials {
public:
    float       Bonds;
    float       Stocks;
    float       MoneyMarkets;
    BankList    Banks;
};
```

Because BankList is now declared, you can use it within the Financials structure.

I've Got Pizza on My Brain

Let's take another look at the pizza application, this time changing it so that it uses structures:

```
//Compute the cost of a pizza.
#include <iostream.h>

//Toppings are always $2 each.
const int PricePerTopping = 2;
//A plain pizza costs $10.
const int PlainPrice = 10;


class Pizza {
public:
    int NumberOfToppings;
    int CostForToppings;
    int Cost;
};

void main() {
    Pizza MyPizzaInfo;

    //Find the number of toppings.
    cout << "How many toppings do you want?\n";
    cin >> MyPizzaInfo.NumberOfToppings;

    //Calculate the cost for the toppings.
    //Use the constant so that it is easier to read.
    MyPizzaInfo.CostForToppings =
        MyPizzaInfo.NumberOfToppings * PricePerTopping;

    //Calculate the total cost.
    //Note that the constant makes it easier to read.
    MyPizzaInfo.Cost = PlainPrice +
        MyPizzaInfo.CostForToppings;

    //Print the result.
    cout << "Your pizza costs $" << MyPizzaInfo.Cost
        << "\n";
}
```

(You can type this program in, or load it from the PIZZA3 directory on the separately available program disk.)

You might notice some other interesting things about this program. First, the Pizza structure is declared before main( ). That's because you need to declare things before you use them. In this case, Pizza is used inside main( ), so it's declared before main. You'll see this over and over again in C++ programs. A class is declared. Its various member functions are defined. And then the class is used.

At first you might think that things seem a little backwards because the lowest, most elementary items are declared first, followed by the items that use them. You'll get used to this as you do more programming in C++. For now, if you want to see the big picture, you might start toward the bottom of a source file and then work your way back up.

Another thing you'll notice is that some code is split across lines. For example, the following statement starts on one line, but the ; (semicolon) doesn't occur until the second line:

```
MyPizzaInfo.Cost = PlainPrice +
    MyPizzaInfo.CostForToppings;
```

That's okay. Sometimes it's easier to read a piece of code if you break a statement into several lines. The compiler knows to keep reading until it finds a semicolon.

Chapter 18

Express Yourself with Expressions

• •

• •

*P*rograms process data — and as part of this processing, they perform a variety of calculations. A set of calculations (or formulas, as they're sometimes called) is called an *expression* in Borland C++. If you've used a spreadsheet, you're probably already familiar with expressions: when you type a formula into a cell, you're typing in an expression.

Expressions are used to calculate new information based on existing information. For example, you could use expressions to calculate the price of a pizza given the price for a plain pizza, the number of toppings, and the price per topping. Or, you could use expressions to calculate the monthly mortgage payment for a $100,000 loan given a 6% mortgage rate. You could also use expressions to calculate far more complicated things, such as the probability of a bridge breaking during a wind storm.

Expressions are important building blocks for creating complex applications. You've already seen a number of simple expressions in the Pizza application. For example, the following line from the Pizza application calculates the price of the toppings. This line uses the expression MyPizzaInfo.NumberOfToppings * PricePerTopping to multiply the number of toppings on the pizza by the cost per topping to find the total cost for the toppings:

```
MyPizzaInfo.CostForToppings =
    MyPizzaInfo.NumberOfToppings * PricePerTopping;
```

Expressions are also used to determine if certain conditions are met. For example, if you want to see if you've exceeded your credit limit, you could use an expression to compare your limit with the amount you've got charged.

When you create a program to match a real-world situation, you usually need to determine the expressions that define what's happening.

Here are some sample expressions:

```
6 + 3
PlainPrice + MyPizzaInfo.CostForToppings
3.1415*Radius*Radius
3.1415*Sqr(Radius)
ChargedAmount < CreditLimit
```

Smooth Operators

Table 18-1 describes five very common *operators* that you'll use over and over again to create expressions.

An operator is simply a math symbol that indicates what type of mathematical operation to use when you write a formula. When you say 4+5, the + is an operator.

Table 18-1: The Math Operators

Operator	Usage	Meaning
*	foo * bar	Multiply two numbers. For example, 6 * 3 is 18.
/	foo / bar	Divide two numbers. For example, 18 / 3 is 6.
+	foo + bar	Add two numbers. For example, 6 + 3 is 9.
−	foo − bar	Subtract two numbers. For example, 9 − 3 is 6.
%	foo % bar	Modulo. Returns the remainder of dividing two numbers. For example, 10 % 3 is 1, because 10 / 3 is 3, remainder 1. See the following tip about modulo.

Modulo is often used to constrain a set of integers to a range. For example, suppose you have a spaceship that moves across the bottom of a screen (such as with the Space Invaders video game). If you want the spaceship to reappear on the left side of the screen once it has gone off the right edge, you can use modulo. If the screen is 10 units wide, and pos is the position of the spaceship, then no matter what you add to pos, pos % 10 will always be between 0 and 9.

Thus, when the spaceship gets to position 9 and you add 1 to the position to move it right, pos % 10 returns 0, and the spaceship shows up on the left. ∎

Complex Operators That You Can Ignore for Now

Table 18-2 describes operators that are more complex than the operators described in Table 18-1. You probably won't need to use these complex operators right away. Later on, as your programming skills increase, you'll find them to be quite useful. Several of the complex operators are described further in their own separate sections outside the table. (You guessed it — they're too complex to describe fully in a table!)

Table 18-2: Increment, Decrement, and Shift Operators

Operator	Usage	Meaning
++	foo++ ++foo	Increment. The increment operator adds 1 to the value of an item. For example, 1++ is 2, and a++ is one more than the value of a. (By the way, the ++ operator is where C++ gets it name.)
−−	foo−− −−foo	Decrement. The decrement operator works the same as the increment operator, but it decreases instead of increases a value. If a is 2, for example, then a −− is 1.
>>	foo >> bar	Bit shift right. When you do foo >> bar, it's the same as finding the integer result of: $$\frac{foo}{2^{bar}}$$ See the "More on >> operators" section for examples and more discussion.
<<	foo << bar	Bit shift left. This is similar to >>, but the numbers get bigger. foo << bar is the equivalent of foo $* 2^{bar}$. See the "More on << operators" section for examples and more discussion.

More on the ++ operator

The increment operator can be kind of tricky, because the amount added depends on the type of item incremented.

For example, if you have a pointer to an item foo, and foo is four bytes long, then incrementing the pointer actually adds 4 to its value, because that way it points to the next foo. Confused? You'll learn more about pointers in Chapter 22.

There are two flavors of ++. You can put ++ before a variable (*preincrement*), as in ++bar, or you can put ++ after a variable (*postincrement*), as in bar++.

++bar increments the value of bar, and then evaluates bar. So if you do this:

```
int bar = 1;
cout << ++bar;
```

bar is set to 2, and 2 is printed on the screen.

By contrast, bar++ evaluates bar and then increments it, so that this:

```
int bar = 1;
cout << bar++;
```

sets bar to 2, but prints 1. That's because bar is evaluated before it's incremented.

++ is often used in loops and iterators.

More on the >> operator

Here are some examples of the >> operator in action:

16 >> 1 is 8

16 >> 2 is 4

16 >> 3 is 2

15 >> 1 is 7

15 >> 2 is 3

These answers are arrived at by determining the binary representation of foo and then shifting all bits right bar times. Note that when you shift bits right, the number gets smaller.

For example, the binary representation of 16 is:

1 0 0 0 0

If you shift these bits right once you get:

0 1 0 0 0

Which is 2^3 or 8.

Thus, 16 >> 1 = 8.

Here's another example. The binary representation of 15 is:

0 1 1 1 1

So 15 >> 2 is:

0 0 0 1 1

Which is 3.

More on the << operator

Here are two examples of the << operator:

16 << 1 is 32

15 << 2 is 60

If the value of the variable exceeds the precision, bits will be cut off. For example, suppose you have only 8 bits to represent a number. If you shift the number to the left 8 times, the end result is zero. That's because all the bits that contained a value were shifted away.

Note that << looks just the same as the << used with *cout*. When used in an expression, it means bit shifting. But the << of a *cout* takes priority (because the expression is evaluated left to right and the *cout* << is found first).

So if you want to print the result of a bit shift, you should enclose the shift in parentheses, as in this example:

```
cout << (16 << 2) << "\n";
```

On and Off Again with Boolean Expressions

So far all the operators you've looked at are for calculating the result of an expression. For example, you've seen how to calculate the price of a pizza by multiplying the number of toppings by the price per topping.

Now you're going to learn about *Boolean expressions*. With Boolean expressions, you're not concerned about the result of a particular expression, but with determining whether the expression is true or false.

For example, you might say "Does he love me?" or "Has my credit limit been exceeded?" or "Did the user ask to print a page?" Boolean expressions are almost always used in conjunction with questions. Generally, these questions are turned into statements that are equivalent to "If the Boolean expression is true, then do a bunch of things."

If the result of a Boolean expression is 0, the answer is considered false. If the result is not 0, the answer is considered true.

The following sections describe the operators used in Boolean expressions. (Naturally enough, these operators are known as *Boolean operators*.)

In Chapter 19 you'll see how to combine Boolean operators with questioning statements, such as the *if* statement.

Something confusing that'll bite you at least once

Note that the Boolean operator == is different from the assignment operator =. The assignment operator = sets the variable on the left equal to the value on the right. The Boolean operator == checks to see if the value on the left is the same as the value on the right, but doesn't alter any variables. Using = where you want == is a common mistake that can make a big mess.

For example, the following fragment always sets *a* to 2. Notice that in the *if* statement, *a* is set to 1.

Since 1 is a Boolean true, the *a* = *a* + 1 line executes:

```
if (a = 1)
    a = a + 1;
```

This is quite different from the following, which only adds 1 to *a* if *a* is 1:

```
if (a == 1)
    a = a + 1;
```

Table 18-3: The Comparison (Boolean) Operators

Operator	Usage	Meaning
>	foo > bar	Greater than. Returns true if the expression on the left is greater than the expression on the right. For example: 3 > 5 is false. 3 > 1 is true. 3 > 3 is false because 3 is equal to, but not greater than 3.
>=	foo >= bar	Greater than or equal to. Very similar to >, but it also returns true if the left and right expressions are equal. For example: 3 >= 5 is false. 3 >= 1 is true. 3 >= 3 is true, because 3 equals 3.
<	foo < bar	Less than. Returns true if the expression on the left is less than the expression on the right. For example: 3 < 5 is true. 3 < 1 is false. 3 < 3 is false.
<=	foo <= bar	Less than or equal to. Returns true if the expression on the left is less than or equal to the expression on the right. For example: 3 <= 5 is true. 3 <= 1 is false. 3 <= 3 is true.
==	foo == bar	Equals. Returns true if the expression on the left equals the expression on the right. For example: 1 == 2 is false. 1 == 1 is true.

(continued)

Operator	Usage	Meaning
!=	foo != bar	Not equal. Returns true if the value on the left is not equal to the value on the right. For example: 1 != 2 is true. 1 != 1 is false.
!	!foo	Not. Takes a single argument. If the argument is true, it returns false. If the argument is false, it returns true. For example: !1 is false. !0 is true.
&&	foo && bar	Logical and. Returns true if the expression on the left and the expression on the right are both true. For example: 1 && 1 is true. 0 && 1 is false. Used for questions such as "If the spirit is willing && the body is weak then...".
||	foo || bar	Logical or. Returns true if either the expression on the left or the expression on the right is true. For example: 1 || 0 is true. 1 || 1 is true. 0 || 0 is false.

Your Assignment, Should You Choose to Accept It

You use the assignment operator (=) when you want to give a variable a value, such as when you want to store some information in a variable or save the results of a calculation. For example, you've already seen it used in lines like this:

```
Cost = PlainPrice + CostForToppings;
```

When you assign a value, the value of the expression on the right side of the = is copied into the variable on the left side of the =.

You can use multiple assignments in a single statement. For example, this line sets several variables to 0:

```
a = b = c = 0;
```

You can only assign a variable a value of the same type as the variable, or a value that can be converted to the type of the variable. The examples that follow illustrate this point.

The following is okay, because *a* and 10 are both integers:

```
int a = 10;
```

This is not legal, however (in fact, to put it in non-C++ terms, you could probably call it a "Bozo no-no"):

```
int a = "bozo";
```

That's because *a* is an integer and "bozo" is not (Bozo's a clown, remember?). ■

Impress Them with Complex Expressions

You can combine all types of operators to make complex expressions. For example, you could determine the cost of a pizza, including the price of delivery and tax, with this:

```
PizzaCost = (1 + TaxRate) * (DeliveryPrice +
    PricePerTopping*NumberOfToppings + PlainPrice);
```

Or, you could print out a complex expression with this:

```
cout << (3*16/7 << 2)*(foo && finished);
```

Handy Self-Operating Operators

You'll probably find that you frequently need to perform some very simple operations on a variable. For example, you might want to add a value to a score, or you might want to multiply a variable by a constant.

Of course, you can always do these things using statements such as these:

```
foo = foo*3;
bar = bar + 2;
```

C++ is known, however, for providing a variety of shortcuts that can help you spend less time typing.

Table 18-4 shows a number of shortcuts you can use to operate on a variable. All these shortcuts replace statements of the form:

```
foo = foo operator bar
```

with statements of the form:

```
foo operator bar
```

For example, instead of doing this:

```
b = b + 1;
```

you could do this:

```
b += 1;
```

Operator and a Haircut: Two Bits

Integers are stored in the computer as a series of bits. For example, a short integer is stored with 16 bits. The number of bits determines the maximum value the integer can take.

Boolean values are typically saved as short integers (16 bits), even though the value of each can only be true or false. If you're using a large number of Booleans, you can save lots of space by using a single bit to represent each Boolean value.

For example, let's suppose you survey 10,000 people, and you ask each person the same 16 simple yes-or-no questions. Saving the results of your survey in a program will require 10,000 * 16 (160,000) integers. That's more memory than computers in the early days ever had!

But, if you instead save the result of each answer as a single bit, where you set bit 0 to true if question 1 was answered yes, bit 1 to true if question 2 was answered yes, and so on, you could save a lot of space. In this particular case, you could save 16 answers in each integer — and you'd require only 10,000 integers to save the results of the survey. That's quite a difference.

When you pack information into an integer in this way, it's sometimes called creating *bit fields* or *bit packing*.

Table 18-4: Assignment Operator Shortcuts

Assignment operator shortcut	Usage	Meaning
+=	foo += bar	Add the value to the right to the variable on the left. For example, this adds 3 to foo: foo += 3;
–=	foo –= bar	Subtract the value on the right from the variable on the left. For example, this subtracts 3 from foo: foo –=3;
*=	foo *= bar	Multiply the variable on the left by the value on the right. For example, this multiplies foo by 3: foo *= 3;
/=	foo /= bar	Divide the variable on the left by the value on the right. For example, this divides foo by 3: foo /= 3;
%=	foo %= bar	Save the modulo of the variable on the left with the value on the right. For example, this sets foo to the modulo of foo and 10: foo %= 10;
<<=	foo <<= bar	Performs a left shift of the variable on the left, by the number of bits specified on the right. For example, this multiplies foo by 4: foo <<= 2;
>>=	foo >>= bar	Performs a right shift of the variable on the left, by the number of bits specified on the right. For example, this shifts foo two bits to the right, thus dividing foo by 4: foo >>= 2;
&=	foo &= bar	Performs a bitwise and with the variable on the left. For example, if foo is 10, this is 2: foo &= 2;

(continued)

Operator	Usage	Meaning
|=	foo |= bar	Performs a bitwise or with the variable on the left. For example, if foo is 10, this is 11: foo |= 1;
^=	foo ^= bar	Performs a bitwise invert of the variable on the left. For example, if foo is 10, this is 8: foo ^= 2;

A little voodoo magic: hex (and binary and decimal)

If you're new to computers, all this talk about binary numbers might be a bit confusing. The number system you use every day is called a *base ten* or *decimal* system. In base ten, every time you move left in a number, it represents ten times as much, so that 10 is ten times as big as 1, and 200 is ten times as big as 20. Each digit represents a power of ten, so, for example, the number 125 is really 100 + 20 + 5. This is the same as $1*10^2 + 2*10^1 + 5*10^0$.

Computers aren't able to represent ten different options for each digit, though. Instead, they can only tell if a number is on or off — each digit can only be a 0 or a 1. Such numbers are called *base two* or *binary* numbers. A digit in a binary system is often called a *bit* (short for *binary digit*). For example, the binary number 1101 is the same as $1*2^3 + 1*2^2 + 0*2^1 + 1*2^0$. Which, in base ten, is 8 + 4 + 1, or 13.

Computers store numbers in groups eight bits long, called *bytes*. A byte can represent 256 unique values (or, 2^8). When two bytes are put together they are called a *word*. A word has 16 bits and can represent up to 65536 values (2^{16}). Four bytes put together is called a *double word*.

2^{10} is a magic number for computer people. This is 1024, which is frequently called a *K*. Even though

K or *kilo* means one thousand, for computer people a K means 1024. So 64K of memory means 64*1024, or 65536 bytes. Likewise, a *mega*byte, or *M*, normally means one million. But for computer people it means 1024*1024, or 1048576.

Because it can be a pain to write out binary numbers (they have too many digits), *hex* or *hexadecimal* notation is sometimes used instead. Hexadecimal numbers are numbers that are base 16. When writing a hex number, every four bits from a number are combined to form a single hex digit, also known as a *hexit*. Because each hexit can range between 0 and 15, the letters A through F are used to represent 10 through 15. In other words, A is 10, B is 11, and so on. When you write a hex number in C++, you precede it with 0x. So, 0x0A is the same as 10 in the decimal system. And 0xFF is the same as 255. If you hang out with enough computer people someone will inevitably ask you your age in hex.

And why are computers binary? A lot of the reason has to do with how chips operate, and in particular, with the characteristics of transistors. It's a pretty involved explanation, so I guess you'll have to read my upcoming bestseller *Solid State Particle Physics for Dummies* to learn more.

You can use the bit operators in Table 18-5 to operate on specific bits within a variable.

Table 18-5: The Bit Operators

Bit operator	Usage	Meaning
~	~foo	Computes a bitwise not. If a bit is 0, it's set to 1. If a bit is 1, it's set to 0. For example, given a four-bit binary number: ~1011 is 0100
<<	foo << bar	Shifts a number left by a number of bits. For example, given a four-digit binary number: 1011 << 2 is 1100 (Also discussed in Table 18-2.)
>>	foo >> bar	Shifts a number right by a number of bits. For example: 1011 >> 2 is 0010 (Also discussed in Table 18-2.)
&	foo & bar	Performs a bitwise and. When the bit on the left and the bit in the corresponding position on the right are both 1, it returns 1. Otherwise, it returns 0. For example: 1011 & 1010 is 1010
|	foo | bar	Performs a bitwise or. When the bit on the left or the bit on the corresponding position on the right is 1, it returns 1. Otherwise, it returns 0. For example: 1011 | 1010 is 1011
^	foo ^ bar	Performs a bitwise exclusive or. When one, but not two, of the bits on the right and left are set, it returns 1. Otherwise, it returns 0. For example: 1011^1010 is 0001 See the tip about the ^ operator in this section.

Note that foo^bar^foo always returns foo. This property is often used with bitmapped graphics.

Also, foo^foo is always 0. In the old days, assembly language programmers used this trick to make programs go faster, because doing this was the fastest way to set a value to 0. ■

For Hardcore Folks Only: The If Operator

The if operator is very similar to the @IF function in a spreadsheet. The if operator takes three expressions. It evaluates the first expression. If the first expression is true, it returns the value of the second expression. But if the first expression is false, it returns the value of the third expression.

In a spreadsheet, this is written:

```
@IF(expr1, expr2, expr3)
```

Which really means: if *expr1* is true, then return the value of *expr2*. Otherwise, return *expr3*.

In C++, this is written:

```
expr1 ? expr2 : expr3
```

So you could write something like this in a blackjack game:

```
UserMessage = (ValueOfCards > 21) ? "You're busted!" :
    "Hit again?";
```

What Do I Do First? Order of Operations

If you recall back to when you studied addition and division in school, you might remember that the order in which you write things *does* matter. (You might even remember words such as noncommutative property and stuff like that.)

The computer follows the same rules that you learned (and probably forgot) from math class. Expressions are evaluated left to right, but some things are evaluated first. For example, if you have 3 + 2 * 3, the answer is 9. Why? Because multiplication takes priority over addition. So the 2 * 3 is evaluated before it's added to 3. If you simply read things left to right, you'd get 15 instead.

You can use parentheses to change the order of operation. For example, you could write (3 + 2) * 3. In this case, 3 + 2 is evaluated first, then multiplied. If you aren't sure about which things are evaluated first, it doesn't hurt to add parentheses.

Table 18-6 lists the *order of operations*. The items at the top of the table are evaluated before (or have a *higher precedence* than) those at the bottom. For example, + appears before >. So, 1 + 0 > 1 is the same as (1 + 0) > 1. The answer (of course) is false.

All items on the same row have the same priority, so they are always evaluated left to right when found in an expression. For example, 3 * 4 / 2 is the same as (3 * 4) / 2.

Table 18-6: The Order of Operations

Highest precedence	( )
	++ −− ~ !
	* / %
	+ −
	>> <<
	< <= > >=
	== !=
	&
	^
	|
	&&
	||
Lowest precedence	?:

If you're not sure about the order of operations, always add plenty of parentheses so you understand what's going on. ∎

Here Are Some Operator Examples

Let's take a quick look at some examples that show operators in action.

Example 1: This statement determines the area of a circle.

```
Area = 3.14*Radius*Radius;
```

Example 2: This statement calculates how much tax you would pay on a purchase of amount Purchase, given a tax rate TaxRate.

```
Tax = Purchase*TaxRate;
```

Example 3: Given the information from Example 2, this statement calculates the total price for the item. Essentially, it is adding the amount of the tax to the purchase price.

```
Price = (1+TaxRate)*Purchase;
```

Example 4: Given the price from Example 3, the following statement checks to see if the credit limit is exceeded. If the credit limit is exceeded, it increases the credit limit by 500. (This is an advanced example.)

```
CreditLimit = (Price > CreditLimit) ? CreditLimit + 500
    : CreditLimit;
```

Example 5: The following statement calculates the position of a spaceship in a Space Invaders game. CurPos is the current position, Vel is the velocity, and ScreenW is the screen width. If the spacecraft goes off the right side of the screen, it will reappear on the left.

```
NewPos = (CurPos + Vel) % ScreenW;
```

Example 6: Given Example 5, this statement increments a counter every time the spaceship goes off the right side of the screen. This example is kind of tricky — it uses the fact that true is 1. So (CurPos + Vel > ScreenW) is 1 if the spacecraft moved off the screen:

```
Counter = Counter + (CurPos + Vel > ScreenW);
```

Here's another way to write this:

```
Counter += CurPos + Vel > ScreenW;
```

Chapter 19

Controlling Flow

● ●

In This Chapter

▶ Learn about keywords used in control statements

▶ Use *if* to create conditions

▶ Create loops with *for* and *while*

▶ Use *switch* to create complex condition blocks

▶ Learn about *case*, *break*, *do*, and *goto*

● ●

*B*y this point, you've learned almost all of the fundamental aspects of pro- gramming. But your programs can still only execute sequentially. That is, your programs start with the first line in main and continue on, statement after statement after statement, never deviating from their course for even one single moment.

But, as you've probably discovered, life doesn't really work that way. Some- times a little variety is called for, in life and in your programs. In some cases, it's okay to have a program flow directly from one line to the next, but in many other cases, you'll probably want to divert or change the flow to suit your needs. That's why C++ has a number of statements that can help you control the flow through your programs. These statements let you perform certain actions only if particular conditions are true, or they let you repeat an action until something happens.

You'll find lots of reasons to use statements like these. Here are some examples of typical scenarios where you might need to repeatedly perform some type of operation:

✔ To continue adding the price of each item until there are no more groceries.

✔ To pump gas until the tank is full.

✔ To find the average grade of the 32 students in a class by repeatedly adding together the grades of each student.

In other situations, you need to make a choice. Such choices are usually of this form: if some condition is true, then perform certain actions. Here are several examples that illustrate this:

✔ If the professor insists that you do your homework, do it. (But not if your professor doesn't insist.)

✔ To give customers who order more than 3000 widgets a discount.

✔ If the light is yellow, speed up. If it's red, stop.

As you can see, there are numerous situations where you need to repeat a task or make a choice. Flow control statements let you write programs to handle these situations.

The Big Three Keywords: if, for, and while

Three flow control statements are used in almost every application: *if*, *for*, and *while*. *if* (which is sometimes referred to as a *conditional*) performs a set of actions when, and only when, a particular condition is true. *for* and *while* (which are sometimes referred to as *for loops* and *while loops*) repeat a set of statements over and over again.

If I were a rich man: the if keyword

The syntax for *if* is pretty simple:

```
if (expr1)
    stmt;
```

(Note that here — and in subsequent sections — *expr* means an expression such as *i* < 1, and *stmt* means a statement, such as cost = cost + 1.)

expr1 can be any expression. If it's true, *stmt* is executed. (An expression is true if its value is not 0. That is, expressions in conditionals are always Boolean expressions.) You can use { } to perform a group of statements. For example, the following code assigns values if the variable IWereARichMan is true:

```
if (IWereARichMan) {
    Deedle = 0;
    Didle = 1;
    Dum = 0;
}
```

And this sets a discount value if a large order is placed:

```
if (OrderSize > 3000)
    Discount = .2;
```

You can make the *if* statement a bit more powerful by using the *else* option along with it:

```
if (expr1)
    stmt1;
else
    stmt2;
```

In this case, if *expr1* isn't true, *stmt2* is executed.

The following code checks a blackjack hand to see if the player has busted. If the player hasn't busted, the dealer tries to deal a new card:

```
if (HandValue > 21) {
    //The player busted.
    UserScore -= Bet;
    Busted = 1;
}
else {
    //Does the player want another card?
    cout << "Hit?\n";
    cin >> HitMe;
}
```

The following routine determines a discount based on the size of an order:

```
//Ordering 5000 units gives a 30% discount.
if (OrderSize > 5000)
    discount = .3;
else
    //Ordering 3000 units gives a 20% discount.
    if (OrderSize > 3000)
        discount = .2;
    //Otherwise, there is no discount.
    else
        discount = 0;
```

And this routine determines what to do given the color of a traffic light:

```
if (LightColor == Yellow) {
    NoCop = LookForCop();
    if (NoCop)
        Speed += 30;
}
else if (LightColor == Red)
    Speed = 0;
```

Sometimes, as in the previous example, you might have *if*s within *if*s. This is called *nesting*. When you nest *if*s, be sure to indent in a way that makes it easy to read the program.

A beginner's guide to formatting programs (1001 ways to indent your code)

Programmers format code in lots of different ways. While there's no official guideline, there are some things you can do to make your programs easier to read.

Any time you place code within {}, indent the code within the {}. That way, it's easy to see that those lines go together. For example, the following is easy to read because of indentation:

```
if (HandValue > 21) {
   //The player busted.
   UserScore -= Bet;
   Busted = 1;
}
else {
   //Does the player want
   //another card?
   cout << "Hit?\n";
   cin >> HitMe;
}
```

Here's the same code, but without indentation:

```
if (HandValue > 21) {
//The player busted.
UserScore -= Bet;
Busted = 1;
}
else {
//Does the player want another card?
cout << "Hit?\n";
cin >> HitMe;
}
```

The first is a lot easier to read, because it's pretty clear what statements are executed if the hand is greater than 21.

You've seen the same rule apply to statements within main() in the pizza program. All the lines within main() were indented. And you've seen a slight variation of this rule when you created structures.

If you have nested statements, indent each time you nest:

```
if (foo) {
   bar++;
   if (bar > 3)
      baz = 2;
   if (goober < 7)
      flibber = 3;
}
```

Another way to make your programs easier to read is to place the } at the same indentation level as the block that started it:

```
if (foo) {
}
```

This makes it easier to see where a particular block ends. Not everyone likes this, though. You might see the following instead:

```
if (foo)
   {
   }
```

There are a variety of papers and books that discuss the pros and cons of the various ways to format code. The code in this book uses a variation of the "Indian Hill" style of formatting.

Forever and a day (well, almost): the for keyword

The *for* keyword is used to repeat statements over and over again. *for* has the following syntax:

```
for (expr1; expr2; expr3)
    stmt1;
```

(This type of repetition is called a *for loop*.)

When the *for* loop starts, *expr1* is evaluated. *expr1* is usually where you initialize variables that will be used in the loop. Then *expr2* is evaluated (it's evaluated each time the loop is entered, which is how you control how many times the loop executes). If *expr2* is true, *stmt1* is executed. And if *stmt1* is executed, *expr3* is evaluated; *expr3* is usually used to modify what happens in *expr2*. If *expr2* is false, however, the loop ends and the program moves on to the next statement after the *for* loop.

Here's a simple for example

Did the previous explanation seem confusing? Let's look at a simple example:

```
int i;
for (i = 0; i < 2; i++)
    cout << i << "\n";
```

Here's what's happening in this example:

1. When the loop begins, *expr1* is evaluated. In this case, *i* is given the value 0.

2. Then *expr2* is evaluated. This expression asks, is $i < 2$? Because *i* was just set to 0, *i* is less than 2. Therefore, *stmt1* is executed. (In this case, the value of *i* is printed to the screen.)

3. Next *expr3* is evaluated. In this case, it's *i++*, so *i* is incremented from 0 to 1.

4. Because *expr2* is always evaluated before the *for* loop repeats, we go back to *expr2*. Is $i < 2$? Well, *i* is now 1, so it's less than 2. Therefore we print the value of *i* again.

5. Then *expr3* is evaluated again, and therefore *i* gets incremented to 2.

6. Once again, *expr2* is evaluated. Is $i < 2$? No, because now *i* is equal to 2. Therefore, the loop ends.

By making *expr2* more complex you can do all types of things to determine when the loop ends. *for* loops are often used when traversing data structures. If you're studying Computer Science, you'll see them over and over again.

The broken-record loop: repeating something over and over and over...

If you want to repeat something a number of times, use the following loop:

```
for (i = 0; i < n; i++) {
    //Statements to repeat go here.
}
```

The variable *n* controls how many times the loop repeats. For example, if you needed to print "I will always do my homework" fifty times, you could do this:

```
for (i = 0; i < 50; i++) {
    cout << "I will always do my homework.\n";
}
```

Sure beats writing it out by hand.

If you want to be fancy, you could ask the user for the number of times to repeat:

```
int n;
cout << "How many times do you want to repeat?\n";
cin >> n;
for (i = 0; i < n; i++) {
    cout << "I will always do my homework.\n";
}
```

While you were out: the while keyword

Like the *for* loop, the *while* loop is also used to repeat something a number of times. It's simpler than the *for* loop, though, as you can see here:

```
while (expr1)
    stmt;
```

When the *while* loop begins, *expr1* is evaluated. If it's true, *stmt* is executed. Then *expr1* is evaluated again. If it's still true, *stmt* is executed. This procedure is repeated until *expr1* is no longer true.

For example, you could do the following to repeat 10 times:

```
int i = 0;
while (i < 10) {
    i++;
}
```

You need to make sure that what happens in *stmt* (the part that executes inside the *while* loop) affects the value of *expr1*. Otherwise, you'll never leave the loop.

A real dandy way to hang your computer

Here's a simple program you can write that will completely hang your computer. If you do this, you'll need to reboot.

```
//Hang the system.
void main() {
   while (1);
}
```

Why does this hang the computer? The program stays in the *while* loop until *expr1* is false. In this case, *expr1* is 1, so it's never false. The computer will never exit the loop. Bummer.

This is called an *infinite loop*.

Probably a Homework Problem: Factorial

Here's a typical Computer Science homework problem: how do you find *n* factorial?

n factorial is n * (n – 1) * (n – 2)...*1. So, 2 factorial (written 2! in math books, but not in computer code) is 2 * 1. And 3! is 3 * 2 * 1.

The awful takes-all-day approach would be:

```
//compute n!
cin << n;
if (n == 1)
   cout << 1;
else if (n == 2)
   cout << 2;
else if (n == 3)
   cout << 3*2;
else if (n == 4)
   cout << 4*3*2;
```

You can see how long it would take to type this program in. A much easier way is to use a *for* loop, as shown in the following program:

```
//compute n!
#include <iostream.h>

void main() {
   int n; //The number the user types in.
   int Result = 1;
   int i; //Loop variable

   //Get the value.
   cout << "What is the number?\n";
   cin >> n;
```

```
//Now loop through. Each time through the loop
//multiply the result by i. This will give
//1*2*3...n because i starts at 1 and increases
//until it is n.
for (i=1; i<=n; i++) {
    Result *= i;
}

//Print the result.
cout << "n! is " << Result << "\n";
}
```

(This program is in the FACTOR directory on the separately available program disk.)

Going with the Flow: The Rest of the Flow Keywords

There are a number of other flow keywords you can use in your programs. These are *switch*, which along with *case* and *break* make fancy *if* statements; *do*, which is a variation of *while*; and the *break* and *goto* keywords, which can be used within flow statements.

I'd rather break than switch (at least in this case): the switch, case, and break keywords

The *switch* statement is like an *if* statement with a lot of branches (each branch starts with a *case* keyword). So if you find yourself with a problem such as "if the topping is pepperoni then ..., else if it is sausage then ..., else if it is onions then ..." you could use a *switch* statement instead of an *if* statement. Here's what it looks like:

```
switch (expr) {
    case val1:
        stmt1;
    case val2:
        stmt2;
    ...
    default:
        dfltstmt;
}
```

First, *expr* is evaluated and compared against *val1*. (Here, *val* is some value, such as 1 or 45.3.) If *expr* is *val1*, then *stmt1* and *all following statements* are executed. If *expr* isn't *val1*, then the process is repeated with *val2* and so on. If you include a "default:" item (as shown in the previous code), then if nothing else has matched, the *dfltstmt* (default statement) will run.

Because all statements following a match are executed, you can use the *break* statement to leave the *switch*.

Here's a quick example that prints the text name of a number. A more complete example is provided in Chapter 20.

```
//For demo purposes, n is only handled for 1..4.
switch (n) {
    case 1:
        cout << "one";
        break;
    case 2:
        cout << "two";
        break;
    case 3:
        cout << "three";
        break;
    case 4:
        cout << "four";
        break;
    default:
        cout << "unknown number";
}
```

Note the use of *break* in each case statement. If the *break* statements weren't used, you'd get the following, undesired results:

n	Result
1	onetwothreefourunknown number
2	twothreefourunknown number

(and so on)

Make sure you don't forget the *break* after you execute a *case* in a *switch*. If you forget it, you'll keep on executing lines in the *switch* even though you didn't intend to. ■

Do (wah diddy diddy dum diddy do): the do keyword

The *do* keyword is very similar to *while*. The difference is that with a *while* loop the expression is evaluated before the statements inside are executed. So, with *while*, it's possible that none of the statements will get executed. With a *do*, the statements are executed and *then* a condition is checked to determine whether to continue. If the condition is true, the statements are run again. Otherwise, the loop stops:

```
do
    stmt;
while (expr);
```

Here's a quick example that loops until *i* is *n*:

```
int i = 0;
do {
    cout << i << "\n";
    i = i + 1;
}
while (i < n);
```

If *n* happens to be 0, a number will still be printed, because *expr* isn't evaluated (in this case *i < n*) until after the statements are executed.

It's best to avoid this one: the goto keyword

The *goto* keyword is usually considered a no-no. It tells the computer to jump to a particular statement, no matter what's happening.

Well-structured programs should be easy to read. You should be able to see where a function starts and ends and see how execution flows through it. When you're looking at main and it calls a function (you'll learn more about functions in Chapter 21), you know that at some point the function will end and the next line of code will be executed — that is, unless there's a *goto*, in which case all bets are off.

goto lets you jump all over a program, ignoring boundaries of loops and conditionals (but not functions or files). It makes it much harder to read and debug an application.

There are a couple of rare cases where *goto* is useful, but in general it's avoided and even looked down on. It's one of the features that BASIC and FORTRAN programmers use a lot but that Pascal, C, and C++ programmers sneer at. So don't use it, okay?

Chapter 20

A Better Pizza Application

In This Chapter

▶ Expand the pizza application so the user can choose toppings

▶ Add more constants to the pizza application

▶ Add conditionals to the pizza application

▶ Add loops to the pizza application

*I*n this chapter, you'll use the various Borland C++ statements you've learned so far to create a better pizza program. The new program lets you choose which toppings you want on the pizza, and lets you assign each topping a different price. The program uses a *do* loop to determine when you're finished adding toppings, and a *switch* statement to determine the price of each topping.

How It Works

The program starts by defining a number of constants, such as the price of a plain pizza:

```
//A plain large pizza costs $14.
const float LargePrice = 14;
```

Next, the program defines some constants that are used to make the program easier to read. These constants aren't used for calculations, but they are used in conditional statements:

```
const int Pepperoni = 1;
const int Sausage = 2;
const int Onions = 3;
```

Using constants like this makes it a lot easier to understand code. For instance, Example 1 (which uses a constant for Pepperoni) is easier to understand than Example 2 (which doesn't):

Example 1:

```
case Pepperoni:
    MyPizzaInfo.Cost += PepperoniPrice;
    cout << "OK, we'll add pepperoni.\n";
    MyPizzaInfo.NumberOfToppings++;
    break;
```

Example 2:

```
case 1:
    MyPizzaInfo.Cost += PepperoniPrice;
    cout << "OK, we'll add pepperoni.\n";
    MyPizzaInfo.NumberOfToppings++;
    break;
```

After the constants are defined, the pizza program declares a structure to store all relevant information describing a pizza:

```
class Pizza {
public:
    int NumberOfToppings;
    int Size;
    float CostForToppings;
    float Cost;
};
```

This is a slightly expanded version of the structure used in the pizza application from Chapter 17.

In the new program, the user is asked for the size of the pizza. A conditional is used to determine the base price for the pizza, based on its size:

```
if (MyPizzaInfo.Size == Large)
    MyPizzaInfo.Cost = LargePrice;
else
    MyPizzaInfo.Cost = SmallPrice;
```

Next, a *do* loop is used to ask the user what toppings to add. The user can add any number of toppings and then enter a 0 to tell the program to stop:

```
do {
    //Execute this stuff until the user says stop
    //adding toppings.
    cout << "What toppings? 1 = pepperoni, 2 = "
        << "sausage, 3 = onions, 0 = stop\n";
    cin >> ToppingChoice;
    .
    .
    .
} //End of do statements.
//Stop when the user enters 0.
while (ToppingChoice != 0);
```

Within this loop, a *switch* is used to determine what topping the user wants, to add the appropriate cost, and to keep track of the total number of toppings. Constants are used throughout to make it easier to read:

```
switch (ToppingChoice) {
    case Pepperoni:
        MyPizzaInfo.Cost += PepperoniPrice;
        cout << "OK, we'll add pepperoni.\n";
        MyPizzaInfo.NumberOfToppings++;
        break;
        .
        .
        .
}
```

The 5th Wave   **By Rich Tennant**

"THAT'S RIGHT, DADDY WILL DOUBLE YOUR ALLOWANCE IF YOU MAKE HIM MORE BORLAND C++ APPLICATIONS."

Finally, the program prints what was ordered and the total cost. Notice that an *if* statement is used to print the size of the pizza and that the last *cout* line mixes text with numbers:

```
cout << "That's a ";
if (MyPizzaInfo.Size == Large)
        cout << "large ";
else
        cout << "small ";
cout << "pizza with " << MyPizzaInfo.NumberOfToppings
        << "toppings. That will be $" << MyPizzaInfo.Cost
        << " please.\n";
```

Note that there are several places in the code where the *cout* text is split over several lines in the source file. When you need to do this, just end the text on the first line with a " (a quotation mark), then continue text on the new line with another << and a ":

```
cout << "What toppings? 1 = pepperoni, 2 = "
        << "sausage, 3 = onions, 0 = stop\n";
```

When this prints out, the text will be continuous.

OK, Here's the Pizza Code

```
//Improved pizza application.
#include <iostream.h>

//A plain large pizza costs $14.
const float LargePrice = 14;
//A plain small pizza costs $10.
const float SmallPrice = 10;

//These numbers represent the different toppings.
const int Pepperoni = 1;
const int Sausage = 2;
const int Onions = 3;

//The costs for the various toppings.
const float PepperoniPrice = 1.8;
const float SausagePrice = 2.1;
const float OnionPrice = 0.5;

//Here are some more constants.
const int Large = 1;
const int Small = 2;
```

```
class Pizza {
public:
    int NumberOfToppings;
    int Size;
    float CostForToppings;
    float Cost;
};
void main() {
    Pizza MyPizzaInfo;
    int ToppingChoice;

    //What size?
    cout << "What size pizza do you want? " <<
        "Type 1 for large and 2 for small.\n" ;
    cin >> MyPizzaInfo.Size;

    //What is the base price?
    if (MyPizzaInfo.Size == Large)
        MyPizzaInfo.Cost = LargePrice;
    else
        MyPizzaInfo.Cost = SmallPrice;

    //Start with no toppings.
    MyPizzaInfo.NumberOfToppings = 0;

    //Now we'll find out what toppings the customer
    //wants.
    do {
        //Execute this stuff until the user says to stop
        //adding toppings.
        cout << "What toppings? 1 = pepperoni, 2 = "
            << "sausage, 3 = onions, 0 = stop\n";
        cin >> ToppingChoice;

        //Now figure what to add to the price.
        //While we are at it, we'll count the number
        //of toppings ordered.
        switch (ToppingChoice) {
            case Pepperoni:
                MyPizzaInfo.Cost += PepperoniPrice;
                cout << "OK, we'll add pepperoni.\n";
                MyPizzaInfo.NumberOfToppings++;
                break;
            case Sausage:
                MyPizzaInfo.Cost += SausagePrice;
                cout << "Some sausage on that.\n";
                MyPizzaInfo.NumberOfToppings++;
                break;
            case Onions:
                MyPizzaInfo.Cost += OnionPrice;
                cout << "Sounds good.\n";
                MyPizzaInfo.NumberOfToppings++;
                break;
            case 0:
                //We check for this case so that
                //default isn't called if the user
                //just wants to stop adding toppings.
                break;
```

(continued)

```
            default:
                cout << "Pardon me?\n";
        }   //End of switch.
    } //End of do statements.
    //Stop when the user enters 0.
    while (ToppingChoice != 0);
    //Now the user has finished ordering, so print
    //the cost.
    cout << "That's a ";
    if (MyPizzaInfo.Size == Large)
        cout << "large ";
    else
        cout << "small ";
    cout << "pizza with " << MyPizzaInfo.NumberOfToppings
      << "toppings. That will be $" << MyPizzaInfo.Cost
      << " please.\n";
}
```

(This program is in the PIZZA4 directory on the separately available program disk.)

Chapter 21

Can't Function without Functions

*P*rograms are often very complex and lengthy. In fact, some programs require thousands or even millions of lines of code. When you're creating a large program, it's a good strategy to chunk it down into manageable sections that you (and other people reading it) can easily understand.

Borland C++ lets you chunk programs down by grouping related statements together and naming them. This type of group is called a *function*. (Functions are also frequently called *routines* or *procedures*; in this book I usually call them either functions or routines, but all three terms are quite common.)

Functions can be called in various ways. *Global functions* can be called from any part of your program. *Library functions* can be called by lots of different programs. However, most of your functions will probably operate with a specific object. These type of functions, called *member functions*, are discussed in Chapter 27.

You can also combine functions to build new functions. Building large functions from small functions can help make your programs easier to write, read, and test.

First, Some Opening Statements

You've seen lots of sample programs by now. Earlier you learned that every time you write a statement you need to follow it with a ; (semicolon). But you might have noticed that this isn't always the case in the sample programs. That's because, as with most things in life, there are exceptions and special cases for almost every rule.

So, once again, here's the general rule:

> ✔ Most statements should be followed by a ;

And here are the exceptions and special cases:

> ✔ If the statement starts with a # (pound sign), don't end it with a ;
>
> ✔ If the statement begins with a //, you don't need to end it with a ; (although it doesn't hurt anything if you do use a ;)
>
> ✔ If the statement ends with a }, you don't need a ; *unless* the reason the statement ends with a } is because you've just declared a *class* (or a *struct* or an *enum*), in which case you *must* end it with a ;

How to Make Functions

And now back to the main subject of this chapter: functions. You define a function by giving it a name, followed by ( ) (left and right parentheses). (Later, you'll be putting some things called *arguments* inside the parentheses.) Then, you list the statements that make up the function. The rules for naming variables (described in Chapter 16) also apply to naming functions. Here's how you define a function:

```
void function_name() {
    stmt;
}
```

For example, to make a function that prints "Hello World" you could do this:

```
void PrintHelloWorld() {
    cout << "Hello World\n";
}
```

Then, whenever you wanted to use that function, all you'd have to do is use its name followed by ( ). The process of using a function is referred to as *calling* (or *invoking*) a function. You can call functions as many times as you want.

Just as with structures, you need to define a function before you use it, as shown in the following program. Here's the Hello World application from Chapter 14, but with the addition of a function. The function PrintHelloWorld is now defined at the top of the program, and then invoked in the main routine:

```
//Prints "Hello World" on the screen.
#include <iostream.h>

//Define the PrintHelloWorld function.
void PrintHelloWorld() {
    cout << "Hello World\n";
}

//Now use the PrintHelloWorld function.
void main() {
    PrintHelloWorld();
}
```

(This program is in the HELLOW2 directory on the separately available program disk.)

Arguments (Yes. No. Yes. No.)

You can pass-in values to a function. These values, called *arguments* (or *parameters*), each need a data type and a name. By passing in arguments, you can create a general function that can be used over and over again in an application. You can pass any number of arguments to a function and you can use any data types that you want to use.

This is how you define arguments:

```
void function_name(data_type1 arg1, data_type2 arg2, ...) {
}
```

For example, the following function prints the factorial of a number. The number, called *n*, is passed in as an argument. Note that this value is then used throughout the function:

```
void Factorial(int n) {
    int Result = 1;
    int i; //Loop variable.

    //Now loop through. Each time through the loop
    //multiply the result by i.
    for (i=1; i<=n; i++) {
        Result *= i;
    }

    //Now print the result.
    cout << Result;
}
```

Anytime you wanted to print the factorial of a number, you could call this function. For example, the following program has a loop that iterates three times.

Inside the loop, the program asks for a number and calls the Factorial function to print the factorial of the number:

```
int Number;
int i;

//Loop three times.
for (i = 0; i < 3; i++) {
    //get the number
    cin >> Number;

    //Call the factorial routine with Number.
    Factorial(Number);
}
```

You can easily write functions that have several arguments. For example, the following function prints the value of foo*n!, where both foo and n are passed to the routine:

```
void Fooctorial(int foo, int n) {
    int Result = 1;
    int i;//Loop variable.

    //Now loop through. Each time through the loop
    //multiply the result by i.
    for (i=1; i<=n; i++) {
        Result *= i;
    }

    //Now multiply by foo.
    Result *= foo;

    //Now print the result.
    cout << Result;
}
```

To Return or Not to Return

All the functions discussed so far have performed actions (such as calculating and printing the factorial of a number). But functions can also return values. This capability is useful because it lets you use functions inside expressions. For example, you could use a mathematical library function such as cos( ) in the middle of a formula, as in 3*cos(angle).

You can write your own functions that return values. For example, you might want to create a routine that reads through a database and returns the name (or names) of customers who have placed three or more orders in the last six months. Or you might want to create a function that returns the moving average of a lot of numbers.

There are two things you need to do if you want a function to return a value:

✔ Precede the declaration with the data type it returns, instead of with *void*.

✔ Use the *return* keyword within the function before you leave it.

The *return* keyword immediately leaves a function and returns a value. If you use *return* in the middle of a function, and the *return* is executed, the code following the return is *not* executed. (Not all *returns* are executed. For example, some *returns* are within code that is executed only under certain conditions.)

Here's an example of a factorial program that returns the factorial of *n*. It's similar to the previous factorial, but instead of printing the value in the function, it returns the value:

```
int
Factorial(int n) {
    int Result = 1;
    int i; //Loop variable.

    //Now loop through. Each time through the loop
    //multiply the result by i.
    for (i=1; i<=n; i++) {
        Result *= i;
    }

    //Now return the result.
    return Result;
}
```

Because the factorial function returns a value, you can use it inside expressions. This provides you with more flexibility regarding the ways and places that you can use the factorial function. For example, this code lets you print the factorial in the middle of a sentence:

```
cin >> Number;
cout << "The factorial of " << Number << " is " <<
    Factorial(Number);
```

Functions that return a value can be used anywhere that you can use a value of the return type. Thus, if a function returns an integer, you can use the function any place that you can use an integer. This could be inside an expression, such as:

```
MyNum = 3*Factorial(Number);
```

You can also use functions to compute values that are passed as arguments to other functions. For example, the Factorial function takes an integer argument. Because the Factorial function returns an integer, you can pass the factorial of a number in as an argument to the Factorial function. For example, the following code computes the factorial of a factorial:

```
cin >> Number;
cout << Factorial(Factorial(Number));
```

And this code determines if the factorial of a number is greater than 72:

```
//Is the factorial greater than 72?
if (Factorial(Number) > 72)
    cout << "It is greater.";
```

Put the return type of the function on a line before the function name. This practice makes it easier to find the function names and the function return types, and will therefore make your program easier to read. ■

Avoid global variables!

After you leave a function, any variables that are declared inside that function (such as Result and *i* in the previous factorial example) are destroyed. Therefore any information they contain is lost. If you need to use this information after the function is called, you should return the information by using the *return* keyword.

For example, suppose you need the name of the highest paid employee in your company. If all you want to do is print the name and never look at it again, print the name inside the function and don't return anything. But if you need to use the name outside the function, such as to incorporate it in a form letter, you should return the name.

There are other ways you could get access to the information besides returning it. One way is to use *global variables*, which are variables that are declared before the main( ). Global variables are called global because they can be used from any part inside a program. Continuing with the example given above, the global variable approach to saving the name of the highest paid employee would be to copy the name into a global variable.

Since the variable is global, it sticks around after the routine is ended and you can then look at its value.

Unfortunately, using global variables can lead to *spaghetti code* (code that's hard to read). When you set a global variable within a function, it's impossible to understand what's happening without looking at every line of code. That's not in keeping with good coding practice, which says that when you look at the arguments passed to a function, you should be able to tell what is used by the function and what is changed within the function. It's important that you be able to do this, because this lets you look at and understand the high-level use of the function without having to examine all the code.

There are all types of hard-to-find logic errors that can occur if you aren't careful when you use global variables. In general, you should return values instead of using global variables. If you need to return lots of values, use a structure. Or use pointers (which are discussed in Chapter 22).

Revisiting the Factorial Example

In this section, you'll look at the factorial program again. But this time, the program is put together using functions. As you read over the program, notice that even though it's getting complex, the main routine is fairly simple. In fact, you can now figure out what main( ) does by reading only four statements (the other stuff inside main( ) is all comments).

The program now contains two functions: Factorial and GetNumber. Factorial computes that factorial of a number. This is the same function you saw in the "To Return or Not to Return" section — it takes an integer as a parameter and returns the resulting factorial. GetNumber is used to get input; it asks the user for a number and then returns that number.

The main routine uses the GetNumber routine to repeatedly ask the user for a number. It then uses the Factorial function to display the factorial of the number. It keeps asking for new numbers until the user types in a 0.

Note that the main routine is using a fancy trick to determine when to stop:

```
while (Number = GetNumber()) {
```

Remember that the *while* statement takes an expression as a parameter. The lines in the *while* statement are executed if this expression is true. In this case, the expression first calls the GetNumber routine to get a number. It then assigns the result to the variable named Number. This has three effects. First, the user is asked for a number. Second, if the user types 0, the *while* loop stops. And third, if the user doesn't type 0, the number entered is already stored in a variable that can be used inside the *while* loop. You'll often see this type of shortcut in C++ programs.

Here's the new Factorial program:

```
//Compute factorials until the user types in 0.

#include <iostream.h>

int
Factorial(int n) {
    int Result = 1;
    int i; //Loop variable.

    //Now loop through. Each time through the loop
    //multiply the result by i.
    for (i=1; i<=n; i++) {
        Result *= i;
    }

    //Now return the result.
```

(continued)

```
        return Result;
    }

    //This routine prompts the user for a number.
    //It returns the value of the number.
    int
    GetNumber() {
        int Number;

        cout << "What is the number?\n";
        cin >> Number;
        return Number;
    }

    //Here is where the program begins.
    void main() {
        int Number;

        //Get numbers from the user, until the user
        //types 0.
        while (Number = GetNumber()) {
            //Now we will output the result.
            //Note that we are calling the function
            //Factorial.
            cout << "The factorial of " << Number <<
                " is " << Factorial(Number) << "\n";
        }

        //Now we are finished.
        cout << "Bye bye!\n";
    }
```

(This program is in the FACTOR2 directory on the separately available program disk.)

Reading Programs That Contain Functions

When programs contain functions, the functions are usually defined before they're used. This means that if you read a program line by line, from start to finish, you'll end up looking at all the nitty-gritty details before you get a chance to see how the whole thing fits together.

Here's several tips to make your life easier:

- ✔ If the file has a main in it, skip to the main first and see what it does. Work backwards from the highest level functions to the ones with the most details.

- ✔ If the file just contains a lot of functions, look at the names of all the functions first. Read the comments to get a clue about what they do. Once you've looked at all the functions, it might be easier to figure out which ones are worth checking out and which ones are low-level utility functions you can ignore.

✔ Usually the highest level functions occur at the end of the file.

Variables and Name Scope

If you're wondering why you can give a variable in a function the same name as a variable that already exists outside the function, don't worry — this is explained in Chapter 26.

Some Lines on Inlining

If you have a small function that's used in a loop or is otherwise called very frequently, a technique called *inlining* can make your program run faster.

But first, some information on storing information

Before you learn about inlining, though, there's a bit of background material you need to know about how the computer stores information and loads instructions, and about how a compiler makes function calls.

Storing information in RAM

One of the ways the computer stores information is in memory (RAM). You can have lots of RAM in a computer, which lets programs store a great deal of information. But accessing RAM can be slow. (Of course, you can access thousands of pieces of RAM in less time than you can blink an eye, but relative to other things that the computer can do, RAM access is slow.)

Storing information in CPU registers

Another way the computer stores information is in *CPU registers*. CPU registers are similar to RAM, only there are a small number of them and they are built directly into the CPU. It takes a lot less time to access a CPU register than it does to access RAM. So, when Borland C++ compiles C++ code, thus turning it into machine code, it creates code that uses CPU registers whenever possible so that the code runs quickly. These CPU registers often store temporary information that is used throughout a function. In a moment you'll learn why that's important.

Storing information in the instruction cache

When the computer runs a program, it essentially reads and executes machine-code instructions one at a time. But since reading instructions from memory one at a time can be slow, the CPU instead reads a bunch of consecutive instructions into an *instruction cache* in memory all at one time. The instruction cache is part of the CPU. The CPU can read and execute instructions from the cache very quickly. Thus, when the computer executes instructions that appear one after the other, most of the time the instructions will be in the cache, and thus will execute quickly. The 486 and Pentium chips have large instruction caches to help them run programs faster.

And how that all relates to function calls

Now let's see how registers and the instruction cache relate to function calls. When you call a function, some special code saves the values of CPU registers. (The compiler generates code that saves the values of any registers that might be changed by the function being called. The compiler uses a complex process called *live range analysis* to determine what registers need to be saved.) Then memory is set aside (in an area called the *stack*) for function arguments and local variables. Next, the arguments are copied into this area. Then, the computer jumps from the section of code that's calling the function to the section of code that contains the function. The code in the function then executes, which changes the CPU register values. Then the computer jumps back to the section of code that called the function, cleans up the stack, restores the values of the registers, and continues operating.

Thus, when you call a function, three time-consuming things happen. First, the CPU usually clears and reloads the instruction cache. That's because most of the time the function you're calling doesn't appear close enough to the code that's calling it for the function code to be in the instruction cache. Second, registers are stored in memory. And third, arguments are copied to the stack. When the function finishes, the instruction cache gets reloaded again, and the register values are restored.

If the function doesn't contain very much code, the time for clearing the instruction cache, saving the registers, and copying arguments can overshadow the time spent in the function.

And now back to inlining

That's where inlining comes in. If you declare a function as an *inline* function, something different happens. Instead of the function being called, the code that makes up the function is automatically inserted where the call is, just as if you copied it there by hand. As a result, the program is larger, because the code is repeated. But, the code is faster, because the instruction cache usually doesn't need to be cleared, registers usually don't need to be saved, and arguments don't need to be copied to the stack because they'll already be on the stack of the function calling the inline function.

(Note that if the function is complex, however, inlining won't help performance much. In fact, the compiler doesn't even bother to inline complex expressions. In this case, it just treats the function as a normal function. When this happens, it's called *expanding an inline function out of line*.)

And now, with that explanation in hand, here's how to make a function an inline function: put the keyword *inline* before the name of the function when you define it, like this:

```
inline int
Factorial(int n) ...
```

Recursion...Recursion...Recursion...

If a function calls itself, it's said to be *recursive*. Recursive routines are often used in situations in which completing a process is made easier if you can repeat the process on a smaller subset of items.

For example, suppose you want to sort a lot of numbers. (This happens to be a classic and time-consuming Computer Science homework problem. I'll probably get into trouble for revealing this, but solving problems by using recursion happens way more often in Computer Science classes than it does in real life.)

Sorting a large set of numbers can be a fairly complicated task. The easiest way to do it is to search through the set for the smallest number, place it in a result list, and repeat this process until all the numbers are sorted. The problem with this approach is that you keep looking at the same list over and over and over again. It takes a long time. That's why there are entire books devoted to finding faster ways to sort numbers.

A common way to speed this process is to use recursion — and thus break the sorting problem into smaller problems. For example, suppose that instead of sorting one list you wanted to merge two sets of already sorted numbers. That's a lot easier.

Why? Well, let's call the set that starts with the smallest number *A*. And we'll call the other set *B*. We'll call the answer Result. To merge *A* and *B*, add the first item in *A* to the Result. Now look at the second item. Is that smaller than the first item in *B*? If so, also add it to Result. Keep doing this until the item in *B* is smaller than the item in *A*. Now add the first item in *B* to Result. Keep looking at all the items in *B* until one in *A* is smaller. It might sound a little complicated on paper, but it's a heck of a lot easier and much faster than traversing all the numbers. In fact, you might want to try it out on paper to prove that it works.

Now the problem is to break the task of sorting numbers into merging two lists of sorted numbers. You can do that by breaking the set of numbers in half and sorting each half. How do you sort a half? Well, you break that half in half and sort it. As you continue this process, you'll eventually end up with a set that has one or two numbers in it. And that's a pretty easy set to sort.

Now you just go backwards, merging the smaller sets into bigger sets. Eventually you'll end up with two halves that you merge together to create one sorted list. So, by using recursion, you made the problem easier by using the same tasks on smaller pieces.

Let's look at this in a little more detail.

1. Start with a set of unsorted numbers:

   1 3 7 5 14 9 2 7

2. Break these into two smaller sets:

   1 3 7 5   14 9 2 7

3. These are still too big. Break them again:

   1 3   7 5   14 9   2 7

4. Now they're easy to sort. Sort each set:

   1 3   5 7   9 14   2 7

5. Now go backwards. Merge the newly sorted sorts together:

   1 3 5 7   2 7 9 14

6. And merge once more:

   1 2 3 5 7 7 9 14

Voila!

The code would look something like this:

```
numberlist
Sort( numberlist) {
    if (NumberOfItemsIn(numberlist) == 1)
        return numberlist;
    if (NumberOfItemsIn(numberlist) == 2) {
        sort the two items //a simple compare
        return sortedlist;
    //The list is larger, so split it in two and call
    //sort again.
    Merge(Sort(first half of numberlist), Sort(second
```

```
        half of numberlist));
    }
```

Determining the factorial of a number, as you did earlier in this chapter, is often done using recursion. The following factorial function is similar to that shown in the section "Revisiting the Factorial Example," but instead of using a *for* loop, the factorial routine calls itself with $n-1$. In other words, $n! = n*(n-1)*(n-2)....$ This is the same as saying $n! = n*((n-1)!)$.

Of course, $(n-1)!$ is the same as $(n-1)*((n-2)!)$. So, the factorial routine keeps multiplying the value passed in by the factorial of that value -1.

```
//Solve factorial using recursion.
#include <iostream.h>

//Here is a recursive function.
//The factorial of 1 is 1, so that is easy.
//For the other ones, call factorial again for
//something easier to solve.
int
factorial(int Number) {
    if (Number > 1)
        //n! = n*(n-1)! = n*(n-1)*(n-2)! ...
        return Number*factorial(Number - 1);
    return Number;
}

void main() {
    int Number;
    cout << "What is the number?\n";
    cin >> Number;

    //Get the result.
    cout << "The factorial is " << factorial(Number)
        << "\n";
}
```

(This program is in the FACTOR3 directory on the separately available program disk.)

Only You Can Prevent Dysfunctional Functions

To indicate that a function can take any number of parameters, you can use **...** (*ellipses*) in the argument list. For example, the following code tells the compiler that any number of parameters can be passed in — it's up to the function to figure out their type and what to do with them:

```
int
factorial(...) {
}
```

In general, though, using ... when you define your own functions is a bad idea because you can inadvertently pass any type of junk into the function. This can cause things to choke pretty badly. Although you'll see ... used in a couple of library functions, such as *printf*, you should avoid using it in functions that you write.

Hey, It's Not My Default

Default initializers specify default values for function arguments. For example, suppose you have a function called foo that takes three integer arguments, *a*, *b*, and *c*, and that in most cases the programmer using your function will never need to use the *c* argument. You can assign a default value for *c*. *c* will always have this value unless a value for *c* is passed in to the function. In other words, you can call foo(1,2), in which *a* = 1, *b* = 2, and *c* is set to the default; or you can call foo(1,2,3), in which case *a* = 1, *b* = 2, and *c* = 3.

Default initializers are useful in functions that contain arguments that are needed only in special cases. Someone who uses the function can ignore these special arguments and the routine will work just fine. But for the special cases, the defaults can be overridden.

To specify default initializers, list the values along with the argument list when you define the function:

```
int
foo(int a, int b, int c = 3) {
}
```

Chapter 22

Some Pointers on Pointers

. . . .

In This Chapter

▶ Learn what pointers are

▶ Find the address of a variable

▶ Dereference a pointer

▶ Dynamically allocate and deallocate memory

▶ Create a linked list

▶ Learn how to use strings

. . . .

Some people think learning about pointers is really really hard. In fact, this is usually the time when many Computer Science majors decide to study Philosophy instead. But actually, pointers aren't so bad — in fact, they're extremely useful. (On the other hand, it's no accident that this chapter contains more technical sections than any other chapter.)

You've already learned a lot of techniques for manipulating data. But as data becomes more and more complex, it becomes harder and harder to process it efficiently using named variables. For example, you might want to have a list of arbitrarily sized pieces of information (like perhaps you know you'll be scanning photographs, but you won't know their size in advance). This type of thing is difficult to handle with named variables but easy to handle with pointers.

As another example, you might need a list of employees in your organization. Because your organization might grow or shrink, you need to make sure the number of employees listed in your program can grow and shrink correspondingly. This is another great use for pointers.

Or, you might want to create a list of words for a spelling checker and need an efficient way to search through the list to see if a word is spelled correctly. Again, pointers make this task easy.

Another reason why pointers are useful is that even though a pointer is small, it can point to a very large thing. For example, let's suppose you have a large computerized collection of patients' medical records, with each record consuming a lot of bytes — some up to several thousand bytes. If you wanted to reorder the records so they were sorted by city, you'd be faced with a very time-consuming job if you had to do it by recopying each record to its new position in the new sort order. But if you had a pointer to each record, you could instead just quickly reorder the pointers. Then, even though the medical records themselves would never move, the changed pointer order would let you view the records in a new sort order.

Wow, I've Already Used Pointers?

You've used pointers in every single program you've written so far. You just didn't know it.

All computer data is stored in memory. When you assign a value to a variable, you fill in a block of memory with the value. When you use the variable, you read the value from memory. So a variable is just a name for a region of memory in the computer.

A pointer is the same thing — it's just the address of something in memory. A pointer points to a portion of memory, just like a variable does. Every time you use a variable you're really using a pointer.

The difference between a variable and a pointer is that a variable always points to the same spot in memory. But you can change a pointer so that it points to different spots in memory.

Figure 22-1 shows three variables called foo, bar, and dribble. You can see their memory address and their values. For example, bar has the value 17 and is located at memory address 4. There are also two pointers in the figure, baz and goo. baz has the value 4, which means it points at memory location 4. Thus, you could use the pointer baz to find out the value of the variable bar. If you changed the value of baz to be 8, you could use it to find the value of dribble (which is "Hey there").

Pointers are one of the most useful items in creating programs because they add great flexibility. You don't need to know details about a piece of data in advance.

Why Pointers Sometimes Freak People Out

There are two reasons why pointers sometimes drive beginning programmers nuts. The first reason is that you often use pointers to obtain *two* different pieces of information. The second reason is that pointers can point to things that don't have names.

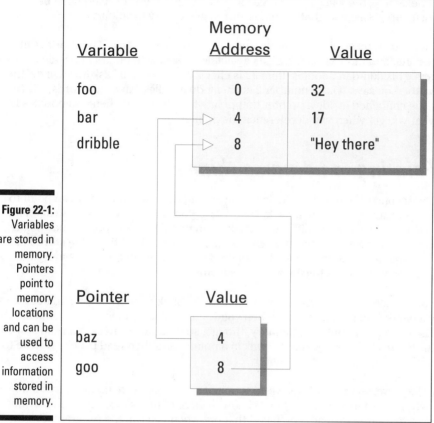

Figure 22-1:
Variables
are stored in
memory.
Pointers
point to
memory
locations
and can be
used to
access
information
stored in
memory.

Double your info, double your fun

As just stated, you can use pointers to get two different pieces of information. The first piece of information is the value stored inside the pointer. This is always the memory address of another piece of information. (For example, if the pointer contains the value 4, that means it's pointing to memory address 4.) The second piece of information is the value of the item pointed to by the pointer. (For example, if memory address 4 contains the value 17, a pointer containing the value 4 would therefore be pointing to an item that had the value 17.)

The value stored in the pointer is simply a memory location. If you print a pointer, you get some funky number that's just the memory address stored in the pointer. But the pointer also points to something — because there's a value stored inside the memory address the pointer contains. This is usually the value you want to get at. Looking at the value contained by what the pointer points to is called *dereferencing* the pointer.

For example, the value of baz (see Figure 22-1) is 4. If you dereferenced baz, you'd get 17 because that's what is stored in memory location 4.

Sound abstract? Nah! You dereference all the time in real life. My favorite Chinese restaurant in Santa Cruz lists available dishes, with numbers beside them. Item #1 is dan-dan noodles. Item #2 is cheng-du noodles. If I ask for item #2, the waitperson says "Okay, number 2 is cheng-du noodles." In other words, 2 is the value contained inside a pointer that points to a dish. And cheng-du noodles is what you get when you dereference the pointer.

Pointing to no-name things

The second potentially confusing thing about pointers is that they can point to things that don't have names. In Figure 22-1, you saw how you can use a pointer to access the values of different variables. In that figure, the pointer baz points to the variable named bar. You can dereference baz to get the value stored in the variable bar. In this case, the pointer is pointing to an area in memory that you've given a name to (the variable's name).

You can also ask the computer to set aside a chunk of information and not give it a name. You'll often do this when you want to allocate memory dynamically. The unnamed chunk is in memory, though, so it has an address. You can store the address of this unnamed chunk in a pointer and then read from and write to this memory by using the pointer.

(There are several reasons why you might want to allocate memory dynamically. For instance, you might not know the size of the data when you're writing the program — instead, you'll find that out when you run the program. Or you might not know how many items you need to create ahead of time. Or you might want to use the memory only when you need it, instead of defining a variable that will immediately use up memory.)

A Specific Pointer Example

Let's look at a specific example in which you use a pointer to access a block of memory. Suppose you want to create a program that stores photographs, and also suppose that when you write the program you don't know how much memory each photograph will require. After all, you can only determine this when the person using the program indicates what photographs will be stored. (Maybe they have a life-size picture of a sumo wrestler, and then again, maybe they have a reduced picture of an ant. Obviously, the small picture of the ant will need less space than the life-size picture of the wrestler.)

In this case, you'll *allocate* (or set aside) a block of memory each time the user tells the program to store a new photograph. So, for each photograph that will be stored, you need to find its size, allocate that amount of memory, and copy the photograph in to that area of memory. Because you allocated the memory instead of creating a variable, you need to make sure you remember where each photograph is saved. You would store the address of each photograph in a pointer.

If you want to examine a particular photograph, you'd just dereference its pointer and look at all the data that describes that photograph.

Okay, that part wasn't too bad. To read in and store a photograph, you just allocated memory for storing the photograph and saved the address of this memory area in a pointer. Now comes the tricky part.

Suppose that now you want to be able to read in lots and lots of photographs. You could have a whole bunch of pointers (say, PhotoPointer1, PhotoPointer2, and so on), and then each time you need another photograph, you could use the next pointer you had. This strategy could get pretty ugly, though, because you'd need to know the number of photographs in advance and you'd need to use a gigantic *switch* statement to figure out what pointer you should use when.

A more elegant approach is to use something called a *linked list*. A linked list is a set of items in which the first item in the list points to the next item in the list. It's kind of like a train. The first car in the train is hooked to the second car in the train and so on (until you get to the caboose).

Another way to trash your computer

Computers keep special information in certain areas of memory. For example, the first thousand bytes or so of memory contain lots of information telling the computer how to process keystrokes, timer clicks, and so forth. Then there is an area where DOS is loaded. In other areas you can find the memory for the video display card. If you know where these areas are, you can point to them with a pointer and start writing in new values. Sometimes this will do good things. For example, most video games know the exact memory area where video information is stored, and use this knowledge to write to the screen very quickly or perform special effects. On the other hand, if you fill these special areas with junk you can cause all types of strange behavior. This is known as *trashing* your computer because you filled really sensitive areas up with trash. When your computer is trashed anything can happen, but what happens is usually not good.

If you ever use a program where all of a sudden real strange characters start flashing on the screen, it's usually because a pointer has gone awry and has written values to screen memory instead of where it is supposed to.

The motto? Be careful when you use pointers.

So, to read in all those swarms of photographs, you could create a linked list of photographs. You'd then keep a pointer to the photograph data and a pointer to the next photograph in the list.

Figure 22-2 shows a linked list of three photographs. Each photograph record (on the left) points to both a photograph and to the next photograph record. And how do you represent a photograph record? With a structure, of course.

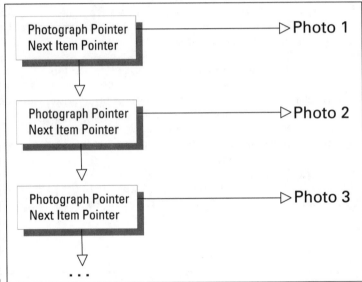

Figure 22-2: Pointers can point to very large and complex data structures. This linked list contains two pointers: one to the next element in the list and one to a photograph.

The linked list is a powerful and common way to store multiple items when the number of items or the size of each item isn't known in advance.

How to Use Pointers with C++

To make a pointer to a data type, create a variable of that data type just like you usually do, but precede its name with a * (pronounced *star*).

For example, to create a pointer to an integer you would do the following, which says that foo is a pointer to an integer:

```
int    *foo;
```

You need to declare the data type that the pointer points to. This makes your programs safer because the compiler will make sure that you don't accidentally point to something of the wrong type (after all, pointers are simply memory addresses).

That way, if you accidentally copy a photograph into an area of memory that's supposed to store a name, the compiler will flag the mistake for you. (This is good, because mistakes of this type could cause very nasty side effects, not to mention create strange names.)

int *foo doesn't mean that the pointer is called *foo. The pointer is called foo. The * tells the compiler that foo is a pointer, but the * isn't part of the variable's name. ■

What's the Address?

When you define a pointer it doesn't have a value. It just points into random space. But an undefined pointer is a dangerous thing. Before you use a pointer you need to assign it a value.

Many times you'll want to use a pointer to point to information stored in a variable. In other words, you'll fill the pointer with the address of a variable in your program. When you dereference the pointer, you can see what's stored in the variable.

To find the address of a variable, precede its name with an & (this is pronounced *amper* or *address of*). For example, you could do the following:

```
//Create a pointer to an integer.
int    *IntPointer;

//Here is an integer.
int    NumberOfToppings;

//Make the pointer point to NumberOfToppings.
IntPointer = &NumberOfToppings;
```

These statements create a pointer called IntPointer that is filled with the address of an integer called NumberOfToppings. If you dereference the pointer, you can find out how many toppings there are.

A pointer can only point to something of the correct data type. That is, if you have a pointer to an integer, you can only fill the pointer with the address of a variable that contains an integer. ■

Values Clarification for Nerds: Dereferencing Pointers

Dereferencing a pointer is easy: you just precede the pointer name with a *. For example, to find the value of what IntPointer points to, you could do the following:

```
//Print the number of toppings.
cout << *IntPointer;
```

This statement dereferences IntPointer. IntPointer contains the address of NumberOfToppings, so the dereference returns the value stored inside the variable NumberOfToppings.

A simple program that dereferences pointers

Let's write a simple program to illustrate the difference between the address contained in a pointer and the value contained in the address the pointer points to.

This program contains an integer and a pointer to an integer. The pointer points to the integer number:

```
IntPointer = &Number;
```

The user types in a value. First the program prints out the value directly:

```
cout << Number << "\n";
```

Next, it prints out the value by dereferencing a pointer. In other words, the pointer IntPointer contains the address of Number. Dereferencing IntPointer prints out the value contained in the address that IntPointer points to — which is the value stored in Number:

```
cout << "Using a pointer " << *IntPointer << "\n";
```

Finally, the program prints the value of the pointer itself. This is the address of Number — the memory location where the integer is stored:

```
cout << "The address is " << IntPointer << "\n";
```

The code

```
//Shows how to declare and dereference pointers.
#include <iostream.h>
```

```
void main() {
    int    *IntPointer;
    int    Number;

    //Have IntPointer point to Number.
    IntPointer = &Number;

    //Get a number from the user.
    cout << "Please type in a number\n";
    cin >> Number;

    //Now print this value back.
    cout << Number << "\n";

    //Now print it using a pointer.
    cout << "Using a pointer " << *IntPointer << "\n";

    //Now print out the value of the pointer.
    //Note that this is a memory address
    cout << "The address is " << IntPointer << "\n";
}
```

(This program is in the POINT directory on the separately available program disk.)

When you run this program, the address will be displayed as a hexadecimal value.

Changing the Value of What You're Pointing At

This section title reminds me of a dumb joke. A programmer shows up outside the library at Princeton University and asks a student "Where are the computer books at?" The student responds "I beg your pardon, but you shouldn't end a sentence with a preposition." So the programmer says "Okay. Where are the computer books at, hosehead?" The moral is: if you're looking at a program with some friends and they say "Hmm, what does this pointer point to?" be sure to correct them with "That's 'What does this pointer point to, *hosehead*?'"

Not only can you look at what a pointer points to, but you can change the value of something that is pointed to. In other words, not only can you read from the memory location, but you can write to it.

To do this, just use the *. For example, if, as in the previous example, IntPointer points to an integer, you could change the value stored in the integer by doing this:

```
*IntPointer = 5;
```

Changing the Value in a Structure

If you have a pointer to a structure, you can change an item in that structure. In the following code, MyStruct is a structure, and foo points to that structure. That means you can use *foo anyplace you can use the structure. To access a member of the structure, you might do this:

```
(*foo).value = 7.6;
```

Here's the code:

```
class MyStruct {
public:
    int    data;
    float value;
};

//Here is a pointer to the structure.
MyStruct *foo;

//Here is the structure itself.
MyStruct Record1;

//Point to the structure.
foo = &MyStruct;

//Change something in the structure.
(*foo).value = 7.6;
```

A Notation Shortcut You'll See Everywhere

Because using the (*pointer).member syntax can be a bit awkward, there's a C++ shortcut for doing this:

```
//Change something in the structure.
foo->value = 7.6;
```

You'll see this pointer->member notation in almost all C++ programs that use pointers.

Memories of the Way We Were

Any time you need to process a number of items but you don't know how many, or any time you need to store something but you don't know its size, you'll end up allocating memory dynamically (this is also called allocating memory *on the fly*).

The linked list of photographs discussed earlier in the "A Specific Pointer Example" section is an example of this: you don't know how many photographs you'll need to store, so each time you take a new photograph you allocate a new photograph record. And you also allocate new memory for storing the photograph itself.

The *new* command allocates memory on the fly. You just tell it the data type that you're trying to create, and *new* returns a pointer to the area it allocated.

If you want to create a new integer on the fly you could do this:

```
//Point to an integer.
int      *IntPointer;

//Now allocate some memory for an integer
//and use IntPointer to point to it.
IntPointer = new int;
```

If you wanted to create a new Pizza structure on the fly, you could do this:

```
//Point to a pizza structure.
Pizza    *MyPizzaPointer;

//Allocate a new Pizza structure and point to it.
MyPizzaPointer = new Pizza;
```

If You Forget This, You'll Lose Your Memory

When you use *new* to create an item, the pointer is the only thing that remembers where the new item is stored. So you need to be very careful that you don't accidentally clear the pointer, or you'll never be able to find the item again.

For example, look at this code:

```
//A forgetful application
//Start with a pointer to an integer.
int      *IntPointer;

//Create a new integer.
IntPointer = new int;

//Set the value to 3.
*IntPointer = 3;

//Now create a new integer.
IntPointer = new int;
```

The last line of this code allocated memory for a new integer. The address of the new integer got stored in IntPointer. But what happens to the integer that got set to 3? It's still floating around in memory, but because IntPointer no longer stores its address, there's no way to access it.

When you forget to save the address for something you created dynamically, that item is left hanging out in memory. This is called a *memory leak*. The item will keep using up memory — and you'll be unable to get rid of it — until your program ends.

When you use *new*, be careful to keep pointers to the memory items until they are no longer needed. When the item is no longer needed, you can get rid of it safely by using the *delete* command, which is discussed shortly.

A Classic Program: The Linked List Example

Here's a small program that shows a typical way to use pointers. The user can type in a set of numbers. These numbers are stored in a linked list and then printed out. This is basically a simple program for storing an arbitrarily long set of numbers.

The program creates a linked list of items. Each item structure contains an integer as well as a pointer to the next structure in the list. The last item in the list has a pointer with the value 0. This is sometimes called a *null pointer*.

How it works

The fundamental part of a linked list is a structure that contains information, along with a pointer to the next item in the list. Here, IntList contains a Number and a pointer to the next IntList:

```
class IntList {
public:
    int    Number;
    IntList        *Next;
};
```

The program contains code to add new items to the list and to display the list. To do this, three pointers are needed. The first pointer points to the beginning of the list. That way, no matter what, the first element in the list can always be found. After all, if you want to print all items in the list, you need to know where the list begins:

```
IntList  *First = 0;
```

The second pointer points to new items when an item is added to the list:

```
IntList  *ListPtr;
```

The third pointer points to the last item in the list:

```
IntList  *LastPtr = 0;
```

This pointer is needed when you add new items to the list. That's because each item in the list points to the next item in the list. The last item in the list contains a null pointer, because nothing follows it. When a new item is added, that null pointer in the last item needs to be changed so that it points to the item that was just added. This establishes the connection between the existing list and the new item. Of course, the new item's pointer is set to null; that's because it is now the last item.

Let's look at this fundamental part of the program. First, the new list item's data is filled in with the number and (because it is the last item) with a null pointer:

```
ListPtr->Number = Number;
ListPtr->Next = 0;
```

Next, if this isn't the very first item in the list, the item is connected to the list, by having the last item in the list point to this item:

```
if (LastPtr)
    LastPtr->Next = ListPtr;
```

If it is the first item, the First pointer is set:

```
else
    First = ListPtr;
```

Finally, the LastPtr is now set to the new item, because this new item is now the last item in the list:

```
    LastPtr = ListPtr;
}
```

Once the user has typed in a set of numbers, the program prints them out by traversing the list. It starts with the first item in the list, prints its value, and moves on to the next item in the list. It does this until the pointer to the next item is null, because that means the end of the list has been reached:

```
do {
    //Print out the number.
    cout << ListPtr->Number << " ";

    //Now move on to the next item in the list.
    ListPtr = ListPtr->Next;
}
```

(continued)

```
//Stop when ListPtr is 0.
while (ListPtr);
```

The code

```
//Read and print a list of numbers.
#include <iostream.h>

//Here is the linked list structure.
class IntList {
public:
    int    Number;
    IntList      *Next;
};

//This function prompts the user for a number.
//It returns the value of the number.
int
GetNumber() {
    int Number;

    cout << "What is the number?\n";
    cin >> Number;
    return Number;
}


//Here is where the program begins.
void main() {
    int    Number;

    //This points to the current IntList item.
    IntList      *ListPtr;

    //This points to the last IntList item created.
    IntList      *LastPtr = 0;

    //This points to the first item in the list.
    IntList      *First = 0;

    //Read in numbers from the user.
    while (Number = GetNumber()) {
        //Create a new structure to hold the number.
        //ListPtr will now point to this structure.
        ListPtr = new IntList;

        //Fill in the structure's values. Note the
        //use of -> because we are using pointers.
        ListPtr->Number = Number;
        ListPtr->Next = 0;

        //If this isn't the first item created,
        //connect it to the list. Otherwise, it
        //is the start of the list.
        if (LastPtr)
```

```
            //LastPtr->Next is the Next pointer from
            //the last item in the list. Connect it.
            LastPtr->Next = ListPtr;
        else
            //If this is the first item, be sure
            //to save where it starts!
            First = ListPtr;

        //Set the LastPtr.
        LastPtr = ListPtr;
    }

    //Now we are finished reading in the list.
    //So let's print it out. We first make sure
    //that it isn't empty.
    if (First) {
        cout << "The list is ";

        //Now use ListPtr to traverse the list.
        ListPtr = First;

        //Read through the list until Next is null.
        do {
            //Print out the number.
            cout << ListPtr->Number << " ";

            //Now move on to the next item in the list.
            ListPtr = ListPtr->Next;
        }
        //Stop when ListPtr is 0.
        while (ListPtr);

        //Now move to a clean line.
        cout << "\n";
    } //end of if

    cout << "Bye bye!\n";
}
```

(This program is in the LINKLIST directory on the separately available program disk.)

You'll see this example again in Chapter 23.

Freeing Your Memory

If you find you no longer need some memory that you've allocated, you should free it so you won't be using more space than you really need. The process of doing this is called *freeing memory*. To free memory, use the *delete* command, which works just like *new* but in reverse:

```
//Pointer to an int.
int    *IntPtr;

//Create an integer.
IntPtr = new int;

//Get rid of the integer we just created.
delete IntPtr;

//Clear the pointer.
IntPtr = 0;
```

Ignore This and You'll GP Fault

When you delete an item, the pointer itself isn't changed. The item that it pointed to, however, is cleared from memory. So the pointer still contains a memory address, but the memory address is now empty. If you dereference the pointer, you'll get junk. Once you've deleted what a pointer points to, you should set the pointer to 0. That way you know not to use it until you make it point to something meaningful.

Passing arguments by reference

In Chapter 21 you learned that modifying global variables within a function is dangerous, and that a better approach is to return a value from a function and set the values outside the function. (This avoids mysterious side effects inside functions.) If you'd rather have a function modify several items, or modify items within an existing structure, you can pass a pointer to those items to the function. The function can dereference the pointer and change the values. This is better than changing global variables (or variables outside the local scope) because when you indicate that pointers are passed into a function, programmers using the function know that the thing the pointer points to might get changed.

Another approach is to use *reference arguments*. When you do this, a pointer to the argument is passed in (not the argument itself). Because a pointer is passed in, any time you change something in the routine, the values themselves are changed. (For more information, see Chapter 26.) Using reference arguments is easier than passing in pointers because you don't need to explicitly dereference the parameters inside the function. To pass an argument by reference, you can precede the name of the item in the argument list with a &:

```
int
Factorial(int &Number) {

}
```

Then, any changes made to Number (or whatever the reference data is) within the function will be permanent—they will have an effect outside the function itself.

Whose GP Fault Is It, Anyway?

If you mess up with pointers you can get some really strange results. If you're running under Windows, you'll probably get a GP fault. Here are some common reasons why you might get yourself into deep water when you use pointers:

✔ You copied something when a pointer is null. If foo is null, *foo = *x* will try to write information to la-la land. Windows doesn't like that. Neither does any system. The end result will be bad.

✔ If you copy something to the wrong place, you can also get some strange results. For example, suppose foo points to the beginning of the list and bar points to the end of the list. If you use bar where you intended to use foo, you won't be doing what you think you're doing.

✔ If you delete memory and forget to clear the pointer, strange things will happen when you write to where the pointer points.

So, don't do these things!

Stringing Us Along

Strings is a computer-speak term for a bunch of text. Or rather, for a set of contiguous characters. "foo" is a string. When you do *cout* << "foo", you're printing a string.

Constant reference arguments: Don't change that structure!

Passing big structures in as arguments can be somewhat time consuming because the computer has to make a new copy of all the items in the structure. To speed this process, pass the structure in by reference. That way, only a pointer is passed (and pointers are very small). The only catch is that now the structure can be changed within the routine. To get around this problem, use a *constant reference argument*. This tells the compiler "I'm only doing this to make it faster. Don't let this thing be changed."

Here's how you do it:

```
int
HeatIt(const Pizza &MyPizza) {
}
```

There are lots of library routines devoted to processing strings. Pointers are also quite useful for processing strings.

Strings are stored in the computer as a contiguous array of characters. Strings are accessed by a pointer to the first item in the string. So if you want to create a string you can do this:

```
//Create a string.
char  *MyWord = "sensitive new-age guy";
```

This will create a string with the text "sensitive new-age guy" in it. The variable MyWord will point to this.

You can print this string out by doing this:

```
//Print out the string.
cout << MyWord;
```

You might want to look at the string library functions to see what else you can do with a string. Most of the library functions for processing strings start with *str*. For example, *strlen* returns the number of characters in a string.

C++ also includes an object called the ANSI string class that can help you create and manipulate strings.

If you allocate memory for a string, remember that the string needs to end with a \0. This takes up one byte, so make sure you include that ending byte in the size of the memory you allocate. If you forget to do this, you'll either crash or trash memory. ■

Avoid the Void *

There sure are a lot of advanced sections here in pointer land! And here's another one.

You might think it'd be handy to create a pointer that can point to anything. These type of pointers are called *void pointers*.

Although void pointers are very versatile (because you can use them anywhere), they're also very dangerous (because the compiler will *let* you use them anywhere).

Here's how you would make one (if you were going to, which I'm sure you're not, right?):

```
//Let foo point to anything.
void  *foo;
```

Pointing at strings

Since you can use a char * to point to a string of text, there are lots of things you can do with pointers to manipulate the text. C++ ends strings with a \0 (a byte containing a zero). That's how the library functions know when a string ends.

If you want to print out the characters in a string one at a time, you can increment the pointer itself. If you have a pointer to a letter in a string, you can add 1 to the pointer to move to the next letter in the string. For example:

```
//A string.
char    *MyString = "hello world";

//Another char *.
char    *CharPtr;

//Change the first character.
CharPtr = MyString;
*CharPtr = 'j';

//Now move on to the next character.
//Do so by incrementing the pointer.
CharPtr++;

//Now change the second character.
*CharPtr = 'o'

//The string is now changed.
//to "jollo world"
cout << MyString;
```

Void pointers are dangerous because there's no type checking for them and their use can accidentally scramble memory.

For example, if you used void pointers in the linked list of photographs, you could accidentally add employee records, integers, pizza orders, and who only knows what else to the linked list of photographs. The compiler would never know you were doing something bad. Your customers sure would, though.

To sum up, unless you really really need to, don't use void pointers.

Tips on Pointers

Here are some simple reminders and tips that can help keep you sane when you use pointers:

- ✔ A pointer contains an address of something in memory. If you add, subtract, or do something else with the pointer, you are manipulating this address. Usually you don't want to do that. Instead, you usually want to manipulate what the pointer points to. You do this by dereferencing the pointer.

- ✔ The name of the pointer isn't *foo, it's foo. *foo dereferences the pointer.

- ✔ If foo is a pointer to an integer, you can use *foo anywhere that you can use an integer variable inside your application. If foo is a pointer to something of data type *x*, you can use *foo anywhere you can use a variable of data type *x*. That means you can do *foo = jupiter;, jupiter = *foo;, and so on.

- ✔ If you create some memory dynamically, be sure to save its address in a pointer. If you don't save the address, you'll never be able to use the memory.

- ✔ When you delete some memory that you've created dynamically, the pointer itself isn't deleted or changed. Just the stuff pointed to. So to avoid problems, set the pointer to null so you don't get confused.

- ✔ If your head feels fuzzy, get some rest or eat some chocolate.

Yea! You've Made It Through!

Guess what? You now know an awful lot about pointers. In this chapter you learned that pointers are simply variables that point to areas in memory. Pointers are used to access memory that is allocated dynamically (for example, when you don't know the amount of memory you need to allocate in advance). Pointers are also used when you want to create linked lists (because you don't know the amount of items in advance).

There are many other uses for pointers. You'll see them used for linked lists throughout this book. You'll also see them in many of the Borland C++ sample programs.

Even though you're now a pointer expert, if you do find yourself getting a little confused, don't be ashamed to look back at the "Tips on Pointers" section every now and then.

Chapter 23
An Even Better Pizza Application

• •

In This Chapter

▶ Add pointers to the pizza application

▶ Use a linked list to store toppings that are ordered

▶ Traverse a linked list to print what type of pizza was ordered

• •

L et's make the pizza program even better. How could that be possible, you
ask? Well, we'll break it into several routines to make it easier to follow.
And we'll use pointers to create a linked list of the toppings that have been
ordered. That way we can print what has been ordered.

How It Works

The major difference between this version of the pizza program and the one in
Chapter 20 is the addition of the linked list.

The class ToppingList is used to create the linked list. It has three data members: Topping stores the type of topping, ToppingPrice stores the price for that
topping, and Next stores a pointer to the next item in the list of toppings.

```
class ToppingList {
public:
    int   Topping;
    float ToppingPrice;
    ToppingList   *Next;
};
```

The function GetToppingList asks users what toppings they want to order. It
builds a linked list of these toppings, using code very similar to the code you
saw in Chapter 22. When the user types in a topping, a new item is created:

```
//Create a new list item for storing the info.
ListPtr = new ToppingList;
```

The relevant information about the topping is stored in the structure:

```
//Store the type.
ListPtr->Topping = ToppingChoice;
    .
    .
    .
switch (ToppingChoice) {
      case Pepperoni:
        ListPtr->ToppingPrice = PepperoniPrice;
```

Then, this new item is connected to the existing list. Or, if the new item is the first item ordered, it's used for the beginning of the list:

```
//Add the new item into the linked list.
if (LastPtr)
   LastPtr->Next = ListPtr;
else
   First = ListPtr;
```

Another function, PrintAndSum, is used to traverse the linked list, compute the total cost of toppings, and echo back what the user ordered. It continues through the list as long as there are items to examine:

```
while (ListPtr) {
```

It then accesses the information it needs from the list item:

```
//Add up the total.
Sum += ListPtr->ToppingPrice;

//Print the topping type.
switch (ListPtr->Topping) {
    case Pepperoni:
          cout << "pepperoni ";
          break;
```

Then it goes on to the next item in the list:

```
//Move to the next item in the list.
ListPtr = ListPtr->Next;
```

Finally, there's a function called CleanUpPizza that traverses the list and frees any memory used by the linked list. This function is used to clean up just before the pizza program ends:

```
while (ListPtr) {
   Cur = ListPtr;
   ListPtr = ListPtr->Next;
   delete Cur;
}
```

The functions you just saw are all used inside the main function.

New and Improved Pizza Code

```cpp
//Improved pizza application.
//This time it will remember what you have ordered.
#include <iostream.h>

//Costs for basic pizzas.
const float LargePrice = 14;
const float SmallPrice = 10;

//These numbers represent the different toppings.
const int Pepperoni = 1;
const int Sausage = 2;
const int Onions = 3;

//The costs for the various toppings.
const float PepperoniPrice = 1.8;
const float SausagePrice = 2.1;
const float OnionPrice = 0.5;

//Here are some more constants.
const int Large = 1;
const int Small = 2;

class ToppingList {
public:
    int   Topping;
    float ToppingPrice;
    ToppingList *Next;
};

class Pizza {
public:
    ToppingList *Toppings;
    int Size;
    float CostForToppings;
    float Cost;
};

//This function asks the user what toppings he or she wants.
int
GetToppingType() {
    int   ToppingChoice;

    cout << "What toppings? 1 = pepperoni, 2 = "
             << "sausage, 3 = onions, 0 = stop\n";
    cin >> ToppingChoice;

    //Return this value.
    return ToppingChoice;
}
```

(continued)

```
//This function gets the list of toppings the user wants.
//It returns a pointer to the list of toppings. It returns
//0 if no toppings are requested.
ToppingList *
GetToppingList() {
    int   ToppingChoice;

    ToppingList *ListPtr, *LastPtr = 0, *First = 0;

    //Execute until the user says to stop adding toppings.
    while (ToppingChoice = GetToppingType()) {
        //Create a new list item for storing the info.
        ListPtr = new ToppingList;

        //Store the type.
        ListPtr->Topping = ToppingChoice;

        //Clear the next pointer because there is nothing
        //that follows.
        ListPtr->Next = 0;

        //Now store the price of the topping.
        //Give some nice chatty responses at the same time.
        switch (ToppingChoice) {
            case Pepperoni:
                ListPtr->ToppingPrice = PepperoniPrice;
                cout << "OK, we'll add pepperoni.\n";
                break;
            case Sausage:
                ListPtr->ToppingPrice = SausagePrice;
                cout << "Some sausage on that.\n";
                break;
            case Onions:
                ListPtr->ToppingPrice = OnionPrice;
                cout << "Sounds good.\n";
                break;
            default:
                cout << "Pardon me?\n";
        }        //end of switch

        //Add the new item into the linked list.
        if (LastPtr)
            LastPtr->Next = ListPtr;
        else
            First = ListPtr;

        //Update LastPtr.
        LastPtr = ListPtr;

    } //End of while statements.

    //Return a pointer to the list.
    return First;
}

//Compute and return the total cost of the
//toppings.
```

```
float
PrintAndSum(ToppingList *ListPtr) {
    float Sum = 0.0;

    //Continue printing as long as there are entries.
    while (ListPtr) {
        //Add up the total.
        Sum += ListPtr->ToppingPrice;

        //Print the topping type.
        switch (ListPtr->Topping) {
            case Pepperoni:
                cout << "pepperoni ";
                break;
            case Sausage:
                cout << "sausage ";
                break;
            case Onions:
                cout << "onions ";
        }

        //Move to the next item in the list.
        ListPtr = ListPtr->Next;

        //If there is another item following, add "and"
        //so the sentence reads better.
        if (ListPtr)
            cout << "and ";

    } //End of while.

    //Return the price.
    return Sum;
}

//Frees memory used by the pizza program.
void
CleanUpPizza(ToppingList *ListPtr) {
    ToppingList *Cur;

    while (ListPtr) {
        Cur = ListPtr;
        ListPtr = ListPtr->Next;
        delete Cur;
    }
}

void
main() {
    Pizza MyPizzaInfo;

    //What size?
    cout << "What size pizza do you want? " <<
        "Type 1 for large and 2 for small.\n" ;
    cin >> MyPizzaInfo.Size;
```

(continued)

```
//What is the base price?
if (MyPizzaInfo.Size == Large)
     MyPizzaInfo.Cost = LargePrice;
else
     MyPizzaInfo.Cost = SmallPrice;

//Find out what toppings the customer wants.
MyPizzaInfo.Toppings = GetToppingList();

//Now the user has finished ordering, so print
//back what he or she ordered, starting with the size.
cout << "That's a ";
if (MyPizzaInfo.Size == Large)
     cout << "large ";
else
     cout << "small ";
cout << "pizza with ";

//If user didn't order any toppings, indicate this.
if (!MyPizzaInfo.Toppings)
     cout << "no toppings.\n";
else {
     //User ordered toppings. Find the price
     //and print what user ordered.
     MyPizzaInfo.Cost +=
          PrintAndSum(MyPizzaInfo.Toppings);
     cout << "for toppings.\n";
}

//Now tell the cost.
cout << "That will be $" << MyPizzaInfo.Cost
     << " please.\n";

//Clean up memory.
CleanUpPizza(MyPizzaInfo.Toppings);
}
```

(This program is in the PIZZA5 directory on the separately available program disk.)

Chapter 24

Enumeration Types and Arrays

*R*ecall that earlier, in our pizza program, you defined a whole list of constants for pepperoni, sausage, and onions to make it easier to read the program. Those constants were assigned by hand. Now you're going to learn how to use something called *enumeration types* (sometimes called *enums* for short), which provide a simple way to create a list of constants.

Also recall that, in the same pizza program, you defined a lot of constants for the price of each topping. You used a *switch* statement to figure out the price given the topping number. You also used a *switch* statement to print out what type of topping it was. Our little pizza program only has a few topping choices, but imagine if there were 500 topping choices — you'd have to create a really gigantic *switch* statement to handle that many choices.

That's why arrays are so helpful. *Arrays* let you create variables that contain many entries of the same type. You can very easily look up the value of any item in the array. So instead of a case statement, you could just say "Look in my pricing array to find the cost of topping number 3."

How Do I Use Enums? Let Me Count the Ways...

To create enumeration types, you just give a list of names you want to use as constants. Borland C++ assigns 0 to the first, 1 to the second, and so on.

For example, instead of having this in your program:

```
const int Pepperoni = 0;
const int Sausage = 1;
const int Onions = 2;
```

you could have this:

```
enum {Pepperoni, Sausage, Onions};
```

Any of the words used in this enum (Pepperoni, Sausage, and Onions) can be used throughout the program — they'll be treated just like constants. That is, Pepperoni would be 0, Sausage would be 1, and Onions would be 2. All the *switch* statements in the pizza program will work just as they did before.

Don't worry, be safe

If you want to be safety conscious, you can also specify that the set of enums represents a specific type. This prevents you from accidentally using one enum constant (say, for pizza toppings) where it isn't expected (say, in an enum for types of motor oil).

For example, you could specify that the various toppings are of type Toppings:

```
enum Toppings {Pepperoni, Sausage, Onions};
```

If you do this, the compiler will make sure that you use these names only with variables that are of type Toppings. For example, the pizza program in Chapter 23 declared the following structure, which uses an integer to store the topping type:

```
class ToppingList {
public:
    int   Topping;
    float ToppingPrice;
    ToppingList   *Next;
};
```

To use enums instead, you could change the ToppingList structure to the following:

```
class ToppingList {
public:
    Toppings       Topping;
    float ToppingPrice;
    ToppingList   *Next;
};
```

Whenever possible, assign a type for enumeration types. That way, if you try to use an enumerated constant with the wrong type of information, the compiler will generate a warning. The program will still work, but the warning message will help you track down what's going wrong. ■

A cin of omission

Before you add types to all your enums, however, note that *cin* only knows how to read in information for the predefined data types. If you try to use *cin* to prompt the user for an enumeration constant with a specified type, nothing will happen. This can lead to strange results.

For example, the following code will run fine with no errors, but you won't get what you expect in foo:

```
//Create an enum list.
enum Toppings {Pepperoni, Sausage, Onions};

//foo is of type Toppings.
Toppings foo;

//Read in what foo the user wants.
cin >> foo;
```

Arrays of Hope

Arrays are a very powerful data type that are used throughout many programs. The concept of an array is very similar to that of a row (or column) in a spreadsheet: basically, there are a lot of cells in which you can store information.

The great thing about arrays is that each element in the array has a number, called an *index*, that you can use to easily access the information in that element. You can also use loops to look at all the elements (or a range of elements) in a particular array. The array index lets you access any of the items in the array immediately. This makes *random access* much faster than using lists to store information.

For example, you could use an array to keep a list of prices for pizza toppings. Then, if you wanted to find the price for pizza topping number 1, you would look at array element 1. Likewise, you could use arrays to store exchange rates for various currency markets, or names of various employees, or any number of other things.

Before you create an array, you need to state how many elements will be in it. So, unlike lists, you need to know the size of the array before you create it.

For example, suppose foo is an array of integers. It might look like this:

Index	Value
0	32
1	10
2	17
3	–5
4	10

As you can see, the first element in the array has an index of 0, the second element has an index of 1, and so on. And in this particular array, element 0 has the value 32, and element 4 has the value 10.

To create an array, you simply list the data type, the name, and the number of elements you want within [ ] (square brackets).

For example, to create an array of integers you could do this:

```
//Create an array containing 20 integers, with indices.
//0..19
int     foo[20];
```

It's important to remember that the first element in an array is element 0, and that if you create an array with *n* elements, the last item is *n*–1. For example, in the array shown above, *n* is 5 (because there are five elements). The first element in the array is 0, and the last element in the array is 4 (which is 5–1).

When beginners first start using arrays, it's very common for them to mistakenly use a 1 (instead of a 0) for the first element and then to wonder why the values in the array aren't what they'd expect.

Likewise, it's very common for beginners to inadvertently use *n* (instead of *n*–1) for the last item in the array, and then to get strange data or GP faults. ∎

Accessing an Element in an Array

To access an element in an array, use the variable name followed by the index in square brackets. In the following code, for example, foo is an array of 20 integers:

```
//foo is an array of 20 integers.
int     foo[20];

//Set the first element to 20 and the second element to 3.
foo[0] = 20;
foo[1] = 3;
```

```
//Print the value of the second element.
cout << foo[1];

//Print 3 times the fifth element.
cout << 3*foo[4];
```

Initializing Arrays

There are several ways to initialize arrays. One way is to set each element by hand:

```
foo[0] = 1;
foo[1] = 3;
    .
    .
    .
```

Another way is to use a loop. Loops are especially powerful if there is some pattern to the values in the array or if the initial values can be read from a data file. For example, if you wanted to create an array containing the numbers 1 through 20 you could do this:

```
//TheIntegers is an array of 20 integers.
int     TheIntegers[20];

//Loop through, setting the value of each element in the array.
//Note that we are setting it to 1 + the array index.
for (int i = 0; i < 20; i++)
    TheIntegers[i] = i + 1;
```

Yet another way to initialize an array is to type in the values for elements when you declare the array. You can type in as few items as you would like (the remaining items are given a default value). For example, you could initialize an array of integers with:

```
int     MyInts[10] = {1, 4, 5, 6, 7, 8};
```

In this case, the first six elements are assigned the values listed (element zero is assigned the value 1, element one is assigned 4, and so on), and the remaining four elements are assigned 0.

Stringing Together Strings in an Array

You can also make and initialize arrays of strings to use in your programs. As you might recall, a string is an array of characters (or a char *). The following code creates and initializes an array of strings, and then prints them out:

```
//Create an array of three strings.
//Assign initial values
char *foo[3] = {"hello", "goodbye", "how are you"};

//Print out the strings.
cout << foo[0] << foo[1] << foo[2] << "\n";
```

A Dr. Lizardo Special: Multidimensional Arrays

(If you're not familiar with Dr. Lizardo, a character in the movie *The Adventures of Buckaroo Bonzai,* your education is sadly lacking; this movie is a real must-see for programmers. Dr. Lizardo travels to other dimensions and encounters all sorts of bizarre creatures named John.)

Techie stuff: the relationship between arrays and pointers

An array of items of type *x* is really a pointer to an item of type *x.* That is, if you do this:

```
int     foo[8];
```

you can treat foo just as if you'd done this:

```
int     *foo;
```

The difference is that when you create an array a block of memory is allocated, whereas when you create the pointer a block of memory isn't allocated. The array variable is a pointer to the first element in the array.

Sometimes pointers are used to iterate through arrays. Consider the following code:

```
//An array of integers.
int     foo[8];
```

```
//A pointer to an integer.
int     *bar;

//Point to the first element in
//the array.
bar = foo;

//This will print out the first
//item in the array.
cout << *bar;

//This will print out the next
//item in the array.
//Note that this is equivalent
//to foo[1].
cout << *(bar + 1);
```

When you use pointers to iterate through an array, each time you add a value to a pointer you are actually adding the size of each array element to the pointer.

Anyway, to return to the main topic, the arrays I've discussed so far have been *single-dimensional* arrays. But there are also *multidimensional* arrays, which are useful in many problem-solving situations. For example, let's say you want to determine how many houses are in each grid of a city map. Since the map is two dimensional, a two-dimensional array would be helpful in this situation, as is shown in Figure 24-1.

Figure 24-1: Each grid in the two-dimensional city map corresponds to an element in a two-dimensional array used to store the number of houses.

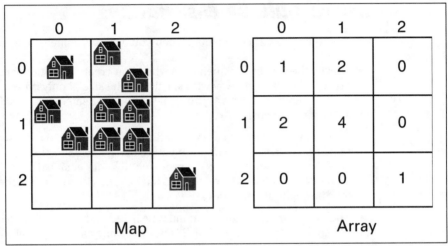

Or, for another example, if you wanted to keep track of how many subatomic particles are in a particular area of space, you could break space into cubic regions and use a three-dimensional array.

You can also use multidimensional arrays when physical space isn't involved. Matrices, which are often used for image processing, are two-dimensional arrays. For instance, if you have a database containing companies, which are divided into divisions, which are divided into business units, that database can also be treated as a three-dimensional array. (In this case, companies would be one dimension, divisions the second dimension, and business units the third dimension.)

I now declare you a multidimensional array

To define a multidimensional array, give as many [ ] as there are dimensions for the array. For example, the following code creates an array for a chess board, which is eight squares high by eight squares wide:

```
int      ChessBoard[8][8];
```

To access an item, you also supply as many [ ] as there are dimensions:

```
//Is the position 3, 4 full?
Full = ChessBoard[3][4];
```

These aren't your average everyday tips, they're multidimensional tips

Here are some tips to keep in mind when you use multidimensional arrays:

✔ Specify the size of all dimensions when you create a multidimensional array. (You can get away with specifying the size of only *n*-1 dimensions for an *n* dimensional array, but you'll usually be safer with specifying the sizes of all dimensions.)

✔ The computer doesn't care which dimension you use to represent a particular property. For example, if you're using a two-dimensional array (with an *x* axis and a *y* axis) to represent two-dimensional space, you can use the first index as *x* and the second as *y*, or vice versa. Just be consistent throughout your code.

✔ The index for each dimension must be listed in its own separate set of square brackets. That is, [1][7] is not the same as [1,7]. [1][7] will access an element in a two-dimensional array. [1,7] is the same as [7].

✔ The compiler doesn't check whether the index you give it is larger than the size of the array. So if you have an array with 20 elements and you set the value of the 500th element, the compiler will generate code that will gleefully trash memory. Make sure that your indices stay within the correct range.

✔ The compiler also doesn't care if you treat a two-dimensional array as a one-dimensional array. It just uses the indices to determine a pointer. You can use this fact to play some interesting tricks and to create faster code. You can also use this fact to confuse the heck out of yourself — that's why it's easier and better to continue using the dimensions you defined when you created the array.

Chapter 25
This Pizza Is Tops

• •

In This Chapter

▶ Add enumeration types to replace some of the constants in the pizza program

▶ Use arrays to simplify topping name and price look-up

• •

*B*ack to the pizza program! This time, you'll be using enums and arrays in the program.

If you compare this latest program to the version in Chapter 23, you'll see how enums make it easier to create constants (which previously had to be given values manually). You'll also see that by using arrays, you can easily expand the number of topping options while reducing the size of the code.

The Pizza Program, It Is a'Changing

To take advantage of enums and arrays, the new program features a number of changes. The following three sections discuss all the changes made to this newest version of our pizza program.

Changes required to add enums

The first change to the program is that now enums (instead of explicit constants) are used for the pizza sizes:

```
enum {Small, Large};
```

Note that nothing else in the program relating to these constants needs to change. For example, anywhere the constant Small was used before will still work. The only difference is that now you don't explicitly assign the constant a value — the compiler does it automatically.

Changes required to use arrays

The second change is that now you use arrays to store the topping types and costs. Instead of having an explicit list of constants for each topping, and *switch* statements to determine the name and cost for each topping, you just store the topping types and costs in an array. The name of topping *n* is found in one array, and the cost for the same topping is found in the other array:

```
const int    NumChoices = 5;
char         *const ToppingNames[NumChoices] =
    {"Pepperoni","Sausage", "Onions", "Extra Cheese",
    "Olives"};
float        const ToppingPrices[NumChoices] = {1.8, 2.1,
    0.5, 1.0, 0.7};
```

For added interest, there's also a change in the number of toppings. Now the program has more toppings than before. If you're a serious pizza consumer, you can add even more toppings by increasing NumChoices further and typing in more toppings and prices.

The arrays are then used throughout the program. For example, the following is used in the GetToppingType routine to print the list of possible toppings:

```
for (i = 0; i < NumChoices; i++)
    cout << i << " = " << ToppingNames[i] <<
        "\n";
```

Note that this loop will work regardless of the number of toppings. So if more toppings are added to the topping list array, they will automatically be printed in this routine — the code doesn't need to change. This is one of the great benefits of using arrays.

The array is also used to echo back what the user selected:

```
if (ToppingChoice >= 0)
    cout << "OK, we'll add some " <<
        ToppingNames[ToppingChoice] << ".\n";
```

The topping arrays are used inside PrintAndSum to find the price and name for a particular topping. This replaces the large *switch* statement in the previous version of Pizza. Once again, the code works no matter how many topping choices you use. If you decide to add more toppings to the list of available toppings (that is, if you change the array size), you won't need to change the code that looks up the name and price from the arrays:

```
Sum += ToppingPrices[ListPtr->Topping];

//Print the topping type. Note that we just
//use the array instead of a huge switch.
cout << ToppingNames[ListPtr->Topping] << " ";
```

Other changes to the program

Several additional changes have been made to the program. First, since it's now much easier to find the price for a topping, you no longer need to keep this information in the ToppingList structure. The new ToppingList structure now contains just the topping number (which is used with the arrays to find the price and name for the topping) and a pointer to the next item in the list of toppings:

```
class ToppingList {
public:
    int    Topping;
    ToppingList    *Next;
};
```

Another change is that a routine called GoodChoice is added to determine whether the user has selected a value that's allowed. GoodChoice checks to make sure the value doesn't go outside the size of the toppings array:

```
if ((ToppingChoice < -1) || (ToppingChoice >=
        NumChoices)) {
    //A bad choice so print a message and return false.
    cout << "I don't understand that choice.\n";
    return 0;
}
```

The last change to the program is that, in GetToppingType, the user now needs to type −1 instead of 0 to indicate that no more toppings are needed. That's because −1 isn't a valid array index, so it's very clear that −1 isn't a requested pizza topping number.

Overall, note that the use of arrays makes the program much smaller and simpler.

And Now for the Code

```
//Improved pizza application.
//This time the list of options is expanded.
#include <iostream.h>

//Constants for pizza sizes.
enum {Small, Large};

//A plain large pizza costs $14.
const float LargePrice = 14;
//A plain small pizza costs $10.
const float SmallPrice = 10;
```

```
//The topping types and prices.
const int  NumChoices = 5;
char       *const ToppingNames[NumChoices] =
   {"Pepperoni","Sausage", "Onions", "Extra Cheese",
   "Olives"};
float      const ToppingPrices[NumChoices] =
   {1.8, 2.1, 0.5, 1.0, 0.7};

class ToppingList {
public:
   int  Topping;
   ToppingList *Next;
};

class Pizza {
public:
   ToppingList *Toppings;
   int Size;
   float Cost;
};

//This function checks to see if the topping choice
//is valid. It returns true if the choice is good.
int
GoodChoice(int ToppingChoice) {

   //It is bad if the number is < -1 or > the number of
   //choices.
   if ((ToppingChoice < -1) || (ToppingChoice >=
         NumChoices)) {
      //A bad choice so print a message and return false.
      cout << "I don't understand that choice.\n";
      return 0;
   }

   //Since we haven't returned, the choice is good.
   return 1;
}

//This function asks the user what topping he or she wants.
int
GetToppingType() {
   int  ToppingChoice;
   int  i;

   //Here is the loop that stops only when the user
   //picks a good topping choice.
   do {
      cout << "What toppings? (-1 to Stop)\n";

      //Display all the topping options.
      for (i = 0; i < NumChoices; i++)
         cout << i << " = " << ToppingNames[i] <<
            "\n";

      //Now get the user's choice.
      cin >> ToppingChoice;
   }
```

```
        //And we'll repeat until the choice is good.
        while (!GoodChoice(ToppingChoice));

        //Repeat back what the user ordered.
        if (ToppingChoice >= 0)
            cout << "OK, we'll add some " <<
                ToppingNames[ToppingChoice] << ".\n";

        //Return the value.
        return ToppingChoice;
}

//This function gets the list of toppings the user wants.
ToppingList *
GetToppingList() {
    int ToppingChoice;

    //Pointers used for maintaining the list of toppings.
    ToppingList *ListPtr, *LastPtr = 0, *First = 0;

    //Execute this stuff until the user says stop
    //adding toppings.
    while ((ToppingChoice = GetToppingType()) >= 0) {
        //Create a new list item for storing the info.
        ListPtr = new ToppingList;

        //Store the type.
        ListPtr->Topping = ToppingChoice;

        //Clear the next pointer because there is nothing
        //that follows.
        ListPtr->Next = 0;

        //We no longer need a switch statement to
        //look up the topping price or name.

        //Add the new item into the linked list.
        if (LastPtr)
            LastPtr->Next = ListPtr;
        else
            First = ListPtr;

        //Update LastPtr
        LastPtr = ListPtr;

    } //end of while statements

    //Return a pointer to the list.
    return First;
}

//Compute and return the total cost of the
//toppings.
float
PrintAndSum(ToppingList *ListPtr) {
    float Sum = 0.0;
```

(continued)

```
            //Keep printing as long as there are entries.
            while (ListPtr) {
                //Add up the total
                Sum += ToppingPrices[ListPtr->Topping];

                //Print the topping type. Note that we just
                //use the array instead of a huge switch.
                cout << ToppingNames[ListPtr->Topping] << " ";

                //Move to the next item in the list.
                ListPtr = ListPtr->Next;

                //If there is another item following, add "and"
                //so the sentence reads better.
                if (ListPtr)
                    cout << "and ";

            } //end of while

            //return the price
            return Sum;
        }

        //Frees memory used by the pizza program
        void
        CleanUpPizza(ToppingList *ListPtr) {
            ToppingList *Cur;

            while (ListPtr) {
                Cur = ListPtr;
                ListPtr = ListPtr->Next;
                delete Cur;
            }
        }

        void
        main() {
            Pizza MyPizzaInfo;

            //What size?  Note the use of the enums.
            cout << "What size pizza do you want? " <<
                "Type " << Large << " for large and " <<
                Small << " for small.\n" ;
            cin >> MyPizzaInfo.Size;

            //What is the base price?
            if (MyPizzaInfo.Size == Large)
                MyPizzaInfo.Cost = LargePrice;
            else
                MyPizzaInfo.Cost = SmallPrice;

            //Find out what toppings the customer wants.
            MyPizzaInfo.Toppings = GetToppingList();

            //Now the user has finished ordering, so print
            //back what they ordered, starting with the size.
            cout << "That's a ";
```

```
    if (MyPizzaInfo.Size == Large)
        cout << "large ";
    else
        cout << "small ";
    cout << "pizza with ";

    //If they didn't order any toppings, indicate this.
    if (!MyPizzaInfo.Toppings)
        cout << "no toppings.\n";
    else {
        //They ordered toppings. Find the price
        //and print what they ordered.
        MyPizzaInfo.Cost +=
            PrintAndSum(MyPizzaInfo.Toppings);
        cout << "for toppings.\n";
    }

    //Now tell the cost.
    cout << "That will be $" << MyPizzaInfo.Cost
        << " please.\n";
    //Clean up memory.
    CleanUpPizza(MyPizzaInfo.Toppings);
}
```

(This program is in the PIZZA6 directory on the separately available program disk.)

Chapter 26

And You Thought Scope Was Just a Mouthwash

• •

In This Chapter

▶ Scope and how it works

▶ Global and local variables

▶ Why you can have lots of variables with the same names in your program

• •

*A*s programs get larger and larger, the number of functions and variables they contain increases. Many of these variables are used temporarily. For example, there are a lot of times when variables are used only to help with loops in a small function, or to temporarily hold what the user typed in. Fortunately, you don't need to give such variables unique names every time you need them. Otherwise, you might need to come up with thousands and thousands of unique variable names.

You can create several variables that have the same name. As long as the variables are created in different functions, they won't conflict. For example, you can define a variable named *k* in a function named foo. And, you can define a variable named *k* in a function named baz. Even though they have the same name, these are different variables — one is only used in foo, and the other is only used in baz.

The two variables are different because they have different *scope*. A variable's scope is the place in the program where it can be used. For example, the *k* that was defined in foo has scope foo. That means it can be used inside foo but it can't be used outside foo.

There are two types of variables: global and local. *Global* variables are accessible from any part of an application. They're useful if you have some constants that you want to be accessible no matter what routine you're in. No two global variables can have the same name.

Local variables are temporary variables used only within one particular function. A local variable is created when the function begins, is used throughout the function, and is destroyed when the function stops. You can have only one variable of that name inside that particular function, but you can use the same name inside a different function. (Changing one of these variables has absolutely no effect on the other variable.)

This is good. Why is that? Well, suppose you have a function called CountUp that prints the numbers from 1 to 10. You would probably use a loop to do this. This loop might use a variable named *i* for the loop counter. If you have another function called CountDown that prints the numbers from 10 to 1, you would also use a variable for the loop counter. Because of local variables, you could name both *i*. This means you don't have to come up for a unique name each time you write a loop. So if you have lots and lots of different functions in your program, some of which were written by other people, you wouldn't have to shout across the room "Hey, did anyone use sdbsdbsdbsdb3 for a loop-variable name yet?"

Any time you define a variable within a function, the variable is *local* to that function. In other words, its scope is that function. You can use it in the function. You can pass it to anything the function calls. But once the function is finished, the variable disappears. The names used for arguments in a function are also local to the function.

Why Bother Talking About This?

Scope might not sound like something worth worrying about. In a way, it isn't, because you'll rarely think about it when you program. But, scope can be confusing to people new to programming, and understanding scoping rules can help you avoid some hard-to-find logic errors.

Consider the following small program:

```
#include <iostream.h>

int x;

void ZeroIt(int x) {
    x = 0;
}

void main() {
    x = 1;
    ZeroIt(x);
    cout << x;
}
```

What happens if you run this program? At first, the global variable *x* is set to 1. Then the ZeroIt function is called, which sets *x* to 0. When you get to the *cout << x*, what will the value of *x* be? It'll be 1.

Why is it 1? The variable *x* within ZeroIt is local to ZeroIt, so it's created when ZeroIt is called. It's assigned the value passed in, which in this case is 1. It's then given the value 0. Then the function is finished, so the variable *x* (which has a value of 0 and is local to ZeroIt) is destroyed. Kaput. Now you return back to the main( ) and do a *cout << x*. That's a different *x*. That's the *x* with global scope.

Likewise, you'd get the same results with the following program. Once again, changes to the variable *x* within ZeroIt don't affect the value of the global *x* that is used in main:

```
#include <iostream.h>

int x;

void ZeroIt() {
    int x;
    x = 0;
}

void main() {
    x = 1;
    ZeroIt();
    cout << x;
}
```

In contrast, consider this program:

```
#include <iostream.h>

int x;

void ZeroIt(int y) {
    y = 7;
    x = 0;
}

void main() {
    x = 1;
    ZeroIt(x);
    cout << x;
}
```

If you run this program, the *cout* will print 0.

Why is it 0 now? Well, this time the argument to ZeroIt is called *y*. So when you pass in *x* to ZeroIt, the value of *x* is assigned to the variable *y*. *y* is given the value 7. Then *x* is given the value 0. Since there's no *x* local to ZeroIt, this is the global *x* that is given the value 0. When ZeroIt is finished, *y* disappears. Since *x* isn't local to ZeroIt, *x* isn't destroyed. And the global *x* is changed.

This example also illustrates a bad coding style. Because ZeroIt changes a value that wasn't passed in to it, if you didn't read through the whole program you might not expect *x* to change when ZeroIt is called. In general, you shouldn't change variables that aren't passed in by reference or pointers. Only change variables that are local to the function.

Scoping Rules: When Is ARose Not ARose?

Fortunately, the C++ scoping rules are fairly straightforward:

- Any variables defined within a function are local to that function. If you define a variable within a function, that variable is created when the function is called, used throughout the function, and destroyed when the function is finished.

- Any arguments for a function are local to that function. For example, if you indicate that a function takes a parameter named ARose, then ARose is local to that function, just as if you had defined ARose within the function. The name of whatever you passed in to the function doesn't matter. The name of the argument does.

- When you're in a function, variables local to that function are used instead of variables of the same name that are global. For example, suppose you define an integer named ARose within a function named foo and that there is a global variable of type float that is also named ARose. If you use the variable ARose within foo, you will use the integer that is local to foo. You will not use (or be able to access without going to some effort) the global variable named ARose that is a float. That is, the local ARose is not the same as the global ARose. They are two different variables that happen to have the same name, and that are used in different places in the program.

- Changes made to a local item don't affect things of the same name that aren't local. For instance, if you have a local variable named ARose and you set it to 0, that doesn't change a thing to a global variable that also happens to be named ARose.

- If, inside a function, you use a variable that isn't local to the function, the compiler will try to find a global variable with the same name. For example, suppose you use a variable named ARose within a function named foo. But ARose isn't the name of one of the arguments passed to foo, and ARose isn't defined within foo. How does the compiler find a variable named ARose to use within foo? It looks for a global named ARose. If it can't find a global named ARose, it prints out an error message.

- If you want to access a global variable from a function that has a local variable with the same name as the global, precede the variable name with

:: (the *scope resolution operator*). For example, if there's a global variable named ARose, and you're in a function that contains a local variable named ARose, ::ARose will refer to the global variable, and ARose will refer to the local variable.

Some Tips on Scope

Here are some suggestions that can make it a lot easier for you to figure out what scope a variable has:

✔ When you define a function, pass in any information it needs to process as an argument.

✔ Avoid global variables. Only use them for constants.

✔ Don't change stuff out of your scope. If you only change local variables and only change reference arguments, things won't get too hairy.

The Scoop on Scope

When you call a function, the variables local to that function are created on the *stack*. (By contrast, memory areas allocated when you use *new* come from a memory section called the *free store*. The free store is just a big chunk of memory that's available for use by the program.)

The stack is an area of memory that is used to help deal with the complexities of calling functions. When a function is called, the address of the item that called it is placed on the stack. Then the function is called. When the function is finished, the address of what called the routine is read from the stack, and the computer returns to this address.

Putting information on the stack is called *pushing to* (or *on*) *the stack*. Removing information from the stack is called *popping from* (or *off*) *the stack*.

A stack is a particular type of data structure. As with a stack of dishes, you can put things on the top one at a time. You can also remove things from the top, but in the reverse order of how they were put on. You can't change this order at all. That is, you can't say "give me the middle of that stack." Another name for this type of a structure is *LIFO*, which stands for last in, first out.

Now back to how the stack makes scoping work. If the function has arguments, the values of the arguments are pushed onto the stack. The argument variable then points to those values on the stack.

Scoping out some files

Global variables and functions are accessible on a source-file by source-file basis. That is, all global variables and functions defined in a source file are said to have *file scope*. By default, they can only be used within the file where they are defined.

To make the routines and variables visible outside a file, you first create a header file. In the header file, list the functions and variables you want to be seen. You need to declare their data types (and argument types, as well). Use the *extern* keyword to indicate that these guys are found from a different file.

For example, if you wanted the GoodChoice function from the pizza program to be used in a different file, you'd make a header file containing the following line:

```
extern int GoodChoice(int);
```

You would then *#include* this header file in the files that you want to use the GoodChoice routine.

Note that you only need to use the *extern* to share variables and functions. This is because *extern* tells the compiler that this item has already been created somewhere else.

When you need to share structures, enums, and classes between files you simply list their declaration in the header file. You don't precede them with the *extern* keyword.

Note that if you have a global variable or function in one file, you can't make a global variable or function with the same name in another file, even if you don't use *extern*.

There are tons and tons of header files that come with Borland C++. Header files are also used in the sample programs in Chapter 33 and Chapter 36. You might want to look at them to see how they work.

For example, suppose you have an argument named foo and you pass in a variable named bar that contains the value 3. The value 3 is pushed onto the stack. foo points to that part of the stack. Changing the value of foo will change the value that is placed on the stack. It won't change bar, because bar isn't on the stack (at least not where foo points). Rather, a copy of bar is placed on the stack and referred to within the function by the name foo. (That is, foo points to the area on the stack where the value of bar was copied.) bar points to some other area in memory. No matter what you do to foo, it will never affect bar, because foo points to one area in memory and bar points to another.

When you define variables within a function, they are also pushed onto the stack. So if you have a variable named baz that's defined within a function, an area on the stack is set aside and baz points to that area on the stack. That's why if there's another baz someplace, the compiler knows that the two are different. The local baz points to a particular spot on the stack, and the other baz points someplace else.

When the function finishes running, all the items it pushed onto the stack are popped off the stack. So all the local variables go away.

You can see that passing in big structures can involve a lot of copying to the stack. If you pass an item by reference, a pointer to that item (instead of a copy of that item) is put on the stack. That's because pushing a pointer takes far less time (and is an example of why using reference arguments can be far more efficient in some cases).

If you push a pointer, it also means that you can change the values of things outside of scope. Why? Well, you can't change the value of the pointer itself, but the pointer points to memory in different scope. (It could point to another part of the stack or to free-store memory.) When you dereference the pointer, you can change things in that other area of memory.

By the way, stacks are used throughout all types of applications. In fact, stacks are how your calculator works. As you type in numbers, they are pushed onto a number stack (which is officially called the operand stack). The operators are pushed onto an operator stack. When enough numbers are in the operand stack, the operator and numbers are popped, the result is computed, and the result is pushed onto the number stack so it can be used by the next operator. Or at least that's how they work in theory.

Part III
Object-Oriented Stuff

The 5th Wave   By Rich Tennant

...AND THESE ARE OUR OBJECT-ORIENTED PROGRAMMING SPECIALISTS.

In This Part

By this point, you've read all about the fundamental elements of programming. In fact, you should be able to read, if not write, some pretty decent programs.

The chapters in Part III discuss the object-oriented specifics of C++. Here you'll learn how to encapsulate things into classes, perform inheritance, and so on. This will help you write programs that are easier to understand, test, and expand.

And let's not forget your favorite pizza program from Part II — we'll transform it into an object-oriented program in this part. By the time you're finished with it, you'll be able to read toppings from a data file, easily write out information about pizza, order regular *and* diet toppings, and protect yourself from nasty user mistakes. Will adding all of this amazing functionality be super hard? Of course not — you'll be using lots of cool object-oriented techniques to leverage your existing work.

If you skipped Part II, here's a quick review of programming fundamentals:

- ✔ Pizza is good. Especially for breakfast.

- ✔ Sugar is good. Especially for dinner.

- ✔ Science fiction is good.

- ✔ Loud music is good.

- ✔ Good music is loud.

So grab your pocket protector, grab a handful of crunchy sugar bombs and a can of Jolt, and jump right in.

Chapter 27
A Touch of Class

*T*here's some good news and some not-so-good news. The good news is that the overall concepts presented in this chapter are easy: you'll be able to create classes in no time. The not-so-good news is that figuring out how to create really well-designed classes can take a long time. That's why most people end up redesigning their first object-oriented programs several times.

If you decided to skip Part II and begin with this chapter, you might actually want to back up a minute and read Chapter 13 first. That's because Chapter 13 describes some of the fundamental reasons for using object-oriented programming, and discusses the basic concepts of object-oriented programming. I'm not going to repeat that stuff here. At least not too much.

Classes are the fundamental organizing unit of object-oriented programming (which is often called OOP for short). A class is a structure that contains some data and some routines to process that data. When people talk about designing objects, they're talking about designing classes. Classes help you model the way real-life things behave. They make it easier for you to test complex programs. And they provide the backbone for inheritance, which helps you reuse code (and reusing code is very cool).

Because the data and the functions are in one spot in a class, it's easy to figure out how to use a particular object. You don't have to worry about what library to look in to determine how to move a picture on the screen, or how to find an employee's home phone number. It's all contained in the object. In fact, the object should contain all routines needed to interact with it.

Not only that, but the only way to change the behavior or data of a class is through the items in the class itself. This avoids confusing situations where a global variable magically changes a whole program. It also means that you can create variables that are read-only to the outside world. This is useful because you can protect data from being inadvertently cleared or altered by someone who doesn't know what they're doing.

Also, because each item is self contained, there's less reliance on global values, and it's easier to create multiple items of each class. Each class contains all the information it needs to do any processing required for that object.

Finally, a well-designed class hides the complexity of underlying structures from the user. The user of the class doesn't need to know what types of data structures or algorithms make the class work. There should just be some high-level calls that manipulate the object.

Welcome to Classroom 101

Surprise! You've already created lots of classes. That's because creating a class is basically the same as creating a structure (which you've already done a number of times). In fact, the only difference between a class and a structure is that you can add functions to classes.

In this section you'll learn everything you need to know about putting together classes. You'll learn about class data members and member functions, how to declare a class, and also how to restrict access to portions of a class by using the *private* keyword. You'll also learn how to define member functions.

Data members

The official name for variables that are part of a class is *data members*. When you analyze a real-world problem and come up with descriptions of an object, the descriptive items turn into data members. For example, color, size, cost, shape, weight, name, and so on are all things that describe an object. They're all things you would save in variables and are what you would use for data members in a class.

Member functions

Member functions are functions that are stored in and used for manipulating a class. When you analyze a real-world problem and come up with actions to manipulate an object, these actions will turn into member functions.

For example, setting the color, computing the size, adding together the parts to find the total cost, and printing are all things that act or control an object. These are activities you would write functions for. These are the things you use for member functions.

Declaring a class

You use the *class* keyword to declare a class, as shown here:

```
class ClassName {
public:
    public data members and member functions listed here
};
```

For example — returning once again to our old favorite, the pizza program — suppose you wanted to make a ToppingList object. You could start with the topping list structure that you've already got, and add a function to add new topping items:

```
class ToppingList {
public:
    int    Topping;
    ToppingList    *Next;
    void Add();
};
```

You would then define what the member function Add does, and use it to add new items to the list of toppings.

Restricting access

Notice that, as the ToppingList class stands now, if someone were to accidentally mess up the Next pointer, bad things could happen.

You can prevent inadvertent access to data members by making them private. Private data members are accessible only from member functions that are part of the class.

In other words, if Next is private, the Add member function could change the value of Next, because Add is a member function of the ToppingList class. But some other class that happened to have a ToppingList in it couldn't change Next directly. Only member functions of ToppingList have that right.

Making a data member private is easy. After you've listed the public data members and member functions, type the keyword *private* followed by a colon. Then list the private data members. (You can have private member functions too.

Private member functions are only callable by member functions in the class. Thus, they are helper functions that are useful for making the public member functions work. But, they aren't so important that they need to be exposed to the outside world via the public interface.)

Let's make Next a private variable. We'll also add a new public member function called GetNext that gets the value of Next. In this way, Next becomes a read-only variable. You can read it from outside the class via GetNext, but you can't directly change the value of Next from outside the class:

```
class ToppingList {
public:
    int    Topping;
    void Add();
    //Use this function to find the next item.
    ToppingList    *GetNext();
private:
    ToppingList    *Next;
};
```

Protected access

So far you've learned two keywords for controlling access rights: public and private. *public* data members and member functions are accessible from outside the class. They provide the public interface to the class. These are the data members and member functions you learn when you want to know how to manipulate a class.

private data members and member functions are for internal use by the class. Only member functions of the class can use these. Private member functions can't be called from outside the class. Private data members can't be read or changed from outside the class. By creating private data members and member functions, you can have a fairly complex class with a very simple public interface — all the internal complexities are shielded from the user of the class because the internal items are private.

There is one more access keyword called *protected*. Protected items in a class can be used only by member functions in that class, or by member functions of classes derived from that class. (You'll learn about derivation in Chapter 30.)

How to make a read-only variable

To make a read-only variable (as just seen with Next in the previous sections), you make the data member private and create a public member function that returns the value of the variable. Don't make a public member function for setting the value of the variable. That way, anyone who uses the class can see what's in the value but will be unable to change it.

Defining member functions

After you've declared what goes in a class, you need to define what the member functions do. Defining member functions is almost the same as defining functions (which you've done in earlier chapters). But because member functions are part of a particular class, you need to specify the name of the class as well as the name of the function. (After all, several different classes could all have a GetPrice function.)

To define a member function, list the class name, followed by :: (this is two colons), followed by the member function name. The official name for the two colons is the *scope resolution operator.* (Now try saying that quickly 100 times.) The scope resolution operator indicates that a particular member function (or data member) is part of a particular class. For example, ToppingList::GetNext( ) refers to the GetNext member function of the ToppingList class, and ToppingList::Next means the Next data member of the ToppingList class.

The following example defines the GetNext member function for the ToppingList class. This function returns the Next pointer for that particular ToppingList item:

```
//Define what happens when NextItem() is called.
//It returns a ToppingList *.
ToppingList *
ToppingList::GetNext() {
    return Next;
}
```

Note that you don't need to say return ToppingList::Next. Within a member function, you don't need to put :: before any of the data member names. The items in class scope are automatically used. Also note that because GetNext is a member function of the ToppingList class it can access the private data members such as Next.

Now How Do I Put These Classes to Use?

Once you've declared a class and defined its functions, you can use the class in your program. Just as with structures, you can create classes either statically or dynamically:

```
//Create a class statically.
ToppingList      foo;

//Create a class dynamically.
ToppingList      *bar;
bar = new ToppingList;
```

The same rules and concepts that apply to static and dynamic variables apply to static and dynamic classes. Creating a class is called creating an *instance* or *instantiating* a class.

Accessing class members

Classes are just like any other data structure. If you want to refer to a data member, just use a . (a period). Note that you can do the same thing to refer to a member function of a class:

```
//Create a ToppingList class.
ToppingList      foo;
ToppingList      *NextOne;

//Find the next item in the ToppingList.
NextOne = foo.GetNext;
```

If you have a pointer to a class, use pointer notation instead:

```
ToppingList      *bar;
ToppingList      *NextOne;

//Create a ToppingList class dynamically.
bar = new ToppingList;

//Find the next item in the ToppingList.
NextOne =  bar->GetNext();
```

Just like variables, classes have *names* (when they are instantiated) and *types*.

At first, beginning programmers often confuse the variable names and class names. If you want to access the GetName member function of object foo which is a ToppingList class, you do this:

```
foo.GetName()
```

not this:

```
ToppingList.GetName()
```

In other words, remember to use the variable name, not the class name. ∎

Accessing members from member functions

When you're in a member function, you don't need to use a . or a -> to access other class member functions or data members. You're in *class scope*, so it's assumed that if you use the name x and x is a member of the class, then that's the x you want to use.

Heading off troubles by using header files

If you have a program that spans more than one source file — such as the program in Chapter 33 — then you should put class declarations in header files. When you need to use a particular class in a source file, *#include* the header file that declares the class.

If you add or remove data members or member functions from a class, always make sure you remember to update the header file. If you forget, you'll get a message like "foo(int *, int *) is not a member of baz". This translates to "Hey, you forgot to update the header file to put the foo member function in class baz." Or "Hey, you typed in some parameters wrong, so what you listed in the class definition isn't what you used when you implemented the thing."

Some Classy Advice on Making Classy Designs

When you create an object-oriented program, you need to think about what's going on in the program. Strive to create objects that model what's being manipulated. (For example, if your object-oriented program takes pizza orders, you might want to create an object that represents a pizza and an object that represents a topping.)

The basic way to design a class is to:

1. Analyze your problem.

2. Look at the data you're manipulating. What is the data? How are you manipulating it?

3. Group data and functions together to define elemental objects.

4. Hide the way things work. Provide high-level functions for manipulating the object, so the user doesn't need to know that names are stored in arrays or that toppings are kept in a linked list. Keep the details and helper functions and details as private data members and member functions.

Object-Oriented Thinking about Pizza

Let's see how you can apply class-design concepts to our pizza program. From a high-level perspective, the pizza program asks the user for the pizza's size and for the type of desired toppings, and then prints this information.

Thus, you'll probably want a pizza object that contains three member functions: one to choose the size, one to choose the toppings, and one to print the order. You might start with a class declaration such as this:

```
class Pizza {
public:
    void ChooseSize();
    void ChooseToppings();
    void PrintOrder();
};
```

Note how similar these member functions are to the functions used in the pizza program in Chapter 25.

As you implement these member functions, you might find that you need to maintain private data members and member functions to store information and to help the user make choices. For example, you might end up with data members for storing information about the size, cost, and toppings:

```
class Pizza {
public:
    void ChooseSize();
    void ChooseToppings();
    void PrintOrder();
private:
    ToppingList *Toppings;
    int Size;
    float Cost;
};
```

In the pizza program in Chapter 25, you kept a list of pizza toppings with the ToppingList structure. The most important things you did with this list were to add new items to the list and to traverse the list. Thus, you might create a ToppingList class that looks something like this:

```
class ToppingList {
public:
    void AddFirst();
    ToppingList *GetNext();
private:
    int    Topping;
    ToppingList *Next;
};
```

The AddFirst and GetNext member functions would contain code for manipulating the list. You used a linked list to store the toppings in Chapter 25. You can just as easily have a linked list of ToppingList objects in your object-oriented pizza program. (In fact, that's what you'll do in Chapter 29.)

Note that the Next data member is a private variable. Any routines that do the dirty work for ToppingList, such as looking up names from arrays or updating pointers in the linked list, would be private items and thus hidden. The person manipulating the ToppingList need not know how any of the information is stored or retrieved.

So far, you've defined two classes for use by the pizza program: Pizza and ToppingList. Pizza is the highest level object. It models the high-level concepts of choosing the size and toppings for a pizza, and printing the order. The other class, ToppingList, models the concept of maintaining a list of toppings.

In Chapter 29 you'll create a full object-oriented version of the pizza program. As you look over that program, be sure to think about the way it was broken into classes.

Let's Review, Class

Here are some things to consider when you start designing classes:

- Look at how other people have designed classes. Examine lots of sample programs.

- Start small.

- Think about how you can reuse your class in other parts of your program and/or in future programs. Sometimes the fewer items that are in a class, the more reusable it will be. You might want to look at the *least common denominator* of characteristics to use for a base class. Remember that, with inheritance, you can build significantly upon an existing framework.

- Are there items in your application that act as stand-alone entities? In other words, if you weren't using OOP, are there certain pieces of data that have a lot of routines for processing them? This could be a good place to try to create a class. For example, suppose you have a structure for containing information about an employee, and various routines that compute the employee's weekly paycheck, update the employee's available vacation time, and so forth. You might combine these into an employee class.

- Once you create an object, all routines for manipulating that object should be member functions. Everything in the object should be self-contained. The object should know everything it needs to know about itself.

- If your object uses global variables, and you keep a pointer to the global inside the object, the object will be more self-contained.

- Determine if your program has certain fundamental things that are repeated over and over with only slightly different variations. If it does, make a generic class that represents this. For example, the pizza program uses arrays to provide lists of choices. You could make a class to represent choices instead, thus hiding the details of using the arrays. Not only would all functions needed to make or print results of choices be in that class, but the same class could be used for choosing the size of the pizza. The linked list is another prime candidate for turning into a class.

✔ Decide whether the users need to understand the internal structure of an object in order to use it. The object will be better designed if the user doesn't need to know anything about the internals. For example, suppose you keep an array of prices inside a choice object. The user should be able to find the price for a particular choice without having to know that there's an internal price array. A member function should take the choice and return the price. This practice makes the interface much easier for others to learn and master.

✔ Remember that it's okay to be confused at first.

✔ Don't be afraid to scrap everything and start fresh; everyone does. It's all just part of the learning process.

Chapter 28

Constructors and Destructors

●●●

In This Chapter

▶ Understand the basics about constructors and destructors

▶ Learn how to create multiple constructors

▶ Pick up some tips for reading object-oriented programs

●●●

*I*t's fun to have people over for dinner, but preparing for it and cleaning up afterward (*especially* the cleaning up afterward part) can sometimes be a real drag. Programming is much the same way: it's lots of fun to design great programs, but the related preparation and cleanup work can seem rather ho-hum in comparison.

But don't let yourself get fooled — preparation and cleanup are very important programming tasks. For example, if you forget to initialize a variable (which is a type of "preparation" task), you might discover to your chagrin that your screen always turns blue or that your program crashes because a pointer is bad. Similarly, if you forget to clean up your program by freeing memory you used, you might discover that although your program ran great the first three times, it now says there's no more memory.

Fortunately (you knew this had to get better, right?), C++ has two built-in features — constructors and destructors — that help you remember to initialize variables and clean up what you've created. *Constructors* are routines that are automatically called when you create an object (instantiate a class). You can put initialization routines inside constructors to guarantee that things are properly set up when you want to start using an object. You can even have multiple constructors, so that you can initialize objects in different ways.

When you're finished with an object — that is, when the function that created it finishes or when you use *delete* — a function called the *destructor* is automatically called. That's where you put all the clean-up code.

To avoid hordes of annoying problems from cropping up in your programs, use constructors and destructors. You'll be glad you did.

A Constructor a Day Keeps the Troubles Away

Constructors are functions that are called every time an object is created. If any of the data members in the object need initializing when the object is created, put that code inside the constructor.

Constructors have the same name as the class name. So the constructor for Pizza is named Pizza::Pizza. The constructor for Bam is Bam::Bam.

Constructors can never return values.

Well, it's that time again. Let's see how you might use constructors with the pizza program. Suppose you define a class for storing information about a pizza, much as you did in the previous chapter. This class will contain information about the size, cost, and toppings on a pizza:

```
class Pizza {
public:
    ToppingList    *Toppings;
    int Size;
    float Cost;
};
```

Now, let's add a constructor that initializes values when the object is created. To do that, add the constructor to the class declaration:

```
class Pizza {
public:
    Pizza();
    ToppingList    *Toppings;
    int Size;
    float Cost;
};
```

Now put in the constructor code:

```
Pizza::Pizza() {
    //Initialize the cost.
    Cost = 0;
    //Make the topping list a null pointer.
    Toppings = 0;
}
```

This code initializes the variables used in the Pizza class.

You need to add the constructor to the list of member functions in the class definition. Constructors can be public, private, or protected. ∎

Increasing flexibility with multiple constructors

Sometimes you might want more control over how an object is created. For example, you might want to be able to pass in the size of the pizza when you create a pizza object. That way you can just say "give me a large" every time you create the object. You can do this by using *multiple constructors*.

You can have as many constructors as you want. Each different constructor, though, needs to take a different set of parameters. (That is, one constructor could take one integer, another could take two integers, a third could take one float, and so on.)

You can pass in parameters when you create the object. The appropriate constructor will be called with the parameters.

For example, you could do this:

```
//Creates a pizza object statically, passing in the
//parameter Large.
Pizza MyPizza(Large);

//Creates an employee record dynamically, passing in
//a name and state.
foo = new EmployeeRecord("Elvis, Young", "Tennessee");
```

In the first case, the compiler will look for the constructor that takes a single integer argument as a parameter, and call it. In the second case, the compiler will look for a constructor that takes two char * arguments, and call that.

You create constructors that take arguments the same way you create regular plain-vanilla constructors. Use the name of the class, and list the arguments you want:

```
//Now we'll add another constructor to the
//list of member functions.
class Pizza {
public:
    Pizza();
    Pizza(int MySize);
    ToppingList   *Toppings;
    int Size;
    float Cost;
};

//If a size is passed in, we'll use it to initialize
//the Size value.
Pizza::Pizza(int MySize) {
    Size = MySize;
    ToppingList = 0;
}
```

Each constructor needs a unique signature

You can have as many constructors as you want, but each must have a unique set of data types as arguments. That is, each must have a unique *signature*.

For example, even though the following two constructors might do different things and have arguments with different names, their data types are the same. This will result in a syntax error:

```
Window::Window(int Left, int Right) {
}

Window::Window(int Width, int Color) {
}
```

Using multiple constructors with lists

One good use for multiple constructors is to create public and private constructors. The public constructor is used when new objects are created by the outside world. The private constructors are used internally as helper functions.

For example, if you're constructing a linked list of objects, you might use a private constructor to add a new item to the linked list. (The constructor would be private in this situation because it's being called only by a list member function.)

Tearing It Down with Destructors

The destructor is a member function that is automatically called whenever an object is destroyed. Objects are destroyed for various reasons. For example, a local object might be destroyed when a particular function finishes. Or an object created with *new* might have gotten *delete*d. Or perhaps the program finished and all static objects were therefore deleted.

The destructor is called automatically by the compiler. You never call it yourself, and you can't pass parameters to it.

The destructor has the same name as the class, but with a ~ (tilde) before it. You can only have one destructor per class, and it must be public.

The destructor is the ideal place to do general clean-up work, such as freeing up memory the class allocated with *new*, saving things to files if necessary, and closing file handles.

Here's a quick example:

```
class Pizza {
public:
    Pizza();
    Pizza(int MySize);
    ~Pizza();
    ToppingList   *Toppings;
    int Size;
    float Cost;
};

//Clean up the list of toppings when the Pizza class
//is destroyed.
Pizza::~Pizza() {
    //Note that when Toppings is deleted, the destructor
    //for the ToppingList class will be called, and
    //we can do more clean-up there.
    if (Toppings)
        delete Toppings;
};
```

Cleaning up your own mess

Because each class has a destructor, each class is responsible for cleaning up after itself. Therefore, you write clean-up code on a class by class basis instead of having to write all the clean-up code at once.

For example, when the pizza program is finished, the Pizza class variable is destroyed. The Pizza destructor only needs to do whatever is necessary to clean up a Pizza class. If the Pizza class has dynamically created other classes, the Pizza class destructor needs to delete those other classes. But the Pizza destructor *doesn't* need to know all the details about how to clean up whatever those other classes have done. That's because the destructors for those classes are called automatically.

Continuing with this example, the Pizza destructor deletes a ToppingList. This causes the ToppingList destructor to be called. The Pizza class doesn't need to know how to clean up a ToppingList — it just needs to delete it. The ToppingList destructor contains the code for cleaning up anything the ToppingList might need to clean up.

Because of how destructors work, you can write the little bits of clean-up code one piece at a time as you design new objects. You don't have to wait until the end of your application and then try to figure out everything in the world that might have been created and how you can possibly clean everything up.

This is similar to the idea that if you just clean and put something away after you use it, you'll never have a desk/room/car piled with papers, half-read books, and soda cans. Only it's easier to put into practice with C++.

Remember to clean the dynamic stuff, too

If you've created a class or a variable dynamically — that is, if you've created it with *new* — you must remember to *delete* it when you're finished using it. Suppose, for example, that you have a class representing photographs, and that when you created the class you used *new* to allocate memory to store the photographs. You'll need to use *delete* to free up this memory, or it'll just hang around. (Of course, the pointer will be gone so the memory will be orphaned, though.)

Or, suppose you have a class that contains a list of pizza toppings. (What a concept, eh?) When you destroy the class, you also need to destroy the linked list so you can free up the memory that it consumes, and also make sure that the appropriate linked-list destructors are called.

The easiest way to do this is to have the destructor of the linked-list class know to destroy the next object in the list. That way, as soon as you *delete* the first item in the list, the rest of the items in the list will also be destroyed. This is a very easy and convenient way to start a domino chain of destruction. If you pronounce that with a deep, serious voice you can even use it as a movie title.

What Happens If I Have a Class in a Class?

As you spend more and more time programming, you'll undoubtedly find yourself creating lots of classes that contain other classes. For example, you might create a class called PizzaIngredients that describes pizza ingredients; this class in turn might contain a Crust class.

The first thing that happens when a class is created is that memory is allocated for all its data members. If the class contains data members that are classes (such as a data member that's a Crust class), the constructors for these data members are called.

Thus, if a class contains classes within it, the constructors for these classes are called first. That's because they need to be created before the class containing them can be created.

When a class is destroyed, its destructor is called. Then the destructors are called for any data members that are classes. For example, when a PizzaIngredients class is destroyed, its destructor is called. Then the Crust destructor is called.

This concept is probably best illustrated with a simple program, like the one that follows this paragraph. (You can type-in and run this program, if you like.)

In this program, the class foo contains another class named bar. When you run this program you'll see that first bar's constructor is called and then foo's constructor is called. And when the program ends, first foo's destructor is called and then bar's destructor is called:

```
//Shows the order of constructor and destructor
//calls.
#include <iostream.h>

//A simple class with a constructor and destructor.
class bar {
public:
    bar();
    ~bar();
};

//Let the world know when bar is created.
bar::bar() {
    cout << "bar created\n";
}

//Let the world know when bar is destroyed.
bar::~bar() {
    cout << "bar destroyed\n";
}

//Foo is a class that contains another class,
//in this case bar. Because it contains another
//class, creating and destroying foo shows
//the order of constructor and destructor calls.
class foo {
public:
    bar    temp;
    foo();
    ~foo();
};

//Let the world know that a foo is born.
foo::foo() {
    cout << "foo created\n";
}

//Let the world know foo has been destroyed.
foo::~foo() {
    cout << "foo destroyed\n";
}

//This is the main function. It simply creates an object
//of type foo. When Temp is created, the constructors
//are automatically called. When the program finishes,
//Temp is automatically destroyed so you can see
//the order of destructor calls.
void main() {
    foo    Temp;
}
```

(This program is in the CTRDTR directory on the separately available program disk.)

How to Read Object-Oriented Programs

You've seen that object-oriented programs contain lots of classes. Each class has a declaration that tells what's in it, followed by a definition for each of its member functions. The class declaration is usually pretty concise, but the member functions can be spread out over a file. Because you need to read the code in the member functions to understand exactly what they do, figuring out what a class does can mean looking back and forth over a file.

Here are some tips that can help you figure out what your classes do:

- If the file has a main in it, skip to it to see what it does. Work backwards from the highest level classes and routines to the ones with the most details.

- If the file contains a number of classes, look at the class declarations first. Read any comments the programmer has kindly provided to get an idea of what the class does. Then quickly glance at what its various public member functions and data members do.

- Make sure you take a quick look at the various types of constructors provided. It's likely that you'll see them used in the program.

- Ignore the private and protected member functions and data members until later.

- You might need to look at a header file to find the class declaration. Look at the beginning of the source file to determine if the source file includes any header files. (Look for statements that begin with *#include*.) The class declarations could be inside one of those header files.

- Usually the highest level classes are declared last, so it's often a good idea to read through the code backwards. Start with the main. Go up to find the first class declaration. (Skip over its member functions to get to the declaration.) See what that does. Then skip up again to find the next class declaration.

Chapter 29
Pizza++

· ·

In This Chapter

▶ Redesign the pizza program so it's object oriented

▶ Add classes to the pizza program

▶ Add constructors and destructors to the pizza program

· ·

*I*t's time once again to revisit our old favorite, the pizza program. This time, you'll make it object oriented. You'll add all types of object-oriented features, and — just for fun — you'll make a couple of other enhancements, too.

It requires one major change to make our program object oriented — you have to combine the data and functions into objects. Any functions used to process an object will be part of that object. (So there won't be any miscellaneous helper routines lying around.)

You'll also have to make a few minor changes to the functions. The new program will feature new objects, with public interfaces and with private helper data members and member functions.

After you make these changes, the program will be longer than it was before. But the number of items users will need to understand will be much smaller, because they'll only need to understand the public interfaces of the classes.

The Classes in Pizza

The key to understanding an object-oriented program is to understand the objects inside it and their relationships to each other.

As shown in Figure 29-1, there are three main classes in the pizza program: Pizza, ToppingList, and Choice. The primary class — and in fact practically the only class used in main( ) — is Pizza, which represents the concept of a pizza. Pizza contains the ToppingList class, which in turn contains the Choice class.

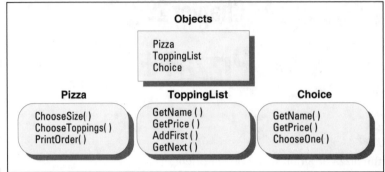

Figure 29-1:
The pizza
program
contains
three main
classes.

In addition to its constructor and destructor, the Pizza class contains three public member functions: ChooseSize( ), ChooseToppings( ), and PrintOrder( ). (I'll bet you can guess what they do!) Since these three member functions are the only public functions, you know that they are the only routines you can use to manipulate the Pizza class.

```
class Pizza {
public:
    Pizza(Choice *PizzaChoices, Choice *TopChoices);
    ~Pizza();
    void ChooseSize();
    void ChooseToppings();
    void PrintOrder();
private:
    ToppingList *Toppings;
    Choice      *PizzaSizes;
    Choice      *ToppingChoices;
    int Size;
    float Cost;
};
```

Not bad so far. If you know how to read an object-oriented program, you can find good information like this quickly.

The big class that pizza uses is ToppingList. How do I know that?

- ✔ I wrote the program, so I better know it.
- ✔ Looking at the comments, I can see that ToppingList is the main class Pizza uses.
- ✔ Looking at the class declaration for Pizza, I can see that ToppingList is used heavily.

Reading the comments about a class is a good way to figure out what's going on. When you write classes, do your fellow programming buddies a favor and include plenty of comments.

ToppingList is used to represent the concept of a topping. In addition to a constructor and destructor, it has four public functions:

✔ GetName( ) returns the name of the topping.

✔ GetPrice( ) returns the price.

✔ AddFirst( ) sets the topping choice for the first item in the list, and then checks to see if more items should be added to the list. If so, it calls the private Add( ) member function.

✔ GetNext( ) returns a pointer to the next topping in the list. Any details about how the list is maintained are hidden. You don't even need to know that a linked list is being used. You just need to know you can get a pointer to the next item in the ToppingList by calling GetNext( ).

```
class ToppingList {
public:
    char *GetName();
    float GetPrice();
    void AddFirst();
    ToppingList *GetNext();
    ToppingList(int Num, Choice *ChoiceList);
    ~ToppingList();
private:
    int    Topping;
    ToppingList    *Next;
    Choice        *ToppingChoices;
    void Add();
};
```

ToppingList also contains a class called Choice. The Choice class is used throughout the program to represent choices of pizza sizes and choices of pizza toppings. Because the Choice class, like all classes, is self contained, the ToppingList class doesn't need to understand how to print information in a Choice class or what the underlying structures in Choice are. It just needs to know the public member functions of Choice. (This makes it a lot easier to program, because the program is built by creating small functional pieces and then combining them.)

Choice is an object that represents the concept of making a choice from a list of options. In addition to the constructor, it contains three public functions:

✔ GetName( ) returns the name of a given choice number.

✔ GetPrice( ) returns the price of a given choice number.

✔ ChooseOne( ) prompts the user to make a selection from the list of choices the object contains.

```
class Choice {
public:
    Choice(const int Num, ChoiceDescription const
```

(continued)

```
    *InitList);
    char  *GetName(int Num);
    float GetPrice(int Num);
    int   ChooseOne();
private:
    int    NumChoices;
    int    GoodChoice(int Num);
    ChoiceDescription    const *List;
};
```

ChoiceDescription is a simple class structure that contains the name and price of an item. It represents a generic choice that can be used to describe anything:

```
class ChoiceDescription {
public:
    //Stores the name of the item.
    char  *ChoiceName;
    //Stores the price of the item.
    float ChoicePrice;
};
```

The ChoiceDescription class is used to create lists of pizza sizes and toppings. Unlike the previous version, the price and name are now combined into a single structure:

```
const ChoiceDescription const Sizes[NumSizes] =
    {{"Small", 10}, {"Medium", 12},{"Large", 14}};
```

So, What Else Is Going On?

To figure out how the program operates, you need to see what the various member functions do. Some of the member functions perform the same role as functions in the previous versions of the pizza program. For example, the new Pizza::ChooseToppings is very similar to the old GetToppingList.

Also, there are now many helper functions. In the previous version of the pizza program, there was a function called GetToppingType that prompted the user to select a topping. In this new version, the idea of selecting a choice is encapsulated in a class called Choice. Choice has a member function ChooseOne that's used to make a selection. Because ChooseOne isn't specific to toppings, it can be used to select any type of thing.

```
int
Choice::ChooseOne() {
    int   i;
    int   Select;

    //Keep asking the users until they pick a good
    //number.
    do {
        cout << "Please make a choice:\n";
```

```
        //Loop through and print all choices.
        for (i = 0; i < NumChoices; i++) {
            cout << i << " = " << List[i].ChoiceName <<
                "\n";
        }

        //Get the selection.
        cin >> Select;
    } while (!GoodChoice(Select));

    //Return the choice.
    return Select;
}
```

Other member functions are used for data hiding. For example, instead of directly accessing an array to determine the price for a pizza topping, you can use the GetPrice member function of the Choice class:

```
//Returns the price for a particular choice.
float
Choice::GetPrice(int Num) {
    return List[Num].ChoicePrice;
}
```

Routines such as this have three advantages. First, you can't inadvertently change the prices because the data is essentially read only. Second, you don't need to understand how the data is stored. If at a later time you want to change the way prices are stored, you can do so without having to change anything outside the Choice class. And third, this strategy makes it a lot easier to read programs, because calling GetPrice makes more sense than reading through data structure code.

Several classes have constructors and destructors:

```
Pizza::~Pizza() {
    if (Toppings)
        delete Toppings;
}
```

How the Linked List Works

As with the previous pizza program, this new pizza program contains a linked list. But adding items to the linked list is done a little differently now. This time, when the Pizza::ChooseToppings routine is called, it asks if the user wants to add toppings:

```
cout << "Do you want to add toppings? (0=No)\n";
cin >> Select;
```

If the user does want to add toppings, a new ToppingList item is created, and the AddFirst member function is called to initialize the first topping:

```
//If yes, start the list.
if (Select) {
    Toppings = new ToppingList(0, ToppingChoices);
    //Find the value
    Toppings->AddFirst();
}
```

Looking at the ToppingList::AddFirst code, you can see that it sets the values for the first item in the list, and then checks to see if additional items should be added. If so, the ToppingList::Add member function is called:

```
if (Select)
    Add();
```

The ToppingList::Add routine creates a new item and attaches it to the linked list:

```
//Now make a new class.
NewOne = new ToppingList(Select, ToppingChoices);

//And now we will hook it up to this item.
Next = NewOne;
```

Then the users are asked if they want to add another topping to the list:

```
//See if the user wants to add another.
cout << "Add another? (0=No)\n";
cin >> Select;
```

If an additional topping is desired, the Add( ) member function is called for the item that was just created:

```
//If the user wants to add another, call Add() for
//the new one.
if (Select)
    NewOne->Add();
```

The Overall Flow

This section briefly describes the overall flow of our new object-oriented pizza program.

First, the main routine creates Choice classes for pizza sizes and toppings:

```
Choice PizzaSizes(NumSizes, Sizes);
Choice Toppings(NumTops, Tops );
```

Then, a Pizza class is created to represent the pizza:

```
Pizza MyPizza(&PizzaSizes, &Toppings);
```

Pizza member functions are then called so the user can choose the size and toppings for the pizza:

```
//Now we will choose the size.
MyPizza.ChooseSize();

//Now we will choose the toppings.
MyPizza.ChooseToppings();
```

Once this is done, the order is printed:

```
//Now we will print the order.
MyPizza.PrintOrder();
```

To figure out what's happening with each of these steps, you need to examine the details of the Pizza member functions.

For example, when ChooseSize is called, it calls the ChooseOne member function from PizzaSizes. Looking at the class definition for Pizza, you can see that PizzaSizes is a Choice class.

Looking at the Choice class, you can see that ChooseOne lists the set of possible choices and asks the user to choose one.

When ChooseToppings is called it creates a new ToppingList and calls AddFirst. This prompts the user for the desired topping and then creates a linked list for any additional toppings the user might want.

It's Pizza! It's Object Oriented! It's the Pizza++ Code

As you read this code, look at main first. Then look at the definitions of the various objects to see what's created. After that (remembering that the highest level objects are created last) you might want to examine the program from the bottom up.

You might also want to compare this version of the program with the previous version (which is in Chapter 25) to track all the changes. You might even want to flip through all the versions of the pizza program just to see how far it's come from its simple beginnings.

```
//Object oriented version of the pizza program.
#include <iostream.h>
//- - Classes are defined here - - - - - - - - - - - -
//
//There are two main classes used:
//     ToppingList - a list of pizza toppings
//     Pizza - info describing the pizza
//We also have helper classes:
//     Choice - used to represent choices that can
//        be made by the user
//     ChoiceDescription - a structure containing a
//        choice name and price


//- - ChoiceDescription - - - - - - - - - - - - - - - -
//We'll use a class to represent the name
//and price of a particular choice. We can then
//use this class for topping and pizza size
//choices.

class ChoiceDescription {
public:
    char  *ChoiceName;
    float ChoicePrice;
};


//- - Choice - - - - - - - - - - - - - - - - - - - - -
//The Choice class contains a list of choices as
//well as functions for returning the name or price
//of a choice and functions for asking the user to
//make a choice. This is a simple generic class that
//can be used throughout to represent different types
//of choice lists.
//
//Choice has the following public interfaces:
//     Choice(int Num, ChoiceDescription *InitList) -
//        initializes the structure with a number of
//        choices
//     GetName(int Num) - returns the name for choice
//        Num
//     GetPrice(int Num) - returns the price for choice
//        Num
//     ChooseOne() - prompts the user to choose one of
//        the items from the set of choices


class Choice {
public:
    Choice(const int Num, ChoiceDescription const
        *InitList);
    char  *GetName(int Num);
    float GetPrice(int Num);
    int   ChooseOne();
private:
    int   NumChoices;
    int   GoodChoice(int Num);
```

```
    ChoiceDescription        const *List;
};

//- - Definitions for Choice member functions - - - - -

//The constructor initializes the class.
Choice::Choice(const int Num, const ChoiceDescription
    *InitList) {
    NumChoices = Num;
    List = InitList;
}

//Returns the name for a particular choice.
char *
Choice::GetName(int Num) {
    return List[Num].ChoiceName;
}

//Returns the price for a particular choice.
float
Choice::GetPrice(int Num) {
    return List[Num].ChoicePrice;
}

//Prompts the user to make a choice from the set
//of options. Prints out what the available choices
//are and makes sure the choice is valid.
int
Choice::ChooseOne() {
    int    i;
    int    Select;

    //Keep asking the user until a good number
    //is picked.
    do {
        cout << "Please make a choice:\n";

        //Loop through and print all choices.
        for (i = 0; i < NumChoices; i++) {
            cout << i << " = " << List[i].ChoiceName <<
                "\n";
        }

        //Get the selection.
        cin >> Select;
    } while (!GoodChoice(Select));

    //Return the choice.
    return Select;
}

//This is a helping function that makes sure
//that a particular choice is valid.
int
Choice::GoodChoice(int Num) {
```

(continued)

```
      if ((Num < 0) || (Num >= NumChoices)) {
         //A bad choice so print a message and return false.
         cout << "I don't understand that choice.\n";
         return 0;
      }
      //Since we haven't returned, the choice is good.
      return 1;
   }

//- - Finished Choice member functions - - - - - - - - -

//- - ToppingList - - - - - - - - - - - - - - - - - -
//The ToppingList class is used to create a linked
//list of toppings contained in the pizza. We'll
//use information hiding so that the Next pointer
//can't be erased accidentally.
//
//Here is a class overview:
//ToppingList(int Num, Choice *ChoiceList) - initializes the
//    class, passing in a pointer to the types of
//    choices that can be used and the topping for the item
//~ToppingList() - frees up memory for the class
//AddFirst() - sets the values for the first element in the
//    list and potentially expands the list
//GetName() - returns the name of the topping
//GetPrice() - returns the price of the topping
//Add() - adds a new element to the list
//GetNext() - returns a pointer to the next item
//    in the list

class ToppingList {
public:
   char *GetName();
   float GetPrice();
   void AddFirst();
   ToppingList *GetNext();
   ToppingList(int Num, Choice *ChoiceList);
   ~ToppingList();
private:
   int    Topping;
   ToppingList *Next;
   Choice      *ToppingChoices;
   void Add();
};


//- - Definitions for ToppingList member functions - -

//Returns the name of the topping. Finds this by
//calling the GetName function of the Choice object.
char *
ToppingList::GetName() {
   return ToppingChoices->GetName(Topping);
}
```

```
//Returns the price of the topping. Finds this by
//calling the GetPrice function of the Choice object.
float
ToppingList::GetPrice() {
    return ToppingChoices->GetPrice(Topping);
}


//This function is used to set the topping for the first
//item in the list.
void
ToppingList::AddFirst() {
    int    Select;

    //First get the selection.
    Topping = ToppingChoices->ChooseOne();

    //See if the user wants to add another.
    cout << "Add another? (0=No)\n";
    cin >> Select;

    //If the user wants to add another, call Add() for
    //the new one.
    if (Select)
        Add();
}

//This function is used to add a new topping to the
//list. It does so by prompting the user for a new
//item from the list of choices, and then adds a new
//element to the list.
void
ToppingList::Add() {
    int    Select;
    ToppingList    *NewOne;

    //First get the selection.
    Select = ToppingChoices->ChooseOne();

    //Now make a new class.
    NewOne = new ToppingList(Select, ToppingChoices);

    //And now we will hook it up to this item.
    Next = NewOne;

    //See if the user wants to add another.
    cout << "Add another? (0=No)\n";
    cin >> Select;

    //If the user wants to add another, call Add() for
    //the new one.
    if (Select)
        NewOne->Add();
}
```

(continued)

```
//Returns a pointer to the next topping in the list.
ToppingList *
ToppingList::GetNext() {
    return Next;
}
//The constructor initializes the class.
ToppingList::ToppingList(int Num, Choice *ChoiceList) {
    Next = 0;
    Topping = Num;
    ToppingChoices = ChoiceList;
}

//This is the destructor. It deletes the next item
//in the list. This will cause all items to be deleted
//and the memory freed.
ToppingList::~ToppingList() {
    if (Next)
        delete Next;
}

//- - Finished ToppingList member functions - - - - - -


//- - Pizza Class - - - - - - - - - - - - - - - - - -
//The Pizza class is used to hold all information
//regarding the pizza. It contains a number of
//data members including a list of toppings.
//
//Here is a class overview:
//     Pizza(Choice *PizzaChoices, Choice *TopChoices) -
//         constructs the pizza class. It takes a
//         pointer to a list of possible sizes and
//         possible choices.
//     ~Pizza() - cleans up
//     ChooseSize() - asks the user for the pizza size
//     ChooseToppings() - asks the user to choose the
//         desired toppings
//     PrintOrder() - prints out the price of the
//         pizza

class Pizza {
public:
    Pizza(Choice *PizzaChoices, Choice *TopChoices);
    ~Pizza();
    void ChooseSize();
    void ChooseToppings();
    void PrintOrder();
private:
    ToppingList *Toppings;
    Choice  *PizzaSizes;
    Choice  *ToppingChoices;
    int Size;
    float Cost;
};
```

```
//- - Pizza member functions - - - - - - - - - - - - -

//Here is the constructor. It expects a pointer to
//a list of possible sizes and toppings.
Pizza::Pizza(Choice *PizzaChoices, Choice *TopChoices) {
    Size = 0;
    Cost = 0.0;
    Toppings = 0;
    PizzaSizes = PizzaChoices;
    ToppingChoices = TopChoices;
}

//Here is the destructor. It deletes the first item
//in the list of toppings. This will cause a chain
//reaction that will free up the whole topping list.
Pizza::~Pizza() {
    if (Toppings)
        delete Toppings;
}

//This asks the user to choose the desired pizza
//size. It uses some of the Choice member functions.
void
Pizza::ChooseSize() {
    Size = PizzaSizes->ChooseOne();
    //Set the initial price
    Cost = PizzaSizes->GetPrice(Size);
}

//This asks the user to select the desired toppings.
void
Pizza::ChooseToppings() {
    int    Select;

    cout << "Do you want to add toppings? (0=No)\n";
    cin >> Select;

    //If yes, start the list.
    if (Select) {
        Toppings = new ToppingList(0, ToppingChoices);
        //Find the value
        Toppings->AddFirst();
    }
}

//This prints out what was selected and the price.
void
Pizza::PrintOrder() {
    ToppingList *Cur = Toppings;

    //Print out the size of the pizza.
    cout << "That's a " << PizzaSizes->GetName(Size)
        << " pizza with ";
```

(continued)

```
      //Are there any toppings?
      if (!Cur)
         cout << "no toppings.\n";
      else {
         //There are toppings, so traverse the list
         //and sum the price.
         while (Cur) {
            //Find the price of the topping.
            Cost += Cur->GetPrice();
            //Print the topping type.
            cout << Cur->GetName();
            //Move on to the next one.
            Cur = Cur->GetNext();
            //If there is a next one, print "and".
            if (Cur)
               cout << " and ";
         } //end of while

         cout << " for toppings.\n";
      } //end of else

      //Print the total price.
      cout << "That will be $" << Cost << ".\n";

}

//- - Finished Pizza member functions- - - - - - - - -



//- - The main function begins here- - - - - - - - - -

//Note that the main function is a lot easier to
//read this time around. That's because all it does
//is create a pizza object and use some of the pizza
//functions.

void
main() {
   //We'll make two lists of choices, one for
   //pizza sizes and one for toppings.
   const int NumSizes = 3;
   const int NumTops = 5;
   ChoiceDescription const Sizes[NumSizes] =
      {{"Small", 10}, {"Medium", 12},{"Large", 14}};
   ChoiceDescription const Tops[NumTops] =
      {{"Pepperoni", 1.8}, {"Sausage", 2.1},
      {"Onions", 0.5}, {"Extra Cheese", 1.0},
      {"Olives", 0.7}};

   //Now we will create the choice objects for
   //toppings and for sizes and pass in the arrays.
   Choice PizzaSizes(NumSizes, Sizes);
   Choice Toppings(NumTops, Tops);

   //Now we will create a new pizza. We'll pass in
   //pointers to the two choices.
   Pizza MyPizza(&PizzaSizes, &Toppings);
```

```
//Now we will choose the size.
MyPizza.ChooseSize();

//Now we will choose the toppings.
MyPizza.ChooseToppings();

//Now we will print the order.
MyPizza.PrintOrder();
}
```

(This program is in the PIZZA7 directory on the separately available program disk.)

Chapter 30
Inheriting a Fortune

● ●

In This Chapter
▶ Learn what inheritance does
▶ Override inherited member functions
▶ Call base constructors

● ●

Conventional programming can waste a lot of time. You write a routine, but can't use it later because you need to make slight modifications. Or, you write a routine that works fine in some cases, but then find you need it to modify a few more things. So what do you do? You end up copying the code, pasting it somewhere else, customizing it, and giving the routine a new name. This is called *copy and paste* programming. In a way it lets you reuse code, but it has several problems. Not only do your programs get bigger from all that repeated code, but it's an easy way to reproduce bugs all over the place.

Object-oriented programming helps you avoid the cut and paste syndrome. You can just take an existing piece of code, inherit from it, and make any needed modifications. No cut and paste. Just reuse of things that work. This strategy is called *inheritance*.

Inheritance is very useful when you build objects. For example, you might write an object that represents a generic car. Then you could inherit from this to create a Chevy. Then you could inherit from that to make a Luxury Chevy. Then you could inherit from that to make the Crazy Eddie Year-End Blow-Out Luxury Chevy. (And anytime you ask the object for its price, it'll ask "What'll it take to make you drive home in this baby?") Each of these objects would inherit behavior from the previous object and would feature some modifications and added special touches.

Also, if you fix a bug in a base class, the fix automatically applies to all derived classes. So if you later discover that your original generic cars honk their horn each time the right turn-signal is used, and then you fix this problem, voila! Not only do all your original generic cars get fixed, but also all your Chevys, all your Luxury Chevys, and all your Crazy Eddie Year-End Blow-Out Luxury Chevys. (And that's a lot better than a product recall, wouldn't you say?)

Nothing Surpasses Reusable Classes

To get reusability, you need to *design* for reusability. As mentioned in an earlier chapter, this is a skill you'll develop over time. Here are some tips and suggestions to keep in mind when you're designing object-oriented programs:

✔ Determine if you can use variations of the object elsewhere. For example, if you have a basic employee information-and-processing object, you could use it as the "core" from which to create other objects. You could add salary information to create a new payroll object. Or you could add health information to create a new health object.

✔ Ask yourself if it really matters what the specific data is. For example, see if you have a fundamental concept (such as a list of choices) that you can generalize. You can always modify your inherited objects later to make them appropriate for specific needs.

✔ Think about your possible future needs. You might want to keep an old object around so you can inherit from it.

✔ Look at the work of other programmers. If you look at ObjectWindows, for example, you can see that it has the basic concept of a window. This then gets specialized into frame windows, control windows, and so on. These in turn get specialized further. You can learn a lot from studying the design strategies used in other programs.

✔ Remember that it takes a great deal of practice to become skilled at writing object-oriented programs. You'll probably write a program, then say "Gosh durn it all, if only I done this and this and this and this then I could have made a real nice object structure I could use inheritance with instead of having these 14 separate objects." That's okay. It's part of the learning process.

It's Time to Claim Your Inheritance

To inherit from an object, use : (pronounced as "is based on") when you declare the new object and list the thing from which you want to inherit:

```
class DerivedClass : public BaseClass {
};
```

Any member function of the base class is now a member function of the derived class. Any data member of the base class is now a data member of the derived class. You just don't have to type all of them in. If you want to add new items to the class, list them in the declaration. These will be the special things that differentiate your class from the base class.

For example, suppose you want to make the CrazyEddiePizza class. It is just like the other Pizza class, but it has a discount. You could do this:

```
class CrazyEddiePizza : public Pizza {
public:
    float discount;
};
```

This class will have all the capabilities of the other Pizza class. You can therefore use the CrazyEddiePizza class much like you would use the Pizza class. For example, here's how you would create the CrazyEddiePizza class and call the ChooseSize( ) member function:

```
CrazyEddiePizza  foo;
foo.ChooseSize( );
```

But now you have an extra data member that you can use, too. Now that wasn't hard, was it?

How Public, Private, and Protected Affect Things

Sooner or later this public vs. private vs. protected thing will bite you, so here are the rules:

- Public items from the base class are fully usable by the derived class and fully usable outside the base class.
- Private items from the base class are invisible to the derived class and invisible outside the base class.
- Protected items from the base class are fully usable by the derived class but are invisible outside the base class.

(Actually, since this *is* C++ you're learning, there are a few additional rules you should know. You can find them in the "Inheriting from Private Benjamin" section later in this chapter.)

Well, I Like It, but Do You Have It in Purple?

If you want, you can change the behavior of an item that you've inherited. This is called *overriding*. For example, if you no longer want Price to be a float, you can turn it into an integer. If you don't like what the ChooseSize( ) function does, you can write a new one.

If an item in the derived class has the same name as that in the base class, the derived class item will be used instead.

This is a great way to customize functionality.

Getting the Most Out of Your Parents

So, you put a new function in because you didn't like what your parent's ChooseSize( ) routine did, but now you wish you could still call your parent's routine. No problem. Just put the base class name, followed by :: and the function name. (By the way, a *parent* is another name for a base class. Maybe next Mother's Day you could try sending your mom a Happy Base Class Day card.)

Let's say you have a class that's derived from Pizza. The following line will call the ChooseSize member function from the base class (that is, from the Pizza class):

```
Pizza::ChooseSize();
```

This is a real nice feature. Not only does it let you call something from your parent, but it also means that if you need to access the functionality that the parent function provides, you don't need to copy and paste the code from the parent class into the derived class. Instead, you can just call the function in the parent class, and then write additional code for performing additional actions.

For example, here's a MilkEmPizza class that tries to get more money from the unsuspecting customer. You could drop this in to our pizza program (hmm, is this a touch of foreshadowing?) and thereby add new capabilities while at the same time taking advantage of the code that was already created:

```
//Start with your basic pizza object.
class MilkEmPizza : public Pizza {
   void ChooseSize();
};

//Get as much money as you can. Here is the
//ChooseSize routine that will be called when
//you create a MilkEmPizza object.
void
MilkEmPizza::ChooseSize() {
   //Start a friendly dialog so they think you are
   //their pal.
   cout << "Whoa. Sure is cold out. Makes you hungry.\n";

   //Now find out what size they want. Use the base
   //class routine so we don't have to repeat the hard
   //work.
   Pizza::ChooseSize();
```

```
      //Did they order a large? If not, pester them once.
      if (Size != Large) {
         cout << "Gee, that might not be enough for you."
            << "Maybe you should try a large.\n";
         //Now ask them once more
         Pizza::ChooseSize();
      }
   }
```

You Won't Need an Attorney to Prove This Inheritance Is for Real

Here's a real small example program that illustrates inheritance and changing the behavior of a function.

There are two classes in this program. You can use the base class to check out one type of behavior, and the derived class to check out the second type of behavior. The derived class also calls the base class:

```
//Illustrates overriding a function through inheritance.
#include <iostream.h>

//This is the base class. It contains a price and a
//way to print the price.
class Base {
public:
   int    Price;
   void   PrintMe();
};

//Print it, letting us know it is the base function.
void Base::PrintMe() {
   cout << "Base " << Price << "\n";
}

//Derived is inherited from Base. But it has a
//different PrintMe() function.
class Derived : public Base {
public:
   void PrintMe();
};

//Let us know the derived one was called. Then
//call the base one.
void Derived::PrintMe() {
   cout << "Derived " << Price << "\n";
   //Now call the parent
   Base::PrintMe();
}
```

(continued)

```
//Here's where it all begins.
void main() {
    Base   BClass;
    Derived        CopyCat;

    //BClass illustrates the base class behavior.
    //CopyCat illustrates the derived behavior.
    BClass.Price = 1;
    CopyCat.Price = 7;
    BClass.PrintMe();
    cout << "Now for the derived.\n";
    CopyCat.PrintMe();
}
```

(This program is in the INHERIT directory on the separately available program disk.)

This Is Important: How to Call Special Constructors in the Base Class

As your programs get complex, you'll start to create classes that have several constructors. Pay attention to this section to learn how to call such constructors when you inherit. You'll find it a very useful technique that will save you many headaches down the road.

When you create a class that inherits from another class, the constructor for the base class is called. The compiler look for the default constructor — that is, it looks for a constructor that takes no parameters.

How to tell if you need to create a default constructor

If you inherit from a class that has a set of specialized constructors, you might need to make sure that the base class has a default constructor.

If all the following statements are true, you need to define a default constructor:

✔ You plan to create derived classes from the class.

✔ The class has some constructors that take arguments.

✔ The class doesn't currently have a default constructor.

✔ You don't plan to explicitly (directly) call one of the specialized constructors from the derived class constructor, as shown in the "This is Important: How to Call Special Constructors in the Base Class" section.

You've seen, though, that sometimes you might want to have specialized constructors.

For example, in the pizza program, there's a special constructor for ToppingList that expects an integer and a Choice pointer. If you derived a new class from ToppingList, you might want to call this special constructor when the derived class is created.

You can do this in the constructor for the derived class. Just list the base class constructor that you want to call, followed by any parameters:

```
Derived::Derived() : Base(....) {
}
```

Here's an example of this, taken from the pizza program in Chapter 33. Okay, so maybe I'm jumping ahead a little bit. But this little snippet of code does illustrate my point quite nicely:

```
//Here is the constructor. It takes several parameters
//and passes these on to the Pizza constructor.
MilkEmPizza::MilkEmPizza(Choice *PizzaChoices,
  Choice *TopChoices) :
  Pizza(PizzaChoices, TopChoices) {
}
```

You can see that when the MilkEmPizza(Choice *, Choice *) constructor is called, it calls the base class Pizza::Pizza(Choice *, Choice *) constructor.

This is a real flexible way to control the way that derived classes are created.

Who's on First: Constructors and Destructors Calling Order

When you inherit from a class, the constructors and destructors for the base class and the derived class are called. It's important to understand the order in which the constructors and destructors are called.

When a derived class is created, first the memory for the class is set aside. Then the base class's constructor is called. Then the derived class's constructor is called.

When a derived class is destroyed, first its destructor is called, and then the destructor for the base class is called.

This Is Also Very Important: Pointers and Derived Classes

If you have a pointer that can point to a base class, you can use that same pointer to point to a derived class. Suppose, for example, that *p* is a pointer that points to a Pizza:

```
Pizza *p;
p = new Pizza;
```

If some other object is derived from Pizza, you can use *p* to point to that, too:

```
p = new MilkEmPizza;
```

"So what?" you might ask. And I'd answer: this is actually very important. It provides you with incredible flexibility because you can have a single pointer type that can be used for many different objects. So you don't have to know in advance if the user will make you create a special, derived object or some other object. You can use the same pointer, and it can deal with the base object as well as derived objects.

For example, suppose you decide to create a SpecialTopping object. This object is derived from the ToppingList object in the pizza program, but also displays the fat content of the object. When you print the name of one of these, it says "Hey, with our new extra-lean bacon, you only get 55g of fat per slice!"

If you wanted to mix some toppings along with special toppings, you can do this without changing the program at all. That's because the Next pointer in the list can point to a SpecialTopping just as easily as it can point to a Topping. You'll learn more about how to do this in the next chapter, which discusses virtual functions.

Pretty cool.

Inheriting from Private Benjamin

When you inherit from a class you can specify access rights. So far, you've used the *public* keyword from inheriting. You can also use the *private* and *protected* keywords.

Table 30-1 shows the effects of using *public*, *private*, and *protected* when inheriting.

Table 30-1: The effect of public, private, and protected on inheritance

If you inherit using...	And the base class's member is...	The inherited member will be this in your class:
public	public	public
	protected	protected
	private	nonaccessible
protected	public	protected
	protected	protected
	private	nonaccessible
private	public	private
	protected	private
	private	nonaccessible

The 5th Wave   By Rich Tennant

"I see you inheriting something soon. But I can't tell if it's a million dollars or a C++ base class."

That pointer thing is cool, but why does it work?

Normally C++ is very strict about types. For example, you can't use an int * to point to a float. But with derived classes, things are a bit different. When the compiler makes a derived class, it makes sure that what is inherited comes first in the class. For example, if the first four items in the base class are integers, then the first four items in the derived class will be those same integers.

If the compiler has a pointer to the base class, it knows how to find the various data members and member functions by determining where they're located in the class. If you take the same pointer and point it to a derived class, then all the base class member functions and data members are still easy to find because the derived class looks like a spitting image of the base class, but with some lucky extras. That's why you have this flexibility. The compiler always knows the offsets of any functions in the base class, regardless of the derived changes.

So what happens if the derived class overrides one of the functions in the base class? Stay tuned for the next chapter.

Chapter 31

Those Virtuous Virtual Functions (or, Polymorphism in No Time)

In This Chapter

▶ Learn what virtual functions are

▶ Determine if you need a virtual function

▶ Make a virtual function

▶ Write a program that shows the difference between virtual and nonvirtual functions

*V*irtual functions are used when a pointer to an object sometimes points to a base class and other times points to a derived class.

Although this might sound a little bit complex at first (after all, you thought you were finished with pointers!), virtual functions are easy to use once you understand the basic concepts.

As you saw in the last chapter, C++ lets you use a pointer to an object to also point to derived objects. So if you have a linked list of pizza toppings, you could have a diet topping that points to a fat-free topping that points to a regular topping that points to a fat-free topping. No problem. And you don't have to change your code — you can use the same pointer type. After all, the toppings are all derived from the topping object.

Sounds great, right? Hmm...there's gotta be a catch.

Of course there's a catch! Almost any time you use pointers there's going to be some little thing that makes your brain hurt. It's just a given.

Okay, here's the catch. Suppose one of the things you did in a derived class was to override the behavior of a member function. For example, suppose you change the PrintName( ) routine for the fat-free toppings so that not only does it print the name, but it lets you know that it's fat free and good for you. Well, if you use a topping pointer, the topping pointer won't use your customized PrintName( ) routine. It'll use the routine that comes from the base class.

This is a bummer. Here's what's happening: inheritance gives you a fantastic ability to reuse code and pointers give you all kinds of flexibility — but when you use them together, blammo! You end up with a problem.

Luckily, *virtual functions* solve this problem. When you use virtual functions, the pointers know that they're supposed to call the member functions that have been overridden by the derived class. When people talk about *polymorphism* being an important feature of object-oriented programming, they really are talking about virtual functions.

Virtual functions are used in almost every object-oriented program that inherits. With Quattro Pro for Windows, for example, you can use your mouse to right-click on an object to get a list of things you might want to do. For instance, when you right-click a cell, you're presented with a list of ways you can format that cell, and when you right-click on a graph axis, you're presented with a list of things you can change about that axis.

How are virtual functions actually being used in this case? Well, Quattro Pro for Windows has a base class from which the various screen objects are derived. Let's call this base class ScreenBase. It contains a virtual function called RightClicked that contains code for reacting when the user right-clicks on the object. A class for cells (let's call it Cell) is derived from ScreenBase. Likewise, a class for graph axes (GraphAxis) is derived from ScreenBase. GraphAxis and Cell override RightClicked.

Quattro Pro also keeps a pointer to whatever object was clicked on. Let's call this CurrentObject. CurrentObject is a ScreenBase pointer. That way, it can point to a ScreenBase object and any of the classes, such as Cell and GraphAxis, that are derived from ScreenBase:

```
ScreenBase      *CurrentObject;
```

So what happens when you right-click on a cell? Because the object clicked on is a cell, CurrentObject contains a Cell pointer. The RightClicked function is called:

```
CurrentObject->RightClicked();
```

Because RightClicked is a virtual function, the RightClicked for Cell is called. That is, Cell::RightClicked() is called. (If RightClicked weren't virtual, then ScreenBase::RightClicked would be called.)

What happens when you right-click on a graph axis? Well, because the object clicked on is a graph axis, CurrentObject contains a GraphAxis pointer. The RightClicked function is called:

```
CurrentObject->RightClicked();
```

Because RightClicked is a virtual function, this time the RightClicked for GraphAxis is called. That is, GraphAxis::RightClicked( ) is called. (Once again, if RightClicked weren't virtual, then ScreenBase::RightClicked would be called.)

Note that in both of these cases, the RightClicked function in the derived objects (Cell and GraphAxis) was called, even though CurrentObject is a pointer to a ScreenBase.

If I Never Use Pointers to Objects, Can I Skip This Chapter?

Yup.

How to Tell if You Need a Virtual Function

By answering the following four questions, you can determine whether or not you should make any particular function a virtual function. If you can answer No to *any* of these questions, you don't need a virtual function:

- ✔ Do you inherit from this class? (Do you think you will in the future?)
- ✔ Does the function behave differently in the derived class than it does in the base class? (Do you think it will in the future?)
- ✔ Do you use pointers to the base class?
- ✔ Do you ever need to use these pointers to point to a derived class? In other words, will you ever mix pointers to base and derived classes?

The family name game

When you have a class *C* that's derived from a class *B* that's derived from a class *A*, it can sometimes be hard to describe the relationship between these classes. One approach some programmers use is to call base classes *parents* and derived classes *children*. (That is, you could say *B* is the child of *A*.) Using such jargon, *C* would be the *grandchild* of *A*. And if *D* and *E* are both derived from *C*, then *D* and *E* are *siblings*. Which leads to great-grandparents, uncles and aunts, and second cousins once removed.

If *all* your answers are Yes, you should use a virtual function. Either that or you could redesign your whole application so that one of the answers is No. (In case you can't guess, using virtual functions is easier than doing this.)

Declaring a Virtual Function

You declare a virtual function in the base class, not in the derived class. To declare a virtual function, precede the function name with *virtual*:

```
class Base {
public:
    int   Price;
    virtual void  PrintMe();
};
```

Now the PrintMe( ) function in the class named Base is virtual.

Suppose you derived a new class from this:

```
class Derived : public Base {
public:
    virtual void PrintMe();
};
```

The compiler will now call the correct thing if you use pointers to these objects:

```
//Have two pointers that can point to a base class.
Base  *BasePtr, *DerivPtr;

//Here we will create a Base class and a Derived
//class. Once again, remember that we are using the
//same pointer type.
BasePtr = new Base;
DerivPtr = new Derived;

//This will call the PrintMe in the Base class.
BasePtr->PrintMe();

//Because we are using a virtual function, this
//will call the PrintMe in the Derived class. If
//PrintMe weren't declared as a virtual in Base, then
//the PrintMe from Base would be called.
DerivPtr->PrintMe();
```

That's all. And magically, it works.

You don't need to include the *virtual* keyword in derived classes when you override functions from the base class that are virtual. It's good to do so, though, because when you read the program it's a lot clearer that you're using virtual functions.

For example, you could use the following declaration for Derived:

```
class Derived : public Base {
public:
    void PrintMe();
};
```

But this is clearer:

```
class Derived : public Base {
public:
    virtual void PrintMe();
};
```

That way, virtu(al) is its own reward. ■

The Proof Is in the Pudding

Just in case you're feeling a bit confused or skeptical about the benefits of virtual functions, the next section provides a sample program that uses both a virtual and a nonvirtual function. If you run it, you'll see that the virtual function is needed when pointers are used.

This program has two classes, Base and Derived. Base contains a member function called PrintMe that is not virtual, and a member function called PrintMeV that is virtual:

```
class Base {
public:
    void  PrintMe();
    virtual void PrintMeV();
};
```

Derived is inherited from Base and overrides both member functions:

```
class Derived : public Base {
public:
    void PrintMe();
    virtual void PrintMeV();
};
```

The main routine starts by creating a Base class. It uses pointers so it can demonstrate the use of virtual functions:

```
Base  *BPtr;

//Create a base class.
BPtr = new Base;
```

Then it calls the member functions:

```
//Call the two functions.
BPtr->PrintMe();
BPtr->PrintMeV();
```

Next, a Derived class is created. Here, the Derived class is pointed to by the base class pointer. This is what makes virtual functions interesting — a pointer to the base class is being used to point to a derived class:

```
BPtr = new Derived;

//Now we will call the two functions. Note that
//the derived PrintMe is never called because it
//is not a virtual.
BPtr->PrintMe();
BPtr->PrintMeV();
```

When this code executes, the PrintMe routine from the Base class is called, even though BPtr points to a Derived class. That's because PrintMe *isn't* virtual. But notice that the PrintMeV routine from Derived is called. That's because PrintMeV *is* virtual.

Finally, a Derived class is created statically and its member functions are called:

```
Derived StaticDerived;

StaticDerived.PrintMe();
StaticDerived.PrintMeV();
```

In this case, the Derived PrintMe is called, because the Derived class is being accessed directly, not through a pointer to its base class.

Once you declare that a function is virtual, it will be virtual for all derived classes. For example, PrintMeV was declared virtual in the class Base. Thus, it is virtual in the class Derived. If you were to create a new class (you could call it DerivedKiddo) that was derived from Derived, then PrintMeV would also be virtual in DerivedKiddo. No matter how deep the inheritance (and it can go as deep as you want), the compiler will determine the correct function to use.

The Code

```
//Illustrates using and not using virtual functions.

#include <iostream.h>
```

```
//This is the base class. It contains two
//ways to print. PrintMeV is a virtual function.
class Base {
public:
    void PrintMe();
    virtual void PrintMeV();
};


//Print it, letting us know it is the base function.
void Base::PrintMe() {
    cout << "Base PrintMe\n";
}


//The virtual version of print me. Nothing looks
//any different here.
void Base::PrintMeV() {
    cout << "Base PrintMeV\n";
}


//Derived is inherited from Base and overrides
//PrintMe() and PrintMeV().
class Derived : public Base {
public:
    void PrintMe();
    virtual void PrintMeV();
};


//Let us know the derived one was called.
void Derived::PrintMe() {
    cout << "Derived PrintMe\n";
}

void Derived::PrintMeV() {
    cout << "Derived PrintMeV\n";
}


//Here's where it all begins.
void main() {
    //Instead of creating classes statically, we will
    //do it dynamically.
    Base *BPtr;

    //Create a base class.
    BPtr = new Base;

    //Call the two functions.
    BPtr->PrintMe();
    BPtr->PrintMeV();
```

(continued)

```
//Delete this object and make a derived object.
delete BPtr;
cout << "Now make a derived object.\n";
//Note that we are using a Base pointer to point to
//a Derived object.
BPtr = new Derived;

//Now we will call the two functions. Note that
//the derived PrintMe is never called because it
//is not a virtual.
BPtr->PrintMe();
BPtr->PrintMeV();

//Now we will delete this and prove that this
//condition only holds when you use a base class
//pointer to point to a derived class.
delete BPtr;

//Statically create a Derived.
cout << "Now we won't use pointers.\n";
Derived StaticDerived;

StaticDerived.PrintMe();
StaticDerived.PrintMeV();
}
```

(This program is in the VIRTFUN directory on the separately available program disk.)

Everything you always wanted to know about pure virtuals (but were afraid to ask)

When you make a pure virtual function (which you do by using *pure virtual* instead of *virtual*), you can't define the behavior of the virtual function in the base class. Any derived class that's going to be instantiated must define what the function does. This is just a way to make sure that programmers fill in the functions for every derived class. A class that contains some pure virtuals that aren't defined is called an *abstract base class*. You can't instantiate the class (because all the member functions aren't defined) but you can use it as a base class for other classes. You probably won't use pure virtuals too much, but you'll see them mentioned in other programming books and in articles.

Sign Up Here for Parenting Classes

Getting ready to inherit? Here's a handy checklist you can use to make sure your base classes are prepared for having classes derived from them. (Kind of like making sure they're prepared for having children. Is the class's diaper bag ready? And what about a stroller?)

- ✔ If you plan to use pointers to the class and to classes derived from the class, use virtual functions whenever you override a function.

- ✔ If you derive from a class with specialized constructors, make sure the derived class's constructors specifically call one of the specialized constructors or that the base class also has a default constructor.

- ✔ If the derived class is going to use some of the hidden data members and member functions, these items need to be protected instead of private.

- ✔ If you inherit a lot of money, send some to me.

Chapter 32
Templates

In This Chapter
▶ Learn what templates are
▶ Create generic classes
▶ Create a templatized linked-list program

● ●

C++ is designed to make your life easier. You've already seen how inheritance and virtual functions can streamline your programming time, because they let you reuse existing code.

The more you can write generic code, the more you can just adapt something you've already written and go home early. *Templates* help you go home early. They let you write a generic piece of code and then use it over and over again with different types of data or different objects.

For example, you could write generic linked-list code that could be used for lists of toppings, lists of names, and lists of vacations. It could even be used for lists of lists. You would write it once, test it once, and then use it many times.

Join the Clean Template Club

The basic idea of a template is that you can create a generic class that operates on some unspecified data type. Then, when you instantiate the class, you specify the type of the object. The compiler does the rest.

So you can write a generic linked list and then use it for integers, floating-point numbers, pizza toppings, and anything else that you can imagine. Not only that, but the generic class is type safe. So if you tried to put a pizza topping into a list of integers, you'd get an error.

Let's take a look at templates in more detail.

You've already seen how you can make a linked list using a class that looks something like this:

```
class IntLinkedList {
public:
    int GetData();
    IntLinkedList *GetNext();
private:
    int   Data;
    IntLinkedList *Next;
};
```

This class has public member functions to return the data and to traverse the list.

Now suppose you wanted to make this class operate on floats instead. To do this, you'd have to change a lot of data types in the class:

```
class FloatLinkedList {
public:
    float GetData();
    FloatLinkedList *GetNext();
private:
    float Data;
    FloatLinkedList       *Next;
};
```

This means cutting and pasting. Cutting and pasting is bad.

If you've programmed in C before, you might say Ahah! I'll just use a void pointer, and keep pointers to all the data:

```
class GenLinkedList {
public:
    void *GetData();
    GenLinkedList *GetNext();
private:
    void  *Data;
    GenLinkedList *Next;
};
```

Well slow down, Sherlock. As I pointed out in an earlier chapter, void pointers are bad. If you use them, your class will no longer be type-safe: you could pass in a pizza topping just as easily as you could pass in a floating-point number. And as a result, you could quickly end up with some really messed-up lists.

Templates solve this problem. They provide a way to create a class that is both generic and type-safe.

The template version of this class would be:

```
template <class T>
class LinkedList {
```

```
public:
    T GetData();
    LinkedList *GetNext();
private:
    T  Data;
    LinkedList     *Next;
};
```

If you wanted to use this for a linked list of integers you would do this:

```
//Make a linked list of integers.
LinkedList<int>  IntList;
```

And you could just as easily make a linked list of floats:

```
//Make a linked list of floats.
LinkedList<float> FloatList;
```

You've Got a Templatized Class Act

To design a templatized class, figure out what data types you need to make generic. For example, in the linked list, the data type was generic. You can have more than one generic type inside a template.

Precede the class declaration with the word *template* followed by a list of the generic types: *<class* type1, *class* type2 ... *>*. Then define the class just as you usually would, using the generic types.

For example, to create a templatized linked list, you would do this:

```
template <class T>
class LinkedList {
public:
    T GetData();
    void SetData(T val);
    LinkedList *GetNext();
private:
    T  Data;
    LinkedList     *Next;
};
```

Defining Member Functions for a Template

When you define member functions for a template, you also need to use the template notation, like this:

```
template <class T>
T
LinkedList<T>::GetData() {
    return Data;
}

template <class T>
LinkedList<T>::SetData(T val) {
    Data = val;
}
```

Sometimes the syntax can get a bit confusing. Don't worry — if you make a syntax mistake, the compiler will give you a syntax error and you can correct your mistake.

Using Templatized Classes

To use a templatized class, just indicate the type to use inside < >, like this:

```
//Generate a linked list of integers.
LinkedList<int>  foo;

//Create a linked list of floats dynamically.
LinkedList<float> *Fptr;
Fptr = new LinkedList<float>;
```

Rules for using pointers to templatized classes

There are three rules you need to know about using pointers with templatized classes:

✔ When you declare the class, you don't need < > when you describe a pointer to the class. For example, suppose you have a template class called LinkedList. You want a pointer to the LinkedList data member in the class so that you can make a linked list. You would say:

```
template <class T>
class LinkedList {
public:
  LinkedList  *Next;
};
```

✔ When you define the member functions, you do need to use < > when you describe a pointer to the class. For example, if you have a member function called GetNext( ) that examines the Next pointer, you would indicate that it returns a LinkedList<T> *:

```
template <class T>
LinkedList<T> *
LinkedList<T>::GetNext() {
    return Next;
}
```

✔ When you create a pointer to a template class, you need to use the < >. For example, if you want a pointer to a linked list of integers, you could have this:

```
LinkedList<int> *foo;
```

These three basic rules can all be summed up by this golden rule:

✔ Unless you're inside the class definition itself, use a < >.

See "The Code" section of this chapter for examples of these rules in action.

Reducing some of the confusion

Sometimes it can be confusing to remember all the rules for when to use < >. That's why you might want to define a new type for each type of template you will instantiate. For example, if you know you'll have a linked list of floats and a linked list of integers you could do this:

```
typedef   LinkedList<float>      FloatList;
typedef   LinkedList<int>        IntList;
```

Then you could use FloatList and IntList as types — for example, like this:

```
FloatList *flPtr, flInstance;
```

Only the type definition needs the < >; everything else uses the new type.

Stick it in a header file

If you want to use a templatized class in more than one file, stick the template class declaration *and* the definition of all its member functions inside a header file. If you forget to put the definitions of the member functions inside the header file, you'll get more error messages than you would ever care to see.

This strategy works when a particular advanced compiler option (the Smart option) is on. The Smart option is on by default, so it should work for any programs you create. If you want to make sure the option is on, select Options | Project. Then expand the C++ Options topic and select the Templates subtopic. Make sure the Smart option is selected. ■

A Templatized Linked-List Program

Let's take a look at a simple program that uses templates to create a generic linked-list class.

This program begins with a LinkedList class. Notice how it uses a template <class T> in the definition, and *T* to represent the generic data:

```
template <class T>
class LinkedList {
public:
    T   GetData();
    void SetData(T val);
    LinkedList    *GetNext();
    void Add();
private:
    T   Data;
    LinkedList     *Next;
};
```

The 5th Wave   **By Rich Tennant**

The template notation is also used when defining the member functions. For example, GetData is a member function of LinkedList and returns a *T* (the generic type used in the template):

```
template <class T>
T
LinkedList<T>::GetData() {
    return Data;
}
```

More ways to prove you're a programmer<g>

Since templates introduce the use of < > in programs, now's a good time to look at some other uses of < >.

Since programmers often communicate by electronic mail, they've developed a set of shorthand symbols to explain situations. Every now and then you'll see this shorthand show up inside program comments.

<g>   Grin. Indicates that something is supposed to be funny. Also used to clarify that a remark is sarcastic, as in: "Oops, gotta go. It's time for another fascinating budget meeting <g>."

:-)   A happy programmer. Something good is going on, as in: "I finally got my program to run with no errors! :-) "

:-o   A surprised programmer: "It worked! :-o "

@#&*   A ticked-off programmer: "What on earth is wrong with my @#&* keyboard! The keys are all sticking. Maybe it's that can of Jolt I spilled on it last night<g>."

NYI   Not yet implemented. Placed liberally throughout programs that aren't quite finished. For example, you might find a comment that reads like this:
       //Balance national budget NYI.

NIH   Not invented here. Used as a disparaging comment about someone else's code: "It's kind of buggy, but then it's NIH."

OTOH   On the other hand. "Maybe Ratbert's idea will make the program run faster. OTOH, it isn't really very safe."

PMFJI Pardon me for jumping in. A polite way to jump in and toast someone. For example, you might say: "PMFJI but you completely missed the point."

RSN   Real soon now: "It will be implemented RSN."

RTFM   Read the fine<g> manual. When someone asks a question, this is used to imply that if he or she had bothered to read the documentation in the first place, they wouldn't need to ask. For example, you might see something like: "Did you see the question Jethro put up on e-mail about how to plug in a monitor? I felt like saying 'What do you mean you don't know how to plug in a monitor? RTFM!' "

As another example, the routine that returns the next pointer also uses the template notation. Note that the definition is slightly different than the one in the class definition, because here you need to say LinkedList<T> *, whereas in the class definition you just say LinkedList *:

```
template <class T>
LinkedList<T> *
LinkedList<T>::GetNext() {
    return Next;
}
```

The generic type *T* is used when asking for and filling data into the list. Also, note the syntax for creating a new LinkedList item:

```
template <class T>
void
LinkedList<T>::Add() {
    T   temp;
    LinkedList    *NewOne;

    cout << "What is the value\n";
    cin >> temp;

    //Create a new one. Note use of <T>
    NewOne = new LinkedList<T>;
    //Hook it up and set the values.
    NewOne->Data = temp;
    NewOne->Next = 0;
    Next = NewOne;
}
```

The main routine uses the templatized linked-list class to create and process a linked list of integers and then a linked list of floats:

```
LinkedList<int>        IntList;
cout << "Integer List\n";
//Set the value of the first one
IntList.SetData(1);
    .
    .
    .
LinkedList<float>      FloatList;
cout << "Floating list\n";
FloatList.SetData(1.7);
```

The example in this section uses *cin* to read data to put into the list (in the Add member function). This will work just fine as long as you are only instantiating the template class for types that *cin* understands. In this example, you create a linked list of integers and of floats. Both are types that *cin* understands.

But suppose you want to read in pizza information so you can have a linked list of pizzas? *cin* doesn't understand how to read in pizza information — you need to teach it how to do this. You'll learn how to do this in Chapter 37, which discusses overloading operators. ■

The Code

```
//This program creates a generic linked list structure
//using templates.

#include <iostream.h>

//Here is where the class is defined.
template <class T>
class LinkedList {
public:
    T           GetData();
    void SetData(T val);
    LinkedList  *GetNext();
    void Add();
private:
    T           Data;
    LinkedList  *Next;
};

//Here we define the GetData member function. It
//returns something of type T.
template <class T>
T
LinkedList<T>::GetData() {
    return Data;
}

//This function assigns a value to the Data item.
template <class T>
void
LinkedList<T>::SetData(T val) {
    Data = val;
}

//This returns a pointer to the next item.
template <class T>
LinkedList<T> *
LinkedList<T>::GetNext() {
    return Next;
}

//Here we will add a new item to the list.
template <class T>
void
LinkedList<T>::Add() {
    T temp;
    LinkedList  *NewOne;
    cout << "What is the value\n";
    cin >> temp;

    //Create a new one. Note use of <T>
    NewOne = new LinkedList<T>;
    //Hook it up and set the values.
    NewOne->Data = temp;
    NewOne->Next = 0;
    Next = NewOne;
```

(continued)

```
   }

//Here is the main
void main() {
   //Create a linked list of integers
   LinkedList<int> IntList;
   cout << "Integer List\n";

   //Set the value of the first one
   IntList.SetData(1);
   //Now add another item to the list
   IntList.Add();
   //Print out the value of the first item in the list
   cout << IntList.GetData() << "\n";
   //Now find the second item and print its value
   cout << (IntList.GetNext())->GetData() << "\n";

   //Do the same exact thing, but now with a list
   //of floating point numbers
   LinkedList<float>       FloatList;
   cout << "Floating list\n";
   FloatList.SetData(1.7);
   FloatList.Add();
   cout << FloatList.GetData() << "\n";
   cout << (FloatList.GetNext())->GetData() << "\n";
}
```

(This program is in the TEMPLATE directory on the separately available program disk.)

Finding Some Good Examples

TIP

For more examples of how to use templates, check out the container-class libraries that ship with Borland C++ 4.0. ■

Chapter 33

This Is Not Your Parent's Pizza++

• •

In This Chapter

▶ Add inheritance to the pizza program

▶ Use protected members

▶ Use virtual functions

▶ Create header files with sentinels

• •

*T*he program in this chapter is an extension to our pizza program. A number of new things are being added to the program. First, a new class is created that is derived from Pizza. This class is the MilkEmPizza class, which tries to pressure customers into ordering a large pizza. The data members and member functions that were private in the Pizza class are now protected so they can be used by MilkEmPizza.

Second, the program now lets you create special DietToppings. These are based on the ToppingList objects but let you know that they're diet toppings. This isn't a major change in functionality, but it shows you how you might use virtual functions. For this change to occur, the DietToppings class is added, and the following changes are made to ToppingList:

✔ Some items are made protected instead of private.

✔ Some of the functions are changed so that they can create either a DietTopping or a ToppingList object.

And third, since the program is starting to get large, it's now broken into files to make it easier to read. Each class is represented in a separate CPP file. This also means there are now a number of header files.

So that you can more easily see the new and changed portions of the program, these areas now have comments that begin with //***NEW.

Figure 33-1 shows the new class structure.

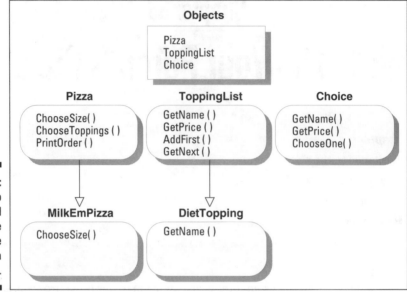

Figure 33-1:
Two inherited classes are added to the pizza program.

How to Read a Program with Multiple Files

Here's how to read a program that consists of multiple files:

1. Look for the file containing main( ).

2. Read this file, paying special attention to classes used in main( ).

3. Look for the files that define classes used in main( ).

4. See what they do. Pay attention to the classes they use.

5. Look for those files and repeat step 4.

6. Hope that there are some good comments to guide you through.

7. Use tools such as the ObjectBrowser from Borland C++ to see the class structure and to navigate through it.

What's Happening in This Program

Except for being broken into multiple files, this program is very similar to the previous pizza program (from Chapter 29). The main difference is that two inherited classes have been added to this newer version: MilkEmPizza and DietTopping.

The MilkEmPizza class

MilkEmPizza is a new class designed to get more money from the customer. It is derived from Pizza:

```
class MilkEmPizza : public Pizza {
public:
    MilkEmPizza(Choice *PizzaChoices, Choice *TopChoices);
    void ChooseSize();
};
```

Its constructor simply calls the Pizza constructor. (If an explicit call to the Pizza constructor wasn't made, the compiler would look for the default constructor Pizza::Pizza( ). Since there isn't one, the compiler would give a syntax error. Therefore, you need to make an explicit call so the compiler knows what constructor to use.)

```
MilkEmPizza::MilkEmPizza(Choice *PizzaChoices,
  Choice *TopChoices) :
  Pizza(PizzaChoices, TopChoices) {
}
```

The ChooseSize function overrides the Pizza choose size function so that it can pester the user. It then calls the base class (Pizza) ChooseSize function. Thus, it easily adds new functionality without having to duplicate code:

```
void
MilkEmPizza::ChooseSize() {
    cout << "Sure is cold out. You look hungry.\n";
    Pizza::ChooseSize();
    if (Size != PizzaSizes->GetMax()) {
        cout << "Are you sure that's enough? "
            << "Why don't you try a large.\n";
        Pizza::ChooseSize();
    }
}
```

The main routine now creates a MilkEmPizza class instead of a Pizza class:

```
MilkEmPizza MyPizza(&PizzaSizes, &Toppings);
```

Because MilkEmPizza is derived from Pizza, you don't need to change anything else in main. It will work just as before, only now the customer is pressured to buy a large pizza. This seamless change illustrates part of the beauty of inheritance.

The DietTopping class

The other new class you'll see is the DietTopping class, which is derived from ToppingList:

```
class DietTopping : public ToppingList {
public:
    virtual char *GetName();
    DietTopping(int Num, Choice *ChoiceList);
    ~DietTopping();
private:
    char *MakeDietName(char *TopName);
    };
```

DietTopping overrides the virtual GetName function to let the user know the topping is a diet topping:

```
char *
DietTopping::GetName() {
    return MakeDietName(ToppingList::GetName());
    }
```

DietTopping::GetName calls a new private member function that's called MakeDietName. MakeDietName takes a string, in this case the topping name, and then adds "special diet" to the name. MakeDietName uses several library functions to help it manipulate strings. First, MakeDietName creates a buffer where the new string will be stored. The buffer needs to be large enough to contain the original string ("special diet") and the ending /0. The *strlen* routine returns the length of a string:

```
//Create a new string.
NewWord = new char[strlen(TopName) + strlen(DietWord)
    + 1];
```

Next the "special diet" string is copied into the buffer, followed by the original topping name:

```
//Copy the DietWord to the beginning of the result.
strcpy(NewWord, DietWord);

//Append the topping name and that string.
return strcat(NewWord, TopName);
```

Because the DietTopping class allocates memory with *new* every time GetName is called, a destructor has been added to free up that memory. You'll find the following lines in the destructor and GetName:

```
if (NewWord)
    delete NewWord;
```

This code checks to see if there is currently any memory allocated for the diet string name. If there is, it deletes it so that memory is not lost.

The DietTopping class behaves similarly to the ToppingList class, but it proudly indicates that the particular topping is a diet topping. Once again, you've added significant new functionality without having to make major changes to the program.

Mixing the objects in the linked list

Because you can use a pointer to a base class to also point to a derived class, you can use a pointer to a ToppingList class to point to a DietTopping. Thus, you can easily mix DietTopping objects and ToppingList objects in a single linked list.

In other words, you don't need to change the code much to mix diet and non-diet toppings. You just need to give the user the chance to decide which type of topping to add next, create the appropriate diet or non-diet object, and then everything in the list code will work just fine.

Two things in our program need to change so that the user can make the diet/non-diet decision: the Pizza::ChooseTopping class and the ToppingList::Add function. As you can see, the Pizza::ChooseToppings class just asks the user whether or not to create a diet or non-diet topping and then creates either a DietTopping object or a ToppingList object, as appropriate. The AddFirst( ) function is then called to find out what the first topping is and then to add any additional toppings:

```
cout << "Do you want to add toppings? (0=No)\n";
cin >> Select;

//If yes, start the list.
if (Select) {
   //Make it diet?
   cout << "Do you want your first topping to be "
        << "a diet topping? (0=no)\n";
   cin >> Select;
   if (Select)
        Toppings = new DietTopping(0, ToppingChoices);
   else
        Toppings = new ToppingList(0, ToppingChoices);
   Toppings->AddFirst();
}
```

The ToppingList::Add function also changes so that DietTopping or ToppingList classes can be added to the list:

```
//Should it be a diet class?
cout << "Do you want that to be a diet topping?"
     << " (0=no)\n";
cin >> Diet;
```

(continued)

```
//***NEW
//Now make a new class. Find out if it should
//be diet or regular.
if (Diet)
    //Make a DietTopping.
    NewOne = new DietTopping(Select, ToppingChoices);
else
    //Make a normal topping.
    NewOne = new ToppingList(Select, ToppingChoices);

//And now we will hook it up to this item.
Next = NewOne;
```

Finally, because you have a linked list containing pointers to objects, some of which are DietTopping objects and some of which are ToppingList objects, you need to make ToppingList::GetName virtual so that the correct GetName is called when a DietTopping object is pointed to by a ToppingList pointer. Note that the functions that used to be private are now protected so that the DietTopping class can use them:

```
class ToppingList {
public:
    //***NEW Now this is virtual
    virtual char *GetName();
    float GetPrice();
    void AddFirst();
    ToppingList *GetNext();
    ToppingList(int Num, Choice *ChoiceList);
    ~ToppingList();
    //***NEW — private items switched to protected
protected:
    int    Topping;
    ToppingList    *Next;
    Choice         *ToppingChoices;
    void Add();
};
```

Store class declarations in the header files

As mentioned earlier in the chapter, the other major change made to this version of the program is that it's now split into multiple files. As a result, header files are used to store the class declarations. For example, toplst.h contains the declaration for the ToppingList class.

Any time a file needs to use a class, it also needs to include the declaration for the class. For example, toplst.cpp uses ToppingList and DietTopping classes, so it has the following includes:

```
#include "toplst.h"
#include "diettop.h"
```

The main routine uses a Choice and a MilkEmPizza class, so it has these includes:

```
#include "choice.h"
#include "milkem.h"
```

TECHNICAL STUFF

That's no ordinary lookout; it's a sentinel in a header file

In C++, it's a no-no to read a header file twice while processing a particular file. That's because the first time the compiler reads the header file, it reads the various class declarations. The second time the compiler reads the header file, the classes have already been declared. So when the compiler reads the class declarations the second time, it tries to declare the classes again. But you can't declare a class two times. This is a conflict, so the compiler will complain loudly.

There are two ways to get around this situation:

1. Make sure you don't load header files twice. There are two parts to this process. First, look at the header files that are included by the files. Make sure that you don't have two *#include* lines that load the same header file. Second, some header files themselves include other header files. Check to make sure there aren't double loads because of this. For example, suppose you include header file foo.h and header file bar.h. If foo.h happens to include bar.h as well, then you will end up loading bar.h twice.

2. Create sentinels.

Approach #2 is far easier and safer. It will work even if some hosehead on your programming team doesn't follow #1.

The idea behind a sentinel is that the first time the header file is read, a preprocessor directive defines some value that says "I've been read." The header file has another preprocessor directive that checks for this value. If the value isn't found, the stuff in the header file is read. If the value is found, everything in the header file is skipped.

Implementing a sentinel is easy. Put this at the beginning of the header file:

```
#if !defined(H_foo)
#define H_foo
```

Only, type the name of the header file instead of foo. The H followed by the underline is used so you don't accidentally use the same name as a variable or class in your program.

At the end of the file put:

```
#endif          //H_foo
```

These lines say "If H_foo isn't defined, then define it and read in the file. But if H_foo is defined, skip everything." Everything is skipped because there is nothing but the big if in the file. So there are no lines to read in if the #if fails.

You'll see sentinels throughout the header files used in this program. You'll also see them throughout the header files you get with Borland C++.

Finally, the Sample Program

This program is broken into a number of files. (If you get the separately available program disk, the files are all part of an IDE file called PIZZA8.IDE.)

The files are:

- PIZZA8.CPP   Contains the main().
- MILKEM.H   Defines the MilkEmPizza class.
- MILKEM.CPP   Code for the MilkEmPizza class.
- PIZZACL.H   Defines the Pizza class.
- PIZZACL.CPP   Code for the Pizza class.
- DIETTOP.H   Defines the DietTopping class.
- DIETTOP.CPP   Code for the DietTopping class.
- TOPLST.H   Defines the ToppingList class.
- TOPLST.CPP   Code for the ToppingList class.
- CHOICE.H   Defines the Choice class.
- CHOICE.CPP   Code for the Choice class.

Here's the code:

PIZZA8.CPP

```
//This version adds a new class called MilkEmPizza
//that's designed to get more money from the customer.
//It also creates diet as well as regular
//topping objects.

//The major changes are:
// A new class MilkEmPizza is added. It is derived from
//    pizza.
// Pizza's private members are now protected so that
//    they can be used by MilkEmPizza.
// MilkEmPizza is used in main() instead of Pizza.
// A new class DietTopping is added. It is derived from
// ToppingList.
// ToppingList::GetName() is now virtual. It is
//    overridden by DietTopping.
// ToppingList's private members are now protected and
// a default constructor is used.
// ToppingList's Add() is modified so that diet toppings
//    can be created.
```

```
#include <iostream.h>
#include "choice.h"
#include "milkem.h"


//There are four main classes used:
//    ToppingList — a list of pizza toppings
//    DietTopping — a special topping that has less
//        calories
//    Pizza — info describing the pizza
//    MilkEmPizza — a special type of pizza that tries
//        to be expensive
//We also have helper classes:
//    Choice — used to represent choices that can
//        be made by the user
//    ChoiceDescription — a structure containing a
//        choice name and price


//----The main routine begins here-----------------------

void
main() {
    //We'll make two lists of choices, one for
    //pizza sizes and one for toppings.
    const int NumSizes = 3;
    const int NumTops = 5;
    const ChoiceDescription const Sizes[NumSizes] =
        {{"Small", 10}, {"Medium", 12},{"Large", 14}};
    const ChoiceDescription const Tops[NumTops] =
        {{"Pepperoni", 1.8}, {"Sausage", 2.1},
        {"Onions", 0.5},{"Extra Cheese", 1.0},
        {"Olives", 0.7}};

    //Now we will create the choice objects for
    //toppings and for sizes and pass in the arrays.
    Choice PizzaSizes(NumSizes, Sizes);
    Choice Toppings(NumTops, Tops );

    //Now we will create a new pizza. We'll pass in
    //pointers to the two choices.
    //***NEW
    //To maximize revenue we'll use a MilkEmPizza.
    //Note that just the declaration has changed.
    //We don't need to change the code anywhere else.
    MilkEmPizza MyPizza(&PizzaSizes, &Toppings);

    //Now we will choose the size.
    MyPizza.ChooseSize();

    //Now we will choose the toppings.
    MyPizza.ChooseToppings();

    //Now we will print the order.
    MyPizza.PrintOrder();
}
```

MILKEM.H

```
//Create a sentinel. Only include the header if it
//hasn't been read yet.

#if !defined(H_MILKEM_H)
#define H_MILKEM_H

#include "pizzacl.h"

//This defines the MilkEmPizza class.
//This class is very similar to the Pizza class. The
//only difference is that the ChooseSize() command will
//now try to make the customer buy a large pizza.
//It inherits all of the data members and member
//functions from Pizza and overrides ChooseSize().

class MilkEmPizza : public Pizza {
public:
    MilkEmPizza(Choice *PizzaChoices, Choice *TopChoices);
    void ChooseSize();
};
#endif  //H_MILKEM_H
```

MILKEM.CPP

```
#include <iostream.h>
#include "milkem.h"

//----MilkEmPizza Class-----------------------------------
//***NEW
//This class is very similar to the Pizza class. The
//only difference is that the ChooseSize() command will
//now try to make the customer buy a large pizza.
//It inherits all the data members and member
//functions from Pizza and overrides ChooseSize().
//The class is defined in milkem.h


//----MilkEmPizza member functions----------------------

//The constructor calls the base class constructor.
MilkEmPizza::MilkEmPizza(Choice *PizzaChoices,
  Choice *TopChoices) :
  Pizza(PizzaChoices, TopChoices) {
}

//The overridden ChooseSize badgers the customer.
void
MilkEmPizza::ChooseSize() {
    cout << "Sure is cold out. You look hungry.\n";
    Pizza::ChooseSize();
    if (Size != PizzaSizes->GetMax()) {
        cout << "Are you sure that's enough? "
```

```
           << "Why don't you try a large.\n";
        Pizza::ChooseSize();
  }
}


//----Finished MilkEmPizza member functions--------------
```

PIZZACL.H

```
//Create a sentinel. Only include the header if it
//hasn't been read yet.

#if !defined(H_PIZZACL_H)
#define H_PIZZACL_H


#include "toplst.h"
#include "choice.h"


//The Pizza class is used to hold all information
//regarding the pizza. It contains a number of
//data members including a list of toppings.
//
//Here is a class overview:
//    Pizza(Choice *PizzaChoices, Choice *TopChoices) -
//        constructs the pizza class; it takes a
//        pointer to a list of possible sizes and
//        possible choices
//    ~Pizza() - cleans up
//    ChooseSize() - asks the user for the pizza size
//    ChooseToppings() - asks the user to choose the
//        desired toppings
//    PrintOrder() - prints out the price of the
//        pizza

class Pizza {
public:
    Pizza(Choice *PizzaChoices, Choice *TopChoices);
    ~Pizza();
    void ChooseSize();
    void ChooseToppings();
    void PrintOrder();
    //***NEW - private items switched to protected
protected:
    ToppingList *Toppings;
    Choice      *PizzaSizes;
    Choice      *ToppingChoices;
    int Size;
    float Cost;
};

#endif  //H_PIZZACL_H
```

PIZZACL.CPP

```cpp
#include <iostream.h>
#include "pizzacl.h"
#include "diettop.h"

//----Pizza Class------------------------------------
//The class is defined in pizzacl.h


//----Pizza member functions--------------------------

//The constructor initializes the class.
Pizza::Pizza(Choice *PizzaChoices, Choice *TopChoices) {
   Size = 0;
   Cost = 0.0;
   Toppings = 0;
   PizzaSizes = PizzaChoices;
   ToppingChoices = TopChoices;
}

//Here is the destructor. It deletes the first item
//in the list of toppings. This will cause a chain
//reaction that will free up the whole topping list.
Pizza::~Pizza() {
   if (Toppings)
      delete Toppings;
}

//This asks the user to choose the desired pizza
//size.
void
Pizza::ChooseSize() {
   Size = PizzaSizes->ChooseOne();
   //Set the initial price
   Cost = PizzaSizes->GetPrice(Size);
}

//This asks the user to select the desired toppings.
//***NEW — now lets you choose diet toppings
void
Pizza::ChooseToppings() {
   int   Select;

   cout << "Do you want to add toppings? (0=No)\n";
   cin >> Select;

   //If yes, start the list.
   if (Select) {
      //Make it diet?
      cout << "Do you want your first topping to be "
           << "a diet topping? (0=no)\n";
      cin >> Select;
      if (Select)
         Toppings = new DietTopping(0, ToppingChoices);
```

```
      else
          Toppings = new ToppingList(0, ToppingChoices);
      Toppings->AddFirst();
   }
}

//This prints out what was selected and the price.
void
Pizza::PrintOrder() {
   ToppingList *Cur = Toppings;

   //Print out the size of the pizza.
   cout << "That's a " << PizzaSizes->GetName(Size)
        << " pizza with ";

   //Are there any toppings?
   if (!Cur)
      cout << "no toppings.\n";
   else {
      //There are toppings, so traverse the list
      //and sum the price.
      while (Cur) {
         //Find the price of the topping.
         Cost += Cur->GetPrice();
         //Print the topping type
         cout << Cur->GetName();
         //Move on to the next one.
         Cur = Cur->GetNext();
         //If there is a next one, print "and".
         if (Cur)
             cout << " and ";
      } //end of while

      cout << " for toppings.\n";
   } //end of else

   //Print the total price.
   cout << "That will be $" << Cost << ".\n";

}


//-----Finished Pizza member functions--------------------
```

DIETTOP.H

```
//Create a sentinel. Only include the header if it
//hasn't been read yet.

#if !defined(H_DIETTOP_H)
#define H_DIETTOP_H

#include "toplst.h"
```

(continued)

```
//----DietTopping----------------------------------------
//The DietTopping is a special type of topping that
//has less fat.
//It is derived from ToppingList, but has a different
//GetName() routine. It also contains a destructor for freeing
//memory used by MakeDietName.
class DietTopping : public ToppingList {
public:
   virtual char *GetName();
   DietTopping(int Num, Choice *ChoiceList);
   ~DietTopping();
private:
   char *MakeDietName(char *TopName);
   char *NewWord;
};
#endif //H_DIETTOP_H
```

DIETTOP.CPP

```
#include <iostream.h>
#include <string.h>
#include "diettop.h"


//----DietTopping----------------------------------------
//***NEW
//The diet topping is inherited from ToppingList.
//It is defined in diettop.h

//The constructor initializes the class.
DietTopping::DietTopping(int Num, Choice *ChoiceList) :
 ToppingList(Num, ChoiceList) {
   //No string is being stored yet.
   NewWord = 0;
}

//The destructor frees the string memory.
DietTopping::~DietTopping() {
   if (NewWord)
      delete NewWord;
}

//This routine is used to convert a topping name into
//the special diet topping name.
char *
DietTopping::MakeDietName(char *TopName) {
   //Here is the string that makes the difference.
   char *DietWord = "special diet ";
   //Is there already a string that we need to free?
   if (NewWord)
      delete NewWord;

   //Create a new string. It needs to be long enough
   //to merge the two strings.
   NewWord = new char[strlen(TopName) + strlen(DietWord)
      + 1];
```

```
    //Copy the DietWord to the beginning of the result.
    strcpy(NewWord, DietWord);

    //Append the topping name and return that string.
    return strcat(NewWord, TopName);
}

//This is the overridden GetName(). It calls
//MakeDietName to add the special diet message to
//the string.
char *
DietTopping::GetName() {
    return MakeDietName(ToppingList::GetName());
}
```

TOPLST.H

```
//Create a sentinel. Only include the header if it
//hasn't been read yet.

#if !defined(H_TOPLST_H)
#define H_TOPLST_H

#include "choice.h"

//----ToppingList-------------------------------------------
//The ToppingList class is used to create a linked
//list of toppings contained in the pizza.
//
//Here is a class overview:
//ToppingList(int Num, Choice *ChoiceList) — initializes the
//    class, passing in a pointer to the types of
//    choices that can be used and the topping for the item
//~ToppingList() — frees up memory for the class
//AddFirst() — sets the values for the first element in the
//    list and potentially expands the list
//GetName() — returns the name of the topping
//GetPrice() — returns the price of the topping
//Add() — adds a new element to the list
//GetNext() — returns a pointer to the next item
//    in the list

class ToppingList {
public:
    //***NEW Now this is virtual
    virtual char *GetName();
    float GetPrice();
    void AddFirst();
    ToppingList *GetNext();
    ToppingList(int Num, Choice *ChoiceList);
    ~ToppingList();
    //***NEW — private items switched to protected
protected:
    int    Topping;
    ToppingList    *Next;
```

(continued)

```
        Choice          *ToppingChoices;
        void Add();
};

#endif //H_TOPLST_H
```

TOPLST.CPP

```
#include <iostream.h>
#include "toplst.h"
#include "diettop.h"

//The class is defined in toplst.h


//----Definitions for ToppingList member functions-----

//Returns the name of the topping. Finds this by
//calling the GetName function of the Choice object.
char *
ToppingList::GetName() {
    return ToppingChoices->GetName(Topping);
}

//Returns the price of the topping. Finds this by
//calling the GetPrice function of the Choice object.
float
ToppingList::GetPrice() {
    return ToppingChoices->GetPrice(Topping);
}

//This function is used to set the topping for the first
//item in the list.
void
ToppingList::AddFirst() {
    int  Select;

    //First get the selection.
    Topping = ToppingChoices->ChooseOne();

    //See if the user wants to add another.
    cout << "Add another? (0=No)\n";
    cin >> Select;

    //If the user wants to add another, call Add() for
    //the new one.
    if (Select)
        Add();
}


//This function is used to add a new topping to the
//list.
//***NEW — now it can make a DietTopping as well
```

```
void
ToppingList::Add() {
   int  Select, Diet;
   ToppingList  *NewOne;

   //First get the selection.
   Select = ToppingChoices->ChooseOne();

   //Should it be a diet class?
   cout << "Do you want that to be a diet topping?"
        << " (0=no)\n";
   cin >> Diet;

   //***NEW
   //Now make a new class. Find out if it should
   //be diet or regular.
   if (Diet)
      //Make a DietTopping
      NewOne = new DietTopping(Select, ToppingChoices);
   else
      //Make a normal topping.
      NewOne = new ToppingList(Select, ToppingChoices);

   //And now we will hook it up to this item.
   Next = NewOne;

   //See if the user wants to add another.
   cout << "Add another? (0=No)\n";
   cin >> Select;

   //If the user wants to add another, call Add() for
   //the new one.
   if (Select)
      NewOne->Add();
}

//Returns a pointer to the next topping in the list.
ToppingList *
ToppingList::GetNext() {
   return Next;
}

//The constructor initializes the class.
ToppingList::ToppingList(int Num, Choice *ChoiceList) {
   Next = 0;
   Topping = Num;
   ToppingChoices = ChoiceList;
}

//This is the destructor. It deletes the next item
//in the list. This will cause all items to be deleted
//and the memory freed.
ToppingList::~ToppingList() {
   if (Next)
      delete Next;
}
//----Finished ToppingList member functions--------------
```

CHOICE.H

```
//Create a sentinel. Only include the header if it
//hasn't been read yet.

#if !defined(H_CHOICE_H)
#define H_CHOICE_H

//----ChoiceDescription----------------------------------
//We'll use a class to represent the name
//and price of a particular choice.
class ChoiceDescription {
public:
   char *ChoiceName;
   float    ChoicePrice;
};

//----Choice----------------------------------------------
//The Choice class is a simple generic class that
//can be used throughout to represent different types
//of choice lists.
//
//Choice has the following public interfaces:
//    Choice(int Num, ChoiceDescription *InitList) —
//        initializes the structure with a number of
//        choices
//    GetName(int Num) — returns the name for choice
//        Num
//    GetPrice(int Num) — returns the price for choice
//        Num
//    ChooseOne() — prompts the user to choose one of
//        the items from the set of choices
//    GetMax() — returns the maximum number
//        allowed

class Choice {
public:
   Choice(const int Num, ChoiceDescription const
      *InitList);
   char  *GetName(int Num);
   float GetPrice(int Num);
   int   ChooseOne();
   //***NEW
   //Now it will return the maximum number allowed.
   int   GetMax();
private:
   int   NumChoices;
   int   GoodChoice(int Num);
   ChoiceDescription       const *List;
};

#endif //H_CHOICE_H
```

CHOICE.CPP

```
#include <iostream.h>
#include "choice.h"


//----ChoiceDescription----------------------------------
//We'll use a class to represent the name
//and price of a particular choice. We can then
//use this class for topping and pizza size
//choices. There are no member functions for this
//class. Note that this is a little bit cleaner than
//in the last program, because the name and price are
//always kept together, making it easier to initialize
//and query.
//The definition can be found in choice.h

//----Choice---------------------------------------------
//The Choice class contains a list of choices as
//well as routines for returning the name or price
//of a choice and routines for asking the user to
//make a choice. This is a simple generic class that
//can be used throughout to represent different types
//of choice lists.
//Any time that you need to represent a set of choices,
//print out a selection, or make a choose, you can use
//this class. Note that this will simplify a lot of
//the process of getting the name and price of toppings
//and so forth.
//
//Choice has the following public interfaces:
//     Choice(int Num, ChoiceDescription *InitList) -
//         initializes the structure with a number of
//         choices
//     GetName(int Num) - returns the name for choice
//         Num
//     GetPrice(int Num) - returns the price for choice
//         Num
//     ChooseOne() - prompts the user to choose one of
//         the items from the set of choices
//     GetMax() - returns the maximum number
//         allowed
// The definition can be found in choice.h


//----Definitions for Choice member functions------------

//The constructor initializes the class.
Choice::Choice(const int Num, const ChoiceDescription
  *InitList) {
  NumChoices = Num;
  List = InitList;
}
```

(continued)

```
//Returns the name for a particular choice.
char *
Choice::GetName(int Num) {
    return List[Num].ChoiceName;
}


//Returns the price for a particular choice.
float
Choice::GetPrice(int Num) {
    return List[Num].ChoicePrice;
}


//Prompts the user to make a choice from the set
//of options. Prints out what the available choices
//are and makes sure the choice is valid.
int
Choice::ChooseOne() {
    int    i;
    int    Select;

    //Keep asking the user until a good number
    //is picked.
    do {
        cout << "Please make a choice:\n";

        //Loop through and print all choices.
        for (i = 0; i < NumChoices; i++) {
            cout << i << " = " << List[i].ChoiceName <<
                 "\n";
        }

        //Get the selection.
        cin >> Select;
    } while (!GoodChoice(Select));

    //Return the choice.
    return Select;
}


//This returns the maximum number that is allowed
//in the set of choices.
int
Choice::GetMax() {
    return NumChoices - 1;
}


//This is a helping function that makes sure a
//particular choice is valid.
int
Choice::GoodChoice(int Num) {

    if ((Num < 0) || (Num >= NumChoices)) {
        //A bad choice so print a message and return false.
        cout << "I don't understand that choice.\n";
        return 0;
    }
```

```
    //Since we haven't returned, the choice is good.
    return 1;
}

//----Finished Choice member functions------------------
```

(This program is in the PIZZA8 directory on the separately available program disk.)

Chapter 34
E-I-E-Iostreams

● ●

In This Chapter
▶ Learn what streams are
▶ Read from and write to files
▶ Read and write different types
▶ Control output format

● ●

*O*ne of the fundamental operations of a program is to gather input and store output. In previous chapters you've seen how *cin* and *cout* do just that. *cin* and *cout* are both from a library that can also read from and write to disks. This library (or set of routines) is called the *iostream* library.

There are lots of different ways that you can get and save input. The iostream library is a particularly nice way because it handles much of the low-level processing automatically.

Quick-and-Dirty Reading from and Writing to a File

There are a number of library routines that can help you read from and write to files. Here's a real easy way to open a file for writing:

```
ofstream foo("filename");
```

ofstream is a special type of class that's used for sending output to files. (That's what the *o* and the *f* at the beginning of the word stand for: output and files.) You can pass ofstream a file name during the constructor, and then use << to write to it:

```
//Write "Hello World" in the file.
foo << "Hello world";
```

ofstream has a buddy named ifstream that is used for getting input from a file. (And, yes, the *i* and *f* stand for input and files.) *ifstream*'s usage is similar:

```
ifstream foo("filename");
//Set up some space into which to read text.
char  buffer[100];
//Read some text from the file.
foo >> buffer;
```

If you wanted to read numbers instead, you could do this:

```
int     MyInt;
foo >> MyInt;
```

But wait a minute! Before you use either of these, you need to do this:

```
#include <fstream.h>
```

Some Other Things You Need to Know

When you destroy a stream variable, its file will be closed. You can close it before the stream goes away by using the close( ) member function:

```
//Close the file used with the stream called foo().
foo.close();
```

Typically you would do this when you want to use one stream for accessing several files. In this case, you would close the first file and then open up a different file using the open( ) member function:

```
//Now open up "foo.txt".
foo.open("foo.txt");
```

If you want to see if there's anything left in the file, use the eof( ) member function, which returns true when the end of the file is reached. You can see an example of this in the program in the "A Quick Example of Reading Numbers and Words" section.

Five Facts on Files

Here are some handy tips about files:

> ✔ It's usually best if you don't read from and write to a file at the same time. It's perfectly legal to do so, but sometimes (especially for beginners) it can

be confusing to figure out which part of the file is being read and which part of the file is being written.

✔ When you write numbers to a file using <<, the numbers are saved as text. But no spaces are put between them. So if you want to see

    3.4 5.6 66.28 8

instead of

    3.45.666.288

then you need to put spaces between the numbers when you write them to a file. For example, you could do this:

```
cout << foo << " ";
```

✔ There's a magic character (called the end-of-file character and sometimes written *eof*) placed at the end of the file to say "Hey, I'm finished." When the >> finds this, it knows to say that the end of the file has been reached.

✔ Strings are read until a delimiter — namely *eof* or \n — is found. If the last string in a file doesn't end with a \n, then the end of file is reached immediately after the last string is read.

✔ When numbers are read in, the end-of-file character isn't included when the last number is read. So, if you're not careful, you'll end up trying to read one more item than is actually in the file and trying to put the end-of-file character into a number. In this case, the >> does nothing, so the number isn't changed. The next example program looks at this situation in a little more detail.

A Quick Example of Reading Numbers and Words

The example in this section writes some numbers and words to files, and then reads them back.

It begins by writing two files. One file contains text and the other file contains numbers:

```
//Open the file new.txt.
ofstream OutFile("new.txt");

//Write some text to the file.
OutFile << "Row, row, row your boat";

//Now close the file.
OutFile.close();
```

(continued)

```
//Open a different file and write some numbers
//in it. Note that these are separated by
//spaces.
OutFile.open("numbers.txt");
OutFile << 15 << " " << 42 << " " << 1;
OutFile.close();
```

Next, the ifstream class is used to open a file for reading. This time, instead of opening the file when the stream is constructed, the open command is used. Both approaches work fine, and you can use whichever method you prefer — the program demonstrates both approaches so you can see how they each work:

```
ifstream InFile;
InFile.open("new.txt");
```

A buffer is created to store the information that is read in from the file. In this case, the buffer is made 50 bytes long. You need to make sure that the buffer is larger than the largest item that you read in. If you know what the data is, just make the buffer larger than the largest item. Otherwise, you can control how much information is read in through programming commands.

The file is read into the buffer, and then printed out, one item at a time:

```
InFile >> p;
cout << p << "\n";
InFile >> p;
cout << p << "\n";
```

Next, the number file is read. A loop is used to read the entire file, regardless of the number of items in the file. The *eof* function indicates when the end of the file is reached. Because the end-of-file character is treated as an integer, a special check is used so that the very last item read from the file (the end of file) isn't printed as being one of the numbers:

```
//Read through the file until there is no more
//input.
while (!InFile.eof()) {
    //Read in an integer.
    InFile >> TempNum;
    //If the end of the file wasn't just reached,
    //print out the integer.
    if (!InFile.eof())
        cout << TempNum << "\n";
}
```

Finally, the text file is read one word at a time. (By the way, if you stored the words in a linked list of word objects, you'd be well on your way to completing the infamous word processor homework assignment given in many Computer Science classes.)

Making >> and << work with your types

By default, >> and << work only with the standard, predefined data types. You can also make them work with your own types by using operator overloading. You can find examples of how to do this in Chapter 37.

The Code

```
//Illustrates use of streams for file i/o.

#include <fstream.h>
#include <iostream.h>

void main() {

    //Open the file new.txt.
    ofstream OutFile("new.txt");

    //Write some text to the file.
    OutFile << "Row, row, row your boat";

    //Now close the file.
    OutFile.close();

    //Open a different file and write some numbers
    //in it. Note that these are separated by
    //spaces.
    OutFile.open("numbers.txt");
    OutFile << 15 << " " << 42 << " " << 1;
    OutFile.close();

    //Now we will open a file for reading.
    ifstream InFile;
    InFile.open("new.txt");

    //Set up a buffer that can be used for reading
    //the text.
    char p[50];

    //Read and print the first two words from the
    //file.
    InFile >>  p;
    cout << p << "\n";
    InFile >>  p;
    cout << p << "\n";
```

(continued)

```
//Close the file.
InFile.close();

//Now we will read through the integers.
int TempNum;
InFile.open("numbers.txt");

//Read through the file until there is no more
//input.
while (!InFile.eof()) {
   //Read in an integer.
   InFile >> TempNum;
   //If the end of the file wasn't just reached,
   //print out the integer.
   if (!InFile.eof())
      cout << TempNum << "\n";
}
InFile.close();

//Now, just for the fun of it, we will read through
//the text file one word at a time.
InFile.open("new.txt");

//Read through the file until there is no more
//input.
while (!InFile.eof()) {
   //Read through the file one word at a time.
   //For reading words we don't need to do the
   //eof check in the middle.
   InFile >> p;
   cout << p << "\n";
}

}
```

(This program is in the FILESTR directory on the separately available program disk.)

Special Things to Toss into a Stream

Here are some things you can include in a stream to change the way reading and writing is handled. These things (called stream manipulators) don't cause anything to be read or written; they just affect the way following items are read or written:

dec   Read or display the next number as a decimal.

hex   Read or display the next number as a hex number.

oct   Read or display the next number as an octal number.

For example, if you know that the user is going to type in a hex number you could do this:

```
cin >> hex >> TempNum;
```

Or, you could use this as an instant hex-to-decimal converter:

```
//Read it in as hex.
cin >> hex >> TempNum;
//Print it out as decimal.
cout << TempNum;
```

Setting Fill and Width for Integers

By default, numbers are printed using as many characters as it takes to print them. If you need to, though, you can use more spaces. This can be useful when you want to keep things in columns. To do this, use the width( ) member function:

```
//Output numbers using 20 spaces.
cout.width(20);
```

Or, you could instead put in a fill character. For example, you might want to print * in unused spaces so that someone doesn't alter your paychecks:

```
//Use * as the fill character.
cout.fill('*');
```

Of course, you can set a fill character the same exact way with file streams.

But Wait, There's More

There are hundreds and hundreds of different ways that you can read from and write to the screen and files, and there are plenty of extra classes not covered here. If you want to become an input/output maestro, read through the stream sections of the various Borland C++ manuals. In addition to the general sections on streams and the stream classes, you might want to pay special attention to the sections on formatting methods, format flags, and manipulators.

Chapter 35

Staying Out of Trouble: Exception Handling

● ●

In This Chapter

▶ Learn what exception handling is

▶ Create exception classes

▶ Examine exception handling in an application

● ●

*Y*ou've already seen how part of the programming process involves testing and debugging your program. But even after your program is bug-free and running fine, it could still run into problems. That's because you can't predict what the user is going to do to your program or what conditions your programs will face. The only thing you really *can* predict is that unexpected things are going to happen.

These unexpected conditions are called *error conditions*. There are lots and lots of reasons why error conditions happen. Maybe the disk is full, or maybe the machine doesn't have enough memory to read in the 75M photograph the user is trying to stuff into a database, or maybe an input file has bad data, or maybe the user typed in "fudge" instead of the pizza number.

The point is, *all* these things (and many more besides) can cause bad things to happen in a program. Often the program will crash or GP fault.

Fortunately, *exception handling* can help you catch and handle errors.

Error Handling the Old Way

So that you can fully appreciate the joys of exception handling, let's take a look at the old, messy way of handling errors.

Error handling can be divided into two parts: detecting the error and then communicating and handling the error. The first part — detecting the error — isn't usually so bad. Some routine deep in the bowels of the application needs to have some extra code added to check for errors and to essentially say "Aha — not enough data. This is an error."

Once the error is found, it needs to be communicated and handled. The communication part can be a pain. The item that finds the error might have been called by some function that was called by some function that was called by some function, and so on. All these functions need to be able to see that an error has occurred and then figure out what to do. Usually, some code is checked — if it indicates that there were no problems, the routine keeps going; otherwise, the routine ends early.

In other words, a straightforward set of code such as this:

```
//Call a bunch of functions.
ReadToppings();
ReadSizes();
ReadMyLips();
```

would need to turn into this:

```
//Call a bunch of functions. Values less than
//0 mean errors.
temp = ReadToppings();
if (temp < 0)
    return temp;
temp = ReadSizes();
if (temp < 0)
    return temp;
temp = ReadMyLips();
if (temp < 0)
    return temp;
```

Now imagine doing that after every single function call in every single routine in your program. Yuck.

To make matters worse, suppose a function is allowed to return a value less than 0. In that case, you'd need another type of error scheme to check after each function is called.

Finally, after going through all this, some function eventually needs to look at the error code and say something like "Aha. I know how to handle this error." This function needs to be able to differentiate the various types of errors.

In short, it's a pain to do this. You might have to spend far more time writing all this crazy error code than writing the important parts of the program. Plus, this type of error-handling code makes the program ugly and hard to read.

Error Handling the New, Improved Way

Exception handling solves these problems. There are two parts to exception handling: one routine throws an exception (it essentially says "whoa, error found!") and a second routine is designated as the handler. When the exception is found, this second routine takes control.

With this new strategy, all those messy return-code checks after every function call are no longer needed. The unique error codes and problems with function return values disappear.

And there's another benefit, too. Any objects that have been created locally — that is, any objects that were created when various functions were called — are automatically destroyed. To illustrate this, suppose function *A* creates a local object called ObjectA, then calls a function called *B*, which creates a local object called ObjectB, which calls a function that finds an error. ObjectB and ObjectA would be destroyed. So any files, memory, data, and so on that they used would be cleaned up.

Try and Catch My Drift

Here's how exception handling works. If you want to turn on exception checking in a section of code, you put the code inside *try { }*. This says "Try out the following routines and see what happens." Following the try, you put a *catch { }*. This says "If any problems occur, catch them here and handle the errors."

An exceptionally well-handled example

Let's take a quick look at an example of exception handling in action. (We'll discuss the syntax in more detail in a moment, in the section called "Just the Syntax, Ma'am.") The program contains a function that tries to allocate 50000 bytes of memory. The function then uses the memory. First, let's look at it without any error handling:

```
void
AllocateBuf() {
    char  *buffer;
    buffer = new char[50000];
    buffer[0] = 'h'; //Set the first character.
    foo(buffer);  //Pass the buffer to function foo.
}

void
main() {
    AllocateBuf();
    cout << "Finished fine";
}
```

What happens if there isn't enough memory to allocate a 50000 byte array? The *new* command will return 0, indicating that it couldn't allocate the memory. Thus, buffer will contain a null pointer. When you try to set the first character to the letter *h*, you'll crash. (Uh oh.)

If you added error handling, you might do something like this:

```
void
AllocateBuf() {
    char  *buffer;
    buffer = new char[50000];
    if (buffer) {
        //Only do this if buffer is not null.
        buffer[0] = 'h'; //Set the first character.
        foo(buffer);        //Pass the buffer to function foo.
    }
}

void
main() {
    AllocateBuf();
    cout << "Finished fine";
}
```

In this case, the routines within the *if* statement won't execute if memory couldn't be allocated. Looks like it's pretty simple to avoid the crash!

Unfortunately, you still have lots of things to change to make this approach work. First, even if you aren't able to allocate the memory, you'll print "Finished fine". So, you'd probably want to return an error code from AllocateBuf( ). And you'd need to check that error code. As you can see, you'll quickly end up with the problems described in the "Error Handling the Old Way" section.

With exception handling, your code would be a lot simpler:

```
void
AllocateBuf() {
    char  *buffer;
    buffer = new char[50000];
    buffer[0] = 'h'; //Set the first character.
    foo(buffer);  //Pass the buffer to function foo.
}

void
main() {
    try {
        AllocateBuf();
        cout << "Finished fine";
    }
    catch (xalloc) {
        cout << "Darn — ran into a problem."
    }
}
```

This version is far less intrusive. The following lines mean run this code with exception handling in action:

```
try {
    AllocateBuf();
    cout << "Finished fine";
}
```

If the memory could be allocated, "Finished fine" will print. But if a problem occurs when allocating memory, *new* throws an exception (which in this case happens to be the *xalloc* exception). Thus, the following lines spring into action:

```
catch (xalloc) {
    cout << "Darn — ran into a problem."
}
```

These lines say "If an xalloc exception happened, I must have had some trouble allocating memory, so print an error message."

Flexibility: exception handling's middle name

C++ exception handling provides great flexibility. You can turn error checking on and off selectively by enclosing only certain sections of code within a *try*. You can easily handle different types of errors. And you can process the same error different ways in different parts of the program by having what happens in the *catch* operate differently.

For example, suppose you call the AllocateBuf( ) routine from two different parts in your program. In one part, you're calling it to allocate memory for a file you want to save, and in another part you're using it to allocate memory for a photograph.

You could do the following:

```
//Here you try to save the file.
try {
    AllocateBuf();
    SaveFile();
}
catch (xalloc) {
    cout << "Couldn't save file";
}
//Here you are allocating memory for a photograph.
try {
    AllocateBuf();
    ProcessPhoto();
}
catch {
    cout << "Couldn't process photo";
}
```

The same AllocateBuf( ) is called in each case. And the same type of error will occur if the memory couldn't be allocated. But the error message that's printed will be different in each case.

Throw up Your Arms if You Run into Trouble

Okay, everything looks pretty reasonable so far. But what do you do if you detect a special error condition within your function? For instance, a previous example calls a function named foo. Suppose foo checks the values inside the buffer passed to it, and knows that if the first letter is x an explosion might occur. How would you indicate that an error condition has occurred?

Inside a function, you use the *throw* command if you find an error. This triggers an exception, and the compiler looks for the *catch* area from the most recent *try* block.

So, if you wanted to throw an error if the first letter in the buffer is x, you could do this:

```
void
foo(char *buffer) {
    if (buffer[0] == 'x')
        throw "Look out!";
    //Process buffer here.
}
```

This code checks to see if the first character in the buffer passed to foo is x. If it is, it throws an exception. If it isn't, foo continues normally.

Another nice thing about exceptions is that you can make as many different types of exceptions as you want. Each *throw* sends an instance of a data type. You can create whatever data types you want, fill them with data, and use that information to help process the error.

You can even use classes. That way you can build routines to help process the error right into the error class that is thrown. For example, you could create a new class called MyError. If you run into a problem you would create a MyError variable, and then *throw* that variable.

The *catch* takes a data type as a parameter. So you could make a ChoiceError class that is caught by one *catch*, and a MyError class that is caught by another.

You can also use inheritance. For example, the MyError class could be derived from the ChoiceError class.

Just the Syntax, Ma'am

Here's the syntax for exception handling:

```
try {
    //Error handling now on.
    statements;
}
catch (error_type_1) {
    statements to handle this error;
}
catch (error_type_2) {
    statements to handle this error;
}
    .
    .
    .
```

To trigger the error, you would do this:

```
throw error_type;
```

Here's a quick example. This program has a loop that asks the user for a number five times. Each time through the loop, it prints the square root of the number. If the user types a negative number, it prints an error message:

```
#include <iostream.h>
#include <math.h>

//Throws an error if n < 0.
//Otherwise returns square root.
float SquareRoot(float n) {
    //If n is bad, throw an exception.
    if (n < 0)
        throw "Can't find root if less than 0\n";

    //n is good, return the value.
    return sqrt(n);
}

void
main() {
    int i;
    int UserNum;

    //Loop 5 times.
    for (i = 0; i < 5; i++) {
        //Turn on exception handling.
        try {
            //Get the number.
            cout << "Please enter a number\n";
            cin >> UserNum;
            cout << "The answer is " << SquareRoot(UserNum) << "\n";
        }
```

(continued)

```
                    //We'll catch any exceptions that throw char *'s.
                    catch (char *Msg) {
                       //Print the message for the user.
                       cout << Msg;
                    }
               }
          cout << "Thanks for entering numbers!\n";
     }
```

(This program is in the EXCEPT directory in the separately available program disk.)

To read this program, look first at the *try* block, where you see a lot of routines that are called. These routines will execute normally unless some problem occurs:

```
try {
   //Get the number.
   cout << "Please enter a number\n";
   cin >> UserNum;
   cout << "The answer is " << SquareRoot(UserNum) << "\n";
}
```

If an error occurs in one of these routines, the SquareRoot routine *throws* a char *. It fills the char * in with an error message:

```
if (n < 0)
   throw "Can't find root if less than 0\n";
```

Right after the *try* block, there's a *catch* area. You can see that there is a *catch* for anything that *throws* a char *. The char * that's thrown is a real variable, so it has a name. The *catch* routine prints out its value.

```
catch (char *Msg) {
   //Print the message for the user.
   cout << Msg;
}
```

So what happens when this program runs? First, the program enters the loop. Within the loop, it tries to execute the code within the *try* block, which asks the user for a number and then prints the square root of the number. If the user enters a number that isn't negative, the SquareRoot function won't throw an exception. In this case, all the code in the *try* block executes, and the square root of the number is printed. Then, execution jumps back to the beginning of the loop (assuming the loop isn't over) and the code in the *try* block is tried again.

If the user types in a negative number, the SquareRoot function throws an exception. In this case, the code inside the *catch* block executes, printing out an error message. Then, execution jumps back to the beginning of the loop (unless the loop has already gone through five times) and the code in the *try* block is tried again. Once the loop executes five times, the program prints a goodbye message and stops.

It Looks Good, but That Type Stuff Is Confusing

Throwing classes solves two problems because you can make as many different types of exceptions as you would like, and because you can pass a great deal of information about an error and how to process it when a problem occurs.

For example, when a disk error occurs you might want to indicate the drive that has the problem. And if a file is corrupted, you might want to indicate the file name and the last place in the file that was successfully read. You might even want to have a routine for trying to fix the file.

But when you throw a class, how does the compiler know which *catch* to use? That's the great part. The compiler looks at the type of the data you threw, and finds the catch that knows how to handle those items. So you can make a DiskErrorClass, a FileCorruptClass, and a MemoryErrorClass, with each class containing information describing the problem that occurred. Each class can contain completely different types of information.

If you then found a disk error, you'd do this:

```
DiskErrorClass.foo;
//In real life, fill it with info here.
throw foo;
```

And if you had a corrupt file, you'd do this:

```
CorruptFileClass.bar;
//In real life, fill it with info here.
throw bar;
```

Then, the appropriate catch will be called, because *catch* looks to match a data or class type:

```
//Catch disk errors here.
catch (DiskErrorClass MyError) { }

//Catch corrupt files here.
catch (CorruptFileClass MyError) { }
```

Using classes is an elegant way to provide great flexibility, because you can make whatever error classes you want and store lots of information in them, while making it easy for the compiler to find exactly what exception type was thrown.

If you want, you can use simple data types like char * for exception types. But you're much better off creating exception classes because you can fill each class with a lot of information to describe exactly what went wrong. The routine that finds the error knows all this stuff. The routine that processes the error knows how to use the information to help the user.

Another great thing about designing your own classes is that you can give them member functions. For example, you can build into the class a set of routines to print out what error has occurred and to help you process or fix the situation.

Let's Look at an Example

The following is an excerpt from the program in Chapter 36. The excerpt shows an exception class that contains data members to describe the problem and a member function to help print what went wrong.

The *try* and *catch* occur in main. A set of routines, in this case for reading choice lists from files, are enclosed in a *try* block:

```
try {
    PizzaSizes = new Choice("sizes.txt");
    Toppings = new Choice("toppings.txt");
}
```

This is followed by a *catch* block to catch any problems that occur when these routines run. If an error does occur, the PrintError member function of the error class is called to print out what happened. Then the application terminates:

```
catch(ChoiceError BadOne) {
    //ChoiceError class to print out what happened.
    BadOne.PrintError();
    cout << "Stopping due to error.\n";
    //Now terminate the program using a library call.
    exit(EXIT_FAILURE);
}
```

That's the only change that had to be made to main to handle errors. No complicated code is required to look at return values or to figure out what to do for different error conditions.

The exception error class, ChoiceError, contains information describing the error and a member function for printing information about the error:

```
//Contains info describing an error.
class ChoiceError {
public:
    int   LastItem;
    char  *FileName;
    void  PrintError();
};
```

Exception type conversion and catch matching

If an exception type can easily be converted to a type in the *catch*, it's considered a match.

For example, it's easy to turn a *short* into an *int*. So the catch will be used if you do this:

```
catch (int k) { }
.
.
.
throw (short i = 6);
```

Likewise, if you threw a class Derived that was derived from class Base, a pointer to the derived class can easily be used as a pointer to the base class:

```
catch (Base *foo) { }
.
.
.
Derived *foo;
foo = new Derived;
throw foo;
```

In this case, the catch will also be called. For this reason, you might want to use virtual functions when you create member functions in exception classes.

The compiler will call the first catch that matches the data type. So if you have a bunch of classes that are derived from a base class, list them first and the base class catch last. That way the special case (the derived class) catch will be called rather than the base class. Because, after all, the compiler just uses the first one that matches, and both will suffice in this case.

The Choice class function GotEOF contains code for throwing an exception if the end of the input file was unexpectedly encountered. This occurs if the file contains bad data or no data at all.

If an error occurs, a ChoiceError object is created, filled with information, and thrown. This immediately destroys objects on the stack and transfers control to the *catch* block, as shown in the following code snippet:

```
void
Choice::GotEOF(int BadItem, char *FName) {
    ChoiceError   Err;
    //Fill in the name and last item that was read.
    Err.LastItem = BadItem;
    Err.FileName = FName;

    //Throw the exception.
    throw Err;
}
```

You can see this code in action in Chapter 36.

Make way for users!

The great thing about users is that they use your software. This provides you a shot at fame and fortune, or at least means you get to keep your job or pass a class. The bad thing about users is that they often do things with your software that you don't expect. That's why you need to add exception handling code.

Here are some common error conditions your program should be able to handle.

✔ The program runs out of memory. This can happen if the user tries to open files much larger than you expect, if the user doesn't have much memory in his or her machine to begin with, or for a number of other reasons.

✔ The user types in a bad file name. For example, when the program asks the user what file to open, he or she might type "Hey, why do you care?" Obviously, that's not a legal file name.

✔ The user types in a number that is outside an acceptable range. For example, you might want numbers between 0 and 5, but the user

types in -17. Consider adding range checking for functions that users will never get near. For example, you could have some internal computation routines that expect numbers in a certain range. Adding error checking will make them safer to use.

✔ Users load a file that isn't the correct type. For example, you might have a program that reads text files, but the user tries to run COMMAND.COM through it. This can happen in other parts of your code if you're expecting data structures to be filled with information of a particular format, and for some reason, it doesn't come to your function that way.

✔ Data files are missing. For example, suppose your program expects a list of passwords in a file called PASSWD.SCT. But for some reason, the user deleted this file, so now the program can't find the password file.

✔ The disk is full. Your program needs to save a file, but there is no more space left on the disk.

Inheriting from Error Handling Classes

You can derive new error handling classes from existing ones. This lets you reuse error handling code quite nicely.

For example, suppose you have a DiskError class that contains a member function for handling the problem and data members describing what happened. You could create a FatalDiskError class by deriving from the DiskError class and adding or overriding existing items.

Be sure to follow the rules for when to use virtual functions (see Chapter 31).

Five Rules for Exceptional Success

Here are five simple rules you can follow to help you when you write exception handling code:

- ✔ Throw classes instead of simple data types. You can provide a lot more information about what went wrong.

- ✔ Throw classes so that you can add member functions if you need to.

- ✔ Create a different class for each major category of error you expect to encounter.

- ✔ Make sure you exactly match the type of what you throw with what you catch. For example, if you throw a DiskError *, make sure you catch a DiskError *, not a DiskError.

  If you mess this up, unexpected things will happen. (Note that if the compiler can convert one error type to another type, such as a float to an integer, it will try to do so in order to find a match for an exception. See the "Exception type conversion and catch matching" sidebar for more information.)

- ✔ If no handler is found for the exception, by default the program will abort. Be prepared for this. Fortunately, since objects on the stack will be destroyed, their destructors will be called and your application will perform clean-up.

Chapter 36
Safe and Flexible Pizza++

● ●

In This Chapter
▶ Use streams to read choice lists from disk files
▶ Add exception handling to process unexpected disk errors

● ●

*I*n earlier versions of our pizza program, if you had wanted to change the set of available toppings or sizes, you would have had to change code and recompile. This might not bother you, but it might be a little much to expect pizza parlors to whip out Borland C++ every time their menu changed.

With this chapter's updated version of the pizza program, you can list the toppings and sizes in text files. That way, anyone can change the text file and the new items will be loaded the next time the program runs. The text files will be read using streams.

Because this new version of the program lets end-users create the topping lists, more mistakes can happen. For example, a user might indicate that there are nine different toppings, but get tired after listing two toppings and then stop. The new program features error checking, so it can now throw an exception if something like this happens.

The Input Files

Let's take a quick look at the two files used for describing pizza choices. One (SIZES.TXT) is read for the list of size choices, and the other (TOPPINGS.TXT) is read for the list of topping choices. Each starts with a number telling how many items are in the list, followed by that many names and prices. Feel free to change these files.

If you want to check out the exception handling, you could make the number of choices much larger than the number of items listed. For example, you could change the first number in SIZES.TXT to 45, but then not add any more sizes.

SIZES.TXT

```
3
Small      10
Medium     12
Large      14
```

TOPPINGS.TXT

```
5
Pepperoni       1.8
Sausage         2.1
Onions          0.5
Extra_Cheese    1.0
Olives          0.7
```

By the way, you'll notice that the TOPPINGS.TXT file contains a _ (an underline) instead of a space between the two words Extra and Cheese (like_this). That's because a space would be read as two separate items and things would get kind of messed up. You can program around this if you want. (Consider it a piece of homework!)

How It Works

There are two main changes to the program. First, streams are used to read the pizza sizes and pizza toppings from disk files. Second, exception handling takes care of unexpected errors while reading the disk files.

Using streams to read choices from disk

A new Choice constructor takes the name of a disk file and reads the file for choices:

```
Choice::Choice(char *FileName) {
```

It begins by opening the file and finding the number of choices:

```
//Open up the file.
ifstream ChoiceFile(FileName);

//Find the number of choices in the file.
ChoiceFile >> NumChoices;
```

It then creates a new ChoiceDescription containing enough entries for the number of choices:

```
//Create a new list that is big enough to hold
//all these choices.
List = new ChoiceDescription[NumChoices];
```

It then uses streams to read the choices from the file. The GetEOF function is called if the end of the file is unexpectedly reached:

```
//Read all the choices out of the file.
for (i = 0; i < NumChoices; i++) {
    //If we've already hit an end of file, then
    //something is wrong.
    if (ChoiceFile.eof())
        GotEOF(i, FileName);

    //Otherwise, read the name into the buffer.
    ChoiceFile >> buf;

    //Create a copy of the name that will hang
    //around permanently.
    temp = new char[strlen(buf)+1];
    strcpy(temp, buf);

    //Use this as the name.
    List[i].ChoiceName = temp;

    //Now read in the price.
    ChoiceFile >> List[i].ChoicePrice;
}

//Be polite and close the file.
ChoiceFile.close();
}
```

This constructor is called in main to create the two choice lists:

```
PizzaSizes = new Choice("sizes.txt");
Toppings = new Choice("toppings.txt");
```

The exception handling

Exception handling is used to make sure errors don't occur when reading the disk files. In particular, the Choice constructor just shown calls Choice::GotEOF if the end of the file is reached unexpectedly. This happens if the file doesn't contain as many entries as it should.

The Choice::GotEOF function throws an exception:

```
//Fill in the name and last item that was read.
Err.LastItem = BadItem;
Err.FileName = FName;

//Throw the exception.
throw Err;
```

This exception is caught in the main routine. The main routine surrounds the routines that read the disk files in a *try* block:

```
try {
    PizzaSizes = new Choice("sizes.txt");
    Toppings = new Choice("toppings.txt");
}
```

That way, if any problems occur they'll be caught in the *catch* block. This block calls the ChoiceError::PrintError function to indicate what went wrong, deletes the PizzaSizes class if it exists, and then terminates the program:

```
catch(ChoiceError BadOne) {
    //Had a choice error. Print out what went
    //wrong.
    BadOne.PrintError();
    cout << "Stopping due to error.\n";
    //If PizzaSizes was created, delete it.
    if (PizzaSizes)
        delete PizzaSizes;
    //Now terminate the program using a library call.
    exit(EXIT_FAILURE);
}
```

This code executes only if there was a problem in the application.

The exception class, ChoiceError, contains information describing the error along with a member function to display the error information:

```
class ChoiceError {
public:
    int    LastItem;
    char   *FileName;
    void   PrintError();
};
```

The Code

Most of the files in the pizza program didn't need to be changed. Only the files that *did* change are listed here. As always, look for //***NEW to find what's changed.

PIZZA9.CPP

```
//This version reads the toppings and sizes from
//a file using streams.
//It uses exception handling in case one of the
//files is incomplete.
```

```
//The major changes are:
// The choice lists are in a try block.
// Choice now reads from files to initialize arrays.
// Choice will throw an exception if it finds a problem.
// A ChoiceError class is created to handle the
// exception.

#include <iostream.h>
#include <stdlib.h>
#include "choice.h"
#include "milkem.h"

//There are four main classes used:
//      ToppingList - a list of pizza toppings
//      DietTopping - a special topping that has less
//          calories
//      Pizza - info describing the pizza
//      MilkEmPizza - a special type of pizza that tries
//          to be expensive
//We also have helper classes:
//      Choice - used to represent choices that can
//          be made by the user
//      ChoiceDescription - a structure containing a
//          choice name and price
//      ChoiceError - used for exceptions



//-----The main routine begins here----------------------


void
main() {
    //***NEW
    //We'll make two lists of choices, one for
    //pizza sizes and one for toppings.
    Choice *PizzaSizes, *Toppings;

    //***NEW
    //We'll read the choices in from disk files.
    //If there is some problem with a file an
    //exception will be thrown. We'll catch that
    //exception.
    try {
        PizzaSizes = new Choice("sizes.txt");
        Toppings = new Choice("toppings.txt");
    }
    //Here we will catch any exceptions thrown by
    //things in the call block.
    catch(ChoiceError BadOne) {
        //Had a choice error. Print out what went
        //wrong.
        BadOne.PrintError();
        cout << "Stopping due to error.\n";
        //If PizzaSizes was created, delete it
        if (PizzaSizes)
            delete PizzaSizes;
```

(continued)

```
//Now terminate the program using a library call.
  exit(EXIT_FAILURE);
}

//No exception thrown, so continue.

//***NEW
//Because we created these dynamically we no
//longer need to get their address — they are already
//pointers.
MilkEmPizza MyPizza(PizzaSizes, Toppings);

//Now we will choose the size.
MyPizza.ChooseSize();

//Now we will choose the toppings.
MyPizza.ChooseToppings();

//Now we will print the order.
MyPizza.PrintOrder();
}
```

CHOICE.H

```
//Create a sentinel. Only include the header if it
//hasn't been read yet.

#if !defined(H_CHOICE_H)
#define H_CHOICE_H

//----ChoiceDescription------------------------------
//We'll use a class to represent the name
//and price of a particular choice.
class ChoiceDescription {
public:
    char  *ChoiceName;
    float ChoicePrice;
};

//----Choice-----------------------------------------
//The Choice class is a simple generic class that
//can be used throughout to represent different types
//of choice lists.
//
//Choice has the following public interfaces:
//      Choice(int Num, ChoiceDescription *InitList) —
//          initializes the structure with a number of
//          choices
//      Choice(char *FileName) — reads entries from
//          a file
//      ~Choice() — cleans up memory used by choice
//      GetName(int Num) — returns the name for choice
//          Num
```

```
//      GetPrice(int Num) — returns the price for choice
//          Num
//      ChooseOne() — prompts the user to choose one of
//          the items from the set of choices
//      GetMax() — returns the maximum number
//          allowed


class Choice {
public:
    //***NEW New constructor
    Choice(char *FileName);
    //***NEW no longer using const for second arg
    Choice(const int Num, ChoiceDescription
      *InitList);
    //***NEW destructor
    ~Choice();
    char *GetName(int Num);
    float   GetPrice(int Num);
    int  ChooseOne();
    int  GetMax();
private:
    int  NumChoices;
    int  GoodChoice(int Num);
    //***NEW private function
    void GotEOF(int BadItem, char *FName);
    ChoiceDescription       *List;
};


//***NEW
//----ChoiceError----------------------------------------
//ChoiceError contains a description of an error.
//It also contains a member function that can be
//used to print out why the error happened.
//
//ChoiceError has the following public interfaces:
//   PrintError() — prints why an error happened

class ChoiceError {
public:
    int    LastItem;
    char  *FileName;
    void  PrintError();
};

#endif  //H_CHOICE_H
```

CHOICE.CPP

```
#include <iostream.h>
#include <fstream.h>
#include <string.h>
#include "choice.h"
```

(continued)

```
//----Choice--------------------------------------------
//
//***NEW
//Choice has a new constructor that will read a
//set of choices from a disk file, giving added
//flexibility. Choice also checks for error
//conditions and throws an exception if something bad
//happens. A private function GotEOF() has been added
//that throws the exception.
//
//If choices are read from files, the expected
//format is:
//   numChoices
//   name1      price1
//   ....
//
// The definition can be found in choice.h.

//----Definitions for Choice member functions-----------

//***NEW
//This routine is called if an unexpected end of
//file is found.
void
Choice::GotEOF(int BadItem, char *FName) {
   ChoiceError *Err;

   //Fill in the name and last item that was read.
   Err.LastItem = BadItem;
   Err.FileName = FName;

   //Throw the exception
   throw Err;
}

//***NEW
//This is a new constructor that takes the name
//of a file containing choices. It uses streams
//to read the choices from disk.
Choice::Choice(char *FileName) {
   int  i;
   char buf[50], *temp;

   //Open up the file
   ifstream ChoiceFile(FileName);

   //Find the number of choices in the file.
   ChoiceFile >> NumChoices;

   //Create a new list that is big enough to hold
   //all these choices.
   List = new ChoiceDescription[NumChoices];

   //Read all the choices out of the file.
   for (i = 0; i < NumChoices; i++) {
      //If we've already hit an end of file, then
      //something is wrong.
```

```
      if (ChoiceFile.eof())
         GotEOF(i, FileName);

      //Otherwise, read the name into the buffer.
      ChoiceFile >> buf;

      //Create a copy of the name that will hang
      //around permanently.
      temp = new char[strlen(buf)+1];
      strcpy(temp, buf);

      //Use this as the name.
      List[i].ChoiceName = temp;

      //Now read in the price.
      ChoiceFile >> List[i].ChoicePrice;
   }

   //Be polite and close the file.
   ChoiceFile.close();
}

//***NEW
//Here is the destructor. It reads through the
//items in a Choice list and frees all memory.
Choice::~Choice() {
   int i;

   //Free all strings.
   for (i = 0; i < NumChoices; i++)
      delete List[i].ChoiceName;

   //Free the array space itself.
   delete List;
}

//The constructor initializes the class.
//***NEW — note that we are no longer expecting the array to
//be constant.
Choice::Choice(const int Num, ChoiceDescription
   *InitList) {
   NumChoices = Num;
   List = InitList;
}

//Returns the name for a particular choice.
char *
Choice::GetName(int Num) {
   return List[Num].ChoiceName;
}

//Returns the price for a particular choice.
float
Choice::GetPrice(int Num) {
   return List[Num].ChoicePrice;
}
```

(continued)

```
//Prompts the user to make a choice from the set
//of options. Prints out what the available choices
//are and makes sure the choice is valid.
int
Choice::ChooseOne() {
    int  i;
    int  Select;

    //Keep asking the user until user picks a good
    //number.
    do {
        cout << "Please make a choice:\n";

        //Loop through and print all choices.
        for (i = 0; i < NumChoices; i++) {
            cout << i << " = " << List[i].ChoiceName <<
                "\n";
        }

        //Get the selection.
        cin >> Select;
    } while (!GoodChoice(Select));

    //Return the choice.
    return Select;
}

//This returns the maximum number that is allowed
//in the set of choices.
int
Choice::GetMax() {
    return NumChoices - 1;
}

//This is a helping function that makes sure
//a particular choice is valid.
int
Choice::GoodChoice(int Num) {

    if ((Num < 0) || (Num >= NumChoices)) {
        //A bad choice so print a message and return false.
        cout << "I don't understand that choice.\n";
        return 0;
    }

    //Since we haven't returned, the choice is good.
    return 1;
}

//----Finished Choice member functions-------------------

//***NEW
//----ChoiceError----------------------------------------
//ChoiceError contains a description of an error.
//It also contains a member function that can be
//used to print out why the error happened.
//
```

```
//   PrintError() — prints why an error happened

//----ChoiceError member functions----------------------

void
ChoiceError::PrintError() {
    cout << "An error was found in " << FileName <<
        " while reading choice # "  << LastItem << "\n";
}
```

(This program is in the PIZZA9 directory on the separately available program disk.)

Chapter 37

Brain Overload with Overloading (and Friends)

*W*hen you overload a function, you can have several functions with the same name, but each with a different set of arguments. You can then invoke the function in a variety of different ways, depending on what your needs are.

For example, let's say you need to write a function that finds an employee's home address. You could write one function that requires the person's last name, and another function that requires the person's employee identification number. Both functions perform a very similar operation, but without overloading, you'd need to give each function a different name.

There are lots of other things you can use overloading for. For example, you can expand the way << works with streams so that you can print complex structures in a stream. Or you can overload operators so that +, *, and - know how to do matrix math.

How to Overload a Member Function

Overloading a member function is easy. You've already done it with multiple constructors. Just provide a set of functions that have the same name, but different argument signatures.

The following example contains two functions for finding and returning the phone number for an employee. Both are called GetPhone. One takes an integer and the other takes a string.

```
class EmployeeArray {
public:
    int    GetPhone(int Id);
    int    GetPhone(char *Name);
private:
    int    EmpId[NumEmployees];
    char *EmpNames[NumEmployees];
    int    Phone[NumEmployees];
};

//Get the phone # given the id #. Return
//0 (operator) if listing is not found.
int
EmployeeArray::GetPhone(int Id) {
    //Loop through to find it
    for (int i = 0; i < NumEmployees; i++) {
        //If find it, return
        if (EmpId[i] == Id)
            return Phone[i];
    }

    //Never found it.
    return 0;
}

//Get the phone # given the name. Return
//0 (operator) if listing is not found.
int
EmployeeArray::GetPhone(char *Name) {
    //Loop through to find it
    for (int i = 0; i < NumEmployees; i++) {
        //If find it, return
        if (!strcmp(EmpName[i],Name))
            return Phone[i];
    }

    //Never found it.
    return 0;
}
```

With this code, you can find a phone number by doing this:

```
//Get # for employee 007.
GetPhone(7);

//Get # for Elvis.
GetPhone("Elvis");
```

So what's so special about this? Well, now you don't need to give different names to functions that more or less do the same thing, except they do it given different data. If it weren't for function overloading, you'd have to create a function called GetPhoneGivenInt, a function called GetPhoneGivenString, and so on. Here, you only need to know that GetPhone returns a phone number. You can pass it an integer, or you can pass it a string.

Overloading a Predefined Function

If you want to, you can overload predefined functions such as *strcpy*. You can also inherit from existing classes, such as the stream classes, and use overloading to add new behavior. Just add a function that has the same name as an existing function, but that takes different arguments.

Operator Overloading

(This is some really hard-core stuff.) You can change the behavior of operators: *, -, +, && and other such funny characters. For example, suppose you do a lot of work with graphics. Points are often stored in matrixes (two-dimensional arrays). Transformations — such as rotate, scale, and so on — are also easily stored in matrixes. Quite often graphics programs do a lot of matrix multiplication because that's an easy way to transform a bunch of points from one spot to another.

To do this, you end up writing lots of functions that perform matrix multiplication, matrix addition, and so on. As a result, if *A*, *B*, *C*, and *D* are matrixes, you end up writing code that looks like this:

```
//D = A*B + C;
MatrixCopy(D, MatrixAdd(MatrixMul(A,B),C));
```

As you can see, this can get kind of confusing. If you wanted to, you could overload the behavior of =, *, and + so that they knew how to operate on matrixes. That way you could just write this:

```
D = A*B + C;
```

And if the values weren't matrixes, the same algorithm would work just fine, too.

Warning: This gets really complex

There are all types of different rules and issues that come up as you start to do operator overloading. In this chapter, you'll learn enough to become dangerous. In other words, you'll learn the basics of overloading, but you won't learn all the 30 or 40 pages of tricks and traps that you might run into. (There are plenty of books that can help you learn about them.)

Be forewarned: I wasn't kidding when I said this operator overloading stuff is complex. It's a good idea to read this chapter carefully before you start trying out the stuff you're learning. And any time you decide to overload the =, watch out! ■

Here's the syntax for overloading an operator that takes one parameter:

```
return_type
operator op (parameter) {
    statements;
}
```

Here's the syntax for overloading an operator that takes two parameters:

```
return_type
operator op (lvalue, rvalue) {
    statements;
}
```

To illustrate this, suppose you want to define how ! behaves for ToppingLists so that you can determine if there's another topping after the current one. Here's what you'd do:

```
//Define that !ToppingList returns 1 if there
//is an item that follows and 0 if there is not.
int operator!(ToppingList &foo) {
    if (foo.GetNext())
        return 1;
    return 0;
}
```

This code means that anytime the compiler sees a ! followed by a ToppingList object, the compiler says "Aha — the programmer wants me to use the special ! that's designed just for ToppingList objects." For example, you could use this in your application to check the ToppingList:

```
if (!myTopping)
    cout << "Still more";
```

If myTopping.GetNext() isn't 0 (that is, if there's an item that follows), !myTopping will return 1 and "Still more" will print. If, on the other hand, there are no more toppings in the list, !myTopping will return 0.

Overloading inside or outside classes

There are two ways you can overload an operator. One way is to add the new operator to the class definition. The other way is to make the operator have global scope, as is done with the << example in the "Teaching streams a thing

Teaching streams a thing or two about pizza

The code in this sidebar is an excerpt from the sample program in Chapter 38. This code overloads << so it knows how to print out information about pizzas so you can just do *cout* << foo (where foo is a Pizza) to print the pizza order.

In this code I've overloaded the way << is used with streams. When you do a *cout* <<, what's really happening is that the << is operating on a stream from the left and a source on the right, and then returning a stream. That's why *cout* << 1 << 2 works — because << just returns a stream.

If you wanted to use << to print out a Pizza class, you could do the following:

```
//Call this if a stream << Pizza is used in the program.
//Simply calls one of the Pizza member functions to
//do the hard work.
ostream& operator<<(ostream& s, Pizza& TheZa) {
        return TheZa.PrintOrder(s);
}
```

Now you can do:

```
cout << MyPizzaInfo;
```

Here, << has a Pizza class on the right, so it calls the special << operator that's designed to take a stream on the left and a Pizza class on the right. This in turn calls a Pizza member function called PrintOrder to output information about the pizza to the stream.

or two about pizza" sidebar. Whether the operator is overloaded inside or outside the class will have absolutely no effect on how you use the operator. But where you overload the operator will change how you define the operator.

To make the overloaded operator part of a class, put the declaration in the class, like this:

```
//Make the operator overload part of the class.
class MyClass {
    int operator!();
};
```

Note that when you overload a unary operator such as ! within a class, you don't need to fill in any arguments for the operator. That's because the object itself is assumed to be the argument.

Converting unbelievers to programmers

One very far-out thing you can do with operator overloading is to create automatic *conversion rules*. A conversion rule is a set of code that converts data from one type to another type. For example, in the following line, the compiler converts the integer 3 to a floating-point number that's stored in the variable *a*:

```
float a = 3;
```

The compiler can do this because it has a rule that it runs to convert integers to floating-point numbers.

You can create your own conversion rules. For example, suppose you have a class called Pizza and you want to convert it to a float. In particular, you want the float representation of a Pizza to be the price of the pizza. (Does it make sense to say the float representation of a pizza is its price? That's up to you — *you* get to decide what the conversion from one type to another

does.) To do this you would add the following member function to the Pizza class:

```
operator float() {return Size;}
```

If you then did the following, where foo is a Pizza object, *a* will be set to the cost of the pizza:

```
float a = foo;
```

You could compute the cost of 3 pizzas with 3*foo.

You can convert any type to another type. For example, if you wanted to convert an Unbeliever class to a Programmer class (assuming you had such classes in your program) you could put the following member function in the Unbeliever class:

```
operator Programmer() {
//Conversion code goes here!
}
```

If you want to define the operator outside a class (that is, if you want to make it global), just define it as in the << example shown in the "Teaching streams a thing or two about pizza" sidebar, and make it a friend to the class (you'll learn about friends later in this chapter):

```
class Pizza {
    friend ostream& operator<<(ostream& s, Pizza& TheZa);
public:
    Pizza(Choice *PizzaChoices, Choice *TopChoices);
```

The official inny and outy guidelines

There are four guidelines that can help you decide whether an overloaded operator should or shouldn't be part of a class. Each guideline is discussed in its own separate section (yes, this is a tip-off that some of them are *long* guidelines!).

Put it in the class if possible

If possible, make the overloaded operator part of a class. This makes the program easier to read and lets you change the behavior of the overloaded operator when you inherit from the class.

The operator can't join the class if its lvalue isn't the class

If the lvalue (the operand to the left of the operator) is not the class, you can't put the operator in the class. For example, when the compiler looks at an expression such as ClassA << ClassB, it essentially looks for a member function called << within ClassA. You can add a << operator to ClassA that can take ClassB as the second argument. (Note, though, that if you want to access any nonpublic members of ClassB, then ClassA must be declared a friend of ClassB. You'll learn about friends later in this chapter.)

Suppose, however, that you didn't write ClassA. In that case, there won't be a << within ClassA that knows how to take a ClassB as a parameter. Putting the overloaded << in ClassB won't do any good — the compiler will still look inside ClassA because ClassA is on the left side of the expression.

In such a case, you need to make the operator global — you do this by defining it outside the class. The compiler will look for a global operator that takes ClassA on the left and ClassB on the right, find this global overloaded operator, and use it. That's why when we made << stream a pizza it couldn't be in the class. The lvalue was an ostream&, not a Pizza&, and we can't change the source code (at least not without a lot of pain) for ostream.

Likewise, if you want to use any of the predefined types (integers, floats, and so on) as lvalues, you'll need to use global overloading. If the operator isn't defined in the class, define it as a friend of the class.

When some things are overloaded, they must be defined within the class

If you're overloading =, [ ], or ( ), they must be defined within the class.

Preserving commutivity in overloaded operators

If you're overloading an operator and you want to preserve commutivity, you should usually use global overloading. Operators such as + and * are *commutative* (you can switch the left and right sides and the result stays the same). In other words, 6 + 5 is the same as 5 + 6.

But what if you want to overload + so that you can do ClassA + 5? Well, if you want 5 + ClassA to be the same as ClassA + 5, you need to overload + for both integers and ClassA's. You can do the latter, but not the former. So in this case, you need to do global overloading.

On the other hand, if you want ClassA + ClassB to be commutative, you could overload + in both ClassA and ClassB. This will work, although you'll end up repeating similar code once in ClassA and once in ClassB. (If you've set up conversion rules that tell the compiler how to convert a ClassA to a ClassB, using global operator loading is better than overloading in the class for ClassA + ClassB. That's because you can write one rule, and the compiler will convert one of the operands to match. Setting up conversion rules is a pretty advanced use of operator overloading that is discussed in the "Converting unbelievers to programmers" sidebar.)

What you can't do

Here are some things that you *can't* do when you're overloading operators:

- ✔ Invent new operators — you're stuck with the list of existing operators.
- ✔ Override existing behavior of an operator. For example, you can't change + so that 1 + 2 is 4.
- ✔ Change the order of operations.
- ✔ Have existing operators take a different number of parameters. For example, you can't make a 4!2.
- ✔ Have existing operators work on the other side. For example, you can have !3, but not 3!.

Get by with a Little Help from Your Friends

As you've seen, only public data members and member functions are accessible outside a class. Sometimes, however, you need to provide access to private and protected items. That's where you need a little help from your C++ friends.

Here's What Friends Are For

In the "Teaching streams a thing or two about pizza" sidebar, you can see how the overloaded << operator is made a friend of Pizza so it can call a private member function of Pizza.

There are other situations where you would also want to provide this type of access. For example, suppose two different classes, Philippe and Bill, each contain a private data member called BestPinballScore. Now suppose you have a function called Connie whose mission is to find out pinball scores. Connie wouldn't be able to find the pinball scores for Bill or Philippe, because the information is private and Connie isn't a member function of both classes.

You can get around this, though, through the use of friends. If Philippe says that Connie is a friend, then Connie can access the private and protected items in Philippe. Likewise, if Bill says that Connie is a friend, then Connie can access the private and protected items in Bill. That way, Connie will be able to find the BestPinballScore for Bill objects and Philippe objects.

How to Make Friends

You declare friends when you declare a class. Anything that's declared as a friend will have full access to any of the private or protected data members and member functions. Note that the class has to declare its friends — you can't ask to be someone else's friend. This might sound cruel at first, but it's necessary for security reasons.

To indicate that a function (such as Connie), a member function, or a whole class is your friend, use the *friend* keyword in the class definition. For example, here's the Pizza class from Chapter 38, with the addition of some friends:

```
class Pizza {
    //This lets the operator be a Pizza friend.
    friend ostream& operator<<(ostream& s, Pizza& TheZa);
    //This makes the ToppingList class a friend.
    friend ToppingList;
    //This makes Connie a friend.
    friend int Connie(Pizza& p, Beer& b);
    //This lets the Foo::Bar() function be a friend.
    friend void Foo::Bar();
public:
    Pizza(Choice *PizzaChoices, Choice *TopChoices);
    Pizza();
    ~Pizza();
    void ChooseSize();
    void ChooseToppings();
    void PrintOrder();
    ostream& PrintOrder(ostream& s);
protected:
    ToppingList *Toppings;
    Choice      *PizzaSizes;
    Choice      *ToppingChoices;
    int Size;
    float Cost;
};
```

You don't have to declare friends before the public section, but it's a little easier to read the code if you do.

Chapter 38

Hot Streaming Pizza

● ●

In This Chapter

▶ Overload << to make it easier to print a pizza order

▶ Use friends to allow stream operator overloading

● ●

*T*his final pizza example demonstrates function and operator overloading. We'll also let pizza orders be printed using << instead of the PrintOrder function. This makes the program a bit easier to read, and, more importantly, lets the order be written to disk very easily as well. Naturally, MilkEmPizza automatically inherits all these changes.

There are a number of changes:

✔ The Pizza class now recognizes << as a friend.

✔ There is a new version of PrintOrder that writes to a stream instead of using *cout*.

✔ << is overloaded.

✔ main( ) now uses << to print the pizza.

How It Works

Operator overloading is used to allow << to print out Pizza information. First, the << operator is declared a friend in the Pizza class:

```
class Pizza {
    //***NEW << is now a friend so that it can be used.
    friend ostream& operator<<(ostream& s, Pizza& TheZa);
public:
```

This lets you overload the behavior of << so it can print Pizza information:

```
ostream& operator<<(ostream& s, Pizza& TheZa) {
    return TheZa.PrintOrder(s);
}
```

To make this function work, you need a new PrintOrder function that sends output to a generic stream. That way, you can use << to output to the screen, to a disk file, or to any output stream. This function is the same as the other PrintOrder function, only it outputs to the stream *s* (this is an example of function overloading):

```
ostream&
Pizza::PrintOrder(ostream& s) {
    ToppingList *Cur = Toppings;

    //Print out the size of the pizza.
    s << "That's a " << PizzaSizes->GetName(Size)
        << " pizza with ";
```

The overloaded << is used in main to print out the pizza order:

```
cout << MyPizza;
```

If you wanted to print the order out to a disk file, you could open an output stream, as discussed in Chapter 34, and then use << to that stream instead of *cout*.

The Code

The following listings show the files that have changed.

PIZZA 10.CPP

```
//This version adds operator overloading so that you
//can print a pizza using cout and <<.

//The major changes are:
//    << is overloaded and is then used in main().

#include <iostream.h>
#include <stdlib.h>
#include "choice.h"
#include "milkem.h"


//There are four main classes used:
//      ToppingList - a list of pizza toppings
//      DietTopping - a special topping that has less
//          calories
//      Pizza - info describing the pizza
//      MilkEmPizza - a special type of pizza that tries
//          to be expensive
```

```
//We also have helper classes:
//      Choice — used to represent choices that can
//          be made by the user
//      ChoiceDescription — a structure containing a
//          choice name and price
//      ChoiceError — used for exceptions


//----The main routine begins here----------------------

void
main() {
    //We'll make two lists of choices, one for
    //pizza sizes and one for toppings.
    Choice *PizzaSizes, *Toppings;

    //We'll read the choices in from disk files.
    try {
        PizzaSizes = new Choice("sizes.txt");
        Toppings = new Choice("toppings.txt");
    }
    catch(ChoiceError *BadOne) {
        //Had a choice error. Print out what went
        //wrong.
        BadOne.PrintError();
        cout << "Stopping due to error.\n";
        //If PizzaSizes was created, delete it
        if (PizzaSizes)
            delete PizzaSizes;

        //Now terminate the program using a library call
        exit(EXIT_FAILURE);
    }

    //No exception thrown, so continue.

    MilkEmPizza MyPizza(PizzaSizes, Toppings);

    //Now we will choose the size.
    MyPizza.ChooseSize();

    //Now we will choose the toppings.
    MyPizza.ChooseToppings();

    //Now we will print the order.
    //***NEW — use a stream
    cout << MyPizza;
}
```

OVERLOAD.CPP

```
//This contains the routine that overloads the
//<< operator.
```

(continued)

```
#include <iostream.h>
#include "pizzacl.h"

//Call this if a stream << Pizza is used in the program.
//Simply calls one of the Pizza member functions to
//do the hard work.
ostream& operator<<(ostream& s, Pizza& TheZa) {
    return TheZa.PrintOrder(s);
}
```

PIZZACL.H

```
//Create a sentinel. Only include the header if it
//hasn't been read yet.

#if !defined(H_PIZZACL_H)
#define H_PIZZACL_H

#include "toplst.h"
#include "choice.h"

//The Pizza class is used to hold all information
//regarding the pizza. It contains a number of
//data members including a list of toppings.
//
//Here is a class overview:
//      Pizza(Choice *PizzaChoices, Choice *TopChoices) —
//          constructs the pizza class. It takes a
//          pointer to a list of possible sizes and
//          possible choices.
//      ~Pizza() — cleans up
//      ChooseSize() — asks the user for the pizza size
//      ChooseToppings() — asks the user to choose the
//          desired toppings
//      PrintOrder() — prints out the price of the
//          pizza
//      PrintOrder(ostream&) — prints an order to
//          a stream

class Pizza {
    //***NEW << is now a friend so that it can be used.
    friend ostream& operator<<(ostream& s, Pizza& TheZa);
public:
    Pizza(Choice *PizzaChoices, Choice *TopChoices);
    ~Pizza();
    void ChooseSize();
    void ChooseToppings();
    void PrintOrder();
    //***NEW — prints order to a stream
    ostream& PrintOrder(ostream& s);
protected:
    ToppingList *Toppings;
    Choice    *PizzaSizes;
    Choice    *ToppingChoices;
```

```
    int Size;
    float Cost;
};

#endif  //H_PIZZACL_H
```

PIZZACL.CPP

```cpp
#include <iostream.h>
#include "pizzacl.h"
#include "diettop.h"

//----Pizza member functions----------------------------

//The constructor initializes the class.
Pizza::Pizza(Choice *PizzaChoices, Choice *TopChoices) {
    Size = 0;
    Cost = 0.0;
    Toppings = 0;
    PizzaSizes = PizzaChoices;
    ToppingChoices = TopChoices;
}


//Here is the destructor. It deletes the first item
//in the list of toppings. This will cause a chain
//reaction that will free up the whole topping list.
Pizza::~Pizza() {
    if (Toppings)
        delete Toppings;
}

//This asks the user to choose the desired pizza
//size.
void
Pizza::ChooseSize() {
    Size = PizzaSizes->ChooseOne();
    //Set the initial price
    Cost = PizzaSizes->GetPrice(Size);
}

//This asks the user to select the desired toppings.
void
Pizza::ChooseToppings() {
    int  Select;

    cout << "Do you want to add toppings? (0=No)\n";
    cin >> Select;
    //If yes, start the list.
    if (Select) {
        //Make it diet?
        cout << "Do you want your first topping to be "
            << "a diet topping? (0=no)\n";
        cin >> Select;
```

(continued)

```
            if (Select)
                Toppings = new DietTopping(ToppingChoices);
            else
                Toppings = new ToppingList(ToppingChoices);
            Toppings->AddFirst();
        }
    }

//This prints out what was selected and the price.
void
Pizza::PrintOrder() {
    ToppingList *Cur = Toppings;

    //Print out the size of the pizza.
    cout << "That's a " << PizzaSizes->GetName(Size)
        << " pizza with ";

    //Are there any toppings?
    if (!Cur)
        cout << "no toppings.\n";
    else {
        //There are toppings, so traverse the list
        //and sum the price.
        while (Cur) {
            //Find the price of the topping.
            Cost += Cur->GetPrice();
            //Print the topping type.
            cout << Cur->GetName();
            //Move on to the next one.
            Cur = Cur->GetNext();
            //If there is a next one, print "and".
            if (Cur)
                cout << " and ";
        } //end of while

        cout << " for toppings.\n";
    } //end of else

    //Print the total price.
    cout << "That will be $" << Cost << ".\n";

}

//***NEW
//This prints out what was selected and the price.
//This is the same as PrintOrder, only a stream is
//passed in and returned.
ostream&
Pizza::PrintOrder(ostream& s) {
    ToppingList *Cur = Toppings;

    //Print out the size of the pizza.
    s << "That's a " << PizzaSizes->GetName(Size)
        << " pizza with ";
```

```
    //Are there any toppings?
    if (!Cur)
      s << "no toppings.\n";
    else {
      //There are toppings, so traverse the list
      //and sum the price.
      while (Cur) {
        //Find the price of the topping.
        Cost += Cur->GetPrice();
        //Print the topping type.
        s << Cur->GetName();
        //Move on to the next one.
        Cur = Cur->GetNext();
        //If there is a next one, print "and".
        if (Cur)
          s << " and ";
      } //end of while

      s << " for toppings.\n";
    } //End of else.

    //Print the total price.
    s << "That will be $" << Cost << ".\n";

    //Return it.
    return s;
}

//----Finished with Pizza member functions-------------------
```

(This program is in the PIZZA10 directory on the separately available program disk.)

And Now the Pizza Is Done

Wow. It's been a long, strange trip since we started off with a bare-bones pizza-ordering program. You've learned a lot, and you've put this knowledge to work to create a pretty classy pizza program. You've used an object-oriented design, complete with constructors and destructors, so that you can easily understand, test, and expand your program. You've used inheritance and virtual functions so that you can have diet and regular toppings, and so you can pressure the customer to order a large. You've used streams and arrays so you can flexibly expand the number of sizes and toppings. You've used exception handling to keep your program safe from user errors. And you've used operator overloading and friends to make it easier to print the final order.

So, congratulations! Why not celebrate? Say, what's the number of the nearest pizza joint?

Part IV
The Part of Tens

In This Part

Ah, the famous "Part of Tens." Here's where the *For Dummies* books give you all kinds of cool tips and ideas, usually in the form of Top Ten lists. You'll probably notice that many of the chapters in this part actually consist of *almost* ten or *more* than ten things, but hey, who's counting, anyway? And you'll be glad to get these nifty tips, even if they don't add up to an even ten.

The first chapters in this Part provide solutions for some of the common (but frustrating) things that might give you some grief in the beginning. After all, sooner or later *all* beginners (and even tired or stressed out experts) run into puzzling situations or make mistakes sometimes. Maybe you can't get Borland C++ to install. Maybe you accidentally deleted something you really didn't want to delete. Or maybe your program just won't compile, no matter what you do. (Or even worse, maybe your program runs, but it goes belly up before you can say durn.) These chapters can help you solve common problems related to installation, syntax errors, program crashes, and more. What's more, they tell you *why* the problems happened, so you can learn from your mistakes and avoid those kind of problems in the future.

Then, the next two chapters list the Top Ten OWL classes and member functions. It's a good idea to familiarize yourself with them so you can recognize them and know what they're doing when you look at the Borland C++ sample programs. (You *are* looking at the sample programs, aren't you? If you're not, you ought to be — examining sample programs is an excellent way to learn a new programming language.)

And, while we're on the subject of sample programs, the last chapter in this Part lists ten really cool sample programs that come with Borland C++. Be sure to check them out.

Chapter 39

(Fewer Than) Ten Reasons
Why It Didn't Install

● ●

In This Chapter

▶ Not having enough disk space

▶ Choosing the wrong drive letter for the CD

▶ Putting too many floppy disks into the drive

▶ Having bad disks

▶ Installing to the wrong drive

▶ Not being able to access the CD

● ●

*I*f you're having trouble installing Borland C++, it's likely that one of these reasons is the cause of your problem. You might also want to consult the README.TXT and INSTALL.TXT files that come with Borland C++ for more information and suggestions.

Not Enough Disk Space

Borland C++ requires a lot of free disk space. When you select an installation option, make sure you've got enough free disk space for that option.

If you need more disk space, you can either install fewer things or free up some disk space on your computer.

Note that if you're installing to a compressed drive (such as those created by Stacker or DoubleStor), the estimated amounts of free disk space can sometimes be off. Because of this, the install program might initially think it has enough room to install Borland C++, only to discover later (when it's almost done installing, naturally) that there isn't enough space. If you're installing Borland C++ to a compressed disk, give yourself some extra leeway to account for this.

Choosing the Wrong Drive Letter for the CD

If you're installing the CD-ROM version of Borland C++, note that the install program doesn't always know what drive you're going to put the Borland C++ CD into. This won't actually prevent the install from working, but once the product installs, various directories will be set up incorrectly. You might need to modify BCW.INI and SYSTEM.INI so that the correct drive is used. See the INSTALL.TXT file that comes with Borland C++ for more information on what's stored in the INI files.

You Put Too Many Floppies in the Drive at Once

Don't laugh, people actually do this! (If you're one of those people, you probably don't want to laugh right now, though. Maybe later. Maybe in another ten years or so.) Anyway, here's the scoop: when the install program says to insert disk #2, it really means that you should take out disk #1 and *then* insert disk #2. If you try to force more than one disk into the drive, bad things will usually happen. Like your disk drive will break.

You Got Hold of Some Bad Disks

This happens only rarely, but it has been known to happen. The symptom is that the install program just refuses to recognize a particular disk or it reports that it can't find a particular file. Call Borland's Customer Service line to get a new disk.

You Installed to the Wrong Drive

If for some reason you have lots of disk drives, you might accidentally install Borland C++ to the wrong one. Maybe you installed Borland C++ to a drive that doesn't have much room or to a network drive when you really wanted it on a local drive.

If you find out that this is what you've done, delete what you just installed and start the installation process again (being careful to install Borland C++ to the correct drive this time, of course.)

You Can't Access the CD

Usually errors about accessing the CD during installation mean that you need to find an updated CD driver. Make sure you have the latest version of MSCDEX or whatever your CD-ROM driver is. You can often find the most recent drivers on bulletin boards such as CompuServe.

The Installation Program Behaves Strangely or Won't Run

Usually this is the result of some type of conflict between the installation program and a device driver, memory manager, or TSR. In this case, you'll need to do a clean boot and then retry the install.

First, to be safe, make backup copies of your current AUTOEXEC.BAT and CONFIG.SYS files (just copy them to a floppy disk).

Then remove any device drivers, memory managers, and TSRs that aren't absolutely necessary from your AUTOEXEC.BAT and CONFIG.SYS. For example, remove memory managers such as QEMM, sound card drivers, and keystroke recorders. Don't remove disk stackers (such as STACKER) or your CD-ROM driver (such as MSCDEX) because your computer won't be able to run if you do that.

Here are two time-saving approaches to removing these things:

1. The first approach is to precede each line you want to remove with a REM statement. That way you can just remove the REM when you're finished installing and you'll have your system back the way it was.

2. The second approach is to use a clean boot disk, which is a floppy that contains the DOS system. To do this, put a formatted floppy in the A drive and do a SYS A: to make the boot disk. Then copy your AUTOEXEC.BAT and CONFIG.SYS to this disk. Remove the extra stuff (the device drivers, memory managers, and TSRs I mentioned before) from the floppy-disk copies of AUTOEXEC.BAT and CONFIG.SYS. Then you can boot from this clean floppy, and you won't need to restore your hard disk files when you're finished.

   Note: if your AUTOEXEC.BAT files or CONFIG.SYS files run programs, make sure the paths point to the hard drive, not to the default drive. For example, if you had SHELL=\DOS\COMMAND.COM /P /E:1024 in your CONFIG.SYS, change it to SHELL=C:\DOS\COMMAND.COM /P /E:1024.

After you remove the device drivers, memory managers, and TSRs, remove any programs that are automatically started by Windows, such as screen savers, ATM, calendar programs, and so forth.

Then reboot Windows and start the install program again. Once you've finished the install, put back the various device drivers, memory managers, and TSRs that you removed.

Chapter 40

Ten Solutions to Try If It Installs but Doesn't Run

• •

In This Chapter

▶ Making sure the path is set correctly

▶ Making sure \BC4\BIN comes before any other version of Borland C++ you might have in your path

▶ Finding out if you need special device driver files for certain Borland C++ tools

▶ Making sure that BWCC.DLL comes before any other version of BWCC you might have in your path

▶ Creating a program group for Borland C++

▶ Checking out your configuration files to make sure they're okay

▶ Making sure you have enough memory

▶ Making sure you have Windows version 3.1 or later and DOS version 4.01 or later

▶ Fixing conflicts with device drivers, memory managers, or TSRs

▶ Handling an occasional GP fault

• •

*H*ere are the most common problems that might prevent Borland C++ from running, and the solutions you can try to fix them.

What to Do If Windows Says It Can't Find Borland C++

If you get this message, it usually means your path isn't set correctly. Look in your AUTOEXEC.BAT and make sure that \BC4\BIN is on the path somewhere, and that it's pointing at the correct disk drive.

You might also want to make sure that \BC4\BIN is the first item in the PATH.

Note that you can only have so many things on a path. Because of that, sometimes the last items in the path get cut off and DOS can't find them.

To find out if this is what's happening, type PATH from the DOS prompt to show all the directories on the path. If you don't see \BC4\BIN listed there, something is wrong and you should put \BC4\BIN first.

An Older Version of Borland C++ Runs Instead of the New Version

If this happens, you've got an older version of Borland C++ on your system, and its directory is showing up before \BC4\BIN.

Make sure that \BC4\BIN is the first item on the path. You might also want to remove the older version of Borland C++, if you don't need it anymore.

When You Start Windows, You Get a Message about WINDPMI.386 or TDDEBUG.386

WINDPMI.386 and TDDEBUG.386 are special device-driver files that are needed for running certain Borland C++ tools. When you get a message like this, it usually means that you've done a partial install of Borland C++ from the CD-ROM, but that the Borland C++ CD is no longer in the CD drive.

You can ignore this message if you don't plan to run the stand-alone debuggers or command-line tools under Windows. Or, you can exit Windows, put the Borland C++ CD in the CD drive, and start Windows again.

If you don't want to receive this message again (regardless of what CD is in your drive), just copy WINDPMI.386 and TDDEBUG.386 from the \BC4\BIN directory on the CD-ROM drive to your \BC4\BIN directory on your hard drive. Then edit the SYSTEM.INI file so that it knows where to find these device drivers. If you're not quite sure about how to do this, see Chapter 2 or look in the Borland C++ INSTALL.TXT file for more information.

You Get a Message that BWCC 2.0 or Later Is Required

Most often, this message occurs when you're trying to run Resource Workshop. BWCC stands for Borland Windows Custom Controls. These are the custom controls that provide the OK button with the checkmark, the Cancel button with the big red X, and the Ignore button with the speed limit sign.

If you get this message, here's what's happening: instead of finding the latest and greatest version of BWCC, Windows is finding an older version first. This older version could come from an older version of Borland C++ or from all types of different software that you might own.

To fix this problem, make sure that the newest version of BWCC.DLL is in your WINDOWS\SYSTEM directory. Then find and delete the older version that you've got on your system. To find the older version, look at the path and in each directory in the path. (Usually, it's hiding away in the \WINDOWS directory, so look for it there first.)

There Aren't Any Icons for Borland C++

The usual reason why you might not see any icons for Borland C++ is that you didn't make a program group when you installed Borland C++.

You can make your own group by hand. Just create a new group and call it Borland C++ 4.0. Add new icons for BCW.EXE, WORKSHOP.EXE, and any other utilities you want icons for. (You can use the browse option to search for these executables so that you know you get the right path. If you don't get an icon, you've got the wrong path.)

It Ran Fine at First, but This Morning It's Busted

If Borland C++ runs fine at first, but then starts acting up, it usually means that one of your configuration files has gotten a little messed up. Try deleting BCW.INI, BCWDEF.*, and any *.DSW, *.BCW, *.~DE, and *.OBR files, and then starting again. BCW.INI is in the WINDOWS directory, and the other files are in the directory where you store your program and the \BC4\BIN directory.

You might also want to make sure that \BC4\BIN is still on your path. If you installed some other software after you installed Borland C++, it might have accidentally changed your path so that Borland C++ is no longer being found.

You've Got One Copy Running, and Now You Want to Start a Second

Sorry, you can't do this. You can only run one copy of Borland C++ at a time.

You're Getting Messages about Not Enough Resources

Uh-oh. This is the expensive message. It could mean you're running low on disk space, but it usually means you don't have enough memory in your machine. You need at least 4M of RAM to run Borland C++, but you're much better off with 8M or 12M of RAM.

It Just Doesn't Work

If none of the other problems described above seem to be what's going on, ask yourself these two questions:

- Do I have Windows version 3.1 or later? (If not, you need it.)
- Do I have DOS version 4.01 or later? (If not, you need it.)

If this still isn't your problem, you might have a conflict with a device driver, memory manager, or TSR. Make sure you have the latest version of CD drivers and video drivers. If that doesn't fix the problem, check out the suggestions for creating a clean system in the section called "The Installation Program Behaves Strangely or Won't Run" in Chapter 39.

If you can get Borland C++ to work with a clean system, iteratively add back in the drivers you took out, reboot, and try Borland C++ again. When Borland C++ no longer works, you'll know what driver (or thing) is causing the problem. If you don't have the latest version of that driver, you can often find them on bulletin boards such as CompuServe.

It Usually Works, but It Gives an Occasional GP Fault

Sometimes when you get a GP fault, it means you've found a bug in Borland C++. Borland releases patches (programs that make changes directly to the Borland C++ files on your machine to fix bugs) and new versions to fix problems. Check Borland's electronic bulletin board, FTP site (ftp.borland.com), or CompuServe area to see if there are patches that you can apply.

Borland also has an electronic technical newsletter and a service that sends information on new versions via e-mail. For information on how to sign up for either of these services, send e-mail to tech-info@borland.com.

Chapter 41

(Way More Than) Seven Deadly Syntax Errors

● ●

In This Chapter

▶ A variety of common syntax errors, including their probable causes and symptoms

▶ Solutions for fixing the problems that caused the syntax errors

● ●

*A*ll types of things can lead to syntax errors. This chapter describes some of the common mistakes made by C++ programmers, the symptoms you're likely to observe as a result of these mistakes, and the solutions to the problems.

If you get a syntax error and you need more help, click on the syntax error in the message window and press the F1 key on your keyboard. Help will pop up to provide you with a lot more information about what went wrong and how you might fix it.

Wrong Include Paths

Symptom:

```
Unable to open include file foo.h
```

Using the wrong include path is a very common mistake. You'll know this is what you've done if you get an error message like the one above, followed by a million syntax errors about things not being defined.

Make sure the header file you need to load is either in the directory in which your source files are located or in the set of directories listed in Options | Project | Directories. (See Chapter 11 for more information on how to change directories.)

The other, less common cause for this problem is that you've used < > to surround a header name instead of " ". Use " " if the header file is in the same directory as your sources, because < > will only search the directories specified in the list of include paths.

Missing ;

Symptoms:

```
Declaration missing ;
Too many types in declaration
```

Having a missing ; in your code is another very common problem. Most often, you'll receive the two error messages shown above, but you might also receive other errors telling you that a line isn't terminated properly or that lines are really messed up. Essentially, what's happening is that the compiler doesn't know where to stop, so you usually get the error for the line *after* you forgot the semicolon.

The solution is simple: look over your code, starting with the line indicated as being in error and moving upward, to find where you need the semicolon.

Probably the most common cause is from forgetting to use }; to end a class definition. (This will cause the "Too many types in declaration" error.)

If you're not sure about the rules on when to use semicolons, refer to Chapter 21.

Forgetting to Include a Header File

Symptoms:

```
Call to undefined function foo
Undefined symbol foo
Type name expected
```

Forgetting to include a header file is another classic mistake. You can find all types of symptoms, usually indicating that a class, type, or function isn't defined, or that a return type isn't what's expected.

This problem frequently happens when you use functions from the runtime libraries, but forget to include the appropriate header file. For example, if you use *cout*, be sure to include iostream.h; if you use *sqrt*, be sure to include math.h.

Look at the lines where the compiler starts spluttering. If these lines use runtime library functions, make sure you've included the appropriate library. You can check the on-line help or the documentation if you're not sure what library to include.

If the problem is with a function or class that you've defined, make sure you've included the appropriate header file. If you define a class, function, or variable in one file, you'll need to use a header file if you want to use that class, function, or variable in another file.

Forgetting to Update the Class Declaration

Symptoms:

```
foo(int, int) is not a member of bar
Undefined symbol bar::foo(int,int)
```

Forgetting to update a class declaration is a common mistake, especially for folks who are moving to C++ from C. The symptom will typically be something similar like "foo(int, int) is not a member of bar" (from the compiler) or an undefined symbol message from the linker.

C++ is very strict about types. If you change the parameters passed into a member function, you need to make sure that you also update the class declaration. If, as is common practice, you have placed the class declaration in a header file, be sure to update the header file. Likewise, if you add new member functions to a class, make sure that you update the class declaration, too.

Using a Class Name Instead of the Variable Name

Symptom:

```
Improper use of typedef 'foo'
```

Using the class name instead of the variable name when accessing an instance of a class is another classic mistake made by C programmers switching to C++. You'll usually get a message like "improper use of typedef 'foo'".

Remember that the name of a variable is different from the name of a type of a class. For example, suppose you have the following code:

```
TDialog foo;
```

Here, foo is a variable of class type TDialog. If you want to call the Execute member function you must do this:

```
foo.Execute();
```

not this:

```
TDialog.Execute();
```

Forgetting ; after a Class Declaration

Symptom:

```
Too many types in declaration
```

If you forget to put a ; after a class declaration, you'll end up with lots of errors. This mistake happens frequently enough to make it worth repeating. Check out the section called "Missing ;" for more information.

Forgetting to Put public: in a Class Definition

Symptom:

```
foo::bar is not accessible
```

Forgetting to put *public:* in a class definition is another common mistake. You'll get messages such as "foo::bar is not accessible".

By default, any data members or member functions in a class are private. So if you forget to put the word *public:* at the beginning of the class definition, you'll get this message.

For example, if you do the following you can access bar only from within a member function of foo (so it's illegal):

```
class foo {
    int   bar;
};

foo      pickle;
pickle.bar = 1;
```

If you do this, you can access bar from anywhere you're using a foo class:

```
class foo {
public:
   int   bar;
};
```

The following will work just fine:

```
foo   pickle;
pickle.bar = 1;
```

Forgetting a Variable's Name and Using the Wrong Name Instead

Symptoms:

```
Undefined symbol foo
Type name expected
Call to undefined function 'bar'
```

Using the wrong name for a variable or function falls in the "oh shoot" category. You'll get messages like "Undefined symbol NumHogs". This mistake usually happens when you're so busy programming that you forget whether you called a variable NumHogs or HogsNum. If you guess wrong and use the wrong name in your program, you'll get a nasty message. Take a deep breath and make sure you spelled your variable names correctly. You'll get similar problems if you misspell the names for classes or functions.

Using -> When You Really Mean .

Symptom:

```
Pointer to structure required on left side of -> or *->
```

You might accidentally use -> instead of . (period) if you forget that you have a reference to a class, not a pointer to a class. You'll start doing this once you get addicted to pointers and hope that everything is a pointer. As a result, you'll get a message such as "Pointer to structure required on left side of -> or *->".

For example, the following code will cause this problem:

```
TDialog   foo;
foo->Execute();
```

This doesn't work because foo is a TDialog, not a pointer to a TDialog. Use this instead:

```
foo.Execute();
```

Using . When You Really Mean ->

Symptom:

```
Structure required on left side of . or *
```

Another common mistake when dealing with classes and structures is to use a . (a period) when you really needed a ->. (This is similar, but backwards, to the situation discussed in the "Using -> When You Really Mean ." section.) Here, you think you have a reference, but you actually have a pointer. You'll get a message such as "Structure required on left side of . or *".

For example, the following code will cause this problem:

```
TDialog   *foo;
foo.Execute();
```

This doesn't work because foo is a pointer to a TDialog, not a TDialog. Use this instead:

```
foo->Execute();
```

Missing a }

Symptoms:

```
Compound statement missing }
Declaration does not specify a tag or an identifier
Declaration terminated incorrectly
Declaration syntax error
```

Forgetting to put an ending } is actually a bit more excusable than forgetting a semicolon. This usually happens when you have lots of nested *if* statements or other blocks within a function. Generally, you just forgot where you needed to end things; you'll get comments like "Compound statement missing }". If you forgot it for a class, you'll get "Declaration does not specify a tag or an identifier".

You need to go through your code to make sure all {'s have matching }'s. You can use the editor to help find matches. (See Chapter 7 for more information on brace matching.)

Forgetting to End a Comment

Symptom:

> All types of strange errors can occur.

Forgetting to end a comment is much more common with C programmers who use /* and */ for comments than with C++ programmers who use //. That's because the C-style comments can extend across several lines, and it's easy to forget to end them. The result will be completely unpredictable. You'll get a variety of really weird error messages that make no sense.

If you're using the Borland C++ editor with color syntax highlighting turned on (the default), you'll know when you have this problem because a whole bunch of your code will be in the wrong color. That is, lots of your code will be in the comment color, when you really don't want it to be.

You need to look through your code to find where you forgot to put the */.

Using the Wrong Type for a Variable

Symptom:

```
Cannot convert 'char' to 'foo'
```

Using the wrong type for a variable is usually the result of sloppy programming. You'll get messages such as "Cannot convert 'char' to 'foo'" This happens when you try to assign a variable of one type some value that is completely incompatible. For example, you'll get it from code such as:

```
TDialog foo;
foo = 1;
```

Take a look at the line that has the problem and make sure that you're using the correct types. Usually you've just forgotten to access a member function or are somehow confused.

In rare cases this occurs when you have an out-of-date or missing header file.

Note that this problem is common when you take a bunch of C code and compile it with a C++ compiler. That's because C is pretty lax about type checking. C++ is strict and will discover all types of potential problems you never knew existed.

As a last resort, use a typecast to resolve the problem.

Passing the Wrong Type to a Function

Symptom:

```
Type mismatch in parameter b in call to foo::whiz(int)
```

Passing the wrong type into a function leads to error messages. (This situation is pretty similar to the error discussed in the section "Using the Wrong Type for a Variable.") What happens here is that you call some function and pass in an argument that's of the wrong type. You'll get a message such as "Type mismatch in parameter b in call to foo::whiz(int)".

Look back over your code. Make sure you're passing in parameters of the correct type. It usually helps to look at the function definitions at the same time you look at where you call them.

It Worked Just Fine as a C Program, but Now It Won't Compile

Symptom:

It won't compile as a C++ program.

If your program compiled fine when it was a C program, but generates errors when you compile it as a C++ program, you're probably using an incorrect type. C++ is much stricter about type checking than C is. Nine times out of ten the mistake is one of the problems discussed in the sections "Using the Wrong Type for a Variable" and "Passing the Wrong Type in to a Function."

Putting Nothing Instead of a void

Symptom:

```
foo::bar(int) is not a member of foo
```

Declaring a member function as void, but defining it without using void as the return type will generate an error. This mostly bites C programmers. If you've declared that a function is a void function in a class, but not when you define the function, you'll get a message like "foo::bar(int) is not a member of foo".

For example, the following code will cause this problem:

```
class foo {
    void Bummer(int a);
};

foo::Bummer(int a) {
}
```

In the declaration Bummer is a void, but in the definition no return type is specified (so the computer assumes it returns an int). The two are different. You need to do this instead:

```
void
foo::Bummer(int a) {
}
```

Forgetting to Define Template Member Functions in the Header File

Symptom:

```
Undefined symbol 'foo<float>::bar(int)'
```

If you use a template class in several files, but you don't define the member functions in the header file where the template is declared, you'll often get an error. You'll usually get a bunch of strange messages about member functions not being defined.

A simple rule is that if you're creating a templatized class that you'll use in several files, you should define the member functions in the header file where the class is declared.

Not Using a Public Constructor When You Need One

Symptoms:

```
Compiler could not generate default constructor for class 'bar'
Cannot find default constructor to initialize base class 'foo'
```

Not creating a public constructor when you need one, or not explicitly calling a base class constructor, will lead to errors. This situation is kind of rare, but it's confusing when you hit it. This problem will only happen when you have derived some class from another class (call it foo). The constructor from the derived class tries to call the constructor for a foo, but can't find it. That's probably because you haven't defined a default constructor for foo. Or perhaps all the constructors for foo take arguments, and you haven't explicitly called one of these constructors.

Check out Chapter 28 for more information on initializing constructors and creating default constructors.

Putting ; at the End of a #define

Symptom:

All types of strange errors.

Putting a ; (semicolon) at the end of a *#define* will lead to all types of problems. This is one of those royally vexing mistakes. You'll get some very, very strange syntax error somewhere in the middle of your code, but the code looks just fine. If you notice that you happen to be using a macro (bad things!) somewhere around where the problem occurred, then it's quite possible that you have a bad macro. Look for the macro definition and make sure that it's correct and that it doesn't end with a semicolon.

In general, using *#define* to create macros is a pretty bad idea because, as I just mentioned, macros are bad things. That's why I don't explain them in this book.

Forgetting to Make a Project File

Symptom:

```
Linker fatal: Unable to open file bidsi.lib
```

Forgetting to make a project file isn't a syntax error per se, but will cause linker errors. Beginners frequently make this mistake.

If you plan to create an actual executable (rather than compile an individual file for fun), you need to make a project. The project lets the compiler know what types of libraries (and so on) to use. If you find you've got a CPP file sitting all by its lonesome with no project, you'll need to create a project and shove the CPP file in it. If you're not sure what projects are all about, see Chapters 5 and 6.

Exceeding the Automatic Data Segment

Symptoms:

```
Automatic data segment exceeds 64K
Group _TEXT exceeds 64K
```

Exceeding the automatic data segment is a real scary message for a fairly simple problem. This problem almost never occurs except when you're used to programming in DOS and move to Windows. The symptom will be a nasty error message such as "Automatic data segment exceeds 64K" or messages that mention _DGROUP overflow.

Basically, you're running out of accessible memory. This isn't because of a lack of memory in your computer, but rather because of the way the x86 chips or Windows works.

There are two common causes for this. One is that you have a large program but you compiled it using the small model libraries. As a result, you generated more code than the small model library could handle. You'll get a message about the _TEXT segment overflowing. All you need to do is switch to the large model. You can use the TargetExpert to help you with this.

Another common cause is that you have a big global array. This array is using up a lot of what is called the automatic data segment. In Windows, you can't store very much there. Here's a piece of code that shows this:

```
int MyNums[31000];

void main() {
   }
```

If you compile this code, you'll get a nasty error ("Automatic data segment exceeds 64K") when you link. In this case you should use a pointer to an array and allocate the memory dynamically:

```
int *MyNums;

void main() {
    MyNums = new int[31000];
   }
```

An even better approach is to use the __*huge* keyword, which will let you use more than 64K of memory at a time:

```
int__huge *MyNums;

void main() {
    MyNums = new __huge int[31000];
   }
```

You're Out of Disk Space

Symptom:

```
Unable to create output file foo.obj
```

It's pretty rare to run out of disk space, but when you do you'll get an error message. When you get messages such as "Unable to create output file" that just don't make sense, make sure that you still have some free disk space. If you don't, erase files that aren't important until you do have some free space.

Things Are Really Messed Up

Symptom:

Error-free code suddenly generates syntax errors.

Sometimes key Borland C++ files get corrupted, leading to some very strange syntax errors. For example, maybe you come back to your computer after a quick game of frisbee golf and nothing compiles any more. And maybe some really simple programs give you errors such as "missing ; in stdio.h". And you know darn well that you never touched stdio.h (or windows.h, or some other file that isn't part of your source code).

This usually means that some Borland C++ information file got corrupted. Go to the File Manager (or the DOS prompt or whatever), and erase the *.DSW and *.CSM files in your directory. If that still doesn't fix the problem, erase the *.IDE file too. You'll need to re-create your project, but the problem will most likely go away.

Chapter 42

(Somewhat Less Than) Ten Ways to Undo Things

• •

In This Chapter

▶ Edit | Undo thousands of mistakes

▶ Change your mind about changing an option

▶ Revive the last version of your dearly (un)departed file

▶ Bring your targets back into view

▶ Regain control of runaway windows

▶ Bring those title bars back into view

• •

*E*veryone makes mistakes. And luckily, some mistakes can be undone. Here's a quick guide to help you undo some of your Borland C++ mistakes.

I Typed or Deleted Some Things in the Editor, but I Really Didn't Mean To

No problem. Just select Edit | Undo. (There are a number of shortcuts for Edit | Undo; see Chapter 7.) You can undo up to the last 32,767 things that you did in the editor. If that isn't enough to correct what you just did, you've been working much, much too hard and should go home and get some sleep.

Durn, I Didn't Mean to Change That Option

If you didn't mean to change an option, and you haven't pressed the Enter key or clicked the OK button yet, just click the Undo Page button. You can also click the Cancel button and start again. If you've already clicked the OK button, you'll need to go back and undo what you changed, action by action.

Blast, I Saved a File by Mistake and It's Wrong

If you saved a file by mistake, look for the backup file. This will have the same name, but with BAK for an extension. Load this to get back the just-before-I-accidentally-saved-it version.

I Dragged a Target Around in My Project File and I Can't Move It Up Again

This will only happen if you have multiple targets in a project file. For example, suppose you have a target named FOO.EXE and one named BAR.EXE, as shown in Figure 42-1.

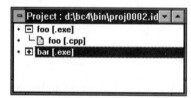

Figure 42-1: A Project Manager window with two projects in it.

Let's say that for some reason you want BAR.EXE to be before FOO.EXE, so you drag it up to FOO.EXE. Lo and behold, it now appears as a dependency of FOO.EXE, as shown in Figure 42-2. That isn't what you wanted!

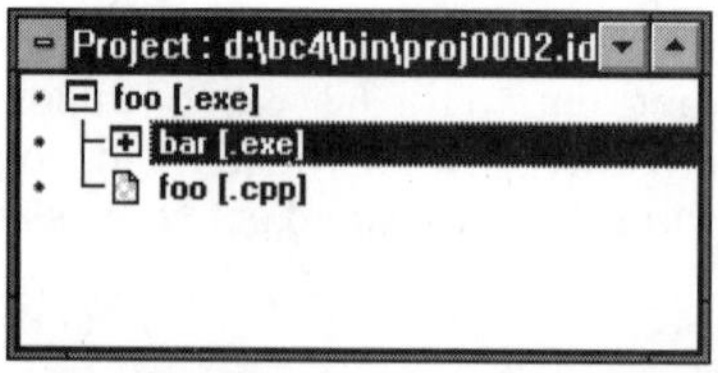

Figure 42-2: Inadvertently making one target a dependency of another target.

If you've accidentally done this, you might find that no matter what you drag, you just can't get BAR.EXE to get out of FOO's dependency list.

Here's what you need to do. Select Options | Environment and then select the Project View topic. Now click on Show project node. This will display an icon for the IDE file itself. If you drag BAR.EXE onto this icon, you'll have what you wanted in the first place, as shown in Figure 42-3.

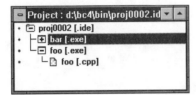

Figure 42-3: Using Show project node, you can make BAR a separate target in the project, not a dependency of FOO.

Now you can go back into the Project View page and turn off the Show project node. You'll have the targets in the order you want, without the IDE file showing.

My Windows Go Off the Screen

This usually happens when you've switched screen resolution. For example, let's say you were operating in 1024X768 and had some windows sized to fit the screen, but then you switched to 640X480. But after you switched, you can't access some of the windows because their title bars are off the top of the screen.

Just exit Borland C++, delete the *.DSW file, and start Borland C++ again. You should be okay.

This can also happen if the DSW file got corrupted for some reason. You might also need to delete your IDE file. (By the way, DSW stands for DeSktop for Windows.)

I Was Typing Away, Turned a Page in the Manual, and BOOM — I Spilled Soda in My Hard Drive

Sorry, you're hosed.

Chapter 43

Almost Twenty Ways to Fix Programs That Crash

● ●

In This Chapter

▶ Initialize variables before you use them

▶ Sometimes one = is better than two

▶ Incorrect use of pointers can cause all types of problems

▶ When you allocate memory, be sure to allocate enough

▶ Don't ignore compiler warnings

▶ Be sure to break out of switches

▶ Look out for infinite loops

▶ Make sure you use the correct variables and functions

▶ Make sure you don't go beyond the end of an array

▶ Avoid changing variables outside a function's scope

▶ Using invalid handles or incorrect parameters causes lots of trouble in Windows

● ●

*T*here are all kinds of reasons why your program might do unexpected (and usually unwelcome) things. This chapter discusses common problems and solutions. If you run into these problems frequently, you might want to purchase a program that automatically helps you find programming errors, such as MemCheck, BoundsChecker, and lint.

You Forgot to Initialize a Variable

Forgetting to initialize a variable is a very common mistake. Anything can happen as a result of this mistake. If the variable was a pointer, you'll GP fault or trash memory. If the variable was a counter, you'll have infinite loops or very strange loops. If the variable was used in a formula, the results will never be correct.

If you forget to initialize a variable, you'll usually get a compiler warning. Be sure to heed it!

Try to remember to always initialize your variables before they're used, especially if they're global variables. It's a good practice to initialize variables when you declare them (for example, int i = 42;) or inside a class's constructor.

You Used = Instead of ==

It's easy to use a = instead of == if you're tired or in a hurry. New C++ programmers also tend to make this mistake if they've previously programmed in a language like BASIC (which doesn't distinguish between assignments and compares).

Note that = means "assign the thing on the left the value that's on the right" and that == means "is this thing on the left equal to the thing on the right?" The two are very different.

For example,

```
if (a = 7)
    cout << "A is 7";
```

will always execute the *cout*. That's because *a* is assigned the value 7 in the *if*. What you meant to do was this:

```
if (a == 7)
    cout << "A is 7";
```

The usual symptoms of this mistake are loops ending prematurely or conditional statements always executing. If these things are happening, look through the *for*s, *while*s, and *if*s in your program to see if you've misused =. If you step through your code with a watch set, you can usually find this type of mistake fairly quickly.

You Used a Null Pointer

Using a null pointer is really just a special case of forgetting to initialize a variable. If you make this mistake and you're running under Windows, you'll get a GP fault or you'll crash Windows. If you're running under DOS, you'll trash memory and usually hang the computer or something else equally nasty. This problem typically occurs the first time you write a linked list or another program in which you have a structure that contains a pointer to something else.

Before you dereference a pointer, make sure the pointer isn't null. In other words, if you have code that does something like this, you need to make sure foo or bar isn't null.

```
//foo is NULL
int     *foo;
*foo = 12;

//Here is another example.
TDialog  *bar;
bar->Execute();
```

You can avoid this problem by always initializing variables. If you have some type of data structure where you don't know if the pointer will be null or not, check the pointer before you use it:

```
if (foo)
    *foo = 1;
```

And of course, never ever do this:

```
if (foo = 0)
    cout << "woops it's null";
```

After all, the (foo = 0) will always turn foo into a null pointer. (If you're not sure why, check out the "You Used = Instead Of ==" section.)

Bad Pointers

You need to be very careful when you use pointers. If you use the wrong one, you'll point to the wrong part of memory, and do something that you didn't really mean to. The typical symptom is that your program crashes, or values get overwritten, or things just don't work. As you can tell, pointer problems can have very confusing and vague symptoms.

To solve the problem, check to make sure that you haven't confused one pointer for another. Make sure that you have it pointing to the right thing.

A related problem is using a pointer that points to something that no longer exists. This happens if you use a pointer to do something, and then free the memory the pointer points to, but then you forget to clear the pointer:

```
//foo points to a dialog.
TDialog *foo;

//Now create the dialog.
foo = new TDialog;
```

(continued)

```
//Now delete the dialog.
//This frees the memory, but doesn't change foo itself.
//That means foo points into nowhere land.
delete foo;

//Here is the really bad thing. The dialog is gone.
//Bad stuff will happen.
foo->Execute();
```

You might want to reread Chapter 22 for some tips on using pointers safely.

You Forgot to Dereference a Pointer

If you forget to dereference a pointer, you'll usually get a syntax error, but sometimes you can sneak these errors by the compiler. The basic problem is that instead of changing the value of what the pointer points to, you changed the pointer itself.

For example, suppose foo points to some integer and you want to add 3 to the integer's value. The following code will compile but it won't work the way you expect:

```
foo += 3;
```

That's because you just made foo point 3 locations ahead in memory. What you really wanted to do was this:

```
*foo += 3;
```

You Forgot to Allocate Memory

If you forget to allocate memory when you're trying to copy some data, you'll end up copying data into a null pointer, which will cause a crash. For example, you might be copying one string to another string. So you have a pointer to the first thing, and a pointer to the second thing, and you copy away. But if you forget to allocate memory for the destination, you'll copy into a null pointer or over some existing structure, and you'll end up in deep trouble.

For example, this type of thing will lead to trouble:

```
//Copy a string to buffer.
char *buffer;

strcpy(buffer, "hello there");
```

Here, you never allocated any memory for the buffer, so you just copied to a null pointer. This will crash or trash.

Here's what you really wanted:

```
//Copy a string to buffer.
char *buffer;

//Allocate some memory for the buffer.
buffer = new char[50];
strcpy(buffer, "hello there");
```

You Overran Allocated Memory

If you didn't allocate enough memory, you'll end up going beyond a variable and into some random space. The symptoms range from GP faults and crashed systems to variables mysteriously having their values change.

For example, the following is dangerous:

```
//Create a 3 character buffer.
char buffer[3];

//Now copy into it.
strcpy(buffer, "hello there");
```

Here you copied a 12-character string (11 letters plus ending null) into a 3-character space. As a result, you'll copy into some memory that could quite easily be occupied by some other variable. If so, bad things will happen.

When you copy into buffers, you need to be very sure that you have enough space in the buffer for the largest thing you'll be copying in to it.

You Ignored a Warning about Suspicious Pointer Conversion

Don't ignore warnings. Especially the warning about suspicious pointer conversion. This warning usually translates into real life as "Danger — I'm about to trash everything inside your program."

Actually, this warning occurs rather rarely. It's most likely to happen if you're converting some old C code to C++. Look at the line that generated the warning and correct it so that you're using proper types.

You Forgot the break Statement in a switch

Forgetting to use the *break* statement in a *switch* is a typical problem experienced by Pascal and BASIC programmers moving to C++. When you have a *switch* statement, the compiler executes all code in the *switch*, starting with the first match it finds and continuing up to a *break* or the end of the *switch*. If you forget to put a *break* in, you'll execute a lot more than you expect. The symptom you'll see is that code is executed for a variety of conditions in addition to the condition that was met. Consider the following:

```
int i = 4;
switch (i) {
case 4:
    cout << "4";
case 3:
    cout << "3";
case 2:
    cout << "2";
}
```

Here, the first case is true — *i* is 4. So 4 is printed to the screen. But there is no *break*, so 3 and 2 are also printed to the screen. What you really wanted was this:

```
int i = 4;
switch (i) {
case 4:
    cout << "4";
    break;
case 3:
    cout << "3";
    break;
case 2:
    cout << "2";
}
```

You Forgot to Increment the Counter in a Loop

Forgetting to increment the counter in a loop is another problem that BASIC programmers are likely to run into. When you make a *for* loop, you need to make sure that you increment the loop counter. Otherwise, you'll end up with an infinite loop.

For example, the following is bad because *i* is never incremented and the loop will therefore never end:

```
for (int i = 0; i < 10;)
    cout << i;
```

What you really wanted was this:

```
for (int i = 0; i < 10; i++)
    cout << i;
```

This is a lot more subtle in *while* loops, as the following infinite loop demonstrates:

```
int i = 0;
while (i < 10) {
    cout << i;
}
```

What you really wanted was this:

```
int i = 0;
while (i < 10) {
    cout << i;
    i++;
}
```

You can also get loop problems if you try to walk a data structure, such as a linked list, and forget to move on to the next item in the list. The following code will print forever:

```
while (foo) {
    cout << foo->x;
}
```

What you really wanted was something like this:

```
while (foo) {
    cout << foo->x;
    foo = foo->next;
}
```

You Changed the Increment Variable in a Loop

Messing with loop counters within a *for* loop can get you into trouble (although this problem doesn't really happen all that often). If you do this, the end result can be that your loops end too quickly or take too long to end.

For example, the following is not a good idea. Because you're changing the loop counter inside the loop, the loop will never end:

```
for (int i = 0; i < 10; i++)
    i = -39;
```

Be really careful of changing the value of a loop counter within a *for* loop. Also, if you change a value within a *while* loop, be very careful to give it the correct value.

The following code is also bad and will never end:

```
int i = 0;
while (i < 30) {
    cout << i;
    i++;
    i = 0;
}
```

Of course, in real life you'll have lots of other code surrounding the offending portion, so it might be harder for you to isolate the code that's changing the loop variable.

Sometimes, you might also run into this problem if you create functions that modify global variables that aren't in their local scope. As discussed in Chapter 26, this is a bad programming practice and can lead to bugs that are difficult to find.

Bad Bounds Check in a Loop

Yup, another loopy loop problem. In the "bad bounds check in a loop" problem, you've got a loop, but it ends either too early or too late. The usual reason for this is that you've used a < when you wanted a <= or vice versa.

As an example, the following code counts from 0 to 9. The stuff inside the loop won't execute when *i* is 10:

```
for (int i = 0; i < 10; i++)
    cout << i;
```

If you really wanted the loop to go from 0 to 10, you should have done this:

```
for (int i = 0; i <= 10; i++)
    cout << i;
```

Another variation of this problem occurs when you just completely mess up whatever the ending condition is. For example, you might slip up and use the maximum width instead of the maximum height. Or you might compare against the minimum, not the maximum, or whatever.

In short, if your loops aren't going as long (or as short) as you expect, check the ending condition to make sure it's correct.

You Used the Wrong Variable

Using the wrong variable can be a very embarrassing problem. You've got a couple of variables in your application, and you just plugged in the wrong one. This usually happens when you don't name your variables well — for example, if you use *i* to represent the width instead of just calling the variable width. The symptom can be anything, but usually you load the wrong value from an array or you loop too long. This problem occurs most frequently when you do loops, because loop-counter variables are often just called *i, j,* and so on.

Here's an extreme example of what can happen if you use the wrong variable:

```
//G is salary.
int G = 10000;

//H is age.
int H = 32;

//Print salary.
cout << H;
```

As you can see, the age is printed instead of the salary. This is actually a simple mistake. If you name your variables well, this kind of thing shouldn't happen very often.

Here's a more typical example:

```
//B is a two dimensional array. The first parameter
//indicates the row and the second the columns.
//Traverse the array and fill it so that it looks like this:
// 1 2 3
// 4 5 6
// 7 8 9
int B[3][3];
int i, j;//Counter variables.

//Go across rows.
for (i = 0; i < 3; i++)
   //Go across columns.
   for (j = 0; j < 3; j++)
      //Fill in the array.
      B[j][i] = i*3 + j + 1;
```

What's happening here is that B[j][i] was used instead of B[i][j]. As a result, the array will look like this:

```
1 4 7
2 5 8
3 6 9
```

instead of like this:

```
1 2 3
4 5 6
7 8 9
```

Bad Bounds for an Array

Believe it or not, if you go beyond the bounds of an array, you'll end up trashing memory. (It's just as if you didn't allocate enough memory.) C++ doesn't do any checking to determine if you're about to go off the end of an array. So if you have an array of three elements and you decide to set the value of a completely nonexistent 500th element, the compiler will generate code that merrily trashes memory. The symptoms of this problem are crashes, GP faults, and variables and structures whose values change in an extremely unexpected fashion. You might also find that your return values are way off the deep end.

Here's an example:

```
//An array of three integers.
int    a[3];

a[57] = 6;
```

And here's another example:

```
char buffer[7];

strcpy(buffer, "hello there");
```

This problem usually occurs when you forget that the first element in an array is 0 and that, if you have an array of *n* elements, the last element has an index of *n*-1:

```
int    a[3];
//This is OK.
a[2] = 1;

//This is not.
a[3] = 1;
```

You'll sometimes run into this problem if you used a formula to calculate the array index and your formula is wrong. Watches can help you quickly figure out what's going wrong — just set the watch to the expression you're using to index the array.

You can get this problem when you're looking up a value in an array, too. For example, the following code won't do what you intended:

```
int Salary[3] = {1000, 2000, 4000};

cout << Salary[3];
```

Instead of printing the value of the third salary, you'll just print out some junk because Salary[3] goes beyond the end of the array.

[x,y] Is Not [x] [y]

If you forget to put each index of a multidimensional array into its own [ ], you're likely to run into problems. You'll either write values into the wrong part of the array or get very strange values when you read from the array.

```
int a[4][5];

//This is not what you want!
cout << a[3,1];

//This is what you really meant.
cout << a[3][1];
```

Changing Variables out of Scope or Changing Globals

Changing variables outside a function's scope (as will happen if you use a lot of global variables) can lead to some very hard-to-understand code and some very hard-to-track bugs. The typical symptom is having variables change out from under you.

Inside a function, don't change globals if you can avoid doing so. Otherwise, you might end up changing values outside the function and having a real bear of a time trying to figure out why the value changed.

Also, if you have a variable that you want to make sure will never change, declare it as a *const*.

For example, the following code will have unexpected results:

```
int a;

void foo() {
    a = 0;
}

void main() {
    a = 1;
    foo();
    cout << a;
}
```

The function foo changes the value of *a*. But you wouldn't know this unless you looked at every line inside foo.

You Did Windows Things inside a TWindow Constructor

Trying to change the size, position, or color of a window inside the constructor for an ObjectWindows window class (such as TWindow) won't have any effect. No matter what you do, the changes will never happen.

When a window (or dialog box) is created, the constructor is called. You can set up all types of variable values here. But when the constructor is called, the window handle is still not valid. So Windows-type calls — things that involve handles to Windows things — won't work yet. If you need to call Windows functions that require a window handle (such as calls to move or size the window), override the SetupWindow virtual function and place the calls there.

For example, the following code won't work as you expect, because you won't be able to change the size of the window:

```
class foo : public TWindow {
public:
    int right;
    int bottom;
    foo();
};

foo::foo() {
    right = 10;
    bottom = 20;
    MoveWindow(0,0,right,bottom);
}
```

What you really want is this:

```
class foo : public TWindow {
public:
    int right;
    int bottom;
    foo();
    SetupWindow();
};

foo::foo() {
    right = 10;
    bottom = 20;
}

foo::SetupWindow() {
    TWindow::SetupWindow();
    MoveWindow(0,0,right,bottom);
}
```

You Passed a Bad Parameter to Windows

Windows calls take lots of different parameters. And sometimes you might inadvertently pass in a bad parameter. There are usually two ways this happens. One way is when you pass in something completely bogus. For example, maybe Windows asked for a handle for a window but you passed in NULL. The other way is when you pass in a perfectly good handle, but for the wrong thing. For example, instead of passing in a handle to the client window, maybe you passed in a handle to the main window.

Whatever way the problem occurred, you're not going to get the results you expected.

If you program in Windows, you need to be real careful that you pass in exactly what's expected. This can be a bit of a pain. If your program just plain doesn't work, this could be the problem. If you've passed in a bad parameter, it can sometimes require an experienced Windows programmer to track down exactly what's going on.

You Have a Bad Date/Time on a File

It's rare to have a bad date or time on a file, but this problem is sure a real mess when you run into it. You'll occasionally get this problem when you copy files from one computer to another or if you're doing development with someone in a different time zone. The symptom is that a problem you *know* you fixed keeps showing up. And your changes don't show up when you debug, either.

What's happening is that the time stamp on a new file isn't older than your current OBJ for that file. So the compiler doesn't think it needs to recompile the file, even though in reality the file is new. If you do a Project|Build all, you'll get around this problem. You can also use TOUCH to update the time stamp.

Chapter 44

The Top Ten ObjectWindows Classes

- -

In This Chapter

▶ TApplication

▶ TWindow

▶ TDialog

▶ TDecoratedFrame

▶ TControlBar

▶ TStatusBar

▶ TDC

▶ TPen

▶ TBitmap

▶ TColor

- -

*B*y now, you might be getting tired of hearing me comment on how difficult it used to be to write Windows programs. In fact, I might be starting to sound like that character in the "Grouchy Old Man" skit from Saturday Night Live in which everything was much harder in the old days (and he *liked* it that way!).

But it's really true; it's much easier to write Windows programs now than it used to be. And one of the many Borland C++ features that makes it easier is ObjectWindows 2.0 (usually called just OWL for short). ObjectWindows 2.0 is a set of classes that encapsulate the Windows API.

Whoa — that class encapsulation stuff sounds pretty complex! Actually, it's not. Basically, OWL just hides the difficult aspects of Windows programming so that you can concentrate on designing your program, instead of on learning all kinds of details about Windows programming. The OWL classes do everything from drawing circles on the screen to displaying status lines and color selection dialog boxes.

This chapter describes the ten most common (out of over 200) OWL classes. It's a good idea to familiarize yourself with them so you'll know what's going on when you look at an ObjectWindows application (for example, when you look at an application created by AppExpert, or when you look at some of the Borland C++ sample programs).

If you want to examine these classes in more detail, or look at the many other OWL classes, check out the *ObjectWindows for C++ Reference Guide* and *ObjectWindows for C++ Programmer's Guide* that Borland provides.

Are you ready? Okay then, from the home office in Silly Valley, CA, here's the list of the top ten most common ObjectWindows classes.

TApplication: Making Your Classes Behave

The TApplication class provides the basic behavior of Windows applications, so it's not surprising that almost every ObjectWindows application includes this class. TApplication handles the Windows message loop and everything else that's involved with simply getting a Windows program off the ground.

You'll often see the following line, where foo is a TApplication:

```
foo.Run();
```

This starts the application running.

If you create applications with AppExpert, the App class is derived from TApplication.

TWindow: OWL Even Does Windows

The TWindow class provides functionality for displaying and moving windows. It's used by almost all the classes that display things — for example, dialog boxes and controls — on the screen. TWindow also handles receiving commands from the user.

You'll often see code like this in OWL programs, where foo points to a TWindow. These lines create and then size the window:

```
foo->Create();
foo->MoveWindow(0,0,5,5);
```

TDialog: The BOXing Champ

The TDialog class is used to create dialog boxes. Lots of OWL classes are derived from TDialog. These include classes for displaying common dialog boxes, printer abort dialog boxes, and so on.

Modeless dialog boxes are created with the Create member function. Modal dialog boxes are created with the Execute member function.

TDecoratedFrame: And Now for That Designer Touch

The TDecoratedFrame class is used for applications that need a status line or tool bar.

TControlBar: Full SpeedBars Ahead

The TControlBar class is used to create SpeedBars. In addition to the usual icons, you can put all types of goodies on a SpeedBar. For example, you can have text fields, combo boxes, and buttons.

AppExpert programs often have code similar to the following line. This code fragment adds a new button to a SpeedBar:

```
foo->Insert(*new TButtonGadget(CM_EDITCUT, CM_EDITCUT));
```

TStatusBar: Status Quo Vadis

The TStatusBar class creates status lines.

TDC: The OWL Graphics Studio

The TDC class is used to display text and graphics within a window. All of the graphics commands for drawing lines, bitmaps, and text are member functions of this class.

When a TDC class is used, you'll often see code like this:

```
dc.SelectObject(pen);
dc.MoveTo(x1,y1);
```

TPen: Etch-a-Sketch, OWL Style

The TPen class controls the behavior of line drawing.

TBitmap: Connect the Dots

The TBitmap class is used to draw bitmaps. A bitmap is a set of dots that define a picture you can draw on the screen.

TColor: Now These Are Some True Colors

The TColor class is used to set the color for pens and brushes. In code, you'll see such things as:

```
TColor GrayColor(10, 10, 10);
```

Chapter 45

The Top Ten ObjectWindows Member Functions

In This Chapter

▶ Run

▶ Create

▶ Execute

▶ MoveWindow

▶ SetupWindow

▶ Insert

▶ Paint

▶ MoveTo

▶ LineTo

▶ TextOut

• •

*I*f Calvin and Hobbes created an application framework they would probably call it GROSS (Get Rid Of Slimy classeS). And it would only have two member functions (whose names should be obvious), mostly designed to throw water balloons. Even though ObjectWindows has more than two member functions, it doesn't have any for throwing water balloons. At least not yet.

In the meantime, here are the top ten most important ObjectWindows member functions.

Run: And They're Off!

The Run member function starts a Windows application running. It is used with the TApplication class.

Create: Monet's Favorite Member Function

The Create member function displays a modeless window. It is used with the TWindow and TDialog classes.

Execute: "Off With Her Head!"

No, this member function isn't something used by the Queen of Hearts in *Alice in Wonderland*. It's actually a mild-mannered member function that displays a modal dialog box and is used with the TDialog class.

MoveWindow: I Want It Next to the Door. No, Over to the Right. No, by the Door Is Better. And It Should Be Larger. No, Smaller. But Narrower...

The MoveWindow member function is used to move or resize a window. It takes four parameters: the left, top, right, and bottom location for the window.

You'll see this with any of the classes that are derived from TWindow. You can use it to position windows, dialog boxes, gadgets, VBX controls, and so forth.

SetupWindow: Looking Out Any Window

The SetupWindow member function is called before a new window is displayed. If you want to change a window's size, or to do some initial drawing, you do it by overriding this member function.

Note that you use SetupWindow instead of the class's constructor when you need to do things that affect screen appearance. That's because the window handles aren't available when the constructor is called, but they are available when SetupWindow is called. ■

Insert: I Want More Stuff on My Control Bar!

The Insert member function is used with TControlBar classes to insert new items in the control bar.

Paint: Painting-by-Windows

The Paint member function is called every time a window is painted. You should subclass this member function when you need to display special data inside a window. Paint is called whenever the window is resized, repainted, or printed.

MoveTo: The Line Starts Here

The MoveTo member function is used to set the starting point of a line. It's used with the TDC class.

LineTo: And the Line Goes to Here

The LineTo member function is used in conjunction with the MoveTo member function to draw a line.

TextOut: Let's Check Out That Text

The TextOut member function is used with TDC to print text to the screen.

Chapter 46
Ten Cool Sample Programs

*T*here's a common saying about software that goes something like this: "If you can, buy it. If not, reuse it. And as a last resort, create it from scratch." In other words, it takes a lot of time and effort to create software from scratch, so only do it if you have to.

Borland C++ includes a lot of sample programs that you can use as good starting points for your own applications. You can modify these sample programs to create new applications or just look at them for examples of specific techniques. And, of course, you're always free to copy and paste portions of the sample programs into your own programs.

Table 46-1 lists some of the many sample programs that ship with Borland C++. Do yourself a favor and check them out.

Table 46-1: Ten good sample programs that ship with Borland C++

Program	Directory	Description
aclock	bc4\examples\owl\owlapps	Shows how to use the multimedia strings to play commands. Also contains some animated bitmaps.
ddeml	bc4\examples\owl\winapi	Shows how to use DDE.
diagxprt	bc4\examples\owl\owlapps	Turns on and off diagnostics for different diagnostic groups. Also substitutes for dbwin.exe or ox.sys. A great tool for hard-core programmers.
dragdrop	bc4\examples\owl\winapi	Shows how to implement drag and drop support.
gdidemo	bc4\examples\owl\owlapps	Shows how to use the various graphics classes to draw on-screen.
help	bc4\examples\owl\winapi	Shows how to implement a help system in your application. You might also want to look at helpex in bc4\examples\windows.
prntprev	bc4\examples\owl\owlapi	Shows how to do print previewing.
steps	bc4\examples\owl\tutorial	An incremental tutorial for learning ObjectWindows, including how to use doc/view.
swat	bc4\examples\owl\owlapps	An arcade-style game where you smack bugs into oblivion. You can turn this into multimedia mayhem with four or five simple lines.
vbxctl	bc4\examples\owl\owlapi	Shows how to incorporate VBX controls into an application.

Glossary

● ●

*I*f you want to hang out with C++ programmers, you need to be able to look and talk like a programmer. Despite rumors to the contrary and movies such as *Revenge of the Nerds*, there isn't a specific way that programmers look. But wearing glasses, mismatched clothes, and forgetting to brush your hair couldn't hurt. More important, though, is knowing the right vocabulary. Here's a review of some of the words you've learned, as well as some additional words you're likely to encounter.

About box. A dialog box, common in most Windows programs, that provides information about a program. Typically it shows the version number, copyright, and quite often the amount of memory available or the names of those who wrote the program.

abstract base class. A base class that contains pure virtual functions.

abstraction. A computer model for a real-world situation.

actual arguments. The actual items passed in to a function; that is, the things you actually end up passing in to a function when you call it from a program, as opposed to the list of things you describe when you define the function.

algorithm. A fancy word for an approach or set of steps for solving a problem.

allocating memory. The process by which a program gets memory it can use for storing information. Typically this is done with the *new* command. *See also* dynamic allocation and deallocating memory.

ANSI. Acronym for American National Standards Institute. There are several ANSI committees for defining computer languages.

The committee that meets to define the C++ language is called the X3J16 committee.

API. Acronym for application program interface, and pronounced A - P - I. These are the set of routines that let you interface with an operating system (as in the Windows API), with a set of classes (as in the ObjectWindows API), or with any library or DLL that provides a set of functions that can be called.

AppExpert. A tool in Borland C++ that automatically creates Windows programs for you.

application. A computer program.

application frameworks. A set of classes, such as ObjectWindows, that makes it easier to build applications. Most often, an application framework's primary function is to make it easier to construct a user interface.

argument list. The list of things that can be passed into a routine. Used when you define a function.

arguments. The things that can be passed into a routine.

arity. The number of parameters an operator takes.

array. A type of data structure that can contain multiple items, all of the same type.

assembly language. A very low-level computer language.

assignment. A line in a program that gives a variable a value.

assignment operator concatenation. A fancy way of saying "set more than one variable to a value all at one time." For example, a = b = c = 0;.

bandwidth. The rate of information flow.

bang. The computerspeak word for !, the not operator. !a is read "bang a." Sometimes, though, it is read "not a."

base class. A class from which another class is inherited. Sometimes called a *parent*.

base constructor. A constructor used to initialize a base class. *See also* base class, constructor, derived class, and inheritance.

bcc. The Borland C++ command-line compiler.

BIDS. Acronym for Borland International Data Structures library, the set of prebuilt classes that implement many common data structures used in programs. Also called the *container class library*.

binary. A base two number. Binary numbers can only be on or off.

bit. A binary digit.

bitmap. A computer graphic image. Bitmaps are a two-dimensional set of dots that can be drawn to the screen. The little icons on SpeedBars are bitmaps.

Boolean. A variable that can only be true or false. If the variable has the value 0, it is considered false. Otherwise, it is considered true. Booleans are often used with conditional statements such as *if*.

browser. A tool that graphically displays the relationships of classes and helps you navigate through an application. The Borland C++ browser is *ObjectBrowser*.

bug. A logic error. *See also* syntax error.

bug free. An application without errors. A myth. Usually followed by "trust me," as in "Yeah, it's bug free, no problem, trust me."

byte. Eight binary digits. The smallest unit of memory in a computer.

caret. Another name for ^, the exclusive or operator.

catch. The process of trapping (that is, catching) an error with the help of C++ exception handling.

catch matching. The way the compiler determines what error handling code to execute when it catches an error.

child. A class that is inherited from something else. Also called a derived class.

class. The C++ keyword (and structure) that defines objects.

ClassExpert. A tool in Borland C++ that makes it easy for you to customize a Windows program.

code. A set of lines telling a computer what to do. The compiler turns code into a program. The term *code* always refers to the source the programmer has typed, whereas the term *program* can be either the source or the resulting application that can run.

command-line compiler. A compiler that is run from the DOS prompt. Options are passed to it by a series of flags (command-line parameters). The command-line compiler, unlike the IDE, does not have a user interface. *See also* IDE.

comment. A line in a program explaining what is happening in source code.

compiler. A program that turns a source file written in a high-level language to a program the computer can understand.

compiling. The process of converting any high-level computer language, such as C++, FORTRAN, or COBOL, to machine language.

composition. Creating an object by combining several other objects.

conditional. A construct used to execute statements only if a condition is true. Conditionals let you control the different paths through an application. Conditionals are often called *conditional statements*.

constant. A named value that doesn't change.

constant expression parameter. A parameter that is used with templates. It is treated as a constant, not as a substitution parameter. Often used to pass constants in while creating templates so as to define the size of something.

constructor. A routine that is automatically called when a class is created. Use it to initialize variables and other things.

container class. A class that implements a data structure that is primarily designed for storing and accessing data. For example, classes that implement bags, lists, queues, and stacks are often called container classes. These are all data structures whose

sole purpose is to provide easy ways to store and access data. *See also* BIDS.

crash. The disheartening result of a bug in the code. A program that busts, usually locking up the computer.

data. Information stored in a program.

data member. A piece of information (variable) that is part of a class.

data structure. Although this term can mean the design for any structure that contains data, it is usually used to refer to a design for storing data that includes specific features to make access and entry of data efficient or convenient.

data types. In C++, there are several different types of variables that you can use. The data type indicates the type of information a variable contains.

deallocating memory. Returning memory that was allocated to the computer so it can be used again. This is done with the *free* command. *See also* allocating memory.

debugger. A program that helps you find out why your program doesn't work.

debugging. The process of tracking down and fixing bugs in a program.

decimal. A base ten number. The kind of numbers you use in everyday life. When you order 130 pizzas (wow!) you are really ordering $1*10^2 + 3*10^1 + 0*10^0$ pizzas. By contrast, computers internally store numbers as binary numbers.

declaration. Telling the compiler the data type for a variable. The declaration is the first time the compiler learns about a particular variable. No memory is allocated for the variable at this time. *See also* definition.

decomposition. Breaking a problem into smaller parts.

default initializers. When you define function arguments you can specify that some have default initializers. If the function is called without values specified for all the arguments, the default values (those specified by the default initializers) will be used for the arguments that weren't passed in.

definition. A declaration indicates what's in a class. A definition actually allocates memory. So you declare classes and you define variables and functions. *See also* declaration.

dependency. A file that, if changed, will make another file have to be recompiled. For example, if a source file includes a header file, and then the header file changes, the source file will need to be recompiled. The header file is a dependency.

dependency list. The set of files that are dependencies for a particular file.

dereferencing. Finding out the value contained in the item a pointer points to.

derived class. A class that is created by inheriting behavior from another class. Sometimes called a *child*.

destructor. A routine automatically called when a class is destroyed. Use it to reset values, free up memory, close files, and do other clean-up work.

dialog box. A window used by programs to display static information or to get input from the user. Dialog boxes are used for answering immediate questions and are then closed; they typically are not resizable.

dialog class. A class (such as the TDialog class in ObjectWindows) that is used for creating and controlling dialog boxes.

DialogExpert. A tool in Borland C++ that helps you easily create a variety of standard dialog boxes.

dialog resource. A component of a Windows program that stores information on where controls (such as buttons and check boxes) appear on a dialog box. It also stores information about the size and appearance of the dialog box.

document/view. An approach to class design that makes it easier to write applications that can display different types of documents. Each document type (such as a word processor file, a database file, or a text file), has an associated document class for accessing the information in the document. There are also associated viewer classes that know how to display the information in documents in various ways (for example, showing hidden codes, WYSIWYG, showing the hex values in lists, and so on).

drag and drop. The process of clicking on an item, moving the mouse while holding the mouse button down, and then letting go of the mouse button. Typically this is used to select some object and perform an action upon it.

dynamic allocation. Allocating a chunk of memory to use in a program on the fly. This chunk isn't created because of a variable definition. That is, the compiler doesn't automatically set aside this memory when you define a variable. Rather, you allocate the memory yourself using the *new* command.

dynamic link library (DLL). A library (containing functions, classes, or resources) that is loaded by the program only when the program needs to access the library. The items in DLLs can be shared by several programs, and only consume memory when they are needed. By contrast, functions (or classes or resources) from static libraries are copied into the program by the linker. They are always part of the application.

early binding. What happens when you don't use a virtual function. To illustrate, suppose you have a pointer to an object that is either itself a foo or derived from foo. When you call a member function of the item pointed to, the corresponding member function in foo is called even if you're pointing to an object derived from foo. *See also* late binding.

EasyWin. A special Borland C++ library that makes it easy to write programs in Windows that use *cin* and *cout* for input and output.

editing. The process of writing and modifying source code. Usually done in an *editor* (or *programmer's editor*), a word processor specifically designed for writing computer programs.

encapsulation. Combining data and functions into a single entity.

enumeration types. Also known as *enums*, enumeration types are constants that are automatically created by the compiler. You list the names for the constants, and the compiler automatically generates a value.

error conditions. An unexpected condition that causes an error. For example, running out of memory is an error condition.

error handling. The process of dealing with (or the set of code for dealing with) error conditions. Note that this isn't the process of handling syntax errors; it's handling problems caused by strange things a user might do with a program.

exception handling. A C++ feature for dealing with error conditions. When an error (an exception) occurs, special code executes to resolve the problem.

exclusive or. A logical operation where the result is true only if one, but not both, bits are true.

Experts. Tools in Borland C++ that make it easier for you to create programs. *See also* AppExpert, ClassExpert, DialogExpert, and TargetExpert.

expression. A set of calculations (sometimes called a formula).

extension. The three letters that appear after the dot in a file name. For example, the CPP in FOO.CPP and the BAT in AUTOEXEC.BAT are extensions.

external reference. A reference to a variable or function that is defined outside the file. In other words, a variable or function whose memory was created somewhere else, but that you need to use in this file anyway.

factorial. A mathematical formula that calculates $n*(n-1)*(n-2)*...*1$.

FIFO. First in, first out. A data structure where the first item put in the structure is the first item taken from the structure. A queue is an example of a FIFO data structure.

FILO. First in, last out. A data structure where the first item put in is the last item taken out. A stack is an example of a FILO data structure.

floating-point numbers. Numbers that have a decimal point, such as 1.3, 4.24445, and 3.14159.

flow statements. Statements that control the order in which lines in a program execute. Normally code executes one line after another sequentially. Flow statements, which use the keywords *for, if, while, do*, and *switch* let you control the order.

foobar. This and the related words foo and bar (along with their cousins bah, baz, and foobah) are used to represent generic-item placeholders. For example, you might say "Suppose I took an object of type foo and...". These names are frequently used as variable names in programs. (Foobar originates from the military term fubar, which roughly stands for fouled up beyond all recognition.)

free store. A fancy name for free memory. This is where memory is dynamically allocated from. When you do a *new* you are getting the memory from the free store.

friend. A function or class that is given special permission to access private and protected members of another class.

functions. A set of named code that can be called from another place in a program. For example, you could create a function for printing a pizza order, and then call this function from a reporting section of the program. Functions are often called *routines* or *procedures*.

function body. The statements inside a function. These are what make the function tick.

function prototype. A description of a function so that the compiler can tell what parameters it requires.

GIGO. Garbage in, garbage out. No matter how good a program is, if you feed it a bunch of junk, you'll get processed junk for an answer.

global functions. Functions that are callable from any place in a file or program.

global variables. Variables that are accessible from any place in a file or program.

GP fault. A message from Windows that tells you that you've crashed big time. Short for general protection fault, which is some mumbo jumbo relating to how 386's work.

GUI. Short for graphical user interface, and pronounced gooey. The part of a program (or operating system) that uses items such as menus, dialog boxes, and icons to make it easier for the user to interact with the program and to choose commands.

hang. The result of a really bad bug. When you get one of these, you probably need to turn off the computer.

header file. A file that contains function prototypes and other definitions used by a source file, so that the compiler has enough information to process source code.

helper functions. Functions that exist for the sole purpose of helping a public function perform tasks. For example, a function for printing a person's name might call helper functions that capitalize the first letter of the name, insert a Mr., Ms., or Mrs. before the name, and so on.

hex. A hexadecimal, or base 16 number.

hexit. A hex digit.

high-level language. A computer language that is easier to understand than underlying machine code. Languages such as C++ and Pascal are high level. Assembly language is low level.

hosed. A computerese term for having a problem, as in "You're really hosed now!"

hosehead. A loser. Note, however, that this is sometimes used affectionately.

identifier. Same thing as the variable's name.

include files. Files that are included by a source file. Typically include files contain declarations of classes and constants.

IDE. Short for Integrated Development Environment. This is the Borland C++ development environment, from which you can edit, compile, debug, and browse programs.

index. A number used to access an element in an array. For example, if you did foo[2] = 1 to set the value of the third element in the array foo, 2 is the index.

infinite loop. A loop that never ends. If you get in one of these, you're hosed.

information hiding. Shielding underlying details from the programmer or end user.

inheritance. Creating a new object by adding on to the capabilities of an existing object.

inline. A technique used to increase the speed of a program. When you inline a function, the function body is copied directly into the code rather than being called.

instance. A specific creation of a class. A class definition tells what the class will do theoretically. An instance is an actual live class. It exists. The process of creating an instance of a class is called *instantiating a class*.

iostreams. The technical name for the routines used to read and write from the screen. *cin* and *cout* are part of the iostream library.

keywords. Official commands in a programming language, such as *for*, *return*, and *template*.

late binding. What happens when you use a virtual function. The program determines at runtime whether to call a member function from a base or derived class. *See also* early binding.

library. A set of commonly used routines that a program can call.

library functions. Functions from a library.

linked list. A data structure used to store an arbitrarily sized number of items. Each element in the list contains a value as well as a pointer to the next item in the list.

linker. A program that combines the results of compiling several files into a single application that the computer can run.

listing. Another name for source code. Usually used when you are "examining a listing."

local variable. A variable that is defined in, and therefore only accessible within, a function.

logic errors. Mistakes caused from an incorrect approach to solving a problem. *See also* syntax error.

loop. A construct used to repeatedly execute a set of statements.

loosely typed languages. Languages that don't require you to declare types before using an item.

low-level language. A language that very closely matches the underlying machine code used by a computer. *See also* high-level language.

lvalue. The value on the left side of an assignment or operator. lvalue is also used to describe the memory address for a variable.

machine language. The actual code that the computer understands. Machine code is actually just a set of instructions that the CPU interprets. For example, there are machine language commands for adding numbers, for copying values from one area in memory to another, and so on.

macro. A name given for a set of user-defined commands. When encountered in a program, the commands making up the program are expanded. Unlike functions, macros expand as actual text, so they are really a cut-and-paste shorthand. Macros allow for parameter substitution.

main. The place where C and C++ programs begin. Sometimes called the main function.

make. The process of recompiling and relinking any source files that have changed since the last time a program was built. Also used to refer to the program (MAKE.EXE) that makes programs.

makefile. A file used by MAKE that lists all the source files that comprise a particular program, along with dependencies and rules for building the files.

mangling. A method for encoding names of data and functions so the compiler can tell what data types they use. Sometimes called *name mangling*.

MDI. Short for Multiple Document Interface. A style of Windows program in which multiple data windows can appear within a program window. The Program Manager is an example of an MDI application.

member function. A function that's part of a class.

memory leak. A logic error that results in memory being allocated but not freed. As a result, less and less memory is available for use as a program runs.

node. A file in the Project Manager. Usually these are source and header files. The word comes from the Computer Science description of a data structure called a *tree*.

null pointer. A pointer that contains the value 0. In other words, a pointer that points to the very beginning of memory — which is a place that you are not allowed to touch. Dereferencing a null pointer will crash a program.

object. The instantiation of a class. *See also* class.

ObjectBrowser. A tool in Borland C++ used for graphically examining the relationships of classes.

ObjectWindows. A set of classes provided with Borland C++ that model Windows. Using these classes makes it easier to write Windows programs. Often called *OWL*.

OOP. Abbreviation for object-oriented programming.

operand. The things in a formula that are operated upon. In 3 * 2, the numbers 3 and 2 are the operands.

operator. The thing that modifies a value. Multiplication (*), division (/), and addition (+) are all operators.

operator overloading. Redefining the way an operator (such as +) behaves, so that it can operate on new types of data.

overloading. Adding an additional behavior to something. For example, if you had a function called GetPhone that could be passed an integer or a string as an argument, you'd have two versions of GetPhone, each performing a similar task with slightly different information.

overloading resolution. Finding which function definition corresponds to a particular usage, when you've overloaded a function.

overriding. Changing the behavior of an item that is inherited; in particular, by using the same name as an item in the base class but just making it behave differently.

parent. Another way to say *base class*.

passing arguments. Giving some values to a function. This is how you can customize or generalize what a function does.

pizza. One of the basic food groups for programmers. Perfect for breakfast. A finer point of programming etiquette: if you order a pizza after midnight and continue eating it for breakfast, it is still considered fresh.

pointer. A variable that contains a memory address. This thing points at a value in memory.

polymorphism. Changing the way a particular routine behaves, depending on the object in use.

pop. To remove an item from a stack.

preprocessor directive. A command that controls the compiler, but does not turn into code. These commands start with a #. For example, #include will include a header file.

private. Something in a class that can be used and seen only by member functions of that class.

project file. A list of executables and their source files. Anytime you need to compile a

program, you first create a project for it. You indicate the name of the executable you're trying to create and the source files to compile to create it. Sometimes just called a *project*.

Project Manager. A tool in Borland C++ that makes it easy to create and manipulate project files.

protected. Something in a class that can be used and seen only by member functions of the class or by derived classes.

public. Something in a class that can be seen and used by everyone.

pure virtual. A virtual function that is declared but not defined for a particular class. *See also* abstract base class.

push. To add an item to a stack.

read-only variable. A data member that can be read, but not modified. This is done by making the variable a private (or protected) data member, and by providing only a public access function for reading the value.

recursion. A technique in which a routine calls itself.

reference argument. A type of argument where a pointer to the value is passed to a function rather than to a copy of the value.

Resource Workshop. A tool that comes with Borland C++ for creating and editing Windows resources.

resources. The components that make up the user interface of a Windows program. Bitmaps, cursors, menus, and dialog boxes are all resources.

return type. The data type of whatever a function returns. In other words, the type of value that is calculated by a function.

reuse. The goal of object-oriented programming (OOP). Taking code you created once and using it again later so you can save time.

robust. An application that is stable and well tested.

runtime library. A library that ships with Borland C++ that contains a set of very common functions for reading, writing, and calculating. For example, the runtime library contains functions for manipulating strings, doing trigonometry, and finding the size of files. Often called the *RTL*.

runtime polymorphism. A fancy name for *late binding*. The behavior of a particular call, when made through a pointer, depends on the type of the object it is used with, and this can't be determined until the program is running.

rvalue. The value on the right side of an assignment or an equation. When a variable is in an rvalue, it's part of a formula that is being evaluated. rvalue is also used to describe the value for a variable.

scope. The area where a variable is usable.

SDI. The abbreviation for Single Document Interface. A style of Windows program where the program only displays one window at a time. Notepad is an example of an SDI application. *See also* MDI.

sentinels. A line added to a header file that prevents the header file from being read twice within a single source file.

signature. A fancy way of saying the type of arguments passed to a function. For example, int, int is one signature. int, float is another. const int, float is a third. The signature is used by the compiler during overloading resolution.

source file. A file containing computer source code.

spaghetti code. Code that is poorly designed and therefore hard to read. A disparaging term often used for code that has lots of *goto*s in it.

splash screen. The screen showing the product name. It appears when an application starts, to let you know what's running. Usually includes some type of corporate logo and copyright information.

squiggle. The computer name for ~, the bitwise not operator. Also called *tilde*.

stack. A FILO data structure used in programs for creating local variables and storing other information.

star. This is how you pronounce *. So, for example, *foo is read "star foo". And ringo * is "ringo star" or "a pointer to type ringo."

statement. A line in a program telling the computer what to do.

static memory allocation. Allocating a chunk of memory through a variable definition.

stderr. Standard error. It's where you write characters when you have an error message that you don't want to be part of your *cout* stream. You can write to it with *cerr*.

stdin. Standard input. It's where characters come from that are read with *cin*.

stdout. Standard output. It's where characters go to when they are written with *cout*.

streams. Another name for iostreams. Sets of characters or other things that are written out to a device.

string. A set of text, such as "hello".

strongly typed language. A language that requires you to declare types before using an item.

subclassing. Another name for inheriting.

sucked in. The automatic process of copying routines from a library, as in "Not my bug; it was sucked in from the library."

symbol table. A table used by the compiler. The symbol table contains information about the variables, classes, and functions that are used by a source file.

syntax error. An error caused by incorrect use of the C++ language. Forgetting a semicolon, passing in the wrong data type, using the wrong include path, and leaving off a } are all examples of syntax errors. *See also* logic error.

syntax highlighting. A feature of the Borland C++ editor that uses different colors for different parts of C++ syntax to make it easier to read source files.

The 5th Wave
Re·al Pro·gram·mers   By Rich Tennant

Real Programmers love to talk "computer-eze" while ordinary citizens are listening.

tag name.   A fancy way of saying the name or data type of a class.

target.   A file that gets created in a project. Usually this is an executable, but it can also be a DLL, library, or help file.

TargetExpert.   A Borland C++ tool that makes it easy to select the type of program to create. For example, you can choose to create a Windows program, an NT program, a DOS program, or a Windows DLL.

template.   A generic class. Sometimes called a parameterized class. Templates perform some type of function on a generic data item; the actual type of the data item is specified when the template is instantiated. Also called a *template class*.

tilde.   The official name for ~.

typecasting.   Converting an item from one data type to another.

type conversion.   Automatic conversion of an item from one type to another.

type specifier.   The thing that tells what data type a variable will be.

uninitialized.   A variable that is defined but not yet given a value.

variable.   A name for a piece of information in a program.

virtual function.   A function that allows late binding. *See also* early binding, late binding, and pure virtual.

word.   Two bytes.

xor.   Another way of writing exclusive or.

Installing the Service Update

• •

In This Chapter

▶ Determine whether you have the original install program or the Service Update install program

▶ Install the Service Update

• •

OK, Which Install Program Have I Got Here?

As mentioned in Chapter 2, a Service Update (also called Borland C++ version 4.02) was shipped in June 1994. Since the install programs for the original release and the Service Update differ, you need to determine whether or not you have the Service Update so you'll know which set of install instructions to follow. Here's how to tell:

✔ If you ordered and received the Service Update CD or disk set from Borland, you have the Service update. (That's the easy one!)

✔ If you bought Borland C++ before the end of June 1994, and you haven't ordered the Service Update, you don't have the Service Update.

✔ If you aren't sure which version you have, put one of the disks (or the CD) in the disk drive. Type DIR A: (or whatever the drive letter is containing the disk). If you see files dated June 10, 1994 or later, you have the Service Update.

✔ If you're still not sure, follow the steps in the Starting Install section of Chapter 2. If the first install screen has an icon containing a pair of sunglasses in front of a text file, then you have the Service Update. (And thus you should follow the Service Update installation instructions in this Late-Breaking News section.)

If you want to install the original install program (version 4.0), return to the Starting Install section in Chapter 2. If you want to install the Service Update, continue reading this section.

Starting Install for the Service Update

You need to start Windows before you run the Borland C++ 4.0 Service Update install program. To start Windows, type:

```
WIN
```

(By the way, if you ever get tired of seeing the Microsoft logo flash by when you start Windows, just type `WIN :` instead.)

To run the install program follow these steps:

1. If you have the floppy-disk version of Borland C++, put the first floppy disk in your disk drive.

    If you have the CD-ROM version, put the CD in the CD drive.

2. Select File|Run from the Program Manager.

3. If you have the floppy version, type `A:INSTALL` and click the OK button. (If your floppy isn't in drive A, use your drive letter instead of A. For example, if your floppy is drive B, type `B:INSTALL`.)

    If you have the CD-ROM version, type `E:\INSTALL\INSTALL` and click the OK button. (If your CD drive isn't drive E, then type its drive letter instead of E.)

4. When the first screen appears asking if you want to read INSTALL.TXT, click the Skip button.

Now — *before* you select any options — continue reading this section of the book so you can understand the various types of installs you can do.

The Full Service Update Install (Or How to Fill a Disk in No Time)

This approach installs all the Borland C++ tools and requires around 88M of free space on your hard disk. Before you do a full install, it's a good idea to determine if this is really the best approach for you. Do you plan to use all the Borland C++ tools and utilities? Can you spare this much hard disk space? Many programmers (and almost all beginners) find that other installation scenarios are better suited for their needs. Simple step-by-step directions for each installation scenario are given in the following sections.

If you've decided that the full install is best for you, then follow these steps.

Remember, you'll need around 88M of free space on your hard disk before you begin.

If you're installing from floppies:

1. Select the drive onto which you want to install Borland C++.

2. Click the Next button. (The Full radio button will already be checked.)

3. Click the Next button again.

4. Click the Install button.

5. Grab a good novel or two and place the disks into the machine when prompted.

If you're installing from CD:

1. Select the drive onto which you want to install Borland C++.

2. Make sure the Full radio button is checked and then click the Next button.

3. Click the Next button again.

4. Click the Install button.

5. Read a few comics or grab a slice of pizza.

The Bare-Bones Service Update Install (Requires CD-ROM)

With the CD-ROM version, you can keep almost everything on the CD-ROM drive. A small number of configuration files will be stored on your hard disk, but everything else will stay on the CD. Performance will be a bit slow because you'll run the compiler and load libraries from the CD, and CDs are slower than disk drives. On the other hand, you'll only need around 75K of disk space!

To do the bare-bones install:

1. Select the drive onto which you want to install Borland C++.

2. Click the CD Only Config. radio button on.

3. Click the Next button.

4. If you don't plan to do 32-bit programming, click the Install Win32s radio button off.

5. Click the Next button.

6. Click the Install button.

If you do the bare-bones install, you'll need to make sure the Borland C++ CD-ROM is in your CD-ROM drive every time you start Windows. That's because Borland C++ needs certain device-driver files that help its command-line programs run under Windows. These files are stored on the hard drive during a full install, but kept on the CD-ROM during the minimal (bare bones) install. If you do the bare-bones install, Windows will look for these files on the CD-ROM drive when it starts. (If you'd like to free your CD from this constraint, see the "Free, free, set your CD free" sidebar in Chapter 2.)

Four Other Service Update Installation Scenarios

This section describes the installation procedures for the four other installation scenarios. Selecting one of these scenarios can help you keep disk consumption down without impacting performance. Instead of installing the full set of Borland C++ tools, these scenarios install only the tools you'll use on a regular basis. If you use these scenarios, you'll be able to perform all the tasks discussed in this book (and in fact almost all programming tasks), yet use far less disk space than the full install requires:

- ✔ **I want Windows tools only:** Installs a reasonable set of tools for creating Windows applications. Requires around 57M of disk space.

- ✔ **I want Windows tools only, but keep stuff on CD:** Installs a reasonable set of tools for creating Windows applications, but keeps some files, such as the help files, on the CD to reduce disk consumption. Requires around 32M of disk space.

- ✔ **I need Windows and NT tools only:** Installs a reasonable set of tools for creating Windows and 32-bit Windows applications. Requires around 76M of disk space.

- ✔ **I want DOS tools only:** Installs what you need to create DOS programs. Requires around 39M of disk space.

The following sections show how to install for these various options.

The "I want Windows tools only" Service Update install

The following steps install the tools you need to create 16-bit Windows applications.

1. Select the drive onto which you want to install Borland C++.

2. Click the Custom radio button on.

3. Click the Next button.

4. Click the Install Win32s option off.

5. If you're running Windows from a local area network, click the LAN Windows Configuration option on.

6. Click the Next button. The Target Platforms dialog box will appear.

7. Click the 32-bit Windows and DOS options off.

8. Click the Next button. The Tools dialog box will appear.

9. Click these options off: Command Line Tools and Debuggers.

10. Click the Next button. The Visual Tools dialog box will appear.

11. Click the Next button. The Run-time Libraries dialog box will appear.

12. Click these options off: Compact, Small, Medium.

13. Click the Next button. The ObjectWindows dialog box will appear.

14. Click these options off: ObjectWindows Source, ObjectWindows 1.0 Conversion Tool.

15. Click the Next button. The Class Libraries dialog box will appear.

16. Click these options off: Class Libraries Source, Obsolete Class Libraries.

17. Click the Next button. The Examples dialog box will appear.

18. Click these options off: Class Libraries, IDE.

19. Click the Next button. The OnLine Help dialog box will appear.

20. Click the Next button.

21. Now click on the Install button.

The "I want Windows tools only, but keep stuff on CD" Service Update install

The following steps are similar to those for the "I want Windows tools only" install, except that help files and sample programs are kept on the CD-ROM drive to save hard disk space.

1. Select the drive onto which you want to install Borland C++.

2. Click the Custom radio button on.

3. Click the Next button.

4. Click the Install Win32s option off.

5. If you're running Windows from a local area network, click the LAN Windows Configuration option on.

6. Click the Next button. The Target Platforms dialog box will appear.

7. Click the 32-bit Windows and DOS options off.

8. Click the Next button. The Tools dialog box will appear.

9. Click these options off: Command Line Tools, Debuggers, Examples, Help, and Documentation.

10. Click the Next button. The Visual Tools dialog box will appear.

11. Click the Next button. The Run-time Libraries dialog box will appear.

12. Click these options off: Compact, Small, Medium.

13. Click the Next button. The ObjectWindows dialog box will appear.

14. Click these options off: ObjectWindows Source, ObjectWindows 1.0 Conversion Tool.

15. Click the Next button. The Class Libraries dialog box will appear.

16. Click these options off: Class Libraries Source, Obsolete Class Libraries.

17. Now click on the Install button.

The "I want Windows and NT tools only" Service Update install

The following steps install the tools you need to create 16- and 32-bit Windows applications. This install is similar to the "I want Windows tools only" install, but adds the 32-bit tools and libraries.

1. Select the drive onto which you want to install Borland C++.

2. Click the Custom radio button on.

3. Click the Next button.

4. If you're running Windows from a local area network, click the LAN Windows Configuration option on.

5. Click the Next button. The Target Platforms dialog box will appear.

6. Click the DOS option off.

7. Click the Next button. The Tools dialog box will appear.

8. Click the Next button. The Debugger dialog box will appear.

9. Click the Remote Debugging option off.

10. Click the Next button. The Visual Tools dialog box will appear.

11. Click the Next button. The Run-time Libraries dialog box will appear.

12. Click these options off: Compact, Small, Medium.

13. Click the Next button. The ObjectWindows dialog box will appear.

14. Click these options off: ObjectWindows Source, ObjectWindows 1.0 Conversion Tool.

15. Click the Next button. The Class Libraries dialog box will appear.

16. Click these options off: Class Libraries Source, Obsolete Class Libraries.

17. Click the Next button. The Examples dialog box will appear.

18. Click these options off: Class Libraries, IDE.

19. Click the Next button. The OnLine Help dialog box will appear.

20. Click the Next button.

21. Now click the Install button.

The "I want DOS tools only" Service Update install

The following steps will install the tools you need to create DOS applications.

1. Select the drive onto which you want to install Borland C++.

2. Click the Custom radio button on.

3. Click the Next button.

4. Click the Install Win32s option on.

5. If you're running Windows from a local area network, click the LAN Windows Configuration option on.

6. Click the Next button. The Target Platforms dialog box will appear.

7. Click the 16-bit Windows and 32-bit Windows options off.

8. Click the Next button. The Tools dialog box will appear.

9. Click the Next button. The Debugger dialog box will appear.

10. Click the Remote Debugging option off.

11. Click the Next button. The Visual Tools dialog box will appear.

12. If you want to run only the command-line tools, you can save 22M of disk space by clicking off the Integrated Development Option. If you do so, also click off Resource Workshop. Note that in most cases, and in all the examples in this book, you'll want to install the IDE.

13. Click these options off: Winsight, Control 3D, Winspector, and Misc.

14. Click the Next button. The Run-time Libraries dialog box will appear.

15. Click these options off: Tiny, Compact, Medium, and Huge.

16. Click the Next button. The Class Libraries dialog box will appear.

17. Click these options off: Class Libraries Source, Obsolete Class Libraries.

18. Click the Next button. The Examples dialog box will appear.

19. Click Class Libraries off.

20. Click the Next button. The OnLine Help dialog box will appear.

21. Click these options off: ObjectWindows Help, Win32 and Windows 3.1 Reference, Resource Workshop Help, Visual Utilities Help, Creating Windows Help.

22. Click the Next button.

23. Now click the Install button.

Index

TM

PROGRAMMING
BOOK SERIES

Borland C++ For Dummies
Disk Offer

Tired of typing code? Tired of creating project files? Get all the major programs in this book on disk and save valuable time.

The disk is in 3 1/2 inch (1.44MB) format and costs $15. To order, send a check payable to *Michael Hyman* to the following address:

> Michael Hyman
> 11500 Homewood Road
> Ellicott City, MD 21042

Maryland residents add appropriate sales tax. (Outside the U.S., add $5 for shipping and handling. Checks must be drawn on a U.S. bank.) This disk cannot be mailed to a P.O. box. In addition, CODs are not accepted.

This offer is not associated with IDG Books.

IDG BOOKS WORLDWIDE REGISTRATION CARD

Title of this book: **Borland C++ For Dummies**

My overall rating of this book: ❏ Very good [1] ❏ Good [2] ❏ Satisfactory [3] ❏ Fair [4] ❏ Poor [5]

How I first heard about this book:

❏ Found in bookstore; name: [6] _____

❏ Advertisement: [8] _____

❏ Word of mouth; heard about book from friend, co-worker, etc.: [10] _____

❏ Book review: [7] _____

❏ Catalog: [9] _____

❏ Other: [11] _____

What I liked most about this book: _____

_____

_____

What I would change, add, delete, etc., in future editions of this book: _____

_____

_____

Other comments: _____

_____

Number of computer books I purchase in a year: ❏ 1 [12] ❏ 2-5 [13] ❏ 6-10 [14] ❏ More than 10 [15]

I would characterize my computer skills as: ❏ Beginner [16] ❏ Intermediate [17] ❏ Advanced [18] ❏ Professional [19]

I use ❏ DOS [20] ❏ Windows [21] ❏ OS/2 [22] ❏ Unix [23] ❏ Macintosh [24] ❏ Other: [25]_____
(please specify)

I would be interested in new books on the following subjects:
(please check all that apply, and use the spaces provided to identify specific software)

❏ Word processing: [26] _____

❏ Data bases: [28] _____

❏ File Utilities: [30] _____

❏ Networking: [32] _____

❏ Other: [34] _____

❏ Spreadsheets: [27] _____

❏ Desktop publishing: [29] _____

❏ Money management: [31] _____

❏ Programming languages: [33] _____

I use a PC at (please check all that apply): ❏ home [35] ❏ work [36] ❏ school [37] ❏ other: [38] _____

The disks I prefer to use are ❏ 5.25 [39] ❏ 3.5 [40] ❏ other: [41]_____

I have a CD ROM: ❏ yes [42] ❏ no [43]

I plan to buy or upgrade computer hardware this year: ❏ yes [44] ❏ no [45]

I plan to buy or upgrade computer software this year: ❏ yes [46] ❏ no [47]

Name: _____ Business title: [48] _____ Type of Business: [49] _____

Address (❏ home [50] ❏ work [51]/Company name: _____)

Street/Suite# _____

City [52]/State [53]/Zipcode [54]: _____ Country [55] _____

❏ **I liked this book!** You may quote me by name in future
   IDG Books Worldwide promotional materials.

My daytime phone number is _____

IDG BOOKS

THE WORLD OF COMPUTER KNOWLEDGE

 **YES!**
Please keep me informed about IDG's World of Computer Knowledge.
Send me the latest IDG Books catalog.